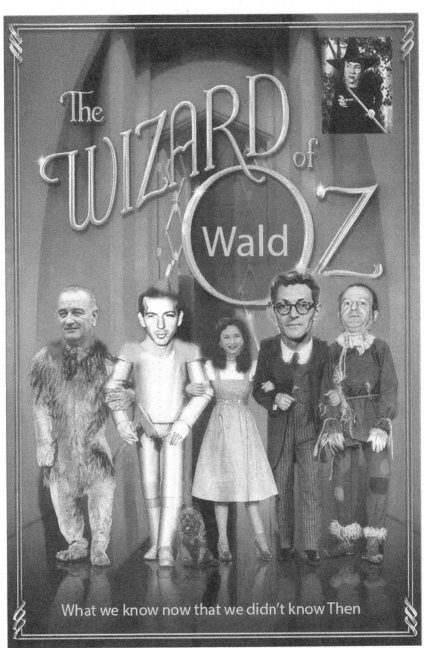

The WIZARD of OZ

Wald

What we know now that we didn't know Then

GARY HILL

The Wizard of Ozwald: What We Know Now That We Didn't Know Then
© Gary Hill 2024, All Rights Reserved

Published by:
Trine Day LLC
PO Box 577
Walterville, OR 97489
1-800-556-2012
www.TrineDay.com
trineday@icloud.com

Library of Congress Control Number: 2024941538

Hill, Gry.
The Wizard of Ozwald: What We Know Now That We Didn't Know Then —1st ed.
p. cm.

Epub (ISBN-13) 978-1-63424-500-5
TradePaper (ISBN-13) 978-1-63424-499-2
1. Kennedy, John F. 1917-1963 Assassination. 2. Lee Harvey Oswald 1939-1963.
3. James Jesus Angleton 1917-1987. 4. Intelligence services – United States. I. Hill,
Gary. II. Title

FIRST EDITION
10 9 8 7 6 5 4 3 2 1

Cover art: Album / Alamy Stock Photo

Distribution to the Trade by:
Independent Publishers Group (IPG)
814 North Franklin Street
Chicago, Illinois 60610
312.337.0747

www.ipgbook.com

BRUTUS: Farewell to you. – And you – And you, Volumnius.
  – Strato, thou hast been all this while asleep.
  Farewell to thee too, Strato. – Countrymen,
  My heart doth joy that yet in all my life
  I found no man but he was true to me.
  I shall have glory by this losing day
  More than Octavius and Mark Antony
  By this vile conquest shall attain unto.
  So fare you well at once, for Brutus' tongue
  Hath almost ended his life's history.
  Night hangs upon mine eyes. My bones would rest,
  That have but labored to attain this hour.

CLITUS: Fly, my lord, fly.

BRUTUS: Hence. I will follow.
  I prithee, Strato, stay thou by thy lord.
  Thou art a fellow of a good respect.
  Thy life hath had some smatch of honor in it.
  Hold then my sword and turn away thy face
  While I do run upon it. Wilt thou, Strato?

STRATO: Give me your hand first.
  (holds BRUTUS' sword) Fare you well, my lord.

BRUTUS: Farewell, good Strato. (runs on his sword)
  Caesar, now be still.
  I killed not thee with half so good a will. (dies)

– William Shakspeare, *Julius Cesear*, Act 5, Scene 5

To my wife Sharon Hill

Thank you for your help, love and support

CONTENTS

Preface

By Paul Bleau

Paul Bleau holds an MBA from McGill University; he owned and ran a leading marketing communications agency for 25 years, and supervised Canada's first "denormalization" campaign of the tobacco industry. Since 2006, he has been professor at St. Lawrence College. His study of how history textbooks cover the JFK assassination and how their authors defend themselves, along with a series of follow-up pieces, are published on the KennedysandKing website. He has also been a guest on BlackOp Radio. Paul teaches Champlain College Quebec City Canada. He holds an MBA from McGill University, Montreal, Canada. He has a long track record of research and writing about the JFK assassination which includes the following:

Has written numerous articles for KennedysandKing;

A regular guest on BlackOp Radio and other podcasts;

Appeared in the documentary JFK Revisited: Through the Looking Glass, Oliver Stone;

Organized the Oliver Stone comes to Quebec City event in 2022;

CAPA Conference 2022 presenter Dallas, Texas;

UKDealeyPlaza keynote speaker, Canterbury, UK, Conference 2023;

Presenter Co-Author of The JFK Assassination Chokeholds that prove there was a conspiracy (2023) at Lancer Conference Dallas Texas, 2023.

I got to know Gary Hill by reviewing his excellent book *The Other Oswald: A Wilderness of Mirrors* for Jim DiEugenio's Kennedysandking. In so doing I discovered one of the most underrated researchers in the field. *The Other Oswald* sheds light on false defector programs, Ruth Paine's sister and her intel tasks that relate to defector Robert Webster, the Rand company and provides a brilliant comparison of Webster and Oswald's defections.

Hill lived through the assassination, the Cold War and the multiple investigations into the case. Through this time, he never stopped researching the conspiracy about the JFK assassination and has been a reliable source of critical information for decades who has lacked the visibility he deserves. When Gary asked me to write a preface for his new book, *The Wizard of Ozwald*, I gladly accepted. This does not mean that I agree with all the opinions he has put forth over time, it does mean that Gary deserves the esteem of fellow researchers because of his professionalism and experience.

After spending over a year writing and promoting *The JFK Assassination Chokeholds that Inescapably Prove there was a Conspiracy* with four colleagues, I could not wait to get back to what has always been my real passion: solving the crime of the last century – instead of proving there was a conspiracy.

In *Wizard*, readers will follow a puppet not only down a road full of intelligence related intrigue but, more importantly, they will move vertically up the strings where they will come face to face with the puppeteer. By presenting documentary records, mining the research of other reliable authors, and linking chronologies, persons of interest, revealing suspicious behaviors and analyzing critically, Hill presents both a flow chart and part of an organizational structure that led to what happened in Dealey Plaza on November 22, 1963.

Two thousand and twenty-three was not a good year for Lone Nut propagandists. The breaches in the law around the JFK Assassinations Act by both Trump and Biden and non-stop gas lighting are pushing this rag tag team of obfuscaters into a very small sandbox where they are the ones who come across as illogical contrarians. People are demanding more and more to know what happened. A book like *Wizard* could not come out at a better time because it is about the truth. The reason the U.S. is so polarized right now is because of the mastery of lying that so many have come to rely on for their quest for money, power and fame. Many citizens have had it with turning on the TV and listening to politicians putting on their most sincere look and then boldly lying to the audience while wars, climate change, mass murders, drug problems, illegal immigration are spiraling out of control. Lies that ramped up into full gear when JFK was assassinated and never stopped. This truth is so important because of what JFK stood for which is on the opposite side of today's national culture that has gripped the world's most powerful country.

Thanks to the author, *Wizard* will guide readers down this road with the most up to date, pertinent and revealing information that allows one to understand both the puppet and his master. Obviously if you are reading this preface then you have already begun your quest for the truth around one of the most important crimes of the last century: Enjoy the ride, you're not in Kansas anymore.

FOREWORD

SEEING INTO THE ABYSS

"These savage nuts have shattered the great myth of American decency."
— Hunter Thompson

I LEARNED THE TRUTH AT 17 [1]

In 1963, the world, like TV and a majority of movies, was still viewed in black and white. We were the good guys. The Russians and Castro were the bad guys. Life was simple and easy to understand.

I was 17 and couldn't fathom why anyone would want to kill the president. I wasn't the only one. Everyone I knew seemed to feel the same way. He was popular, and he and his wife were perceived as movie stars or royalty to youngsters like myself. I'm sure that, had I lived in the South, my views would have been different. Still, the whole thing was baffling. Years later, when the subject of JFK was brought up in a local barroom discussion, I was very surprised to be attacked by a majority of the patrons for defending him. By this time his posthumous assassination had commenced in the right-wing media. I now recognize it as a negative propaganda campaign assault likely instigated by the CIA. This propaganda operation was designed to destroy his image and counter his growing martyrdom. Why hadn't I noticed this local negativity before? Why hadn't I perceived this right-left dissension as a youth?

During the Cuban Missile Crisis, I remember wondering why the Russians would risk a nuclear war by implementing their aggressive military endeavors in the Caribbean. Were they crazy or just evil? What did we do to instill fear and hatred in the Soviet regime? Didn't they know we were good guys? As an adult, it's now obvious that the Bay of Pigs, Operation Mongoose and its raids of sabotage, assassination attempts on Castro and threats of another invasion, not to mention imperialistic profiteering, might all be valid reasons for the Russians to aid in the defense of an ally under threat of invasion.

---

1   I was 17 when JFK was shot. Appologies to Janis Ian.

When Oswald was arrested and labeled the lone assassin, I was confused. Why would a liberal kill a liberal? It didn't make sense. He had no motive. I guess I wasn't the only one that came to that conclusion. The Warren Commission struggled with it as well.

When the scarecrow,[2] Jack Ruby, shot tin man, Lee Oswald, in a police station surrounded by an army of *protectors,* I began to get the feeling that something was very wrong here. What weren't we being told? Although surrounded by police, Oswald was a sitting duck. Years later, when the Zapruder film was finally available to the public, it became blatantly obvious that JFK, like his supposed assassin, was also *made* an easy target and met the same fate. Then it hit me. Neither he nor Oswald were protected ... *on purpose.* They were two sitting ducks helplessly exposed on a pond of political vulnerability. The reality of it hit me like a slap in the face. It was then that I realized I had been lied to growing up. In truth, the good guys *don't* always win. It seems that the bad guys were the winners most of the time. Being bad guys, they don't have any moral codes to slow them down. They can lie, cheat, steal, and kill to achieve their goals. When they find themselves in danger of losing, they simply liquidate their opponents by any means necessary. They don't play fair. It was at that point that I came of age and realized life isn't fair. Not in the real world.

Was I the only one left in the dark back then? In retrospect, it turns out we all were. In many ways, our leaders were as well. What were some of the black ops and dirty tricks being perpetrated that even the Warren Commission was kept in the dark about?

Let's take a look at what the WC wasn't told. The CIA had been working with the mafia to kill foreign leaders.[3] The Military had proposed launching an all-out first strike against the Soviets and Chinese (shades of Pearl Harbor), in essence a sneak attack! What was even more unbelievable was the fact that our military leaders were willing to accept 30 or 40 million American casualties as collateral damage. The CIA and FBI were opening US citizen's mail and spying on them using wiretaps.[4] Drugs were being imported into the US by our intelligence agencies to finance covert intelligence operations.[5] Domestic terrorism was being considered against our government and its people for use as a *false flag* operation to validate

---

2   Ruby wanted to be important, be looked up to, recognized as having a brain. So he fits the scarecrow profile in our quest for the Wizard.

3   CIA/Mafia plots. ZRRIFLE.

4   Operation CHAOS, HTLINGUAL (CIA), HUNTER, Z-covers and COINTELPRO (FBI), SHAMROCK (NSA)

5   GLADIO

an excuse for a war with Cuba.[6] Nazi war criminals were being smuggled out of Europe after the war and incorporated into US intelligence, playing an influential role in our foreign policy. The CIA was performing sadistic experiments with drugs and hypnosis to achieve mind-control in unsuspecting civilians and vulnerable incarcerated subjects.

This work will take a fresh look at what we know now as opposed to what we knew then. It will show that JFK was not killed randomly by a lone nut, nor by a foreign government, but by his domestic enemies and under the rationale of patriotism. His executioners were rogues in the *National Security Establishment,* who considered him a security risk. It will also expose the hand of James Jesus Angleton as a ghostly entity who ran this show from behind the scenes. He will be revealed through his cut-out, David Atlee Phillips, and Phillips cut-out George Joannides, to be Lee Harvey Oswald's puppeteer. This can be done by following the trail of handlers in reverse. Each time this is done, no matter who you start with, the result leads us to the Poet Spy.

Son of Spam

Our government betrayed us in 1963. They used our black-and-white view of the world against us. We were manipulated by psychological warfare professionals to successfully shape our opinions and viewpoints. David Phillips was one of these propaganda wizards but he was not alone. Alex Sill describes the use of *verbalisms* he calls " *'emotionally charged shielding phrases,' designed to shut down critical thinking and quash an argument, whether well founded or not."* An example would be questioning the critic's patriotism.[7]

Similarly, Victor Marchetti described what he called *"Limited Hangout Strategy"* as spy jargon for releasing some hidden facts to distract the public from bigger, more explosive information.[8]

Similar techniques are used effectively today as marketing strategies to endorse political con men. A popular one is called *"Psychological Sets."* This mechanism is used to effectively hinder cognitive performance, decision making and problem-solving. For example, as a business man, Donald Trump has at his disposal professional Madison Avenue marketers that could sell you the Brooklyn Bridge.

---

6   NORTHWOODS

7   "For reasons of National Security-Reframing the Assassinations of the 1960s and the Case Against the CIA," Alex Sill, Kennedy and Kings Website, June 12, 2023

8   This techniques was used in a CIA effort to sacrifice E. Howard Hunt in a civil trial against him initiated by Mark Lane.

In 1967 The CIA released a dispatch that coined the label "*conspiracy theory*" and "*conspiracy theorists.*" It instructed journalists to attack anyone who challenged the official narrative from the Warren Commission. it's interesting to note that the document is labeled "*psych,*" for psychological operations or disinformation. it's also marked "*CS copy*" at the bottom, meaning "*Clandestine Services*" Unit.

The author of this treatise was Ned Bennett of the CA (Covert Action) Staff in close conjunction with CI (Angleton's Counter-intelligence) /R&A (Research and Analysis). Lamar Waldron says that,

> Bennett was chosen because he had written an important article for the *London Spectator*, entitled "The theories of Mr. Epstein," that trashed the book *Inquest* by Edward Epstein.[9]

In a subsequent memo, Bennett attached the article as an example of the type of piece that could be written to attack critics. He encouraged subordinate media assets to use this technique. Bennett *just happened* to be present and participate in the debriefing of Robert Webster. In addition he was allowed to interview Webster separately.[10] The usual suspects surface time and time again in this saga when they are needed to control the course of events.

---

9   *Legacy of Secrecy,* Lamar Waldron, p.380
10   104-10182-10075

PART I

WACK A MOLE

INTRODUCTION

THE TIN MAN AND THE WIZARD

Oz never did give nothin' to the Tin Man, that he didn't already have.
– "Tin Man," Dewey Bunnell of America

The charm of Frank Baum's *Wizard of Oz* has endured for far more than a century. It's narrative encompasses the conflict of good vs evil as well as the power of the innocence and loyalty between its characters. Its success is contingent on these eternally endearing themes. An innocent young girl is caught up in a tornado and dropped into an enchanted land far more colorful and exciting than that of her previous drab existence in Kansas. With the help of a group of misfits who selflessly aid and defend her to the death, she undertakes a journey to seek the help of a legendary wizard whose powers and benevolence are mythological. However, in reality the wizard turns out to be a mere mortal, a flawed egotist who means well but possesses no magical powers. In essence, a fraud. The innocent child loses her innocence and must face the harsh reality of life. But in the end, her dream of going home is achieved simply because she wanted it badly enough to never give up.

THE THREE MEN I ADMIRED MOST

The parallels to my quest for the truth regarding the assassination of my childhood idol are striking. Growing up in an age of innocence, the '50s and '60s, I, like Dorothy, was a naive child living in a drab world of black and white. Like Dorothy, I believed in the dreams of the leaders I saw as hope for the future. John F. Kennedy, Martin Luther King, and Robert Kennedy all held ideals that provided that hope. I believed that with dedication and perseverance, I could achieve my goals as well. Anything was possible. However, in my world, like Dorothy's, a tornado called the Cold War wreaked havoc on those dreams and even on life itself. This conflict took the lives of the three wise men and with them my innocence. I had to face the harsh reality of the real world. Hate had prevailed over love. I discovered that in real life the bad guys sometimes win. Like Shakespeare's hero, *Hamlet*, I endeavored to avenge my fallen father's image and solve the crime of the century. Where to start? *Just follow the yellow brick road.* Go where the research takes you. My quest for truth had begun.

During the Cold War, anti-Communist fanatics were locked in a life-and-death struggle against the evil Red Empire. In the previous decade hatred and paranoia fueled this struggle, perceived to be a terminal one, between East and West. All-out war was believed to be inevitable. That was a given. Nuclear annihilation seemed an acceptable solution to the problem by those in the Security State and Military. Throwing gasoline on the flames, the CIA connived to create false flags designed to justify actions against their adversaries that would otherwise be unthinkable to the American people.

Amidst this firestorm, a lowly Marine became a pawn in a game of world supremacy. Manipulated by a paranoid mastermind of counterintelligence, he would become one of the most important and misunderstood characters in world history.

Part I of this diatribe will deal with the pawn and his puppeteer … in essence, a tin man called Ozzie and a Wizard we shall call *Oz the Great and Powerful.* This pawn was a vest-pocket asset of a bespectacled, cadaverous, super-secretive icon of the world of counterintelligence. James Jesus Angleton and his CI/SIG station controlled and monitored Lee Harvey Oswald for *four* years *before* the assassination of JFK.

At the height of the Cold War, the US Military and Security State were convinced that war with the USSR was inevitable. Once the U-2 flights over Russia established that the US had a huge advantage in nuclear missiles, the war hawks concluded that *now* was the time to strike first and wipe Communism off the map, not only in the Soviet Union but China as well. Action had to be taken before the Russians closed the *missile gap.* Under the Eisenhower regime, *massive retaliation* had been the military protocol. Kennedy and McNamara were now promoting a *limited response* doctrine.[11] This was *strike one* for JFK. Kennedy failed to pursue military intervention at the Bay of Pigs, Laos, Vietnam, Berlin and in the Cuban missile crisis. *Strike two.* JFK was negotiating a test ban treaty and a cutback of nuclear weapons on both sides. To the US hawks, this would mean throwing away the missile advantage they held over their adversaries. *Strike three.* Add to this the President's bypassing the Joint Chiefs and CIA to deal directly with Kruschev to avoid war and making peace overtures to Castro. This proved the straw that broke the camels back. To JFK's Security State adversaries, this amounted to appeasement. They regarded the idea of peaceful coexistence as unacceptable. They saw Kennedy as a traitor and a threat to national security. To the

---

11   Conventional weapons instead of a nuclear strike.

Cuban exile commandos, accepting Castro and his Communist regime was a despicable act of betrayal. With a second term on the horizon, followed by eight years of RFK and then eight more of Teddy, the establishment of a Kennedy dynasty seemed inevitable. There was little recourse left to these *patriots*. It was their duty to *save* the country. There was only one solution, and that was the initiation of a coup d'état.

As Steven Grant, author of a JFK assassination comic book series called *Badlands*, so eloquently put it;

> American history is an hourglass, the center of which is the first Kennedy assassination. Not that things, including political murder, only went on afterwards that did not go on before – any good student of American history can uncover and chart the non-democratic molding of our country over its first two centuries – but the immediacy of information transfer in 1963 shattered the taboo against rubbing the public's face in it. The public's face was rubbed, and rubbed hard. This was complicated by the idealism that Kennedy spoke to, whether that was a sincere gesture or, as some have charged, a cynical political ploy. The murder of Kennedy was such a rabbit punch at idealism, a mocking of the naïveté of those who thought they could effect a change. So idealism, in the face of political reality, went underground, flipping the bird at the powers that be as it dropped out, put on gaudy clothes, and grew its hair.

Grant's portent that: *The man who killed President Kennedy midwifed the Sixties."* is a brilliant take. He also wonders why Oswald was chosen to be the patsy? His query ponders the dichotomy of conflict in Oswald's resumé. Yes, he was a perfect patsy, being a commie and Castro sympathizer. However, if the CIA, FBI or mafia were behind the crime, why would they choose someone with links to themselves? The answer is brilliantly simple. The names Oswald and Hidell would assure a cover-up. To seriously investigate the assassination would result in uncovering Oswald's connections to these very groups. The *country* was not ready for that much information in 1963, and the agencies who had surreptitiously manipulated the scapegoat, had to keep their clandestine evils a secret. Oswald was chosen as the patsy *because* of his connections and not in spite of them. These agencies would *have* to cover-up to protect themselves. Not because they were involved in the assassination as agencies but to hide their dirty dealings and protect their reputations. Since Oswald was a creature of James Angleton as early as 1959 and maybe earlier, it is obvious who chose him and why. His very name would invoke a cover-up.

CHAPTER 1

MINSK MELODRAMA

I have never personally known an individual more motivated by what appeared to be a genuine concern for the human race.
— Kerry Thornley's take on Lee Harvey Oswald

swald's Russian sojourn is but one mysterious episode in the life of the quintessential poster boy for mystery. Researchers have wondered what really went on behind the iron curtain during Oswald's residence there. Robert Oswald told Jay Edward Epstein that his brother's hair texture had changed when he returned from the USSR, something he attributed to possible electroshock or other medical treatment by the KGB. He brushed aside Lee's opinion that it was due to the cold Russian winters. Were the Soviets attempting mind control under the guise of therapy on this defector? Perhaps with cranial implant devices? Robert may have been suspicious of the time Lee spent in a hospital in Minsk. Why was he there and what went on while he was? Could it be that Robert's lack of remorse after Lee's death was an indication that he didn't truly believe that the man who returned from Minsk and was killed in the DPD basement was actually his brother? Lee's half-brother, John Pic, also claimed that physically Lee wasn't the same sibling he had known before his Soviet tour. Several researchers, including British writer Michael Eddows, believed that the real Oswald was replaced with a Soviet doppelganger who was sent here as a spy, perhaps one with a deadly mission.

What is known about Oswald's time in the USSR? The Warren Commission said that he went there as a discontented defector who offered to give secrets to the Soviets. This is a fairy tale. If this were true, they certainly would have debriefed and probably arrested him upon his return. They didn't. They even lent him money to help him get home. The "official" version of events is that the Russians weren't interested. They considered him unstable. A KGB officer[12] who claimed to have handled

Oswald's case, conveniently defected to the West at a time coinciding with the release of the Warren Report. His version of events supported the Commission's conclusions. Oddly, there was no mention of this KGB defector in the Commission's report. In addition, factions of the CIA as well as the FBI were divided in their takes on this defector's authenticity.

A newly released CIA document[13] quotes as its *source* a former KGB officer who revealed that Lee Harvey Oswald *was* an agent of the KGB. In addition, the document reveals that the UKGB[14] recruited Marina as a "*swallow*" (Soviet female prostitute) for use in sexual entrapment operations.

This *source* was informed of this by senior staff officers from the Minsk KGB Counterintelligence School (Minsk CI School) and department 1 (American targets) of the Second Chief Directorate (internal security and counterintelligence -SCD) headquarters. They revealed that Oswald was an agent even before he met Marina and that their meeting was not accidental. Marina was *directed* in her relationship with Lee. However, he did fall in love with her in spite of the fact that he originally pursued her on the rebound in an effort to hurt his true love, Ella German, who had rejected his marriage proposal.

SCD headquarters stated that it was not clear whether the local or regional UKGB was involved. The KGB considered Marina a reluctant agent and came to the conclusion that although she was interested in Oswald, she was more interested in escaping the USSR and poverty.

Soon after Oswald's defection in 1959, he was given an apartment on the Svisloch river, close to the Minsk CI School and Victory Square. There he was placed under surveillance by the Minsk UKGB. The Second Department – (foreign counterintelligence) considered Oswald an agent because he provided them with information on his past.

The *source* stipulated that it was common practice in UKGB to claim a foreigner living in its region as an agent. The regional UKGB would forward the subject's physical description, age, and any other information gathered to KGB Headquarters, claiming the subject as a foreign agent. These regionally claimed agents *were not agents in the classic sense*, rather they were an attempt by regional UKGB to obtain prestige.

In the early 1980s, Colonel Yurshak, an instructor at the Minsk CI School, stated that he had been involved with the Oswald case when he was with the Minsk UKGB. Their files on Oswald included agent, surveillance, monitoring reports as well as other information. When the

---

13   104-10014-10056
14   Ukrainian KGB

source questioned headquarters about the rationale for running Oswald, an ex-marine with little access to information, he was merely assured that Oswald was run in Minsk as an agent.

Yurshak had a low opinion of Oswald and considered him crazy and unpredictable. He revealed that Oswald was never required to sign an agreement to cooperate, even though he was cooperating. Yurshak believed Oswald knew he was in contact with the KGB.

Oswald was interrogated several times in Moscow by officers from KGB Headquarters (NFI). Oswald's KGB handlers considered passing him to the First Chief Directorate (Foreign Intelligence – FCD) to be handled by a KGB Residency in the United States, but the proposal was ultimately rejected because Oswald was considered too unstable. Upon Oswald's return to the US, Marina angered the KGB by refusing to continue cooperating with them.

At least six KGB and former UKGB staff officers told the *source* about the Oswald case. The stories were consistent. Each of these officers told Source that the KGB did not handle Oswald after his re-defection to the US and had no further contact with him. They also said that the KGB never tasked Oswald, and certainly never tasked him to kill President Kennedy. The *source* stated that rumors in the West, suggesting that the KGB was involved in Kennedy's assassination, were absurd. The KGB would never risk the scandal of assassinating a major world leader.

EVALUATION

What is to be made of this document? It is ridiculous to believe the WC version of events. Their contention is that the Soviets weren't interested in a defector eager to give them U2 secrets which they coveted is absurd. We are also to believe that, although his acts were treasonous, he was not debriefed or even interviewed when he returned. In fact, he was lent money to do so. This during the McCarthy witch hunt era when wearing a pink shirt could cost you your employment?

The Soviet version of events, provided by defector Yuri Nosenko, a likely agent provocateur, is in essence, just as lame. The Soviets weren't interested in this lunatic defector. The Russians were clearly covering their ass to prevent WWIII.

This document puts a more believable spin on their party line. It is saying: *yes we were interested and got some information from him, but in the end, we decided to drop him and what he did upon returning to America had nothing to do with the KGB.*

From Oswald's perspective, he was giving information provided to him to achieve his assignment as a false defector, and from the CIA's perspective, he was being used as a dangle in a mole hunt.

But even more valuable is what this document tells us about Marina. It has been suspected by many researchers that Marina was part of a KGB program to attach Soviet wives to returning defectors. These women would then become sleeper agents once in the USA. This document provides convincing proof that Marina was one of these.

MARINA AND WEBBY

In my research on defectors, particularly Robert E. Webster, I became intrigued by the connection between Webster and Marina Prusakova (Oswald). After marrying Oswald and immigrating to America, Marina told a friend, Katya Ford, who was part of the Dallas Russian exile community, that her husband Lee had defected while working at a trade exhibition in Moscow. It was Webster who defected while working at a trade exhibition in Moscow, not Oswald. So, it seems logical to assume that, at the very least, she was acquainted with Webster well enough to be familiar with his background. Still, it is certainly strange that she would confuse his story with her husband's. Further suspicion that a link exists between Marina and Webster is fueled by the fact that her address book contained a listing corresponding to Webster's Leningrad apartment. This book was found among Marina's possessions during an investigation into her background by US Intelligence officials.

At the time of Webster and Oswald's defection, US Intelligence, in particular ONI and CIA, were involved in sending false defectors to Eastern bloc nations as intelligence dangles. The number of these individuals increased radically circa 1960. Soviet Intelligence countered the increase in defectors with a program of their own. They began attaching Soviet women to these defectors when they returned to the US. Was Marina Prusakova one of these feminine "sleeper" agents? In the game of counterintelligence – all is fair in love and war.

According to a CIA memorandum:

> ... at the time (1960, the Agency) was becoming increasingly interested in watching develop a pattern that we had discovered in the course of our bio (graphical) and research work; the number of Soviet women marrying foreigners, being permitted to leave the USSR, then eventually divorcing their spouses and settling down abroad without returning "home." ... we eventually turned up something like two dozen similar cases.

Taking a closer look at Marina's life before and up to her meeting Oswald is enlightening. The "official" story is that seven months after leaving Leningrad and moving to Minsk, she was introduced to Lee Harvey Oswald at a trade union dance at the Palace of Culture in Minsk. Marina said they spoke in Russian and she believed him to be from the Baltic States by his accent, in essence, a native of the Soviet Union. An acquaintance, Yuri Merezhinsky, introduced her to him. Later, when asked who it was that introduced her to Oswald, she couldn't remember. Even when asked if it was Merezhinsky, she didn't recognize the name. The second time she was asked, she did recognize it. But later her mind went blank once again. How could she not remember how she met her husband and who introduced her to him? She also didn't remember when Lee asked for her hand. Even worse, how could she think she met Oswald at the Moscow Trade Exhibition, thus confusing him with Webster?

I began to wonder why Marina had left Leningrad, a city she had said she loved, and moved to Minsk to live with her uncle, who was an MVD official. Marina's version of the story given in Priscilla McMillan's book, *Marina and Lee*, was that her step-father, whom she lived with in Leningrad, threw her out because he wanted to remarry after Marina's mother's death. But according to Yuri Merezhinsky, Marina was deported from Leningrad for prostitution.[15] Norman Mailer wrote that her step-father evicted her after an argument in which he called her a prostitute.

Bells went off in my head as I recalled another incident involving Robert Webster and a prostitute named Nancy Jane McClain in Cleveland, Ohio, as revealed by a 1964 FBI report.[16] The document raises suspicion that Webster was using Oswald's name in a tryst with a call girl in Cleveland in 1963.

An entry in Marina's address book coinciding with Webster's Leningrad apartment building was listed under the name, "Lev Prizentsev" The address listed was; Kondrat 'yevskiy Prospeckt 7, Apt. 63 or Kondrat 'yevskiy Prospeckt 63, Apt. 7, Leningrad. A CIA document dated May 8, 1964, for Lee J. Rankin concerns "traces" on the addresses found in Marina Oswald's notebook. The CIA compared them against their international index looking for "traces" and found that the address under the name of Lev Prizentsev was the same as that of Robert Edward Webster.

15   The presenter in the TV program *The Way It Was* aired over the ORT channel from Moscow in February 2001 said that according to his information Marina Prusakova was deported from Leningrad, where she had resided before, because of her relationship with a foreigner. After that she went on being under the KGB surveillance. See *Oswald's Russian Episode*, Ernst Titovets, Mon Litera Publishing House.

16   See *The Other Oswald, A Wilderness of Mirrors*, Gary Hill, TrineDay books, Chapter One.

Marina told the FBI in an interview on 17 December 1963, that she met Prizentsev at the rest home near Leningrad (October 1960) and that *"he had an amorous interest in Irina Volkova (a friend of Marina), who unfortunately was already married."*

Traces: (1. No traces on Prizentsev. (2. Robert E. Webster, who renounced his U.S. citizenship in 1959 when he defected to the USSR and returned to the U.S. as an alien under the Soviet quota in May 1962, claimed to have resided in a three-room apartment at Kondrat 'vevskiy Prospeckt 63, Apt. 18, Leningrad, during his stay in the USSR.

At first, as stated above, Marina explained that Lev was in love with a girlfriend of hers, Irina Volkova, who was already married, and that was her connection to him. Prizentsev lived in Apartment 7 and Webster and his mistress Vera Platanova in Apartment 18. Another explanation she gave was that Lev was an elderly gentleman she met in a "rest home" near Leningrad. In reality, the CIA found no references or traces on this man. Was Lev Prizentsev actually Robert Webster? Was Webster using this name as an alias, or did she make up the name rather than reveal who it was she was visiting? Was Lev an acquaintance who acted as a translator for Marina and Webster? Any way you look at it, Marina was entangled with two American defectors. Why is there no mention of this interlude or "Prizentsev" in McMillan's book *Marina and Lee*?

Marina denied knowing Webster. However, in his last days, Webster nodded affirmatively when asked by journalist, Dick Russell if he knew Marina. Also, in a phone conversation with Carol Hewitt, Marina queried, *"How is he?"* when Hewitt told her of a visit to his nursing home.

When Marina left Leningrad and moved to Minsk in August 1959, Webster had not yet arrived in the city. So she had to have visited his apartment at a later date. She did. A close look at her travels shows that Marina went on *"holiday"* in the fall of 1960 to Leningrad. Can it be a coincidence that once there, she frequently visited a friend who happened to live in the same apartment building as Webster. At this time Webster *was* living in Leningrad. Marina had not yet met Oswald. Was she being used to seduce an American defector to attach herself to him when he returned to the US? Was she seeing him as a prostitute or both? There is speculation that Webster may have used prostitutes in the US, as the Nancy Jane McClain episode suggests. Was Marina part of the Soviet Intelligence program to send women home as *sleeper* agents with US defectors? Was she used as a *"swallow"* (prostitute) to get information from an American defector? Did the KGB have a hold on her due to her previous deportation out of Leningrad?

In the vastness of the Soviet Union, it seems unlikely that a simple girl of Marina's age would find herself, by mere chance, in the proximity of two personages as rare as American defectors were at the time. If they had occupied the same city, such an encounter might be plausible. However, considering the distance between Leningrad and Minsk and the difficulties routinely involved in travel throughout Russia at that time, coupled with the brief time frame overlapping the stay of the two men in her country, it seems an unlikely coincidence.

If Oswald's Soviet interlude and ease of return were mysterious, Marina's story is close to unbelievable. Marina Prusakova's birth certificate lists Severodvinsk as the city of her birth. However, the city wasn't named Severodvinsk until 1957, and she was born in 1941. A KGB legend? The birth certificate Marina brought to the United States was issued on July 19, 1961. Since she had to have one to obtain a marriage license before April 30, 1961, Jay Edward Epstein concluded; *"It thus seemed that new documents – and possibly a new identity – were furnished to Marina after it was decided that she would accompany Oswald to the United States."* In the middle of all this turmoil, Marina decided to take her annual *"holiday"* and travel alone to Kharkov, not a garden spot in October, to visit her aunt. As disclosed earlier, her *"holiday"* the previous year was in Leningrad. There she stayed at a government *"Rest House."* Odd that a 19-year-old needed to stay in a *"Rest House."* It was in October 1960 while on that *"holiday"* that she frequented Robert Webster's apartment building in Leningrad.

The only reliable sources for what transpired are the witnesses who were there and observed the events of Marina and Oswald's meeting. As previously stated, the man who introduced Marina to Lee was Yuri Merezhinsky. He was a medical student like Oswald's friend Ernst Titovets. Merezhinsky's mother was Professor Lydia Cherkasova. She was head of a laboratory at the Academy of Sciences engaged in classified research and a Communist Party member who rubbed shoulders with Khruschev himself. Old enough to be Oswald's mother, she was giving a lecture on the evening he met Marina at the Palace of Culture. She had only recently returned from the United States. The dance at which Marina met Oswald took place after the lecture. Yuri ran a slide projector from the orchestra pit as a visual aid to his mother's lecture. There are contradicting versions of how Yuri met Lee and how Lee met Marina.

HOW DID LEE MEET YURI MEREZHINSKY?

Merezhinsky's version is that Lee showed up out of nowhere, approached Yuri, and introduced himself. Yuri's mother, Lydia Cherkasova, agreed with his account that Lee magically appeared, approached Yuri, joined him in the orchestra pit, and helped him run the projector. However, a friend of Yuri and Marina, Kostya Bandarin, an anesthesiologist, said that Yuri knew in advance that Lee was coming over. According to this version, Yuri had gone in search of Lee and brought him to the orchestra pit. Marina corroborated Kostya's version saying it was Yuri who asked Lee to the lecture to hear his mother talk about America. According to Lee's friend, Ernst Titovets, Yuri, having been briefed (KGB) about Oswald, located Oswald and brought him to the orchestra pit.

HOW DID LEE MEET MARINA?

Yuri and Marina said that Lee met Marina on the dance floor. However, Bandarin and Professor Cherkasova said that Marina showed up and was introduced by Yuri to Lee in the orchestra pit. Wherever it happened, it was Merezhinsky that introduced Marina to Lee. Titovets agreed and said the two were friends.

THE ENTOURAGE OF THE LADY IN RED: WERE THEY *SUITORS OR ACCOMPLICES?*

Titovets accompanied Oswald to the dance. However, he did not accompany him to the lecture, and therefore was not privy to whether Lee and Marina had already met in the orchestra pit. At the dance, he and Oswald became separated in their search for girls to dance with. Titovets was conversing with an attractive girl when Lee interrupted him and asked Ernst to follow him to another area of the building, ostensibly to act as a translator. The object of this discourse was a beautiful Russian girl with a bouffant hairdo and a red dress. Titovets observed that Marina was surrounded by a small group of what Marina described in the book *Marina and Lee* as suitors. These were Yuri's and Marina's friends and included Kostya Bandarin, Sasha Peskarev as well as Yuri. Titovets thought it odd that these suitors never interfered with Lee's advances toward Marina and did not act competitively. He felt that they seemed to be there to see to it that nobody got in the way of her courting the American. This seems odd, particularly in the case of Sasha, who was said to be in love with her. Marina, at first seemed uninterested in Lee. Yuri perceived that she was anticipating the arrival of Anatoly Shpanko, who was Marina's current love interest. Eventually, she warmed to Lee and gave him her telephone number.

There are different versions of what happened after the dance. Apparently, Lee and a couple of the suitors walked Marina home. However, Yuri tells of a party they attended at his mother's apartment. It's not clear if Lee was invited by Yuri or by his mother, whom Oswald had carried on a conversation with after the lecture. She said she had spoken to Oswald about the kind of research she was engaged in. This is particularly intriguing. Would a Communist party member involved in classified projects be discussing those projects with an American defector who might possibly be a spy? Would she invite him to her home? Cherkasova had admitted she was routinely in touch with the KGB. No foreign contact would be tolerated to a person of her position during the Cold War.

INFORMANTS OR PATRIOTS?

Titovets portrayed himself as Oswald's friend and would lead us to believe he did not inform or spy on him. However, he felt that he or any of his peers would assume it was their patriotic duty to help their country in this way if they were asked to do so. Oswald was no dummy and suspected, correctly, that his apartment was bugged. He and Titovets spent time trying to find listening devices. He also stated that it was he who had invited Lee to the dance. The KGB would have known this from the bugs in Lee's apartment. Let's take a look at the others associated with the meeting of Lee and Marina.

Kostya Bandarin collected pornographic pictures as a teenager. He had quite a collection. This resulted in someone squealing on him and Capt. Nikolayev of the KGB extracted his collection and used it to blackmail him. He was likely manipulated into obtaining information about Oswald and aiding in connecting Oswald with Marina.

Lydia Cherkasova and her son, Yuri Merezhinsky, were KGB-connected. It may have been Yuri who approached Lee and invited him to attend the lecture. It was Yuri who introduced him to Marina.

Sasha's role is not clear, but the fact that he made no attempt to compete with Lee for Marina, even though he was in love with her, says volumes.

Marina herself would have to have been in collusion with the machinations going on at the dance. Marina's story is that she didn't know Lee was an American when she met him. But Yuri said that when he introduced them he told her Lee was an American. Someone is lying.

Titovets didn't like Marina and found her conniving and shallow.[17] He believed she wanted, all along, to go to America as much or more than Lee. After only about a month of marriage, Oswald revealed that he wanted to return to the US. Marina had no objection.

After the assassination, a Moroccan student, Mohamed Reggab came forward and claimed to have been a boyfriend of Marina Oswald. Romance took place in Moscow in the first half of 1961 while Reggab was studying cinematography there. He stated that he has photos of Marina and a letter from her in his effects in Casablanca and has written his brother-in-law to find them and send them to him. Marina denied she ever knew Reggab but certain details he related about her and her background lend credence to his story. The CIA was anxious to follow up his story and was willing to pay him to fly to Casablanca and back to find the picture and letter if necessary. However they soon became suspicious of him and feared he was stalling.

"*Reggab has number of complex financial, documents and personal problems which are leading him to consider return to Moscow for further study at cinematography institute. Believe he would definitely return if encouraged by us and that he would be susceptible recruitment as KUBARK agent during Moscow sojourn and possibly as long range asset in Morocco.*" (Doc CIA 104-10020-10052 & 104=10020-10006). The CIA concluded Reggab's story was a fabrication.

MATERIAL GIRL

I think that there is plenty of evidence to suggest that Marina was a Soviet dangle used as bait to lure first Webster and later Oswald into taking her back to the US. We now know that such a program existed as a response to the fake defector programs of the ONI and CIA. We can also perceive that Marina wanted to go to the US, and once there would stay and be useless to the KGB as a "*sleeper*" agent. She wanted all the material goods America had to offer; TVs, appliances, clothes, cars, etc. She was probably chosen for this project by her uncle, an MVD official. Or possibly she was blackmailed by the KGB when she was deported from Leningrad for prostitution. In an interview with Ernst Titovets, Yuri Merezhinsky related that; "Marina was sent out from Leningrad in twenty-four hours for prostitution with a foreigner. *She was in a jam and came to Minsk to stay with her uncle.*" He went on to say, "*We call it 101 Kilometers – which means being sent very far away... from Leningrad. She came to Minsk with four other*

---

17   A shallow swallow?

people who were sent out of Leningrad together. She was part of a group. Two young men and two women. Her uncle worked for MVD (Ministry of Internal Affairs). That is why she was privileged to come to Minsk and not 101 Kilometers. One hundred and one Kilometers means you have to cut trees in the forest. A labor camp for prostitutes and people who don't work. You are sent out of big cities to work hard labor. She was seen regularly in Hotel Leningrad and they told her to leave because of foreigners." Kostya Bandarin told Norman Mailer that the foreigner she was involved with was a Georgian. He said that Marina's uncle helped to hush it up and it was he who saved her from the labor camp. However, the price derived from the KGB may well have been blackmailing her to get her to take part in the *sleeper* agent program.

HEADLINE-AUG 19, 1965 – *THE EXCELSIOR*

"WIDOW OF LEE OSWALD HAS BEEN HIT BY HER NEW HUSBAND (KENNETH PORTER) AND HE THREATENED SUICIDE. PORTER IS PUT IN THE SAME JAIL AS JACK RUBY"

Apparently Oswald wasn't the only one who beat Marina. Maybe she deserved it as Marguerite Oswald and George de Mohrenschildt contended.

In 1965 Marina married Kenneth Porter. Although he never adopted Junie and Rachel, they took his last name. Probably Marina's way to keep them from knowing the real identity of their infamous father as well as protecting them from harassment. She and Porter divorced in 1974 but reunited six months later and have been together ever since.

There is a strange coincidence involving Porter's employment at Collins Radio. On the day of the assassination, an Oswald double was seen driving a car owned by Tippit's best friend, Carl Mathers. It couldn't have been Oswald because at that time he was on his way to the Dallas jail, having been arrested at the Texas Theater. The investigation of this incident opened a can of worms tying the Military-Industrial Complex to the events of November 22, 1963, via Collins Radio. Collins Radio had tentacles that reached out to J.D. Tippit (through Mather), Lee Oswald (through the double, Admiral Bruton of Collins, and the MDC Pontchartrain camps and their raid involving the CIA flagship, The *Rex*), Jack Ruby, who hosted a Collins party at the Carousel, David Ferrie (through phone calls to Belcher Oil who owned the *Rex*), LBJ (General Dynamics), George de Mohrenschildt (through Bruton), Cuban exiles and the CIA plots to kill Castro (raids by the *Rex* on Cuba led by Rolando Martinez of Watergate fame), D.H. Byrd and the Texas School Book Depository, and eventually to Marina Oswald Porter. Why did the DPD Intelligence Division pay an informant to spy on fellow workers at *Collins Radio* who were suspected of being subversive? Was there a link between the Navy's nuclear sub radar and communications HQ, where Admiral Bruton was working on a top-secret communications project, and Michael Paine, whose family owned an island nearby? Why were Robert E. Webster's final days spent near the same location?

Was Operation Paper Clip another link between *Collins* and the Paines? Michael's boss at Bell Helicopter was Walter Dornberger, a Nazi general sentenced to die at Nuremberg for war crimes and rescued by Allen Dulles and Paper Clip along with Werner Von Braun, General Reinhard Gehlen and many others?

A report in the *Wall Street Journal* in April '63 revealed that *Collins* was planning to construct a radio communications system to link Laos, Thailand and South Vietnam. After JFK's murder *Collins Radio* would become a major benefactor of LBJ's escalation of the Vietnam War.

A connection between Oswald, *Collins* and the *Rex* mission of October 63 was MDC, the Movement Democratico Christiano, who had a commando training camp near Lake Ponchartrain in Louisiana. Oswald tried to infiltrate this camp at the behest of some US intelligence agency, most likely the FBI under RFK's orders to close these training camps and stop raids of sabotage against Cuban targets.[18]

What was the nature of Tippit's relationship to Carl Mather? Mather worked for *Collins Radio,* who had a connection with the Military Industrial Complex and US. Intelligence projects supporting anti-Castro Cubans in raids against Cuba.

The Mystery of Albert Schweitzer College

Man can hardly even recognize the devils of his own creation.
– Albert Schweitzer

Lee Harvey Oswald was a man of mystery. I believe that one of the reasons he was chosen for clandestine undercover assignments was that he kept his mouth shut. The numerous inconsistencies in his life have been the subject of debate for close to six decades. While there are many, one incident stands out as a possible clue to the real forces controlling his

---

18   According to Peter Dale Scott.

actions. This was his application to Albert Schweitzer College in Churwalden, Switzerland. What was the purpose of this strange endeavor? Was someone behind his actions? Was he on a mission? Was the real purpose of his assignment different from what he believed it to be? Was he being manipulated by invisible forces, whose identity is speculative to this day?

Albert Schweitzer College (ASC) was an experimental school created to allow students from all nations to meet and study together in the interest of promoting world peace and goodwill. That statement alone resulted in them being seen as a threat in the eyes of military hawks, the CIA, and Cold War profiteers. They had little interest in peace and a paranoid fear of it breaking out.

ASC was not a traditional degree-granting four-year college. It was non-accredited and ran on a trimester schedule. You could enroll for one trimester or a whole year. The college was very small with fewer than 50 students and a few staff members.

According to the Warren Commission (WC), on September 4, 1959, even before he left the El Toro base in California, Oswald applied for a passport under the pretense of attending the Albert Schweitzer College[19] in Switzerland and the University of Turku in Finland; also included were travel in Cuba, the Dominican Republic, England, France, Germany, and Russia. Although his passport was authorized on September 10th, he did not get his discharge until September 11th. The Marines never questioned the discrepancy between these travel preparations and the purpose of his discharge, which was to take care of his "ailing" mother.[20] After staying home with Marguerite for just three days, he told his mother that he was going into the "import-export" business. Her WC testimony was that *import export* was already stamped on his passport. His brother Robert, wrote that Lee planned on going to New Orleans and working for an export firm.

On September 17th, Oswald departed for New Orleans, on the first leg of his defection.[21] On September 20, he embarked on a freighter to La Havre, France. The journey took sixteen days. He arrived in France on October 8th. The Warren Commission said that he arrived in Southampton, England, on October 9 and set off for Helsinki, Finland, arriving and checking into the Torni Hotel the same day.

---

19   It seemed odd to me that Oswald was accepted at a college with no high school diploma. However, Robert Oswald disclosed in his book *Lee,* that his brother had earned a GED while in the Marine Corps in March of 1959.

20   A box of candy fell off a shelf in a store she worked in and hit her on the nose.

21   He made the travel arrangements through "Travel Consultants," a New Orleans based travel agency also used by Clay Shaw. On the agency's questionnaire he gave his occupation as "shipping export agent."

However, on Oswald's passport, the British immigration stamp reads; "Embarked 10 Oct. 1959." He then flew to Helsinki, Finland, arriving on October 10th at 11:30 P.M.[22] The CIA, in response to a Warren Commission request, said that they could not identify any direct flights from London to Helsinki that would have allowed Oswald to arrive at his Helsinki hotel on the evening of October 10, 1959. So, was this a military flight? Or was it an indirect flight with a stopover?[23] Another question is why, after taking a slow boat to China, err... *France,* did Oswald suddenly take quick flights to England and Finland? He told English customs agents that he was staying in the UK for one week before departing for Switzerland to attend Albert Schweitzer College. Instead he departed the same day to Finland. Oswald requested his Soviet visa on Monday, October 12th, the first business day after his arrival at Helsinki. His passport shows that his Soviet entrance visa was issued on October 14, a mere forty-eight hours later. The usual time for tourist visas was five to seven days. How did he get his in only 48 hours? In reality, it may have been even sooner. In his book *Passport to Assassination,* KGB Colonel, Oleg Nechiporenko reproduced a photographic copy of Oswald's 1959 application. The form is dated and signed by Oswald on October 13, one day later than previously thought. This document shows that Oswald's visa was granted within 24 hours instead of 48! Once in the Soviet Union, Oswald was initially rejected and given a deadline to get out of town. An apparent suicide attempt caused the KGB to reconsider to avoid an international incident.

When Oswald didn't show up at Albert Schweitzer College in Switzerland, his mother became concerned about him. A $25.00 check she sent him on January 22, 1960, was returned. The FBI knew this because they had been opening her mail. John Newman discovered an FBI memo that revealed a program for "siphoning of bank account information." George Michael Evica believed that this "program," together with the specific history of Oswald's background, trip to Europe, and his subsequent disappearance, points to a Bureau counter-espionage operation. At this point, Mrs. Oswald was interviewed due to Bureau's concern that her missing son's identity was being used by someone else. She revealed that she believed he had taken his birth certificate with him. If not, it was missing. This is the origin of Hoover's June 1960 memo that an impostor might be using Oswald's birth

---

22   CE2677

23   What is mysterious, is why the CIA did not identify nor collect the passenger lists for these flights, which would have still been available in 1964. (Or if they did, why were they not submitted to the Warren Commission?) It would prove or disprove that this was his method of travel. Or was there a sensitive name on the same flight with Oswald?

certificate. Why, after the suspicious suicide attempt by Oswald, did the Soviet officials ask him if he had any identification other than his passport? Did they, like Hoover, believe someone was impersonating him?

So what is going on here? Most researchers now believe Oswald was a "fake" defector, probably part of an ONI project designed to lure the Soviets into accepting them as real or turning them as double agents in a cold war game consisting of mutual efforts to "fake the other guy out." In addition, recently released documents incriminate James Jesus Angleton and his Counterintelligence unit of handling Oswald from the get-go. Oswald being Angleton's singleton agent. For more on this see my book, *"The Other Oswald, A Wilderness of Mirrors."*

How did Albert Schweitzer College, or ASC, fit into all of this subterfuge?

THE CROWN JEWEL OF THE UNITARIAN CHURCH[24]

ASC was owned and operated by the Unitarian-controlled IARF[25]. The main supporters of ASC in the US were the *American Unitarian Association Department of World Churches* and the Unitarian-operated *Friends of Albert Schweitzer College.* As George Michael Evica observed, *"Over the years, Allen Dulles and the OSS/CIA used the Quakers, the Unitarians, the World Council of Churches and other religious groups as sources of intelligence and information.* According to Evica, *The Unitarian Church was the mainstay of the Albert Schweitzer College."*[26] It now seems apparent that Oswald registered at Schweitzer to use it as a reason for travel to Europe in the fall of 1959. It is obvious that he never intended to attend.

Richard Boeke of the *International Association for Religious Freedom (IARF)*, said that the college had 25-30 students when he visited it in 1964. He elaborated that the college was in "a bit of trouble" with the Swiss" due to American students introducing marijuana. This fits Walt Brown's description of Albert Schweitzer College as *"a hippie commune with a curriculum."* The *weed* incident became a *drag* and resulted in ASC moving to a new location near Geneva. When Boeke later revisited the institution he found no students at all, only a director who lived very well. Soon after this, lack of financial support resulted in ASC going broke.[27]

Evica believed ASC was being watched by FBI and CIA due to alleged communist affiliations of Schweitzer himself. In particular, his denunciation of the

---

24   Description of ASC provided by Richard Boeke of the International Association for Religious Freedom (IARF)..

25   International Association for Religious Freedom.

26   *A Certain Arrogance*, George Michael Evica, p.72.

27   *Lee Harvey Oswald's Cold War*, Greg Parker.

nuclear arms race was seen as a threat to Cold War activists. Evica also believed that ASC may have been infiltrated since this was the case with many other institutions espousing the *commie* view on peace.[28] Perhaps the original plan was to have Oswald infiltrate this institution as a spy or agent provocateur.

The *Unitarian Service Committee* was used by the OSS and CIA in various operations, mainly involving relief and refugee work. One prominent member of the USC was Dr. Winfred Overholser, a professor of Psychiatry at George Washington University and Director of St. Elizabeth's Hospital in Wash, DC.[29] Overholser was instrumental in establishing alcoholism as a disease. One of his patients was the poet Ezra Pound.[30]

In October 1942, the OSS established a "truth serum" committee headed by Overholser. This later evolved into project ARTICHOKE, which eventually escalated into MKULTRA. After the Korean War, Overholser worked to ensure US soldiers would be inoculated against communist brainwashing techniques. As stated earlier, Overholser was a Unitarian and active member of the *Unitarian Service Committee*.

If you think all of this may just be a coincidence, then explain Overholser's secret employment by the Warren Commission as a consultant on the lives of both Oswald and Ruby? In addition, Commissioner John McCloy wanted to use Overholser to explain certain anomalies regarding the wounds and the autopsy report, something Overholser was certainly not qualified to do as a psychiatrist.

I'LL GET BY WITH A LITTLE HELP FROM MY FRIENDS

So how did Lee Oswald find out about ASC? The school was practically unknown, even to the Swiss police. The school didn't advertise. The only influx of applicants came from word of mouth and *Friends of Albert Schweitzer College*. Could it have been through CIA channels that he was manipulated into applying?

Oswald's Marine Corps. buddy, Kerry Thornley, told the Warren Commission that he had been attending the "far left" First *Unitarian* Church in Los Angeles around the time he was friendly with Oswald. The church was led by Stephen Fritchman. Fritchman was a peace activist who had been before the *House Un-American Activities Committee* twice and was involved in the Test Ban talks.[31]

28   *A Certain Arrogance, George Michael Evica, p.72*
29   It was Overholser, as Chairman of the American Psychiatric Association, who concluded that United States Secretary of Defense, James Forrestal, "came to his death by suicide while in a state of mental depression."
30   Close friend of James Angleton
31   Fritchman's name was found in the note book of Richard Case Nagell.

The head of the college, Hans Casparis, had attended the University of Chicago at a time concurrent when Kennedy supporter, Paul Douglass was on the faculty. Douglas, a Quaker turned Unitarian and anti-communist became involved in Operation Brotherhood, a CIA project involving medical charity to benefit the Diem regime in South Vietnam. The CIA's front for this venture was the *"International Rescue Committee."*

The Friends of ASC acted as a cutout for CIA money. Not difficult with Percival Flack Brundage[32] involved. He later helped set up CIA proprietary in Miami to support Cuban ops of JMWAVE.

Ruth Paine's sister, Sylvia Hoke, worked for the CIA under Air Force cover on surveillance flight manpower issues. One project she worked on was FICON. FICON was the predecessor of the U2 program. Her role dealt with manpower and recruitment research for the project. My research also found links between Hoke's work for the Air Force in personnel records and a project called LONGSTRIDE that involved another defector, Robert Webster.[33]

THEY'RE EVERYWHERE, THEY'RE EVERYWHERE

Can it be just a coincidence that Unitarians and Quakers are everywhere in the background of the JFK assassination? How many people do you know personally that belong to these groups? How many individuals with CIA ties do you count among your friends and associates? Lee Oswald, portrayed as a loner by the WC, was surrounded by contacts who were both.[34]

Quakers, for instance, keep popping up in strange places in Oswald's world. Ruth Paine was a Quaker and she asked a fellow Quaker, Ruth Kloepfer, to check on the Oswalds while they were in New Orleans. Kloepfer's husband was a professor at Tulane University. Oswald reportedly passed out FPCC leaflets near the homes of professors at Tulane who were members of leftist groups. Richard Nixon, a Quaker, was in Dallas on the day of the assassination. At one time, Jack Ruby worked for Nixon as well as for LBJ. Robert Webster was of the Quaker faith. When Oswald was in Mexico City, he reportedly made contacts with Quakers studying at the Autonomous University. One Quaker student at the University was an active agent of the CIA at the time. Priscilla McMillan, who got an exclusive interview with Oswald when he was in Moscow and befriended Marina after the assassination to collaborate on the book *"Marina and Lee,"*

32   President of Friends of ASC. A Unitarian.
33   *The Other Oswald, A Wilderness of Mirrors*, Gary Hill
34   Also popping up were Trotskyites: George Lyman Paine, Harold Issacs, Harry Power etc.

was a Quaker. Another wealthy Main Line Quaker and philanthropist, Dr. Dee Dee Sharples, later a Temple University Trustee, was once married to George de Mohrenschildt, one of the accused assassin's best friends.

How about Unitarians? Oswald's Marine Corps buddy, Kerry Thornley, and CIA mercenary, Gerald Patrick Hemming were Unitarians. William Lowery, Dallas's answer to Herb Philbrick, was a Unitarian. He ran a shoe store near the Texas Theater.[35] As noted by George Michael Evica, the Unitarian Church was the pillar supporting the Albert Schweitzer College and Patrice Lumumba University. Oswald applied to both.

Another suspicious example of the connection of religion to the JFK assassination is the *Abundant Life Temple* in the Oak Cliff section of Dallas. After breaking the world record for the mile, killing Tippit, and escaping the scene of the murder, Oswald, or whoever the shooter was, reportedly was seen entering the church. Dallas Police were about to search the building when they were called to the Texas Theater.

Eric Tagg labels these

> "old church" organizations as "*a clandestine substructure developed to serve the intelligence community's concept of national security.*"[36]

Tagg continues;

> ... *like all churches are virtually free from official inquiry by the Constitution, not to mention American custom. The "ministers" and "bishops" can accumulate money (religious fund-raising) without serious inquiry as to the source, ...they are free to operate in relative seclusion from the expected social involvements, free to engage in obscure crusades or missions. ... they may be a home structure for the particular church, one would have the most natural of safe houses.*" Was the Abundant Life Temple a safe house where the real shooter of J.D. Tippit found *sanctuary*?

Less mainstream religions, born of con men who were ordained by mail, are prevalent as well. David Ferrie was a "priest" in the *Old Orthodox Catholic Church*. His vestments were found in his apartment after his death. Peter Lavenda made an interesting observation pertaining to Ferrie's religious obsessions. His take is that Ferrie was preoccupied with *ritual* rather than *theology*. He belonged to the Order of St. John, which is a *military* religious order. It was heir to the Knights Templar. Ironically, the Templar were disbanded by the pope on the *22nd of November, 1312*.

---

35   *The Other Oswald, A Wilderness of Mirrors*, Gary Hill
36   *Brush With History*, Eric R.Tagg p154

Guy Banister's investigator, Jack Martin, was also a member of the *Old Orthodox Catholic Church* clergy and he encouraged Thomas Beckham to join and be ordained as well. Later "Bishop" Thomas Beckham set up his obscure ministry in the *Holy Orthodox Christian Church*. Fred Chrisman was a minister in the non-existent *Universal Life Church*.[37] An employee of Jack Ruby and Oswald look alike, Larry Crafard, was affiliated with the *General Assembly and the Church of the First Born*." Is it yet another coincidence that five peripheral characters in the JFK assassination story just happen to be members of "Old Church" ordination mills? Beckham, it seems, was a patsy and later concluded that his "*Old Catholic Church*" was just a front for a group of Cuban Exiles. John Bowen was affiliated with the *Council of Christian Churches*. Bowen was an apparently self-ordained minister who ran several *missions* in Mexico and founded "*The Campfire Council*" a youth group that promoted fascist ideologies.[38] Bowen was also known as Albert Osborne and it was he who sat next to Oswald or an impersonator on a bus to Mexico City. He also may have run a school training assassins in Mexico.

United Missions of America, a Texas Corporation located in Dallas and represented by O.B. Graham (president) purchased the Oak Cliff Christian Church in April 1962 and renamed it the *Abundant Life Temple*. One of the incorporators of the United Missions of America was Walter C. Tucker. Tucker was a mechanic with the Continental Trailways which was located across the Stemmons Expressway from the TSBD. Continental Trailways also employed a man named Kenneth Cosy as a bus driver. Cosy's telephone number (FR5-5591) appears twice on the last page of Lee Oswald's notebook.[39]

Now that we know more about ASC, let's speculate about the mystery of Oswald's involvement with this institution. Why would he apply to a tiny, unaccredited school in a remote village in Switzerland? Even more intriguing is how he even knew of its existence.

The possibilities are few. The College was dependent on the Unitarian Church for support. A group called *Friends of Albert Schweitzer College* helped recruit and raise funds. As stated, there was no advertising or promotion in the US. It is almost a certainty that LHO used personal contacts in making his application. Who could it have been? Kerry Thornley is a possibility. As mentioned before Thornley was a Unitarian and told the

---

37   Beckham and Crisman were subpoenaed by Jim Garrison to testify in the Clay Shaw trial.
38   For a complete biography of Osborne/Bowen see- https://kennedysandking.com/john-f-kennedy-articles/the-dual-life-of-albert-osborne
39   *Brush With History*, Eric Tagg, p157-158

Warren Commission that he had been attending the "far left" First *Unitarian* Church in Los Angeles around the time he was friendly with Oswald.

Another source of ASC students was Antioch College in Yellow Springs, Ohio. It seems ironic that researchers would find connections between Antioch and Lee Harvey Oswald. There were reports of sightings of him at a demonstration there in the early 60s. One FBI report contained an "unverified" statement that Oswald had attended the college briefly in 1957. That would be a good trick since he was in the Marines at the time. Ruth Paine, of course, attended Antioch from 1949 to 1955. In addition, a Navy Department document revealing that Ruth Paine had been requesting information about the family of Lee Oswald in 1957 was found by researcher Michael Levy. Officially, Ruth didn't know of the Oswalds until she met them in 1962. Could it be that Ruth was infiltrating left-wing institutions as far back as the mid-50s and reporting back to the CIA, to whom her family had so many ties? Was Angleton or ONI beginning to consider Oswald for intelligence work in 1957 and needed to know more about him and his family? Was Paine the source of this information? Was Oswald's treatment at Bordentown in 1953 a catalyst in these maneuvers?[40]

ASC was being watched by the FBI and CIA due to the alleged communist affiliations of Schweitzer himself. Could Oswald have been manipulated by one of these agencies to apply?

If so, why? Spying on ASC is a possible reason, but he never attended. I began to look at Oswald's strange behavior from a conspiratorial viewpoint. When you consider that the leftist organizations he was involved with or corresponded with, such as *The Fair Play For Cuba Committee, ACLU, CPUSA* etc. were all groups being investigated and discredited by the CIA and or FBI, you become aware of a connection. Oswald's Clinton, LA escapade may have been part of an assault on *CORE (Congress on Racial Equality)*, a target of Hoover and Angleton's COINTELPRO. Tying these institutions to a commie defector to the Soviet Union created an indirect link to Moscow and the Communist Party. It is a standard intelligence practice to use defamation to discredit your enemies. After the assassination and Oswald's conviction in the media, the FPCC ceased to exist.

So, is this evidence of an intelligence involvement in the Oswald-ASC saga? As a matter of fact, there is a smoking gun. In 1995 the AARB was in the process of reviewing FBI documents related to the JFK assassination in general and ASC in particular. The 1960 release of

---

40   For details on the Bordentown incident, see chapter 16.

these docs had been heavily redacted and portions blackened out. The review board decided it was time for a full release. The FBI balked. Why after 35 years or more would they resist the release? They went as far as appealing to President Clinton. When the smoke cleared, they finally released the materials uncensored. The new releases were surprising. Especially an October 12 memorandum from the American Embassy in Paris to the FBI. It contained three statements that were contrary to the official story about Oswald and the ASC. The memo said that Oswald had originally registered for the Fall trimester of 1959, that he had originally written to ASC from Moscow, and that Marguerite had written directly to Oswald at the ASC address. A November 3 memo to the Director contradicted the October 3 version. This one said Oswald applied from Santa Ana for the Spring trimester and that Marguerite had written, not to Lee, but to college personnel to ask about Lee's whereabouts.

These new documents reveal two things. First, the findings of the 1960 investigations were changed dramatically within a few weeks. Second, they were covered up by the Bureau for 35 years. As researcher Dennis Bartholomew put it,

> ... these documents mean that many of the documents printed in the WC exhibits would have been false and intentionally manufactured to support an incorrect description of Oswald's ASC activities.[41]

WHY DID THE CHICKEN CROSS THE ROAD?

So, there is still no definitive answer. Who told Oswald about ASC? Why did he apply if he had no intention of showing up? Did he apply for the spring or fall trimester? Did he apply from Santa Ana or Moscow? Why did the FBI cover up for 35 years? If only Oswald had had a trial. If only we could ask him questions. Instead, there are a multitude of critical inquiries that will never be answered. Jack Ruby, what have you done?

REEVALUATING MARINA'S ROLE

In 1959, Marina met Robert Webster at the Moscow Trade Exhibition. We can assume this because she told a friend that she met her husband there. But Lee wasn't there. Webster was. I could find no evidence that Marina visited Moscow in 1959. But either she did or Webster told her about the Trade Exhibition in 1960 when she saw him in Leningrad. it's not clear what the date was since Webster went to Moscow three times;

March 59, May/June 59 and July 59. The last time was when he defected. If they met the 2nd or 3rd time, Webster was already involved with Vera Platanova and possibly rejected Marina's advances. In October 1960 she likely met him again several times at his apartment building in Leningrad. By then Vera was a permanent fixture.[42] Perhaps during one of these visits, she discovered that Webster already had a wife in the US and therefore could not bring home a Soviet bride. Perhaps she was visiting him as a prostitute, repeating her behavior with *"foreigners"* that had resulted in her deportation from Leningrad in 1959. Webster may have had a penchant for women of the oldest profession as his involvement with a harlot in Cleveland, Ohio in 1963 indicates.

So, Marina changed her objectives and focused on Oswald instead. In March of 1961, Marina's uncle, a MVD colonel, "encouraged" her to go to a dance at the Palace of Culture in Minsk. There she met, had a whirlwind romance with, and soon married Lee Oswald, another defector. Oswald, in turn, brought her to America.

After the assassination, one of the first people investigated by the FBI as a suspect in the JFK case was Robert Webster, whom they believed knew Oswald in Russia. They checked out his activities on the day of the assassination. Obviously, they suspected he may have been involved.

Was Marina coerced or blackmailed by Soviet Intelligence into developing a relationship with an American defector to spy on him and subsequently accompany him in his return to the US? Did she, in turn, use this as a mechanism to escape the Soviet Union, defect to the United States and live the American dream?

TIMELINE

March 59 – Webster's first trip to Moscow.

May-June 59 – Websters 2nd trip to Moscow.

July 59 – Webster's 3rd trip to Moscow.

Aug 59 – Marina moves to Minsk.

September 59 – Webster moves to Leningrad. Lives at the Baltiskaya Hotel.

October 59 – Oswald and Webster defect. Webster moves to Kandratievski Apartment in Leningrad on Oswald's birthday, October 18.

October 60 – Marina's holiday in Leningrad.

April 61 – Marina and Oswald married.

October 61- Marina's holiday in Kharkov to visit aunt.

---

42   An Apartment Permit shows Platanova living with Webster at 18 Kondratievskii Prospect, No. 63 as of 12/11/59.

DEFECTORS TO THE SOVIET UNION IN ADDITION TO LEE OSWALD, 1959-60

1. Joseph Dutkanicz – He and his wife defected in May 1960. He had been in the Army (Military Intelligence Branch) in Germany. Was recruited by KGB prior to defection. Later applied to return to US. His wife arrived in America in March 1962. However Soviets never let him leave. It is reported that he died there in November 1963.

2. Vladimir Sloboda – Defected May 1960 a few days after Dutkanicz. Like Dutkanicz, he was also stationed in Germany in Army Intelligence and recruited by KGB prior to defection. Sloboda said he had been blackmailed and framed before going to Russia. His English wife managed to leave the Soviet Union.

3. Robert Webster – See my book; *The Other Oswald, A Wilderness of Mirrors.*

4. Bruce Frederick Davis – Served in US Army for 5 years. Left his post in W. Germany and defected in May 1960. Lived in Kiev. Returned to US July 1963.

5. Nicolas Petrulli – Lived in Long Island, NY. Defected September 5, 1959. Renounced his US citizenship after being turned down by Soviets for Russian Citizenship, returned to US Sept 21, 1959,

6. Ricardo Riccardelli- Served in US Air Force. Defected August 1959. Lived in Kiev. Returned June 1963

NOTE:

In 1957, Martin Greendlinger was a mathematician at NYU. While attending the World Youth Festival in Moscow in 1957 he met Yelena Ivanova Pyatnitskaya (Kapustina), a student of the Lenin Pedagogical Institute. He returned to the USSR in April 1958 to marry her. He returned to US in July 1959. Research: US Defector Machine Program and CIA File on Soft Defectors.

TRIVIAL PURSUIT

A letter to Richard Helms from J. Lee Rankin, May 19, 1964:

> *The commission wishes to consider the possibility that during his stay in the Soviet Union, Lee Harvey Oswald may have received medical or psychological treatment or conditioning designed to reinforce or accentuate his apparent hostility to authority and thereby rendering him a disruptive factor in this country after his return. We think a study of*

35

the latest Soviet techniques in mind conditioning and so-called brain-washing would be helpful in that regard. We would greatly appreciate you making such materials as you may have on the subject available to Mr. Wesley J Liebler of our staff. Perhaps a conference on this subject between appropriate members of your organization and members of the staff would be desirable. (Doc 32357059)

Chapter 2

Somewhere Over the Rainbow

However much you deny the truth, the truth goes on existing.
— George Orwell

The Redskins are Coming

Yet another Angle for the Angler.[43]

The suspicious behavior of Oswald's wife Marina and the mysterious connections of his cousin, Marilyn Murret, are an indication that all of these players were being manipulated by US and Soviet Intelligence in a game of Cold War espionage.

I found links between the ONI's false defector program and James Angleton's mole hunt in Oswald's case. Webster, on the other hand, appeared to be handled by James Rand, ATIC (LONGSTRIDE), as well as CIA counterintelligence (Angleton). Hints of CIA involvement in Murret's travels were abundant. As for Marina Prusakova Oswald, it now seems evident that she was used by the KGB as a Swallow in a project whose purpose was to send Soviet women home with U.S. defectors and who eventually would become sleeper agents.

Marilyn Dorothea Murret

Oswald's cousin, Marilyn Murret, led a bizarre lifestyle as a freelance teacher who traveled the world. A 1964 syndicated article, called the *Allen-Scott Report,* that dealt with defectors to the Soviet bloc, listed Murret and Webster among the ten "Most Wanted." Even though Webster had already repatriated and Murret was a tourist and never a defector at all.

In an interview with the FBI, Scott said he had information that there was a "tie-up" between her and Lee Harvey Oswald. A logical assumption since she was his cousin. Scott continued that he also had *information* that indicated Murret was linked to the *"communist apparatus"* of Profes-

---

43   The Angler and Mother were monikers used by associates when referring to James Angleton.

sor Harold Isaacs of the Massachusetts Institute of Technology. Isaacs, a former Communist spy, later became a paid agent of the Japanese. An ex-editor of *Newsweek*, who worked in the United States at MIT in 1953, he also maintained a network in Japan and possibly throughout the world specializing in youth movements. Since 1950, he had also been involved in classified projects for the CIA. Isaacs wrote articles for *The Militant*, the organ of the Socialist Worker Party, which certainly made him known to a subscriber named Lee H. Oswald.

I suspected that since Oswald had been involved with a group of Japanese Communists in Japan while stationed at Atsugi, it was possible this was the Isaacs apparatus and that Murret may have encouraged this contact. Had either or both of them infiltrated this group?

In 1975, William Gaudet, the same CIA agent who was in front of Oswald in line to get a Mexican Visa in October 1963, told Attorney Bernard Fensterwald that Marilyn Dorothea Murret may have worked for the CIA in New Orleans. He should know since he did. Evidence that Murret was a CIA agent comes from a classified Warren Commission document (1080) that was released accidentally through a misfiling error.

I wondered if the CIA had a project involving "tourists" visiting Russia. This would go a long way toward explaining the travels of Marilyn Dorothea Murret. As it turns out, they did have such a project.

OCEANS, REDWOODS AND REDSKINS

Enter Thomas B. Casasin. Casasin became Chief of the CIA's Soviet Russia SR6 Branch in 1960. Casasin told the HSCA in an interview conducted on August 17, 1978, that "the function of Section 6 was operations in support of the Soviet Russia Division of the CIA," including 'classical espionage work.'" As we shall see, Casasin was closely linked with William Crowley, who in turn, was joined at the hip with James Angleton. Casasin also played a role in the debriefing of Webster, and if Joan Mellen is right, Oswald as well. Furthermore it was he who was investigating links between Soviet women marrying foreigners and the KGB. So it seems Casasin played a role in the lives of each of the subjects of this article; Webster, Oswald, Marina. But what about Marilyn Murret?

In the early 1960s, *"Thomas B. Casasin (chief of SR/6) identified the REDSKIN cryptonym as the legal travelers program. It involved using persons to give information about the Soviet Union who had a 'very legitimate' presence in the Soviet Union, such as scientists, etc."*[44]

---
44   180-10143-10227: 180-10143-10227

Richard Bissell, in a memo dated 9/2/59, described a program called *REDSKIN* as follows: "*Operations directed against the USSR proper, whether our own or liaison assets are involved, requiring the specialized knowledge and accumulated experience of the SR Division ... (this includes) CI operations designed to place or recruit sources inside the USSR, legal travel operations into the USSR using nationals of third countries or US citizens, and operations based on the use of Soviets traveling legally from the USSR into the Free World. The various types of legal travel operations into and out of the USSR are considered to constitute an integrated program (REDSKIN).*"[45] Was Murret one of these people? What about Oswald?

Here we have Bissell saying that legal travelers were used to get information from the USSR and that this program included *CI* (Counterintelligence. ... *Angleton*) operations to *PLACE* or recruit sources inside the USSR. Sounds like Oswald.

According to Joan Mellen, "*Casasin also refers in his 25 November 1963 memo to a program called AEOCEAN 3, then run out of SR10, and referring to Oswald in particular: this was the legal travelers program, i. e. the intelligence use of legal travelers to the Soviet Union. It seems apparent that Casasin, a pseudonym, was not in the loop, and is struggling to make sense of Oswald and his defection.*"[46]

Casasin like Otto Otepka, was unaware Oswald was a dangle and considered recommending him for "*REDWOOD.*" A project involving Legal Travelers to the Soviet Union. *REDWOOD* was part of Operation *AE-OCEAN. REDWOOD* also featured an assassination program.

Casasin recalled that he thought Oswald's behavior struck him as "odd" and "unusual" after reading a dispatch on him following Oswald's return to the United States from the Soviet Union. He told his subordinates something along the lines of, "Don't push too hard to get the information we need, because this individual looks odd." Casasin therefore decided not to use him in operations in the REDWOOD target area. REDWOOD was an action indicator for the SE Division. Of particular interest was what information Oswald could provide on the Minsk factory where he had been employed.

Like Otto Otepka, Casasin was not privy to Angleton's vest pocket operations. The Oswald project was one of these.

45   180-10143-10227
46   Joan Mellen, "Who Was Lee Harvey Oswald?" The Wecht Institute, Duquesne University, Pittsburgh, PA. October 5, 2008

CRYPTONYMS

- REDWOOD/REDSKINAERODYNAMIC/OPERATIONAL – Was a CIA source program based in legal travelers to the Iron Curtain countries.

- REDWOOD was an action indicator for the SE Division. (SED was a CIA geographic designation for the Soviet Union and the Soviet Bloc countries of Eastern Europe). It seems now a case of one hand not knowing what the other was doing, a not infrequent CIA situation.

- AEOCEAN – Run out of SR10, and referring to Oswald in particular: this was the legal travelers program, i.e., the intelligence use of legal travelers to the Soviet Union. As stated, it seems apparent that Casasin,[47] was not in the loop, and had a hard time making sense of Oswald and his defection. The definition provided to the HSCA staffers by the CIA was; "people traveling legally or planning travel to the USSR."

- REDSKIN – Operations directed against the USSR proper, whether our own or liaison assets are involved, requiring the specialized knowledge and accumulated experience of the SR Division...(this includes) CI operations designed to place or recruit sources inside the USSR, legal travel operations into the USSR using nationals of third countries or US citizens, and operations based on the use of Soviets traveling legally from the USSR into the Free World. The various types of legal travel operations into and out of the USSR are considered to constitute an integrated program. (Note: There were 30-35 REDSKIN trainees at an SR safe house in New York).[48]

OCEAN 3[49]

AEOCEAN-3 was the agent used by CIA Officer Jacques Richardson, aka Thomas B. Casasin, for the CIA's Legal Travelers Program inside the Soviet Union. A CIA document identifies him as Philip R. Neilson.[50] His was the first notable case of a defector immigrating with Soviet women and these women possibly being sleeper agents. This agent, similar to Lee Harvey Oswald, was able to marry a Russian wom-

---

47   104-10067-10212 Reveals Casasin's true name as Jacques Richardson

48   104-10120-10373- A Memorandum for the Record dated 2/28/61, from Ervan E. Kuhnke, Jr., Chief, SB/2 Desk stated; After discussion between Howard Osborne (Deputy Chief, SR Division) and Jack Southard, Chief, CCG/NC (Central Cover Group, Nonofficial Cover)

49   I wonder if Frank Sinatra was OCEAN 11?

50   104-10429-10239

an named Tamara Kungarova and later immigrate to France with her. Another document[51] states, "*On his second trip to the USSR in January 1959, Philip Robert Neilson, REDSKIN agent, was given an INTOURIST interpreter/guide Tamara Stepanova Kungrova. A romance developed between them and Neilson became determined to marry her, which he finally did in the spring of 1962.*"

In a memo (11/25/63) from Casasin to Walter P. Haltigan during the time Oswald was in the USSR, Casasin said that he was "*increasingly interested in watching a pattern that we had discovered in the course of our bio and research work in (SR) 6: the number of Soviet women marrying foreigners, being permitted to leave the USSR, then eventually divorcing their spouses and settling down abroad without returning "home."* Although the OCEAN 3 case was among the first of these, something like two dozen similar cases eventually turned up. SR6 established links among some of these women and the KGB.. KUDESK[52] became interested in the developing trend SR6 had come across. Casasin closed his addendum to the memo with this line, indicating that he was not aware of Angleton's program: "*It was partly out of curiosity to learn if Oswald's wife would actually accompany him to our country, partly out of interest in Oswald's own experiences in the USSR, that we showed operational intelligence interest in the Harvey story.*"

Other REDSKINNERS

Another document[53] I found recounts a former "*Redskinner*" for the Agency's Soviet Russia Division named Warren Harshman who was a bus tour guide using a route from Helsinki to Warsaw and back. He made five visits to Minsk and stayed at the Hotel Minsk. He was later debriefed and used the cryptonym AEHOLLY 152 or 52 according to the file.

Days before 11/22/63, the FBI investigated[54] another REDSKIN traveler and informant. A note dated 4/28/58 requesting an Investigation and Approval from "*sources*": asks the CI/Operational Approval and Support Division[55] to OK the use of Priscilla Johnson "legal traveler" as a "REDSKIN traveler and informant." Interestingly, her CIA application was ultimately disapproved for security reasons. An 11/29/63

51   104-10012-10111
52   CI staff and CI operations.
53   104-10007-10336
54   104-10173-10145
55   Another link to Angleton

memo[56] from SAC, Boston, to Director, re: approximately 30-year-old female American tourist of interest to KGB for possible recruitment: The Washington field office had been doing a background check on *Priscilla Johnson* between late October 1963 and November 1963 in the days before 11/22/63. Looking at her relationship with Harvard University. Could this have been related to Oswald's Mexico City trip and the subsequent investigation of him by the FBI?

The research of Chad Nagle and Peter Voskamp exposes McMillan's role in REDSKIN. They show that the CIA considered her as a possible "legal traveler into the USSR – spotter" for a *counterintelligence* program (104-10310-10192) involving the placement or recruitment of sources inside the USSR, legal travel operations into the USSR using nationals of third countries or US citizens, and operations based on the use of Soviets traveling legally from the USSR into the Free World. The various types of legal travel operations into and out of the USSR are considered to constitute an integrated program (REDSKIN).

> In April 1958, the CIA's Soviet Russia Division asked the Counterintelligence Staff's Operational Approval and Support Division for authorization to use Priscilla Johnson as a "REDSKIN traveler and informant.

The document above was only released in 2022.

The CIA's chief of the Soviet Russia (SR) Division, Donald Jameson, described a meeting with Priscilla Johnson in Dec. 1962, in Cambridge, Massachusetts. The Agency's Domestic Contacts Division (OO), informed Jameson that Johnson *"had been an OO source and they had a clearance on her for contact and debriefing."*

Proof that Priscilla Johnson (later McMillan) was working the CIA's domestic Contacts Division (OO) is confirmed by this document:

APPROVED FOR RELEASE 1993
CIA HISTORICAL REVIEW PROGRAM

CONTACT REPORT

Meeting with Priscilla Johnson on 11 December 1962

1. _Circumstances of Meeting:_ Priscilla Johnson was selected as a likely candidate to write an article on Yevtushenko in a major U. S. magazine for our campaign. I took advantage of being in Boston on 11 December for the AEWILDFIRE Board meeting to go to the OO Office and inquire about her. She had been an OO source and they had a clearance on her for contact and debriefing. Having talked to them and explained that I was first interested in discussing Soviet literature with her, they agreed to place me in contact. Mr. Butler of the Boston OO Office called Priscilla Johnson who agreed to see me almost immediately. I spent approximately an hour and a half with her in her room at the Brattle Inn, 48 Brattle Street, Cambridge, Massachusetts where she is now living. OO informed me that she is allowed to use the Harvard-Russian Research Center for her own work, mainly the writing of articles and a book, but that she has no other official relationship to the center.

2. _Impressions and Assessment:_ Miss Johnson impressed me as being able, astute and conscientious, qualities that I have noted in the articles of hers that I have read. She is however rather nervous and shy, giving one the impression of a lack of self-confidence, although the evidence of her numerous and important Soviet contacts certainly indicates that she knows how to meet people and how to talk to them. Although concerned about making her articles accurate as to fact and free from any external influence, I think she might be worked around to writing an article in which she genuinly believed, but which would also further our purposes for Yevtushenko. She also has other information that would be well worth getting on several young Soviet writers. The great interest of her life is Soviet literature and primarily its writers. She is personally concerned about many of them and dedicated to the cause of

Even as she was writing *Marina and Lee* in 1975, the CIA documented her role as a witting writing collaborator.

McMillan denied her connection to the CIA until her death. But there is no doubt she was lying. She, like Marilyn Murret, was a *REDSKINNER*. But she was more. She was a media asset.

DEBRIEFINGS; OSWALD AND WEBSTER

Whereas there is no *official* evidence of a debriefing of Oswald, Webster was debriefed in Ohio by CIA and Air Force officials. This was reported by Cleveland Resident Agent, Eugene Rittenburg. He revealed that two unidentified agents "…*talked alone with Webster in the INS offices for about one hour. During this time, no attempt was made to secure and FPI, rather it was a general 'get acquainted' type session. Webster was very well dressed but extremely nervous. His nervousness was not caused by our presence, as Mr. O'Brien had previously told us that he was having difficulty getting Webster's fingerprints as he was perspiring so profusely – even through his fingertips."*[57]

A short time after his return he was first questioned at his home in Zelienople, PA by agents of the FBI. Webster was transferred to CIA Headquarters and was debriefed there for two weeks.[58] He told the FBI that he was never questioned by the KGB: "*The only time I was questioned concerning American defense matters occurred when some Moscow engineers asked me what government work was handled in the Rand Development Corporation. I denied any knowledge of this, because I had none.*" Webster informed the HSCA that the KGB never contacted him, that there was no reason for them to do so as the government officials who aided him in his defection had his entire story. He said he had never been questioned relative to intelligence matters. He signed this Secrecy Agreement. Strangely, the word *Secrecy* is crossed out in the document.

As for Oswald, a program in the PBS documentary series, *FRONTLINE*, entitled "Who Was Lee Harvey Oswald?," revealed a document detailing how a man, a defector (his name was not mentioned),[59] but who had been working at a radio factory in Minsk, had, upon his return to the United States, been debriefed by one "Andy Anderson," a CIA employee with a *00* designation.[60] Richard Helms was confronted with this docu-

---

57   CIA Pitts F.O. 6.28.62
58   One source says he was debriefed for a week at a Washington Hotel by the CIA. So possibly the second week was at Langley. The CIA's main interest was in Russian personnel. They had photographs of Russians whom they wished to know if he had talked with. Webster signed a secrecy oath not to reveal the substance of the CIA debriefing. Related to this, I found an interesting Dept. of Justice document dated August 8, 1962, the subject of which is a KGB agent named "Sasha." Though partially blacked out it states that photos were shown to Webster in at his father's home in Zelienople. He denied knowing who they were. However, the same document states that in May 62, he stated he was in contact with (name blacked out) at the American National Exhibition in Moscow in 1959. It then goes on to say that Webster recanted on July 31, 1962, stating he had been mistaken concerning the name of this individual and that he should have identified him as.. (name blacked out).
59   It was Donald Deneselya (CIA) who came forward first to Senator Richard Schweiker of the House Select Committee, and later to "*FRONTLINE.*" Deneselya told Mellen what he had seen. When he asked his Agency confreres about the document, he was told that the subject was Robert Webster, although Webster was located not in Minsk, but at a plant in Leningrad, and there was a parallel document mentioning Webster by name.
60   00 (Overt Operations-Contacts Division) synonymous with KUJUMP. it's interesting that the existing record shows George de Mohrenschildt reported to the Domestic Contact Service (00) in Dallas on Haitian matters.

ment on the show and, the great actor that he is, pretended to know noth-ing about it. Joan Mellen has done extensive research on the "Anderson" moniker. Mellen believes "Anderson" was a pseudonym used by a woman named Eleanor Reed,[61] a deputy chief of the Section 6 Soviet Russia re-search branch who was near the age of retirement.[62]

Mellen states that the "Anderson" who debriefed Oswald was, strictly speaking, not working directly for Robert T. Crowley, who headed up the CIA Contact Division, Support Branch, the primary function of which was Counterintelligence. But she may have acted on his behalf in the de-briefing. Mellen found that Oswald's debriefing was ordered by E.M. Ash-craft, Chief of the Contact Division. He and Robert Crowley, OSB/CI, Operational Support Branch, Counterintelligence, were on the same lev-el. Eleanor Reed's overall boss would have been David Murphy, Chief of the Soviet Russia Division. Robert Crowley may have just about left 00/OSB (Operational Support Branch) where he was replaced by George S. Musulin by the time Oswald returned from the Soviet Union in June of 1962.

Mellen concluded that; "*Further corroboration that the CIA Soviet Russia Division, Soviet Realities, SR6, in the person of Eleanor Reed, debriefed false defectors is contained in a document that I have just discovered that the CIA released "as sanitized" in 1998. The document resides in Robert Webster's file, is dated 17 August 1962, and is telling for several reasons; the cases of Oswald and Webster are so similar that we can await, with reasonable expec-tation, that a parallel document of Oswald's debriefing by Reed (with, perhaps, her frequent debriefing partner, Rudy ("Valentino") Balaban, may well sur-face. This document demonstrates beyond doubt that Reed ("Anderson") was an SR6 debriefer.*"[63]

SUMMARY

Toto, I don't think we're in Kansas anymore

These memos show that Thomas B. Casasin (Richardson) was look-ing for links between Soviet women marrying foreigners and the KGB. It is clear that he was instructed by CIA not to reveal to HSCA in-formation about a tourist guide he ran in the Soviet Union under a pro-

---

61   Eleanor Reed's pseudonym Eleanor Anderson.

62   **Reed joined SR6 in 1956 and transferred out in 1964; she retired in 1970.**

63   Joan Mellen, "Who Was Lee Harvey Oswald?" The Wecht Institute, Duquesne University, Pittsburgh, PA. October 5, 2008

gram called REDSKIN, and who, like Oswald, married a Soviet woman. The involvement of Casasin and Crowley in all this and the interest of *KUDESK* (Counterintelligence) operations leads to James Angleton. Casasin (Richardson) was not only involved in the debriefing of Webster and likely Oswald, he was also behind the investigation of Soviet women being sent home with defectors as sleeper agents. In addition he played a major role in the OCEAN/REDWOOD/REDSKIN projects. Thus he is tied to all the key players in Angleton's Oswald Project (Oswald, Webster, Marina, Murret). Casasin was closely linked to Crowley and Crowley to Angleton. Cut-outs like Crowley and Casasin insulated the *Angler* and kept him in the background where he could spin his webs unnoticed.

In addition to Casasin (Richardson), Crowley, Murphy, Balaban and Eleanor Reed (Anderson), another interesting name surfaces in the debriefing of Robert Webster. Ned Bennett not only was present but was allowed to interview Webster separately.[64] Bennett is yet another link to Angleton. As a CA (Covert Action) officer, he worked in close conjunction with CI (Angleton's Counterintelligence)/R&A (Research and Analysis). It was Bennett whose memo to media assets coined the term "*Conspiracy Theorists.*" As mentioned earlier, Lamar Waldron believes that "*Bennett was chosen because he had written an important article for the London Spectator, entitled "the theories of Mr. Epstein, that trashed the book 'Inquest' by Edward Epstein.*"[65] In a subsequent memo, Bennett attached the article as an example of the type of piece that could be written to attack critics.

It seems clear to me that Angleton was using Oswald as a vest-pocket agent in his *own off the books* operations. The CIA was opening, reading and copying Oswald's mail while he was in Russia. They were part of a dossier kept on him by CI/SIG, the Super-Secret Counterintelligence unit run by Angleton himself. The agent intercepting Oswald's mail was Reuben Efron. Efron was working for CIA counterintelligence chief James Jesus Angleton at that time. After the assassination, Angleton used Efron to spy on the Warren Commissions interviews with Marina Oswald. He was fluent in many languages including Russian since he had been born in Lithuania. Efron, it turned out, was identified by name but not by affiliation as an attendee at the testimony of Oswald's widow, Marina, on February 5, 1964.

It is now evident that Oswald was not only part of a mole hunt, he was also being used to obtain information. A co-worker at Jaggars-Chil-

---

64   104-10182-10075
65   *Legacy of Secrecy,* Lamar Waldron, p.380

es-Stovall, Dennis Ofsteen, revealed that Oswald had shown him photos of military installations in Minsk. He also passed on information about the radio factory he worked at in Minsk involving radar applications. Oswald was clearly a *Redskinner*.

New Orleans police Lieutenant Francis Martello's son gave Joan Mellen a copy of the note Oswald handed his father to give to the FBI in the summer of '63. In it Oswald used the term "AMEP," which refers to American Express. Mellen deduced that Oswald was communicating with the CIA while in Russia through a CIA asset at American Express named Michael Jelisavcic who ran The AE office in Moscow. The note also included the word "pouch." An FBI document[66] dated 12/17/68 to the Director from SAC, New York, was placed in Oswald's 105 file. It indicated a relationship between Oswald and Jelisavcic. The document relates to the Bureau's attempting to, quote, "*resolve all facts concerning possible compromise of Jelisavcic by Soviet intelligence during his employment within the USSR.*" The Bureau knew that Oswald possessed Jelisavcic's name and room number, and were doing the usual damage control. Mellen wonders if "*American Express was the conduit for funding, for Oswald's orders, or simply provided the "pouch" for intelligence information from Oswald going back to Headquarters.*"

CIA agent Donald Deneselya told Mellen he witnessed a document describing a CIA debriefing of Oswald. This alone places Oswald as a participant in US intelligence. She further disclosed that at a meeting of the National Board of the Communist Party, USA, held on December 4, 1963, the party's National Secretary," Benjamin J. Davis, rejecting the idea that Oswald was one of their own, commented, "Oswald was with the Central Intelligence Agency." (This comes from a 12/11/63 FBI confidential document). Among the details Deneselya added was that some time after he witnessed the Oswald debriefing document, he asked James Angleton where he might find a copy so that he could peruse it again. Angleton's response was "*You'll never find that document.*"

CONCLUSIONS

Casasin, who didn't know Oswald was a dangle, considered recommending him for "REDWOOD."

A project involving Legal Travelers to the Soviet Union, REDWOOD, was part of Operation AEOCEAN.

REDWOOD featured an assassination program.

---

66   65-69127-13 Malcolm Blunt revealed to Mellen that "65 serial is FBI filing system-speak for espionage.

Crowley was "joined at the hip" with Angleton and was involved in Webster's debriefing as well.

Eleanor Anderson (Reed) debriefed Robert Webster and may have debriefed Oswald as well.

Rudi Balaban was involved as well as Crowley.

On Aug 10, 1962, Reed wrote up an analysis of Webster. She came to the conclusion that he was a sociopath.

An Aug. 27 report stated that intelligence gained from Webster involved a radar storage plant and a previously unknown naval installation. It was decided that *"positive intelligence from Webster could be of real value if his bona fides could be established."* Webster was ordered to never admit to anyone he participated in a CIA Counterintelligence Program. CISIG (Angleton).

According to Donald Denzlia, Marina met Webster and Vera at "rest home." This fits in nicely with her "Lev Prizentsev" story.

CHAPTER 3

THE MAN BEHIND THE CURTAIN

Paranoia strikes deep
Into your life it will creep
It starts when you're always afraid
You step out of line
The man come and take you away
  –"For What it's Worth," Buffalo Springfield

THE WIZARD

It was James Angleton and CI/SIG that controlled all the information on Oswald from at least 1959 until he died in 1963. Inexplicably there was no 201 file created for Oswald until 1960. There can be little doubt that LHO was Angleton's vest-pocket agent. It's doubtful that anyone else in the agency, outside of CI/SIG, was aware of him or who was running him. The mole hunt had to be protected. False information needed to be distributed so that the identity of the impostor, embedded in the agency, could be exposed. No one handled secrets better than *Mother*.

The cold war began even before WWII ended. In the latter's waning days plans were already being implemented for the former. The Dulles brothers and their like-minded OSS, military Intelligence, remnants of the defeated Nazi regime, and right-wing factions of government and industry (the military industrial complex), began planning for the demise of the Soviet Union. Projects like Gladio and Operation Paperclip were born of the ashes of the doomed alliance between East and West. The Yalta Conference was seen as a betrayal. The Dulles faction began to believe there was communist infiltration of our government. The McCarthy era would soon arise from this train of thought. Paranoia ruled both Eastern and Western thinking. This is the environment into which the CIA was born. Spies and betrayal were the backdrop in a world of mistrust and suspicion. Kim Philby, Pyotr Popov, Alger Hiss and the Rosenbergs fueled the growing paranoia. The Prince of Paranoia was James Jesus Angleton.

This mindset of suspicion and mistrust was not only prevalent among the cold war adversaries on both sides of the globe, it manifested itself among the various US intelligence agencies that were supposed to be interacting for the common good. As Peter Dale Scott pointed out in his book, *Dallas '63*, these agencies not only didn't cooperate with each other, they each had their own agendas and secret projects. This lack of communication and internal secrecy may explain the bizarre story of a victim of cold war paranoia named Lee Harvey Oswald.

It appears Oswald became a pawn in the extremely complex world of intelligence while stationed at Atsugi in Japan. From what is now known, we can piece together evidence of his manipulation in a game of espionage that commenced with his being approached by Japanese communists. It looks as if he came to the attention of ONI when he was approached and seduced by a waitress at a Japanese club called the Queen Bee. This Nipponese vixen was attempting to get him to talk about his work at the U2 base. When he reported this to his superiors, he was encouraged to play along and infiltrate a Tokyo commune. Oswald took to this line of work like a duck takes to water. Since his youth, he had escaped the oppressiveness of his mother's clutches by creating a fantasy world. He fancied himself a spy living multiple lives like his idol Herb Philbrick on the TV show, *I Led Three Lives for the FBI*. Aware of his successful portrayal of a soldier with communist sympathies, the ONI enlisted him in their false defector program and sent him to the Soviet Union as a dangle. In turn, the paranoid guru of CIA Counterintelligence, James Angleton, aware that Oswald had worked in the secret U2 project, as well as his psychological profile, determined by MKULTRA doctors at Bordentown as a youth, saw an opportunity to utilize him in a mole hunt. The goal was to expose what Angleton believed to be a leak in the U2 project itself. His knowledge of the existence of such a mole came from the ramblings of an intoxicated counterintelligence spy named Pyotr Popov. Behind the scenes, the CIA may have been aware of Popov's impending arrest by the Soviets which happened on the very day Oswald arrived in Moscow. Was this part of his mission?

Researcher John Newman has just recently concluded that Popov's Mole was Bruce Solie. Newman's take is that it was Solie, not Angleton, who was behind the mole hunt. If true, this means that Angleton was duped not only by Philby but by Solie as well. No wonder he was paranoid! Solie was Chief of the Research Branch in the Security Research Staff of the Office of Security. If Newman is right, Solie manipulated An-

gleton into creating a *"FALSE* mole hunt" using "false defectors," primarily Oswald, steering Angleton to believe the KGB's mole was in the Soviet
Russia Division of the CIA. Thus Solie, the actual mole who resided in the
Office of Security, was not only shielded from exposure, but kept abreast
of its progress. He may even have controlled it. When Yuri Nosenko was
sent by the KGB as damage control to assure the US that the KGB had
no interest in Oswald, as well as no involvement in JFK's assassination, it
was Solie who vouched for his bona fides as a real defector. The fact that
Solie was backed up by the FBI's resident agent, FEDORA, who later was
found to be a double agent provocateur, speaks volumes.

> *The U-2 crisis serves as an historic example of how the outcome of one
> celebrated international incident can damage the prospects for progress
> between the superpowers.*
>
> – E. Bruce Geelhoed

Another operation involving Oswald, without his knowledge, may
have been the sabotaging of the 1960 Paris Peace Talks via the downing
of Francis Gary Powers U2 spy plane. The plan here was probably not to
have Oswald give secret information to Russians enabling them to shoot
the plane down, but for the CIA to sabotage the plane itself in Turkey before takeoff and use Oswald as a patsy to take the blame. This strategy had
the side effect of proving the defector's worth as an informant to the Soviets, who were to believe that the information he provided was responsible
for their achieving success in shooting down the *Black Lady of Espionage*.

However, as Scott so perceptively observed, other agencies may also
have played roles in this charade. After JFK was assassinated, agencies
who may not have been aware of ONI's or Angleton's operations and may
have been forced into cover-up mode to protect themselves. This was due
to the compartmentalization and lack of communication between agencies, and even between different departments in the same agencies. The
right hand seldom knew what the left hand was up to. They were forced
to protect top secret ops and sources as well as their own deficiencies and
dereliction of duty.

As Scott observed, problems began when Oswald threw down his
passport on Richard Snyder's desk at the US Embassy in Moscow and
loudly proclaimed that he intended to give secrets to the Russians. This
should have set off alarms and Oswald, still technically in the Marine Reserves, should have been arrested on the spot. That didn't happen. Scott's

use of the analogy, *the dog that didn't bark,* is perfect. This is a reference to a Sherlock Holmes mystery entitled *"The Adventure of Silver Blaze."* In this story a race horse is kidnapped from his stable in the middle of the night. No one saw the crime taking place so it seemed unsolvable. Holmes, however, deduced that it was an inside caper. His reasoning was that the stable dog never barked. In essence it proved that the dog was familiar with the perpetrators and felt no threat. The innuendo in Oswald's embassy escapade is that the *dog* didn't bark because it knew Oswald was not a real defector and that his threats were just a ploy for Russian ears since it was known that the embassy was bugged. The dog, in this case being Snyder, the State Department and US and or military intelligence. In fact, Snyder later stated that that was what he thought at the time. The Soviets shared the same perception. Oswald's charade was meant for the Russian microphones hidden in the embassy.

It is also possible that by leaving his passport with Snyder for two years, the CIA could have given the passport and the "legend" to someone else.

But there was more going on here. It seems that there was also a paranoiac relationship going on between the FBI and Marine G2 with the State Department. In spite of the fall of McCarthy, Hoover was still obsessed with communists under every bed and their infiltration of the State Department in particular. Oswald's vocal threats gave credence to Hoover's convictions and he blamed the State Department for not acting on this subversive traitor. Later, Hoover's mole in the State Department, Otto Otepka ended up losing his position after trying to determine whether Oswald was really a defector giving secrets to the enemy or if he was working for us. Other allies of Hoover in his game were Martin Dies Jr., chairman of the House Committee on UN-American Activities, James O. Eastland and Thomas Dodd of the Senate Internal Security Subcommittee, and J. G. Sourwine, chief counsel for many years to that Senate subcommittee. Their goal was to uncover subversion and communism, and utilized what amounted to a witch hunt to do so. All this inter-agency paperwork on Oswald resulted in a multitude of files. Some shared and others held secret. In the case of Angleton's CI/SIG. These files, with different versions of Oswald's name, and the insertion of false information was used as a barium meal in a mole hunt. In Oswald's case, it is likely that ONI and CIA (Angleton's counterintelligence group in particular), were in the know and that the FBI was out of the loop. Marine G2 may have been in the loop if Oswald's act was part of their efforts to expose liberals in the State Department. In fact, CIA asset Snyder may have been one of those suspected. SISS and HUAC were also using this lowly marine in their pogroms against the left. In that case Oswald would be putting on his show at their behest as well. So, even though FBI and Marine G2 may have been running the same type of operation, FBI may not have been in the loop as to Oswald's game. All this led to the confusion involving Oswald's files to this day. Some released, others not. Marine intelligence files remain elusive.

IN THE MERRY OLD LAND OF OZ

Trying to make some sense of it all
But I can see it makes no sense at all
Is it cool to go to sleep on the floor?
'Cause I don't think that I can take anymore
– "Stuck in the Middle with You" Stealer's Wheel

Since it seems likely that some or all of these operations were piggy-backed with Angleton's mole hunt, Oswald being set up as the assassin of JFK set in motion what amounted to an automatic cover-up. Was this a coincidence or did someone "in the know" manipulate it to happen? Was this Machiavellian puppeteer able to maneuver a forced cover-up as part of a coup, not only sure to be successful, but safe from prosecution as well?

What if someone was not only setting up Oswald, the Cubans and/ or Russians, but the CIA, FBI, ONI and Marine G2 as well. A plot within a plot within a plot? I feel the presence of a genius lurking in the background here. Someone who had manipulated Oswald before in a mole hunt as his personal *singleton* agent. Someone who understood all the levels of the intelligence complex.

To make it all work, it was necessary to link Castro and, or the Russians to the assassination. A scenario along the lines of Operation NORTHWOODS. The device used to make this work was Oswald's trip to Mexico City and supposed contact with Kostikov and KGB Department 13, whose specialty was sabotage and assassination. This puppeteer knew the inner workings of the Mexico City apparatus intimately. His brilliant but paranoid mind always working behind the scenes, spinning webs, never in the limelight. An invisible ghost and catalyst of evil.

In order to accomplish all of this, the puppeteer needed a cut-out. Someone to not only handle Oswald on a personal level, but someone who knew the Mexico City Station and its inner workings as well as he did. Someone who was in charge of *photographic and audio surveillance* of Cuban Diplomats. Someone who was, at the time, running Cuban Ops out of Mexico City. Someone who had just been promoted to Operations Officer on September 29th, 1963 at the *exact* time the episode was beginning. Someone who, a CIA memo in fact revealed, "...*would be assigned to CA (Counterintelligence) Staff (Mexico City) to develop Ideological Warfare.*" Someone who had been seen talking to Oswald in Dallas shortly before he left for Mexico City. Someone named David Atlee Phillips.

According to P. D. Scott,

> David Phillips is the one man who seems to cover all aspects of the CIA-Oswald operation and cover-up in 1963. David Phillips even had one friend, Gordon McLendon, in common with Jack Ruby. McLendon, a sometime intelligence officer and Dallas owner of radio stations, had known Phillips since both men were in their teens. (The two men would in the 1970s join in forming the Association of Former Intelligence Officers. McLendon was close to two other wealthy men in Dallas who have attracted the attention of JFK researchers. They were Clint Murchison and Bedford Wynne.
>
> What was not yet known is why McLendon, whom Ruby described as one of his six closest friends, embarked on a sudden and surprising trip with his family to Mexico in the fall of 1963."[67]

The initial response to the assassination came in two phases. Scott points out that these were, in essence, two interpretations of "who done it." He calls these phase *one* and phase *two*. The phase *one* solution was that Castro and/or the Russians were behind the president's demise. This scenario was promoted by the likes of Win Scott, David Phillips, William Harvey and Dave Morales. It's Mafioso proponents included Richard Cain, John Roselli, Sam Giancana and John Martino. Others like Gerald Ford and Henry and Clair Booth Luce later jumped on this bandwagon. It was based on events like Oswald's Mexico City trysts with Kostikov and Duran as well as other jury-rigged events like the Bayo-Pawley raid. LBJ used this phase *one* information to convince Earl Warren and others on the commission to pursue a cover-up to avoid a nuclear war.

Phase *two*, as Scott describes it, was the lone assassin scenario. This quickly replaced the phase *one* version and was pursued by the FBI and Hoover, with President Johnson's blessing. In essence this is when the intelligence agencies began to scramble to hide the family jewels under the bed.

67   *Dallas '63*, Peter Dale Scott, p. 54

But Peter Dale Scott believes there was also a phase *three* scenario. This one also came out of the Bayo-Pawley raid and may have been its purpose all along. In the 1970s, Johnny Roselli began feeding a story to columnist Jack Anderson. It was an altered version of the Bayo-Pawley raid. Roselli's story was that an assassination team was part of the mission and the goal was to kill Castro. This version claimed that Castro had captured the hit team and *turned them,* sending them back to the US to kill JFK in retaliation. The intention of the Castro retaliation motive was aimed primarily at embarrassing the CIA, and Robert Kennedy in particular, exposing their efforts to murder Castro. It may actually have worked preventing RFK from going after the real culprits. He would be forced to deal with the possibility that his efforts to kill Castro backfired and resulted in his brother's death.

It seems clear that the *phase one* and *phase three* stories resulted in the false *phase two* cover-up. But the deeper truth is that unless there was a massive governmental conspiracy, one of the intelligence agencies would have followed leads that exposed the truth. Instead those agencies were manipulated into a frenzy of self-preservation to protect top secret operations and sources from being exposed.

Were they all outsmarted by one of their own? Was the mole hunter a mole himself in the world of intelligence ... two chess moves ahead at all times? James Angleton would have been the perfect choice for the lead part in the movie ... *The Sting.*

It is now apparent to me that Angleton was running Oswald from the start. It started when Oswald was stationed in Japan and may initially have been under the auspices of the ONI. He was used to infiltrate Japanese Communists and possibly to assist in convincing a Soviet General, Nikoli Eroshkin, to defect to the West. Whether by his own initiative, or under the guidance of Popov's mole who may well have been Bruce Solie, Angleton/Solie sent him to Russia in a false mole hunt. When Oswald returned to the US, he was dangled once again to the Soviets as an employee at Jaggars-Chiles-Stoval.

At that point he was shared with the FBI as an informant and sent to New Orleans to spy on the gun-running apparatus of Guy Banister and infiltrate the Anti-Castro Cuban training camps. At the same time, Oswald was used as a tool in the operation known as COINTELPRO as is evident by his activities in Clinton, LA in the summer of 1963.

But what we didn't know then and only recently have become aware of is that COINTELPRO was not solely the creation of J. Edgar Hoover. Jefferson Morley has exposed that it was, in fact, a joint enterprise with the CIA, and specifically with counterintelligence chief James Angleton.

As Morley points out, COINTELPRO, after all, stands for "*Counterintelligence Program*."

Exposure of this revelation began with a story that broke in *Newsweek* unmasking CIA recruitment of Richard Gibson, a CBS News writer and co-founder of the Fair Play for Cuba Committee. Morely's work has exposed Gibson as a key part of the US Government's plans to destroy the FPCC. After the assassination of JFK, George Joannides' AMSPELL assets went to newspaper reporters with evidence of Oswald's support for the FPCC. The innuendo that Kennedy had been killed by a communist was implanted. Oswald and Castro were "*the presumed assassins.*" A month later, the FPCC disbanded, its work forever tainted by association with the suspected (and now conveniently dead) assassin. The operation to destroy the FPCC had succeeded.

George Joannides got a medal for his covert work in Miami and his manipulation of the HSCA. He retired until needed again to sabotage the HSCA's investigation into Oswald's New Orleans activities involving the Directorio Revolucionario Estudiantil (DRE).

So as we now see, Oswald's final mission was embedded in the operation to discredit the Fair Play for Cuba Committee which was, as it turns out, a joint operation by both the CIA and FBI with Jim Angleton's *ghostly* involvement behind the scenes once again.

Was this another goal, layer or phase of the assassination? To destroy the FPCC? Angleton is once again behind the curtain, manipulating and conniving. He is involved in a mole hunt and Oswald's defection, CIA/Mafia plots to kill Castro, the Mexico City mystery, Operation CHAOS, his own assassination squad handled by Boris Pash, COINTELPRO, the cover-up involving the Warren Commission, and God knows what else. Yet he's always behind the curtain. The master puppeteer.

THE UNHOLY GHOST

> *Sometimes a lie is more important than the truth.*
> –Jim Angleton

Don't be misled. The above diatribe is not a religious one. It doesn't involve the Father, Son or Holy Ghost of religious scriptures. On the contrary, it involves *Mother, Jesus,* and a *Spook.* James *Jesus* Angleton, known as *Mother* in his CIA Counterintelligence work, is the *Ghost* who is the subject of this missive.

Angleton was a shadowy, ghost-like figure that was feared, even by his superiors. Richard Helms often asked John Whitten to investigate Angleton's operations that *"didn't look right."* Whitten said he did so with great trepidation and usually *"fingering his life insurance policy."* In turn, when Whitten asked Helms to look into Oswald, Helms reacted in a way that Whitten interpreted as nervousness and fear.

Although the defections of Lee Oswald and Robert Webster likely started out unrelated, they soon became tools of the espionage apparatus of Jim Angleton. It was he that turned them into "doppelganger dangles" to confuse the Soviets. James Jesus Angleton, the CIA's counterintelligence chief, worked closely with ONI[68] in Oswald's case, and with Rand & ATIC[69] in Webster's. Oswald was sent to Russia as part of a false defector program being run by ONI and Angleton who then used him in a mole hunt. Rand sent Webster to Moscow and he either defected on his own with KGB encouragement through his Russian girlfriend, Vera Plantanova, or was encouraged to do so by James Rand. He was then manipulated by Rand-connected ATIC in a project called LONGSTRIDE. Once Webster was in place, Angleton saw it as an opportunity to use both defectors to initiate his mole hunt.

To catch the "mole," the clever Angleton devised a "mole trap." He would "dangle" false defectors with knowledge in areas of interest to the Soviets. Lee Oswald (radar and the U2 spy plane) and Robert Webster (plastics/fiberglass) were two of these.

As revealed in the last chapter, Angleton was a paranoid[70] genius of counterintelligence. He knew more about Lee Harvey Oswald before Kennedy was killed than anyone in the CIA or the US government. Angleton's aides, in a secret office known as *Special Investigations Group*, monitored Oswald's movements and correspondence from October 1959 through November 1963.[71] Behind-the-scenes Angleton ran his own personal, off the books projects such as his mole hunt and used singleton agents[72] to do

---

68   CIA officer, Victor Marchetti, told Author Anthony Summers, that in 1959 the US was having difficulty acquiring information out of the Soviet Union and were resorting to various activities,. One of these activities was an ONI (Office of Naval Intelligence) program which involved three dozen or so young men who were made to appear disenchanted, poor, American youths who had become turned off and wanted to see what Communism was all about. They were sent into the Soviet Union or eastern Europe, with the specific intention the Soviets would pick them up and "double" them if they were suspected of being US agents, or recruit them as KGB agents.

69   Air-Force Intelligence

70   Often, this paranoia was alcohol fueled.

71   *The Ghost: The Secret Life of CIA Spymaster James Jesus Angleton Jefferson Morley*

72   Gordon Novel, Jerry Patrick Hemming and Lee Oswald are examples.

so. He likely had ties to the CIA/Mafia plots as attested to by J.C. King. He controlled key journalists and had assets inside the FBI.

King said that Angleton had ties to the mob and that it had something to do with Cuba. Could this be the CIA/Mafia plots to kill Castro? If so, Angleton was involved behind the scenes and unnoticed.

A November 1, 1988, article by syndicated columnist Jack Anderson and Joseph Spear exposed the CIA/Mafia collaboration in the public eye. Anderson used the testimony of Joe Shimon, a well-connected Washington cop and ex-police instructor who was close to John Rosselli, Robert Maheu and others involved in those plots. Joseph Shimon, a partner in Operation Mongoose, told Anderson that Jack Ruby had received specific orders from a famous former Havana crime boss. "Santos Trafficante called in the mob's chits with Ruby and ordered him to kill Oswald," Anderson wrote in his 2000 memoir, *Peace, War and Politics*.

Shimon ran an organization known as the International Police Academy on R-Street in Washington, D.C., according to Ross Allen Schoyer who worked with Shimon on 1958-59. The IPA was a CIA front organization that specialized in training foreign operators such as the Iranian Secret Police in dirty tricks and other Gestapo-type operations. Anderson wrote:

> After a 25-year silence, a witness has stepped out of the shadows to tell how a covert CIA mission to liquidate Cuban President Fidel Castro backfired. The Marxist ruler was tipped off that the CIA was trying to kill him. Instead, he may have turned the hired guns against President John F. Kennedy. The witness, a Washington police officer named Joseph Shimon, played an undercover role in the bizarre tragedy. He sat in on the meetings where the Central Intelligence Agency's William Harvey and the Mafia's Johnny Rosselli plotted the assassination of Castro. The covert operation had the blessing of two of America's most notorious crime figures: Sam Giancana, boss of the Chicago mob, and Santos Trafficante, who controlled the Cuban underworld before Castro came to power. Shimon quotes Trafficante as saying, "I'll get you the contacts, give you a lot of names. But keep me out of it."

Joe Shimon's daughter, Toni, when interviewed regarding the death of JFK's friend and lover, Mary Meyer,[73] said; "My dad knew everything about the plan to kill Mary Meyer through Bill Harvey (very close to Angleton). Whatever Bill Harvey was up to, it always came out of Jim An-

---

[73]   It was Angleton who broke into Mary Meyer's studio and stole her diary shortly after her death.

gleton's office." She added,"Dad once remarked that Angleton ran everything, controlled everything in the CIA."

In the early 1960s, the CIA created a program of *"Executive Action,"* code-named ZR/RIFLE and put Bill Harvey at its helm. The purpose of this project was to remove foreign leaders by various means, including assassination.

Angleton was known to run his own private, *off the books* operations. He may even have been running his own assassination team. E. Howard Hunt accused Angleton of running an assassination program unit headed by Col. Boris Pash[74] to eliminate double agents in the CIA.

Investigative journalist Joseph Trento's testimony in a 1984 court deposition revealed that, according to CIA sources, James Angleton was the supervisor of a CIA assassination unit in the 1950s. The "small assassination team" was headed by Army colonel Boris Pash.... Trento testified that his sources confirmed, 'Pash's assassination unit was assigned to Angleton.[75] In 1963 Angleton went with Bill Harvey to London to ask MI6 how to set up an assassination team!

ZRRIFLE and the CIA/MAFIA plots to kill Castro had been active since at least 1961. It may have been sometime in 1962 that rogue elements of the plots; Rosselli, Harvey, Morales, Trafficante, Giancana and Marcello[76] decided to change the target from Castro to JFK. Harvey's mechanism was already in *place.[77]*

SOUTH OF THE BORDER

No lie can live forever.

– MLK

It was one thing to kill the president. It was another to get away with it. The two went hand in hand. With ZRRIFLE and Operation Mongoose still active, the machinery was in place. Its tools were the Cuban exiles, mafia hired guns and Corsican assassins. Harvey, Rosselli and Morales

---

74   It is known that US Intelligence assassination expert, Otto Skorzeny, met with Pash, an Army officer detailed from the military to Wisner's OPC in Fall of 1948. Pash handled a project called PB7. Called before the Senate Select Committee on government intelligence activities in 1976. Called because of E.Howard Hunt's claims that PB7 handled assassinations. Hunt was in federal prison in Florida for participation in Watergate.
75   *JFK and the Unspeakable,* James Douglas
76   Marcello is not generally recognized as part of the plots but he and Trafficante were joined at the hip. So it's hard to believe he wasn't. Least of all when JFK, whom he hated, became the target.
77   In a 1975 interview with Frederick Boron, William Harvey revealed that "the Rosselli assassination operation was funded by ZRRIFLE."

were the commanders. But who masterminded the project? In particular the false flag scenario that in effect neutralized the CIA, Secret Service and FBI once the deed was done? The smoking gun is Mexico City.

The Mexico City episode was a brilliant plan designed to ensure a cover-up. So brilliant, that I suspect only one mind could have conjured it up, James Angleton. It assured that no real investigation would take place by setting up the investigators and forcing them to cover up. Essentially to protect themselves from looking bad and having their dirty secrets exposed.

What links are there to Angleton? It was he who was behind the Oswald project. Oswald had been his singleton agent in his mole hunt false defector program in 1959. It was an example of his skills at long-term planning. Always two chess moves ahead of everybody, he controlled Oswald's pre-assassination file a full year before a 201 file was created for him.

Angleton controlled the CIA's flow of information to the Warren Commission by making his close friend, Ray Rocca, liaison to it. He also knew what to cover up after the Commission had finished its work.

Always thinking ahead, he foresaw the flaws in the "official" story and anticipated them to stay one step ahead of the critics. "*The Trust,*" was patterned after a technique used by the Bolsheviks. After the Russian Revolution, the Bolsheviks realized there would be a counter-revolution and created their own *fake* anti-Bolshevik group to suck in dissidents and single them out for liquidation before they became dangerous.

There is a revealing correlation between the *Trust* and the Angleton's handling of the FPCC that exposes his web spinning. Angleton used Jay Edward Epstein's work as a cutout to create flytraps for researchers who pointed the finger at the CIA in JFK's assassination (a technique of the *Trust*). Similarly, he used Oswald as bait to draw out Castro sympathizers by creating his own fake FPCC branch in New Orleans. The FPCC was an organization the Agency was out to discredit and destroy.[78]

Angleton also had to control the FBI and Hoover's investigation. *The Angler* used FBI agents like Bert Turner as direct contacts to counter-intelligence. Turner effectively turned off information to the FBI. He failed to follow up on Mexico City and was eventually censured by Hoover. Sam Papich, liaison to the FBI, was also more loyal to the CIA than the FBI. The CIA convinced him that the unshared information

---

78   This was accomplished when Oswald was identified as both the assassin of JFK and a member of the FPCC.

was *"too sensitive"* for the FBI. In addition Angleton may have been able to control Hoover via a blackmail threat. Gordon Novel, another Angleton *singleton* agent, said that Angleton showed him a photo of Hoover having sex with his companion and number 2 man in the FBI, Clyde Tolson. This was corroborated by former OSS officer John Wertz to author Anthony Summers. It has long been rumored that Meyer Lansky used this same technique to blackmail Hoover into denying organized crime even existed.

In his book, *Handsome Johnny,* Author Lee Server astutely assessed the cover-up as follows:

"In retrospect, so much had been held back it was surprising that the commission was still able to find Oswald guilty, or Kennedy dead ... evasions proved ill advised, the cover-up causing more damage than the truth. The Warren Commission would be scorned and dismissed. The intelligence services disgraced. Secrets, when they came to be exposed, would serve only to confuse and complicate. The more people knew, the less they believed. History had been thrown to the wolves."

Angleton was not only setting up Oswald, the Cubans and the Russians, but the CIA and FBI as well.

Through this brilliant subterfuge, a cover-up was assured. Reasons: Protecting sensitive sources? Hiding incompetence? Preventing a nuclear war?

In addition Rosselli laid a paper trail in the Castro plots that would later be used to force a cover-up. He and the mob would push the "Castro did it" theory to veil their own involvement and encourage an overthrow of the bearded leader.

Angleton dodged all the bullets by thinking ahead. He confiscated Mary Meyer's diary, Win Scott's papers and manuscripts, and actually ran background checks on the jurors in the Garrison probe, which he feared more than the Warren Commission. He was also likely behind the deaths of individuals and witnesses who knew too much. People like Mary Meyer.

Warren Commission lawyer, David Slawson, who, along with William Coleman, investigated the Mexico City incident and heard the tapes of the Oswald impostor, became angry at the CIA's deceptions and evasive tactics. In a *New York Times* interview in 1975 he called for a new investigation into the JFK assassination.

In a Nov. 6, 2013 article for *Salon,* David Talbot wrote: "Within days of the story breaking in the *Times,* Slawson received a strange and threatening phone call from James Angleton, the spectral CIA counter-intelligence chief. Angleton ... adopted a decidedly sinister tone during his call with Slawson, making it clear to the lawyer that he would be wise to remain "a friend of the CIA."

The threat seems to have served its purpose. When interviewed by the AARB in 1994 and asked about the tapes, Slawson replied; "I'm sorry, but I'm not at liberty to discuss that."

An assessment by someone who knew Angleton well is revealing. Fellow OSS recruit, Dr. Bruno Uberti, evaluated Angleton in this way;

> I considered him brilliant but a little strange.....I met a lot of important Americans from Donovan on down, but Angleton was the personality which impressed me the most. He made a terrific great impression. A very exceptional man. He had something more. He had a strange genius I would say—full of impossible ideas, colossal ideas. I would have liked to have been friends with him, but he never gave me a chance because he was so secretive.

SUMMARY

CIA owes no allegiance to rule of law.
– Jim Angleton

James Jesus Angleton was unhindered by the normal chain of command. His authority was such that he developed an unshakable power base within the CIA. With Angleton at it's helm, CISIG[79] would become undeniably the most powerful office within the agency.

What is the evidence to support my hypothesis that Counterintelligence Chief, James Angleton was the mastermind behind the scenes in key aspects of the JFK assassination? Let's take a look:

- He ran the Oswald project. He was behind the use of Oswald as a false defector in a mole hunt in the Soviet Union. He ran him as a singleton agent with no 201 file for a year before Otto Otepka's investigation forced his hand and a 201 was created. He was also involved via David Atlee Phillips and George Joannides in Oswald's FPCC activities to smear that group. Angleton used David Phillips as his cutout. David Phillips was running Oswald according to HSCA investigator Gaeton Fonzi. I'm not sure what Fonzi knew of Joannides back in the 70s.

• He was the architect of the Mexico City episode and the framing of Castro, Kostikov and Oswald as well. A secondary benefit was the manipulation of US Intelligence including FBI and CIA.

• The CIA's J.C. King, as well as Mongoose participant, Joe Shimon and his daughter link Angleton with the CIA/Mafia plots to kill Castro. Plots that were turned on John Kennedy. Recently I found further proof of this while reading *Handsome Johnny*, by Lee Server. On page 334 Server tells of a meeting between Joe Kennedy, Sam Giancana and John Rosselli. The purpose of the meeting, requested by Kennedy, was to gain the support of the mob in helping get his son Jack elected in 1960. Specifically to influence the Illinois vote. Also present at this meeting was a lawyer named Mario Brod. Brod was present to represent the interests of Jimmy Hoffa. What the others present didn't know was that Brod was an undercover CIA operative working for *James Angleton*. A former OSS operative, Brod's job was that of an underworld penetration agent.

• William Harvey worked closely with Angleton as observed by Joe Shimon, a soldier in the CIA/Mafia plots, and expressed by his daughter, Toni, *"Whatever Bill Harvey was up to, it always came out of Jim Angleton's office."* She added, *"Dad once remarked that Angleton ran everything, controlled everything in the CIA."* Helms and Whitten feared the Counterintelligence Czar and actually knew little of many of his operations.

• Logic dictates guilt by association: Bill Harvey and Angleton worked together. Harvey ran ZRRIFLE, an Executive Action assassination program. According to E. Howard Hunt and others, Angleton is said to have run his own private assassination team headed by Boris Pash. Harvey and Rosselli were thick as thieves and essentially ended up running the assassination plots by themselves with help from David Morales and the JMWAVE station in Florida.

• Angleton controlled the CIA's flow of information to the Warren Commission by making his close friend, Ray Rocca, liaison to it. He also knew what to cover up after the Commission had finished its work. He was a cleaner. He personally confiscated Mary Meyer's diary and likely had her killed. He personally confiscated Win Scott's papers as well. His actions are those of a man protecting himself and show evidence of guilt.

Angleton was in complete control and no one was paying attention to *the man behind the curtain.*

MISSING FILES

William K. Harvey ran CIA assassination operations from 1960 to 1963. According to the ARRB, CIA Director Richard Helms ordered Harvey's "notes and source material" to be destroyed in the 1970s. Harvey's widow also burned his personal papers on his orders.."

Angleton's JFK files were also purged. According to the 1998 report of the Assassination Records Review Board, the CIA "reviewed Angleton's records and incorporated a small percentage into the files of the Directorate of Operations. CIA destroyed other records, either because the records were duplicates or because CIA *decided not to retain them."*

Nearing the end of his life, the *"Angler,"* reflected on the essence of his own evil...

> *"Allen Dulles, Richard Helms, Carmel Offie and Frank Wisner were Grand Masters. If you were in a room with them you were in a room full of people that you had to believe would deservedly end up in hell. I guess I will see them there soon."*

-James Jesus Angleton[80]

---

80   Allen Dulles, Ray Rocca, Richard Helms and Miles Copeland were all in Angleton's will. He actually carried Warren Commission member Dulles' ashes around after he had passed away. The CIA differed uniquely from it's rivals. As noted by David C. Martin in *Wilderness of Mirrors*, it was made up of "academics and Wall street lawyers, many of whom were heirs to family fortunes." They were Ivy Leaguers and scholars.

CHAPTER 4

MISSION POSSIBLE

The better you lied and the more you betrayed, the more likely you'd be promoted. I did things, that in looking back on my life, I regret. But I was part of it and I loved being in it.

−James Jesus Angleton

Although Angleton was predominantly pulling strings behind the scenes, he was sometimes forced to take action to maintain the secrecy of his operations. The cover-up had to be controlled. When people in the know were about to spill the beans, action needed to be taken. For instance, Win Scott's postmortem exposé of the CIA's Mexico City shenanigans needed to be acquired and suppressed. The Angler had to do this himself. This was one of the few times Angleton actually carried out a clandestine task personally, exposing his own personal involvement. In the case of Mary Meyer, wife of Cord Meyer and mistress of JFK, she also knew too much and was threatening disclosure. Win Scott was dead of natural causes, so once his papers were obtained there was no longer a threat from *him*. However, Meyer was still alive in 1964 and extremely dangerous.

Peter Janney, in his excellent book, *Mary's Mosaic*, came to the conclusion that the CIA was responsible for the death of Mary Meyer. A murder most foul. In his astute observations, he concluded that the endeavor was carefully planned and executed with precision. A professional hit designed to look like a random murder. He compared the perps of Mary's demise to that of a highly trained team. A team akin to that of the IMF[81] of the '70s TV show, *Mission Impossible*. He believed that the operation was one of standard CIA procedure. This conclusion seems reasonable being that the crime involved *"Painstaking calculations and details that were involved in the extensive planning of professional assassinations."* Nothing was left to chance. Janney is not just a writer. His father was a CIA agent. Both he and his father knew Cord and Mary Meyer personally. He even suspected that his father may have been involved in some way in her liquidation, or at least was aware of the operation.

The parallels to the murder of JFK are obvious. Both murders took place in a public location. The planners wanted to create the impression that they were random acts. Both Mary and JFK were in motion and slain when they entered a "kill zone." Janney believed Mary had been under surveillance prior to her death. Most researchers believe that a surveillance team was monitoring the motorcade in Dallas. Both cases were "solved" almost immediately with the arrest of a patsy by local police.

Janney believed that the team consisted of at least five operatives, not including the actual architects of the plan or the monitors. The whole undertaking required *Mission Impossible* precision.

Did the CIA have these capabilities? Absolutely. They had been building such a force since at least 1954 in the coup against Jacobo Arbenz in Guatemala. Other coups were successful in Iran, Congo, the Dominican Republic, South Vietnam, Brazil and Allende's Chile. The attempted Cuban coup was the first to fail. However, although it was unsuccessful against Castro, evidence suggests that, in 1963, it's target was changed from Castro to JFK. To the CIA, the elimination of the president became essential, and if successful could possibly lead to a solution to the Cuban problem as well. The NORTHWOODS scenario in a nutshell.

Did the CIA have a Mission Impossible Force? It did. It was called TSD, the Technical Services Division. Under the direction of Dr. Sidney Gottlieb. *"They could do almost anything, from preparing lethal poisons that left no trace, to creating undetectable disguises, articles of clothing etc., all on short notice."*[82] No other entity on earth had resources like the CIA.

In my book, *The Other Oswald, A Wilderness of Mirrors*, I used the real-life exploits of CIA agents Antonio and Jonna Mendez as an example of the CIA's use of twins and disguises. In their book, *Moscow Rules*, they revealed some of the tricks of the spy trade that were used in Moscow during the cold war. Mendez, CIA department chief of *disguise*, describes the use of "twins" in cases where KGBV surveillance made clandestine meetings between case officers difficult. This method involved the use of techniques used by Hollywood magicians to fool their audiences.

If Janney is right, witnesses were manipulated into position to observe the murder and identify the patsy, Ray Crump, through the use of a disguised double. Janney surmised that *"Specialized team from TSD had the capability of transforming almost anyone into whatever was called for, includ-*

ing changing someone's race from white to black if necessary... Someone assigned with a radio to keep tabs on the patsy."

This could also have been the case in Dealey Plaza. Monitoring of Oswald would have been necessary to assure he had no witnesses to his innocence. In both cases doubles and alternate patsies were in place in case things went wrong. In both cases there was likely more than one candidate for patsy.

The plans were brilliant. The attention to detail is immaculate. Sounds like something within the capabilities of James Jesus Angleton, the CIA's mastermind of plotting. Like a chess master, he was always three moves ahead. Cold and calculating, he was the paranoid genius in the background. It was he who controlled Oswald from the very beginning, as early as 1959. As I postulated earlier, he was the likely mastermind of the Mexico City intrigue that effectively neutralized the CIA and FBI after the assassination of JFK. It was he who covered his tracks by confiscating Win Scott's papers in Mexico City. He knew Mary and Cord Meyer intimately. He knew Ben Bradlee and his wife Tony, Mary's sister. They were his neighbors in Georgetown. He stole and suppressed Mary's diary after her death.

BEN BRADLEE

*W*ashington Post editor, Ben Bradlee was a friend of Angleton as well as JFK. His wife Toni was Mary Pinchot Myers sister. It was he or his wife that gave Angleton Mary's diary after they caught him endeavoring to obtain it in multiple break-ins. Bradley had been in service of the ONI during the war. According to Major Ralph Ganis, Bradlee, Thomas Braden (journalist) and Cord Meyer all worked on covert projects carried out by Frank Wisner at a time when Otto Skorzeny was being utilized as an asset within Wild Bill Donovan's Secret Paramilitary Group (SPG). Bradlee replaced Braden as head of the International Organizations Division (IOD), a covert group that handled clandestine activities of global corporate entities. Bradlee was a childhood friend of Richard Helms, and worked in Paris with Richard Ober, veteran OSS and CIA officer. There has been speculation that Ober was Watergate's Deep Throat. Ober was also a deputy of Angleton. Bradlee's wife, Tony Pinchot Bradlee and her sister Mary were close friends with Angleton's wife Cicely. All three were Vassar girls. Mary's husband Cord Meyer was assigned to Frank Wisner's Office of Policy Coordination. Meyer was also a deputy to Braden in the IOD. IOD was the CIA group that handled Skorzeny.

So it is apparent that Bradlee was an insider and friends with Angleton, Helms and Wisner. Wisner and Cord Meyer were the architects of MOCK-

INGBIRD, a CIA mechanism to control the American press. The Washington Post and Phil Graham were the first enlistees in this enterprise. Thus it is obvious that Bradlee was a willing participant. Another point of argument that the Nixon coup was CIA backed using the *Post* as a MOCKINGBIRD vehicle for that goal. Time-Life's C.D. Jackson also worked with Wisner in Mockingbird. This was set up to counter Soviet propaganda and was at the forefront of psychological warfare. It was Jackson who played roles in convicting Oswald in the minds of Americans with the backyard photos and with the purchase and suppression of the Zapruder film.

The CIA's charter forbade domestic covert activities. But Angleton answered to no one. An internal CIA investigation, prompted by the 1970s' Church Committee, verified the far-ranging power and influence that Angleton wielded during his long tenure as counterintelligence Czar. The exposé revealed that Angleton planned infiltration of law enforcement and military organizations in other countries to be used to increase the influence of the United States. It also confirmed past rumors that it was Angleton who was in charge of the domestic spying activities of the CIA under Operation CHAOS. He may also have been running his own assassination teams as E. Howard Hunt suspected.

This paranoid genius of counterintelligence was feared even by his superiors. He controlled key journalists and had assets inside the FBI.

If, as Janney and many others believe, Mary Pinchot Meyer's death was part of a cover-up of the assassination of JFK, it would be logical that the same people responsible for Kennedy's death would be her assassins as well. E.Howard Hunt's death-bed confession to his son, Saint John, fingered Cord Meyer as being in on the plot. Although Cord and Mary were no longer together in 1963, Mary's indiscretion in her affair with the President surely angered him. Cord was placed very high in the CIA hierarchy. He was conveniently out of town at the time of Mary's death. He was friends and worked with James Jesus Angleton. It is known that Mary believed the Warren Report to be a cover-up and suspected the CIA's hand in the assassination. She was keeping a diary that posed a threat to the Agency. Angleton broke into her studio and stole this document. Why do so unless it was a threat to him? Why steal Win Scott's papers unless exposing the Mexico City charade was a threat to him? It is a law of philosophy that every effect must have a cause. Cui Bono? It was reported that on his deathbed, when asked who he thought was responsible for his wife's death, Cord Meyer replied, "...the same people that killed Kennedy."

Part II

Ruthless Paine

Introduction to Part II

The Wicked Witch

Truth is like the sun, you can shut it out for a time, but it ain't goin away.
– Elvis Presley

Part II deals with Ruth and Michael Paine. No one's testimony incriminated LHO more than that of Ruth Paine. Whenever evidence was needed to damage Oswald's image, Ruth came up with it in a timely manner. This overtly selfless angel of mercy was a virtual stranger who generously took Marina in, enabling her isolation from Lee while he was being sheep-dipped for the big event.

In stark contradiction, this peace loving Quaker and her husband were connected to a community of intelligence operatives as were their parents and siblings. While it would seem that her physical attraction to Marina might explain taking her in and separating her from her husband, there seems to be more to her defamation of Lee than meets the eye. The *"Wicked Witch"* was a consummate actress whose credits continue to this day.

Researcher William Gallagher is convinced that the Paines were "rolled over" assets assigned to Dallas for the specific purpose of babysitting the Oswalds. The FBI, unable to get cooperation for Marxist Oswald was hoping to gain information through the Paines as cutouts. In 1963 the FBI considered the Paines to be high priority and may have used pressure to get them to cooperate in an Oswald project. Gallagher writes; "While Ruth was reading the Oswald's mail, Mike was attending any meeting that sounded interesting to the FBI office. One day, he was at a Bircher's meeting. The next night, he was making notes on the ACLU. And, on Sundays, he was eating breakfast at a restaurant across the street from SMU and accosting the students in heated discussions about America's treatment of Cuba."

The Warren Commission considered conducting their own probe of Ruth and Mike. It never happened. For some reason, the Paines seem to be untouchable. They remain fiercely protected to this day. Dallas Assistant DA Alexander wanted to "look into the Paines and felt more should have been done with them," but no one supported him. Alexander also had a signed pass to Ruby's club, found among Ruby's possessions, and had spoken to Jack the day before the assassination. (CE 1628, CE 1322, pp.735-36 A microfilm of the actual cards revealed a signed card for every name listed, except that of Alexander's card is curiously missing. JFK microfilm, Vol. 5, pp R 13-28). The HSCA made excuses as to why they could not subpoena the Paines and the AARB excused them saying it was not their responsibility. Their tax records for 1963 are unattainable.

CHAPTER 5

PAINEFUL POSSIBILITIES

I still do not know why or how, but Mr. and Mrs. Paine are somehow involved in this affair.[83]

– Robert Oswald, shortly after the Assassination

ENTER THE WICKED WITCH

After the assassination of President Kennedy, Dallas Deputy Sheriff Buddy Walthers took part in the search of the home of Ruth Paine. Walthers told author Eric Tagg that they *"found six or seven metal filing cabinets full of letters, maps, records and index cards with names of pro-Castro sympathizers."*[84] James DiEugenio concluded that this *"cinches the case that the Paines were domestic surveillance agents in the Cold War against Communism."*

Walthers also found a big pasteboard barrel filled with leaflets saying "Freedom for Cuba." These were gold colored paper with black printing.

If this is true, it opens up a whole new can of worms that could explain what was really going on in Dallas in November of 1963. Using deductive reasoning, let's reconsider and evaluate what is known.

We know that Oswald was being used in New Orleans as an agent provocateur to flush out pro-Castro sympathizers by handing out FPCC pamphlets, participating in street fights, being interviewed on TV and radio, and approaching left-wing students at Tulane University. All of this had an additional purpose of sheep dipping Oswald as a Marxist and pro-Castro sympathizer.[85]

---

83   Robert told the Warren Commission that he had read in the paper about a man passing a rifle to Oswald over a fence where he was standing inside the rifle range. "As I read this description in the newspaper, I reached the conclusion from that description that it was Mr. Paine." Robert recalled Paine as about 6 feet tall and weighing 160-165 pounds. The incident under discussion appears to be at the Sports Drome in Grand Prairie, Texas, where Oswald supposedly engaged in target practice on November 9, 10 and 17, with someone handing Oswald his rifle over the fence on at least one occasion. Grand Prairie is the town where Michael Paine moved after his break-up with Ruth.

84   *Brush With History*, Eric Tagg, Shot in the Light Publishing 1998

85   It is likely that it was Dave Ferrie that encouraged Oswald to "play the role" of a student of the manifesto by ordering Communist literature. The goal being to become an undercover spy like Lee's idol Herb Philbrick. Ferrie likely encouraged Lee to follow through with his plan to enlist in the Marines as well.

We now know that the CIA as well as the FBI were trying to smear the FPCC by linking it to Communists. That, in fact, was Oswald's purpose. Linking him, an avowed Marxist who had been to Russia, with organizations like the FPCC, ACLU, CORE, American Communist Party etc., insinuating guilt by association. Furthermore, visiting the Cuban and Soviet embassies in Mexico City projected guilty association linking Castro and Khrushchev to the upcoming assassination of JFK.

We also know that the Paines were deeply involved with US Intelligence.[86] Particularly the CIA. We know Ruth Paine was a babysitter for the Oswalds and played a role in separating them, getting Lee the TSBD job, incriminating Lee by providing whatever evidence was needed to DPD and testifying against him.

The actions of the Paine's on the day of the assassination are very suspicious. During his lunch hour that day, Michael Paine and fellow employee, Ramond Krystinik,had been discussing, of all things, assassins! When Oswald was captured, Krystinik hear Paine say, "The Stupid… (something or other)" and also "He is not supposed to have a gun." or "He is not supposed to own a gun."

When Buddy Walthers and other law enforcement officers arrived at Ruth Paine's house, she opened the door and said, "Come on in. We've been expecting you." Walthers found this very unusual since he was sure that she and Marina had not yet been told that Oswald was arrested.

But what if the Paines were playing a dual role and were also working with Oswald in his efforts to denigrate groups like the FPCC? It was Michael Paine that encouraged Lee to join the ACLU. It was Michael that took Lee to a Walker rally as well. In addition, the Paines, like Oswald, portrayed themselves as liberals (Quakers in their case), which in retrospect seems a complete sham. It seems that in reality they were tools of right-wing Intelligence. Were there others involved in this Dallas ring of counter-espionage?

THREE RING CIRCUS

Oswald wanted to be a spy like his idol, Herbert Philbrick.[87] By coincidence there was a Philbrick clone in Dallas at the same time as Os-

---

86   Ruth's sister and brother-in-law worked for the CIA. Ruth's father was an "executive agent" of the CIA according to her admission. Ruth Paine's father and brother worked for AID (Agency for International Development), a CIA cover for clandestine activity abroad. Other AID operatives were George de Mohrenschildt, E. Howard Hunt and LAPD officer, Manny Pena and Antonio Veciana. Micheal Paine had one cousin who was president of United Fruit and another cousin that was it's director. Allen Dulles and John McCloy were also directors of United Fruit. United Fruit is a CIA front company.

87   His favorite TV show was "I Led Three Lives." The show was an anti-communist propaganda series about Herbert Philbrick, who infiltrated the Communist Party for the FBI. Philbrick became Lee's idol and it seems he patterned his life after him as a Herb Philbrick wannabe. He later told his

wald. William Lowery spied on the American Communist Party and the ACLU – two groups Oswald had contact with. Lee had written to CPUSA and gone to an ACLU meeting and joined.

Lowery came out of the cold just weeks before the assassination.[88] It was Oswald's *"I Led Three Lives"* fantasy come to life. Lee was waiting for the day when *he* could come out like Philbrick and Lowery – his visit to Eugene Murret's seminary in August 1963 may have been a dry run in preparing for his debut as an anti-Communist.

One of Lowery's assignments had been "surveillance" of Joseph Rodriguez Molina. Molina worked at the Texas Schoolbook Depository. Did Ruth's getting Oswald that job open the door for him to take over Lowery's assignment? Is that why he took the job? Was he placed in the TSBD to spy on Molina at the behest of Hosty or Lowery and the assistance of Ruth Paine? Molina's home was searched in the middle of the night after the assassination and he spent most of the next day under interrogation at DPD. He was, in fact, fired by the end of the year.

Lowery said he received about $200 a month in cash from the local Dallas FBI office. That is the amount that Texas Attorney General Waggoner Carr told the WC Oswald was rumored to be getting as an informant. Did they mix up Lowery with Oswald or were they both on the payroll? Lowery recalled that S.A. James Hosty paid him on street corners or park benches.[89] Carr's source, journalist Lonnie Hudkins, later said he made up Oswald's FBI Informant number 172 or 179.[90] However, a member of the FBI's office in New Orleans, William Walter, claimed that he had seen an FBI teletype that showed that Oswald had been an informant for that office.[91] Lowery said that the (Communist Party) CP held some meetings in the Oak Cliff YMCA and he speculated that it was possible Oswald, known to frequent the YMCA, may have attended some of the meetings.[92] Was Oswald, like Lowery, a paid FBI informant? Was James P. Hosty the FBI contact for both

---

brother Robert that once he was out of the Marine Corps, "I know what I want to be and how I'm going to be it, which I guess is the most important thing in life." He soon would be going to Russia.

88   Lowery's emergence as a Herbert Philbrick style informant occurred on Sept 23, 1963, at a Subversive Activities Control Board hearing in DC called by RFK to force a Dallas CP member to register pursuant to the McCarran Act.

89   Adrian Alba of the Crescent City Garage in New Orleans said that he saw an agent in a government car hand Oswald an envelope in the summer of 63'. (Earl Golz, *Dallas Times-Herald*, August 7, 1978)

90   The FBI denied Oswald was an informant (of course) and said the 179 informant number belonged to Velma Yvonne Graham, a negro "madam" who ran a house of prostitution in New Orleans. FBI 105-82555-2087

91   NARA RIF no. 180–10076–10413

92   Oswald stayed in room 415 and Dallas CPUSA head Lowery in room 607 on 10/15/62. Lowery admits he might have met LHO at the Oak Cliff YMCA Branch, because the Communists used to have meetings there and he might have "drifted in..." (CE1963) See WC Vol. XX p.198 (list of room numbers)

Lowery and Oswald?[93] Were Lowery, Hosty, Oswald and the Paines working together in anti-Communist activities?

Lowery and his fellow CP members in Dallas were promoting the idea of further establishing their ties to the local ACLU starting in August 1962. Could it be that Ruth and Michael Paine were aware of Lowery and his fellow CP members? Were the six or seven metal filing cabinets found in the Paine house after the assassination, full of letters, maps, records and index cards with names of pro-Castro sympathizers part of a surveillance effort involving Lowery, the FBI, Oswald and the Paines? Did Oswald join the ACLU to link it to the CP via his membership in the FPCC?[94]

As mentioned earlier, Lowery was closely connected to Joseph Rodriguez Molina. During the early investigation, Molina was suspected of being a co-conspirator with Oswald in the assassination. He was interviewed by the FBI and lost his job at the depository in December of 1963. Molina worked for the G.I. Forum.[95] Lowery was spying on this group and apparently tried to link them to CPUSA. Lowery was also a member of the American G.I. Forum.

Lowery gave testimony against other members of the Communist Party that he had infiltrated and helped organize. The people whom he testified against in September 1963, were represented by John Abt. Abt was the attorney Oswald asked Ruth Paine to call to represent him.[96] One of the questions Marina Oswald was asked by the HSCA was; *"Prior to Lee's being arrested, did he ever discuss with you, are you familiar with the name William James Lowery?"*

MYSTERIOUS MATINEE

Oswald's capture in the Texas Theater was made possible by an alert shoe clerk named Johnny Calvin Brewer. Legend has it that Oswald

93   Lowery was informant DL-2-S. Another informant, DL-15-S (later DL T-4) was Lowery who who may have been Lowery's sister. All in the Family. Both infiltrated GI Forum meetings of which Joseph Rodriguez Molina was a member. Was Molina spying on Lowery's CP group or vice-versa? What goes around, comes around. Molina was elected Chairman of the Forum after being nominated by Lowery! However, it seems he never actively served in the office.

94   Harold S. Sawyer was a congressman who worked for the HSCA. It seems he questioned J. Lee Rankin about a story in Dallas Newspapers about an "informant" who destroyed the Communist Party in Texas by informing on them to the FBI and that he was living just two blocks from the Tippit shooting. It seems Sawyer suspected Oswald was on his way to "kill" the informant when Tippit intercepted him. The newspaper article also mentioned that a New York lawyer representing the Communists just happened to be the same lawyer Oswald wanted to represent him. Though Sawyer didn't seem to know the identities of these individuals, it is obvious that they were Lowery and Abt. So. ... where did Lowery live? was it two blocks from 10th and Patton?

95   The American G.I. Forum (AGIF) is a Congress chartered Hispanic veterans and civil rights organization founded in 1948. Its motto is "Education is Our Freedom and Freedom should be Everybody's Business." AGIF operates chapters throughout the United States, with a focus on veterans' issues, education, and civil rights. Its two largest national programs are the San Antonio-based Veterans Outreach Program, and the – based Service, Employment Redevelopment-Jobs for Progress, Inc. (Wikipedia)

96   John Abt was a member of the Progressive Party and spent most of his career as the chief legal counsel of the Communist Party.

ducked into his store foyer to hide from police cars patrolling Jefferson Boulevard. According to Brewer, he suspected Oswald was acting guilty and followed him to the Texas Theater several doors down the street. He claimed he saw Oswald duck into the theater without paying for a ticket and convinced the ticket seller Julia Postal to call the police. Why would Oswald not buy a ticket when he had the money? To draw attention to himself, of course! What amounted to a SWAT team arrived to arrest someone for not buying a 35-cent ticket.

However, William J. Lowery, who, like Herb Philbrick, led three lives for the FBI as an informer, Communist Party member and mild-mannered shoe salesman – was also employed in a shoe store on West Jefferson Boulevard. The Shoe Haven at 620 West Jefferson Boulevard was approximately three blocks west of the Texas Theater and also three blocks away from Hardy's Shoe Store where Johnny Calvin Brewer[97] worked.

Is it possible Oswald went to the wrong shoe store before or even *after* entering the theater?[98] Was he trying to contact Lowery?[99] Lowery was also a member of the Dallas chapter of the *Unitarians*[100] for Social Justice.[101] *Quakers* and *Unitarians* are everywhere in the JFK case.[102]

Lowery's contact with the "ultra-right" was Earl Lively.[103] Lively told Lowery that he had had contact with Philbrick in March 1964. He report-

---

97   As mentioned, it was Brewer who followed Oswald from his store to the Texas Theater and had Julia Postal call the police. An interesting side note is that Brewer had just taken delivery of a brand new car – a 1964-model Ford Galaxy XL500 – and wanted to put it through its paces. Brewer asked for Friday, November 22nd off to do so. An assistant was a substitute for him. So why was he there when Oswald entered the shoe store lobby? http://allthingswildlyconsidered.blogspot.com/2013/11/johnny-brewer-humble-hero-of.html

98   Is it possible that Oswald bought a ticket, entered the theater looking for his contact who may have been Lowery? Did he then leave the theater and enter the lobby of Brewer's shoe store thinking it was Lowery's? When he saw his mistake he then would have re-entered the theater without paying since he already had a ticket. That would explain the discrepancy between Brewer's and Butch Borroughs version of Oswald having and not having bought a ticket. It would also explain Julia Postal's confusion on the same matter.

99   Reportedly a new pair of shoes was among Oswald's possessions after his arrest. Could they have been purchased from Lowery?

100   The Unitarian Church was connected to The Albert Schweitzer College and Patrice Lumumba University. According to George Michael Evica, Oswald applied to both of these institutions. See *A Certain Arrogance*, p. 31 for details. Evica says that "while residing in the Soviet Union, Oswald reportedly applied to this new college (Patrice Lumumba University). His letter has not been found in any American public record, though he did receive a rejection notice dated May 3, 1961 informing him that the school only accepted students from Third World Countries." Evica also points fingers at the Quaker's and Unitarians as targets in US Intelligence's manipulation of religious groups.

101   124-90108-10016

102   See *The Other Oswald, A Wilderness of Mirrors*, Chapter 11

103   Lively was a member of the Air National Guard and at that time was a student of the Air Command and Staff College, Maxwell Air Force Base, Alabama. Lively showed Lowery a letter from Herbert Philbrick, former Communist Party member who had testified on behalf of the Government concerning communist activities. According to Lively, Philbrick was planning to be in Dallas

ed that Philbrick had come across information that Marguerite Oswald had been a communist at one time.[104] It seems that Lively was an OSI (Air Force) officer and was writing an anti-communist book stressing the Fair Play for Cuba Committee connections of Lee Harvey Oswald. He was being helped in this project by Dr. Robert Morris[105] and Lt. George Butler of DPD.[106]

Hosty's caseload in Dallas included the handling of Lowery and Oswald. If there was a relationship between Lowery and Hosty, it seems obvious that there should be one between Lowery and Oswald. Oswald's favorite TV show as a child was *"I Led Three Lives for the FBI"* which starred Richard Carlson as Herbert Philbrick.[107] The show was an unashamed venture into cold war propaganda. It told the story of how Philbrick infiltrated the Communist Party for the FBI while living a private life as a business man with a family. His Dallas counterpart Lowery, helped create the Dallas Communist Party chapter and reported to Hosty about its activities.

I began to wonder if Oswald was involved in an FBI program to flush out CP sympathizers in Dallas. After all, he had done so in New Orleans. His FBI contact in New Orleans was Warren DeBrueys. Was he involved in the same type of program in Dallas under the auspices of Hosty?

So, it seems painfully possible that Ruth and Michael Paine, Lee Oswald, William Lowery and James Hosty may have been working as a team in a clandestine operation involving surveillance of communists and pro-Castro sympathizers in the Dallas area. This might explain sightings of Oswald at the house on Harlandale Avenue that was being used by Alpha 66 just prior to the assassination. Was he reporting to Hosty about them when he dropped off his infamous note at the Dallas FBI office in early November of 63? Had he infiltrated their group? Had he learned of the upcoming assassination plan? Did they discover him and turn him into a fall guy? One thing is apparent. After the assassination, the FPCC ceased to exist. After Lee's arrest, his brother Robert told Lee at the jail house that "I don't think they're (the Paines) any friends of yours!" According to Robert, Lee replied, "Yes, they are."[108]

---

soon and desired to meet Lowery.
104   FBI 105-82555
105   Former counsel to the Senate Internal Security Committee under Senator McCarthy.
106   George Butler claimed that he tried to give Lively any information he could that the FBI turned over to the Dallas Police Department in connection with the Lee Harvey Oswald case.
107   Philbrick was also a member of Ed Butler's INCA's advisory committee, a key source of Propaganda in New Orleans in 1963 with Dr. Alton Ochsner as it's chairman.
108   To me this is an indication that they were in cahoots all along.

CHAPTER 6

THE DEVIL WENT DOWN TO ANTIOCH

….the craziest things make perfect sense.

– David Ferrie

In March 1959, Lee Oswald registered at the Albert Schweitzer College of Churwalden, Switzerland, using it as a reason for travel to Europe in the fall of that year. However, he never showed up for classes.[109] Instead he traveled through Europe to Finland and from there crossed over to the Soviet Union.

On September 4, 1959, even before he left El Toro in California, Oswald applied for a passport under the pretense of attending the Albert Schweitzer College in Switzerland and University of Turku in Finland, and to travel in Cuba, the Dominican Republic, England, France, Germany, and Russia. Although his passport was authorized on September 10th, he did not get his discharge until September 11th. The Marines never questioned the discrepancy between these travel preparations and the purpose of his discharge, which was to take care of his "ailing" mother.[110] After staying home with Marguerite for three days, he told his mother that he was going into the *"import export"* business and her testimony was that *import-export* was already stamped on his passport. His brother Robert, wrote that Lee planned on going to New Orleans and working for an export firm.

These strange actions raise some puzzling unanswered questions. Why did Oswald apply to this little known college in the first place? Why did he apply for the spring semester then travel to Europe in September? Why didn't he attend after being accepted? Why would this institution accept an applicant with so few academic credentials?[111] But most mysteriously,

---

109   It seems unusual behavior for the parsimonious Oswald to pay the $25 registration fee and then forfeit it.

110   A box of candy fell off a shelf in a store she worked in and hit her on the nose.

111   It seemed odd to me that Oswald was accepted at a college with no high school diploma. However, Robert Oswald disclosed in his book "Lee," that his brother had earned a GED while in the Marine Corps in March of 1959.

how did Oswald even know of the existence of this elusive institution? ASC was a tiny, unaccredited school in a remote village in Switzerland.

In March of 1960, Oswald's mother received a letter from ASC addressed to Lee. Wondering where her son was, she opened and answered the letter. ASC officials informed her that Lee never arrived at the college and they had no idea where he was.

Off the Beaten Path

Walt Brown described Albert Schweitzer College as "*a hippie commune with a curriculum.*" When the Warren Commission questioned the Swiss Police about the institution, they said they had never heard of it! So how did ASC recruit its students? Because of its small size and limited funds, the college seemed to do little or no advertising in the United States. It turns out that the primary sponsor of ASC was the *Unitarian* Church. When researcher Dennis Bartholomew, contacted the UUA (Unitarian Church) officials, he discovered that many of the records involving Schweitzer College came from an organization known as *Friends of Albert Schweitzer College* or FASC.[112] The purpose of FASC, it seems, was to assist ASC in recruiting and fund-raising in the United States. Thus ASC recruited American students primarily through personal contacts of the *Friends of Albert Schweitzer*. As George Michael Evica observed, "*The Unitarian Church was the mainstay of the Albert Schweitzer College.*" He discovered that "*Over the years, Allen Dulles and the OSS/CIA used the Quakers, the Unitarians, the World Council of Churches and other religious groups as sources of intelligence and information.*"

The history of Albert Schweitzer College suggests that American espionage assets helped establish the college and then used it, possibly with the knowledge and even cooperation of some of its religious supporters in the Unitarian Church movement and those who worked for the college in Switzerland. One of the Unitarian founders of ASC, Percival Brundage, was a former director of budget for the CIA.[113] He worked closely with both US Intelligence and the military in the '40s and '50s was, in fact, President of the American Friends of Albert Schweitzer College at the time when Lee Harvey Oswald applied.

Another influential Unitarian, James R. Killian, was part of a group in control of US space programs, including the U2 overflights, and in

---

112   Dennis Bartholomew, "LHO on Campus," *Fourth Decade*, vol. 4, nr. 3, 1997
113   His work for the Agency involved in black budgets.

the early '60s. Oswald was joined at the hip with the U2 spy plane and bragged that he would be working for NASA when he left New Orleans.

In essence, those who directed the policy for Albert Schweitzer College were, in fact, elite members of the establishment and allies of the Central Intelligence Agency. In retrospect, Oswald's registration at ASC provides a direct link between that institution and American intelligence.

Whoever was behind the Oswald/ASC connection was knowledgeable about both the OSS's and the CIA's use of Quakers, World Council of Churches, and Unitarians as contacts, assets and informants. They were also cognizant of the FBI's responsibility in tracking down and identifying Soviet illegals and double agents. Thus it is clear that Oswald was being manipulated by someone in American counterintelligence who possessed precisely that double body of knowledge. Could that be James Jesus Angleton?

Another frequent source of recruitment of ASC students was Antioch College in Yellow Springs, Ohio. Researchers had previously found links between Antioch and Lee Oswald, such as an Oswald "sighting" at a demonstration in Yellow Springs in the early 60s.

On November 29, 1963, Sgt. Donald Swartz, Intelligence Unit, Columbus Police Department, advised that he had received the following unverified information from a source he declined to identify: Lee Harvey Oswald allegedly attended Antioch College, Yellow Springs, Ohio, using his true name for a short period of time in 1957 and was dismissed because he was unable to prove his graduation from high school.[114] In addition, an FBI report (#CI 105-25-5) of S.A. Thomas B. Estep of the Cincinnati office included an unverified statement that Oswald attended Antioch in 1957.

It is nearly impossible that Oswald attended Antioch in 1957 since he was in the Marines at the time, but someone he knew attended Antioch from 1949-55. It was Ruth Paine. Was she the anonymous 1963 source that linked him to the institution? What is going on here?

But there is more. Researcher Michael Levy found a Navy Department document reporting that Ruth Paine had been requesting information about the family of Lee Oswald in 1957. This was long before she had been introduced to the defector and his wife by George de Mohrenschildt in the Spring of 1963.

---

114   Oswald was constantly incriminated by anonymous sources. See *The Other Oswald, A Wilderness of Mirrors*, Gary Hill, TrineDay, 2020

SATAN'S LITTLE IMPS

So how do we explain the shenanigans involving ASC, Antioch, Oswald and Ruth Paine? The common denominator is most likely Allen Dulles, whom, along with his colleague James Angleton, manipulated these entities like pawns on the Devil's chessboard. Dulles once referred to himself and his CIA cohorts as *Satan's little imps.*

Dulles' name permeates the Paine family closet of secrets. Let us count the ways;

- The Paine family's involvement with United Fruit. Dulles was on the board of directors.

- One of Ruth Forbes Paine's best friends was Mary Bancroft, secretary and mistress of Allen Dulles.

- Operation Paperclip was a Dulles inspired project to bring Nazi scientists and intelligence operatives into the US after the war to work for the CIA and NASA. Walter Dornberger, convicted Nazi war criminal, was one of these. He was Michael Paine's boss at Bell Helicopter.

- It was revealed by an FBI document dated Dec. 1963, that two friends of the Paines, Fred and Nancy Osborn, vouched for them when questioned by the FBI. Their father, Fred Osborn Sr., was a close friend of Allen Dulles. They attended Princeton together. In addition they were co-founders of the "Crusade for Freedom." Like "Radio Free Europe," Crusade for Freedom spewed CIA propaganda and used the power of radio as a tool of indoctrination. In fact, the two projects merged in 1962. Osborn was the first president of Crusade for Freedom. Allen Dulles and Henry Luce of Time-Life were on its board of directors.[115] *Life* magazine was responsible for convicting Oswald in the eyes of the public by displaying the Neely Street photo of Oswald and his rifle on the cover of its February 1964 issue. Time-Life also purchased the Zapruder film for more than $100,000 in 1963 dollars only to hide it away from the public for years. Former CIA operative, C.D. Jackson[116] was the catalyst behind this venture.

---

115   New Evidence Regarding Ruth and Michael Paine-Steve Jones

116   Jackson was in the OSS during WWII and after the war became Managing Director of Time-Life International. In 1948 he worked with Frank Wisner in what became the counter-intelligence branch of the CIA. It was Wisner that established Operation Mockingbird, a program to influence the domestic American media. According to Spartacus International, Jackson also successfully negotiated with Marina Oswald after the assassination for the exclusive rights to her story. Peter Dale Scott writes in his book *Deep Politics and the Death of JFK* that Jackson, on the urging of Allen Dulles, employed Isaac Don Levine, a veteran CIA publicist, to ghost-write Marina's story. This story never appeared in print.

Ruth Paine's older sister, Sylvia Hyde Hoke, was living in Falls Church, Virginia in 1963. In September of 1963 while traveling across the country, Ruth stayed with Sylvia. Falls Church adjoins Langley, which was then the new headquarters of the Central Intelligence Agency, a prized project of Allen Dulles. When Ruth Paine traveled to New Orleans to pick up Marina Oswald, she made the trip from Falls Church. After picking up Marina, she took her to her home in Irving, Texas, successfully separating Marina from Lee at the time of the assassination.

FRIENDLY PERSUASION

As we saw in chapter one, Unitarians, Quakers[117] were continually popping up in Oswald's world. Ruth Paine and her friend Ruth Kloepfer, Robert Webster, Pricilla McMillan, Dee Dee Sharples de Mohrenschildt are examples.

The list of Unitarians includes William Lowery, Kerry Thornley, and Gerald Patrick Hemming.

Another odd connection of religion to the JFK assassination is the *Abundant Life Temple* in the Oak Cliff section of Dallas.

Old church organizations included more of Oswald connected individuals. David Ferrie, Jack Martin, Thomas Beckham, Fred Chrisman, Larry Crafard and John Howard Bowen (aka Albert Osborne).

CONCLUSIONS

What is to be made of the Antioch incident? It raises a red flag that can easily be construed as a false one. Oswald could not have been a student there in 1957. The anonymous sources that incriminated him had to have come forward much later than that. The omnipresent Ruth Paine was always handy when evidence against Oswald was needed. She is certainly a link to Antioch, being an alumni. If we follow the thread of the Antioch incident, it will lead us directly to Allen Dulles via Ruth Paine. Antioch was a "liberal" college. Beatnik liberals, the 1950s version of Hippies, were always a threat to the establishment. When the CIA and FBI felt threatened by these groups, their usual course of action was to tarnish their reputation with disinformation by linking them to communist front organizations. One of their secret weapons to do this were agents like Lee Oswald. Oswald was used for this purpose to discredit the Fair Play for Cuba Committee. His ordering of a weapon via mail was likely another assignment to aid in the prosecution of interstate weapon sales by

---

117   Others were Trotskyites: George Lyman Paine, Harold Issacs, Harry Power etc.

providing evidence that these businesses were supplying subversives with weapons. Klein's Sporting Goods and Seaport Traders were on a Senate Subcommittee's list to be investigated.[118] We will explore these activities in a later chapter. In turn using Oswald as the agent provocateur, insinuates the presence of James Angleton via his use of Oswald as a singleton agent.

In his book, *CHAOS*, Tom O'Neill linked CIA/MKULTRA doctor, Jolly West to Charles Manson via a clinic run by Dr. David Smith in Haight-Ashbury. Manson had been encouraged to go to the Haight and become part of the hippie drug culture by his parole officer, Roger Smith. West started the *Haight-Ashbury Project*, which was financed by the Foundations Fund for Research in Psychiatry, INC. This Fund was a CIA front.

MHCHAOS was established under President Johnson and expanded under Richard Nixon. It was launched by *James Jesus Angleton* under the reign of Richard Helms, and the project was run by Richard Ober. Angleton is once again in the background inducing *chaos*.

CHAOS was a domestic spying project targeting Americans and ran from 1967 to 1974. The mission of CHAOS was to uncover possible foreign influence on domestic race, anti-war and other protest movements. Of particular interest was the hippie movement and drug culture as well as groups like the Black Panthers. CHAOS was complimented by Hoover's COINTELPRO (counterintelligence program) which Oswald may have been used in against CORE[119] in Clinton, Louisiana. The goal of CHAOS and COINTELPRO was to destroy the anti-war movements of the '60s and '70s. Drugs were given to the hippies and behavior control used to encourage acts of violence and crime. The project was clearly illegal as the CIA's charter forbade domestic activities. Is it possible that the Manson murders were an MKULTRA experiment gone wrong? Or was it, as forensic psychologist and law professor Allan Scheflin described it, *an MKULTRA experiment gone right.*[120]

It is now apparent that Dulles was using religious groups as fronts. Angleton ran an illegal domestic spying project targeting Americans. Hoover's device was COINTELPRO. The purpose of these activities

---

118   Oswald supposedly ordered these weapons using the alias Alik Hiddell. He was first called Alik in Russia, by his fellow workers at the Minsk radio factory who couldn't pronounce Lee. Alik came from "Likoy "(daring in Russian) from anagram of his 3 names. Lee-H-O pronounced Li-kh-o-y in Russian. It may also have become the KGB nickname for Oswald.

119   Congress On Racial Equality

120   Could it be that other MKULTRA subjects; Whitey Bulger, Ted Kaczynski, Rev. Jim Jones, Charles Whitman, Arthur Brenner and David Chapman and Tim McVeigh were victims or tools as well.

was to destroy the credibility of left-wing groups. The Antioch incident was indicative of this effort. Just Satan's little imps running amok behind the scenes with their mischievous games of intrigue. And what we didn't know then that *we do know now* is that: COINTELPRO was not just the creation of J. Edgar Hoover. It was a joint enterprise with the CIA, and specifically with counterintelligence chief James Angleton.

According to FBI documents, while Ruth Paine was a student at Antioch College, in Yellow Springs, Ohio, her mother was telling neighbors that she was a "Communist." (From SA Hosty Report 12-11-63, Field Office File No. DL 1051716).

In June of 1953 an Assistant US Attorney wrote to the FBI to request an investigation of Carl Dudley Hyde to determine the validity of his claim of "Conscientious Objector" in connection with his classification under the Selective Service System. Hyde apparently had run off to England that year to study the possibility of living in a religious community, the Society of Brothers. This may have been a side effect of a *Dayton News* article indicating that Carl Dudley Hyde had sent his draft registration cards to Representative Joseph Martin, Speaker of the House along with a letter stating "We see any military program involving peacetime conscription as a drastic violation of civil rights and a threat to the peace-making efforts of the United Nations."

Carl Dudley Hyde later became a doctor, a general practitioner. But his fame lies in being Ruth Hyde Paine's brother.

CHAPTER 7

THE NIXIE NEXUS

We seek a free flow of information.... We are not afraid to entrust the American people with unpleasant facts.... For a nation that is afraid to let its people judge the truth and falsehood in an open market is a nation that is afraid of its people.

— JFK (February 26, 1962)

If Lee Harvey Oswald had lived long enough to face a jury, one of the lynch pin exhibits of the prosecution would be the paper sack supposedly found on the sixth floor of the Texas Schoolbook Depository near the alleged sniper's nest.[121] The importance of this sack was that it was the link making it possible for Oswald to sneak his Manlicher Carcano into the building on the day of the assassination.

That Oswald carried some kind of package to work that morning is certain. He was seen doing so by Wesley Frazier,[122] who drove Oswald to work that morning. Frazier's sister, Linnie Mae Randle, saw it as well. However, their description of the sack he carried did not correspond in size with the one to be used as evidence. It was smaller and could not have hidden the rifle even if it had been disassembled. When shown the alleged wrapping paper found on the sixth floor, Frazier said it was too big to be the package he saw Oswald carrying in his car that morning. In addition, TSBD employee, Jack Dougherty observed Oswald enter the building that morning and stated he had nothing in his hands.

Incredibly, a second paper wrapping for the rifle turned up in the dead letter section of the Irving Post Office a few weeks after the assassination. It was addressed to Lee Oswald with no return address and mailed before November 22nd.

---

121   The actual existence of the bag is questionable. The bag does not appear in any of the crime scene photos taken of the sniper's nest after the assassination. In addition, the police officers who said they saw the bag gave contradictory testimony about its size, location, and condition. Some of the policemen who searched or saw the sniper's nest after the shooting didn't see a bag there. Also their was no tape on the bag found and it had no oil present even though Oswald's rifle was well oiled.
122   I asked Frazier if it could have been his lunch in the bag. He said no, it was too big. But it was too small for even a disassembled rifle.

Anthony Summers wrote:

> *On December 4, 1963, an deliverable package addressed to "Lee Oswald" was retrieved from the dead-letter section to a post office in a Dallas suburb. It was wrongly addressed to 601 W. Nassaus Street, which could approximate to Neches Street, which was near where Oswald had lived. When opened, it turned out to contain a "brown paper bag..." Since no postal worker is likely to have tossed aside a package addressed to "Lee Oswald" AFTER the name became world famous on November 22, it is reasonable to assume the parcel arrived before the assassination. Who sent it to Oswald, and why, are questions which appear especially pertinent with the knowledge that another paper bag became key evidence. But the Warren Report did not even mention the mystery parcel, and there is no sign that it was forensically tested or further investigated.*[123]

In 1963, the Dallas post office's dead letter department was referred to as The *Nixie* Room. The package was discovered by C. G. Twilley on December 4, 1963. It was addressed to Lee Oswald, seemingly in his own handwriting, but the address was for 601 West Nassau Street. A street that did not exist in Dallas, or anywhere in Texas. Below the address label, the words *"Irving Texas"* were scrawled in different handwriting. The package was due 12 cents postage. It was metered postage and not stamps. The Depository metered the postage on its shipments. The package had no return address. It would seem that someone at the post office knew Oswald and was aware of his connection with Ruth Paine's Irving address and possibly added *"Irving, Texas"* below the label.

The ubiquitous Dallas Postmaster, Harry Holmes opened the package after the assassination. Besides being the only non-police officer to question Oswald, he was also an informant for the FBI.[124] The FBI had been illegally opening Oswald's mail in the US, just as the CIA had done when Oswald was in Russia.[125] The package contained a long, empty paper bag similar to the one supposedly found in the sixth floor of the Texas school book depository building. There were some smudged prints on the package but they were not of a quality useful to identify Oswald as the sender or handler.

What was the purpose of this postal predicament? Why was Oswald himself, or someone else, mailing this package to him prior to the as-

---

123   *CONSPIRACY*, Anthony Summers,Paragon House Edition, pp. 71-72.
124   Holmes, FBI informant T-7, continually lied and doctored evidence to incriminate Oswald.
125   CIA project HTLINGUAL

sassination? If, as the Warren Commission intimated, Oswald made the package with shipping materials utilized by the Schoolbook Depository to mail books, was his purpose to use the facilities to mail it to himself to avoid paying postage? Did he mail it to himself in order to avoid being seen carrying it home? If so, why not mail it to his Beckley Street rooming house? None of these theories make sense. The first because the postage was inadequate and the second because he still had to mail it and could have been seen carrying it to a mail box. And why would he use a non-existent address?

However, if approached from a different perspective, it is easy to see the usefulness of this maneuver as a tool for incrimination. Was it more planted evidence to be used against the patsy? Conspirators who knew ahead of time that planting the gun wasn't enough. The weapon had not only to be tied to Oswald but there had to be evidence that he secreted it into the building ahead of time. With the FBI tracking his mail,[126] a package with his name on it mailed to a phony address would be sure to draw attention to Oswald's premeditation in the crime of the century. Taking into account that Harry Holmes was the Dallas postmaster as well as an FBI stoolie brings this weird odyssey into more focus.

In spite of Anthony Summers' claim, the paper of the un-delivered package *was* examined and found *not* to be identical to the paper used in constructing the gun sack found on the 6th floor of the TSBD. However, because rolls of paper used at the Depository lasted an average of about three days and varied in composition, this did not prove the Nixie parcel wasn't created there. Like the package Frazier saw Oswald with on the morning of the assassination, the Nexie package was too small, measuring 18" in length, to hold even a disassembled Manlicher Carcano.

But there is more. On November 23rd, a 12-cent postage due card arrived at Ruth Paine's house at 2515 W. 5th Street in Irving. This is the same amount of excess postage due as on the Nixie package. Someone at the post office, probably Holmes, had to know that Oswald's family lived with the Paines, since the FBI was opening his mail. Although the card was discovered by Dallas police the

126   The FBI's domestic mail interception program was called HUNTER. Today they use- electronic surveillance of email with a computer program called CARNIVORE.

weekend of the assassination, I could find no mention of police questioning of Ruth or Marina about it at that time. In fact, it wasn't until February 20, 1964, that the card was mentioned by postal inspector Roy Armstrong in an FBI interview. He told the *Fee Bees*[127] that in his inquiries in Irving and Dallas he had somehow determined that the delivery slip of November 20 was related to a magazine delivered to Oswald on the 21st or 22nd of November. Marina was then finally interviewed five days later (February 25th) and, ever cooperative with Hoover's minions, stated the card was for one of Lee's magazines and that she had paid the over-due to 12 cents. Since Lee's magazines were purchased by subscriptions and paid for in advance, this is a weak story. But it wouldn't be the first time statements made by Marina were laced with contradiction or confusion. In addition she stated that when she paid the excess postage she accepted the parcel. If the card arrived on November 20 and the package wasn't discovered until December 6, this defies logic. If it were a magazine, it just happened to be 12 cents light in postage which conveniently coincided with the amount due on the Nexie parcel. As for Ruth Paine, she wasn't interviewed about the card until July 31, 1964. In the interview she skillfully avoided the issue by changing the subject and wasn't asked anything further.

Researcher Garrick Alder believes that Marina's lie and Ruth's evasiveness were deliberate efforts by the FBI and Holmes to separate the witnesses from the parcel, the parcel from the delivery card, and the postal service from the whole affair. The reason is obvious. It might reveal that the FBI was intercepting Oswald's mail, and that is how they knew of his connection to Paine's Irving home. When someone saw his name and the fictional address on the package, this postal employee knew where he could be found. The package may have actually been delivered there with the wrong address displayed. This would certainly draw attention to the FBI's illegal intercept program after the assassination. It needed to be swept under the rug and with Marina's and Ruth's help it was. Who was this postal employee who knew Oswald's whereabouts? The obvious suspect is Harry Holmes, Dallas postmaster and FBI informant.

So, why would Oswald mail the package to a non-existent address and fail to pay full postage? As with much of the evidence against him, it appears he was trying to get caught. Like the rifle, revolver, ID cards, backyard photos, etc., there is too much evidence. Dropping his wallet at the Tippit shooting scene is another example. What is more likely is that conspirators were using the parcel mailing to link the Paine house to the

---

package and to trick Oswald into handling the package and thus obtain his fingerprints on it. Later it could be planted in the 6th floor sniper's nest as proof of this guilt.

Researcher John Armstrong had a different take on this bizarre episode. He seems to speculate that there were two postage due slips delivered to the Paine home, one on November 20 and the other on the 21st. Ironically, both were for 12 cents postage due. This unlikelihood lessens the strength of the theory. However, it provides strength for an axiom I promoted in my book "*The Other Oswald*," that the evidence against LHO always came in pairs.

THE ATTEMPTED DELIVERY ON THURSDAY, NOVEMBER 21

This package was addressed to Lee Oswald, 2515 W. 5th St, Irving, Texas and was not in his handwriting. It didn't arrive because of insufficient postage. The postage due delivery card was discovered by police on Saturday at the Paine house in a blue suitcase owned by Oswald. Officers were sent to the post office to pick up the parcel. They were told it had already been picked up. When interviewed by the FBI in February, Dallas Postal Inspector Roy Armstrong said the package was delivered on either November 20 or 21 to Marina Oswald and that it was a magazine. This agrees with Marina's version of the event. However, if that was the case, how do you explain the postage due card that arrived on November 23? Armstrong's take is that the gummy label with the Nassau Street address was pasted over the original "*Lee Oswald, 2515 W. 5th St, Irving, Texas*" address. That would explain the *Irving, Texas* scrawl below the pasted on label. This interpretation leads to a scenario that makes more sense than others. It goes like this; The conspirators knew in advance that Oswald's gun would be planted on the 6th floor of the TSBD. They needed to provide evidence that he clandestinely transported it from the Paine garage to the crime scene. Thus, they shipped him the package manufactured from materials that could be linked to his place of employment. Oswald was told to expect a package on Wednesday the 20th. This would explain his Thursday visit to Irving which was out of his normal routine. The postage deficit caused the package not to be delivered and it ended up in the Nixie room at the post office. When the mistake was discovered, a gummy label with a phony address was pasted over the original address, that of the Paine house. If the package had arrived on the 20th, Oswald would have opened it on the 21st and handled it, linking his finger prints to the package which would later be planted on the 6th floor. However, if the undelivered package were discovered after the assassination there would be a problem. The official version is that Oswald did not know the motorcade route would include Elm Street until a day or two before the assassination. Hence he needed to go to Irving to get his gun to take advantage of a golden opportunity. If the package were discovered after the assassination, it would be assumed it was sent by conspirators or that he mailed it to himself before he knew the motorcade route was changed. Either way, the lone nut theory would go down the drain. The package had to disappear.

STRANGER THINGS

Although there was no West Nassau Street in Texas, there was one in Tampa, Florida. The zip code was 33607. It was in Tampa that an apparent assassination attempt on Kennedy's life was thwarted on 18 November 1963, just four days before the president was killed in Dallas. The would-be assassin was one Gilberto Policarpo Lopez.[128] Like Oswald, Lopez was a member of the Fair Play for Cuba Committee. A very reliable FBI undercover asset Joe Burton, reported that on November 17, 1963, Oswald visited Tampa and attended a Fair Play for Cuba Committee meeting and met with a key member of the FPCC. Lopez attended the same meeting.[129] John Kaylock claimed to have met Oswald in Punta Gorda, Florida, shortly before the assassination.[130] Frank Sturgis also alleged that he had met Oswald in Florida in the days prior to the assassination itself. Sturgis, of course, was a disinformation agent intent on blaming the assassination on Castro.

Could Oswald have been in Florida on the 17th? The Warren Commission was unable to determine Oswald's whereabouts on the 15th, 16th or 17th of November 1963. Why Marina did not want Lee to visit that weekend is unclear. The WC never bothered to ask her. There is evidence that he visited Abilene, Texas that weekend and met with Cuban exiles. Chapter Nine will explore the Abilene episode.

---

128   For more on the fascinating parallel between Lopez and Oswald see *The Other Oswald, A Wilderness of Mirrors*, Gary Hill, TrineDay Books, 2020
129   "The Ghosts of November," Anthony and Robbyn Summers, *Vanity Fair*, Dec. 1994
130   http://www.maryferrell.org/showDoc.html?docId=59624&relPageId=24&search=kaylock

CHAPTER 8

THE OTHER SCHOOLBOOK DEPOSITORY

This is the night I should go to the theater.

– JFK[131]

I n my book, *The Other Oswald, A Wilderness of Mirrors*, I explored the strange occurrence of paired evidence. There were two rifles, two pistols, two wrappings for the rifle, two or more Oswalds, two (or three) wallets, two sets of incriminating I.D.'s linking Oswald to Hidell in those wallets, two jackets, two shoe stores, two Marinas, etc. Since the book was published, I discovered another example of this duplication. It seems there were actually *two* Schoolbook Depositories in Dallas and both were on JFK's motorcade route on November 22, 1963. *The Texas Schoolbook Depository*, where Oswald worked, was on Elm Street. The *Lone Star Schoolbook Depository was* located further along the motorcade route at 4646 Harry Hines Boulevard.[132] Both warehouses were owned by right-wing radicals. The Lone Star's owner was Ross Carlton, who also acted as vice-president of the company. The Texas Schoolbook Depository was the property of right-wing oil tycoon, D.H. Byrd. Its president was Jack Cason. Cason's wife Gladys[133] was openly quoted as saying, "*Someone ought to shoot President Kennedy.*"

The excellent research of William Weston has uncovered evidence, however, that Carlton was actually running things in the background at the TSBD as well as the LSBD, and that Cason was merely a front man. Carlton was anti-Kennedy, anti-Johnson, anti-integregation, a gun collector, and was accused by a close acquaintance of being a suspect in JFK's murder.

The memoirs of Oswald's employment counselor, Laura Kittrell, reveal that she had in years past sent applicants to the Texas School Book

---

131   (After his decision to remove missiles from Turkey and Italy in exchange for Russian missiles in Cuba.) *Thirteen Days: A Memoir of the Cuban Missile Crisis*, RFK

132   Ruth Paine actually was surprised when she heard on the news that Oswald worked at the Dealey Plaza facility. She had assumed he was located at the other schoolbook warehouse on Harry Hines Blvd.

133   Cason, Gladys, *One Life*, (GSC Creations, 2004), pp. 67-71

Depository. Checking into the background of these applicants was done not by Jack Cason nor Roy Truly, but "the Ross Carlton family" who, she said, were the owners of the Texas School Book Depository.[134] According to Kittrell, the Carltons sold the depository "a year or so before the assassination" but apparently still maintained control over the screening of applicants. If she tried to send someone to the TSBD "who was not a 100% red-blooded, true-blue American," the Carltons would loudly complain.[135]

Kittrell was therefore surprised at the ease with which Lee Harvey Oswald got his job at the TSBD in spite of his undesirable discharge from the Marine Corps. She wondered why the Carltons had hired Oswald. Were they finally relaxing their standards in order to fill job positions that earned very little pay? Weston concluded that what Kittrell did not know was that Oswald had been recommended by the CIA, according to George de Mohrenschildt, whose source was Domestic Contacts Service Chief J. Walton Moore. An additional contributing factor was that Oswald was also an undercover informant for the FBI. The Carltons were probably aware of Oswald's counterintelligence background when Roy Truly hired him on October 15, 1963.

Weston uncovered several links to US intelligence agencies involving the schoolbook business. It seems that CIA agent William Harvey[136] worked as a law editor for Bobbs Merrill in Indianapolis in the late 60s.

McGraw-Hill occupied the third floor of the TSBD in 1963. This company not only published schoolbooks but was a contractor for the Foreign Technology Division and collected data on Soviet aerospace technology.

Van Nostrand schoolbook salesman, Newcomb Mott,[137] like Lee Oswald, entered the Soviet Union by a little known and remote route. He crossed the Norwegian[138] border without a visa and was arrested by the Soviets who were convinced he was a CIA agent. Mott was put on trial for entering the country illegally. He was convicted and sentenced to a forced labor camp. Like Oswald, he attempted suicide with a razor blade. Unlike Oswald, he was successful. Strangely, the blade was included in a gift package from the American Embassy. Hmm. ... A real care package.

Behind-the-scenes intelligence connections of several of Oswald's fellow employees at the TSBD are intriguing as well. William Shelby

---

134   Laura Kittrell's typewritten memoirs consisting of ninety pages is designated as FBI record no. 124-10057-10339; Agency file no. 62-109060-4052

135   *On the Death of JFK: Spider's Web at the Trade Mart,* William Weston

136   William Harvey obituary in the *New York Times,* June 14, 1976.

137   Newcomb Mott story in the *Chicago Tribune,* January 29, 1966.

138   Oswald crossed the border in Finland.

had connections to the CIA. Joe Molina, the building's credit manager, worked with Bill Lowery to infiltrate the G.I. Forum.[139] Molina was arrested on the weekend of the assassination and suspected of being an accomplice of Oswald. Billy Lovelady was involved in an illegal weapons deal while in the Air Force and stationed in Washington, DC.[140] Roy Truly's right-wing and racist leanings are well documented.

At the time of the assassination, the *other* Schoolbook Depository (Lone Star) had recently moved from downtown Dallas to Harry Hines Boulevard. The old location was 703 & 707 Browder Street. This was not far from Jaggars-Chiles-Stoval, which was located at 522 Browder Street. Oswald had worked there from October 1962 to April 1963. The new location was part of Market Hall which, along with the Trade Mart and a Home Furnishing Mart constituted the Dallas Market Center. LSBD, NAPA and Binswanger Glass were the three buildings making up the complex. The 12 story high Stemmons Tower was also included in the project and financed by real estate developer, Trammell Crow. Crow hobnobbed with conservative republicans such as Richard Nixon, Gerald Ford and H.W. Bush.

In 1956, Binswanger built the Cabana Motel with the help of Teamster funds approved by Jimmy Hoffa. This was the same Cabana Motel that was visited by Jack Ruby, Eugene Hale Brading, Lawrence Myers and Jean Aase on the night before the assassination.

The choice of the Trade Mart as the site of the luncheon on November 22nd was not decided until the last minute. Connally wanted the Trade Mart, while Secret Service advance man, Jerry Bruno, preferred the Woman's Building. The motorcade routes for both buildings would have passed through Dealey Plaza. However, had the Woman's Building been chosen, there would have been no hairpin turn onto Elm Street. The motorcade would have continued down Main Street and not slowed down. This would have made a shot from the TSBD much more difficult. Therefore, it is logical that a contingency plan be in place possibly involving the LSBD further along the route. Weston believed that the possibility of a kill zone at the railroad crossing near the LSBD was a real possibility. He cites Jerry Bruno's statement in his memoirs *The Advance Man*. In this manuscript, Bruno said that of the five cities the president was planning to visit in Texas, the least likely for a plot to occur was in Dallas. This was because of the

---

139   For more on this see *The Other Oswald, A Wilderness of Mirror*, Gary Hill, Chapter 6.
140   Rivera, Larry, "Billy Lovelady: A Troubled Past," 28 September 2012 on oswald-innocent.com.

long uncertainty over whether the Women's Building or the Trade Mart would be selected for the president's luncheon.

• • •

I came across a little known item in Vince Palamara's book, *Survivors Guilt* that struck me as a possible connection. Vince quoted an article from the *NY Times* on 12/20/63:

> *A 21-year-old Dallas machinist was arrested by the Secret Service to-day on charges of threatening to kill President Kennedy. The machinist, Russell W. McLarry, said the threat had been made "in jest" on Nov. 21, the day before Mr. Kennedy was assassinated here. Two women to whom Mr. McLarry allegedly made the statement reported it to the po-lice in Arlington, about 15 miles west of here, soon after they heard of the assassination."*
>
> Mr. McLarry was alleged to have told the women that he would be working near the Trade Mart the next day and would be waiting with a gun to "get" the President.
>
> The coincidences are striking. McLarry worked at the Dahl-gren[141] Manufacturing Company, which makes Lithographic print-ing equipment in a plant three blocks north of the Trade Mart. In Chicago, potential patsy Arthur Vallee worked in a lithograph printing building overlooking a planned motorcade route in Chica-go. Oswald worked at Jaggars, Chiles and Stoval, another printing enterprise. Just strange coincidences?
>
> Furthermore, McLarry was unmarried and lived in the Oak Cliff section of Dallas, making him a neighbor of Lee Harvey Os-wald as well as Jack Ruby.[142]

ASSASSINATION BY THE BOOK

Oswald would never have been found guilty of killing Tippit or JFK at the time of his death.
— DPD Homicide Detective James Leavelle, 1988

Logistically, planning for the assassination would have had to take into account the fact that the motorcade route was not yet decided and might be changed at the last moment. Therefore, there had to be a sepa-rate plan prepared for each route. If the Woman's Building had been the site of the luncheon, Oswald would not have been the patsy since a suc-

---

141   The role of the Dahlgren raid in the demise of Abe Lincoln is just another weird coinci-dence between the histories of the two Presidents who were killed 100 years apart but shared so many odd connections.

142   *Survivors Guilt*, Vince Palamara p. 372-373

cessful attempt from the TSBD would have been extremely difficult. A second location for the crossfire would be needed. A second warehouse controlled by the same people and a second patsy would be essential. Note that it was *after* Oswald started working at the TSBD that the motorcade route was changed. Not until November 19 was the Elm Street route made public.[143] Was Russell McLarry a backup patsy? Was the backup team of shooters to be located in the Dallas Market Center and the Lone Star Schoolbook Depository? Was this site to be used in the event that the Woman's Building was the site chosen for the luncheon? Were these locations Plan B and the Dealey Plaza and Texas Schoolbook Depository Plan A? Was Plan A activated when the Trade Mart was finally chosen as the luncheon site? Since the Trade Mart was chosen, Plan A was carried out to perfection. As a result we will never know for sure if there was a Plan B. But if Einstein was right and parallel universes occur whenever historic forks in the road apply, there may well be another version of events where the LSBD is famous and the TSBD just another warehouse.

UP ON THE ROOF

In 1963, fellow Dallas County Deputy Sheriff Pat Boyd told Roger Craig that he had made a silencer for a .30 caliber carbine owned by Harry Weatherford. Weatherford, also a Deputy Sheriff, was stationed on the roof of the Courthouse with a rifle on November 22, 1963. I have always wondered why, if Sheriff Decker had his charges standing down, Weatherby wasn't. Years later, a roofing construction crew found an expended rifle shell on that roof.

> If the American people knew the truth about Dallas, there would be blood in the streets.
>
> – Robert F. Kennedy

---

143   This is strong evidence that Oswald could not have planned the assassination ahead of time. He didn't know the motorcade would go past his job site until a couple days before the assassination.

Part III

Hands off Cuba

INTRODUCTION TO PART III

THE CRIME AGAINST CUBA[144]

The United States has the possibility of doing as much good in Latin America as it has done wrong in the past. I would say we alone have this power – on the essential condition that communism does not take over there

– JFK

JFK and Cuba will forever be linked in history. The Caribbean Island involved his greatest defeat as well as his greatest victory. The Bay of Pigs disaster was the first stage of his evolution from Cold War Hawk to Peacemaker. John Kennedy was a young and inexperienced president when he took office. However, he was an extremely intelligent and savvy man. He could be fooled *once* but caught on quickly. Being taken advantage of by experienced conman Allen Dulles and his CIA cronies, the young president wised up. Dulles and Bissell persuaded JFK into rubber stamping Ike and Nixon's illegitimate offspring, the planned invasion of Cuba at the Bay of Pigs. When this fiasco failed, it was Kennedy who accepted the blame. But he didn't take the humiliation lying down. He fired the *Godfather of the CIA* as well as his cohorts Bissell and Cabell and began a campaign to limit the Agency's power. This evolution from hawk to dove would continue through the Cuban Missile Crisis and consummate in his greatest victory, that of ending the crisis through negotiation and avoiding a nuclear holocaust. Had any other of the leaders of our generation, Eisenhower, Johnson, Ford, Nixon or Reagan been in his shoes, I am sure they would have listened to their military advisors and congressional hawks and taken the road to annihilation. This course of action saved millions of lives but cost JFK his own.

You and I are alive today, my friend, because of his sacrifice.

Pamphlet by Corliss Lamont that WC said motivated Oswald into revolutionary mode.

CHAPTER 9

FAIR PLAY FOR CUBA

I know....Kennedy is a man you can talk with.... Other leaders have assured me that to attain this goal (coexistence) we must first await his reelection.... If you see him again, you can tell him that I'm willing to declare Goldwater my friend if that will guarantee (his) election.

– Fidel Castro to Jean Daniel

THE HORSE OF A DIFFERENT COLOR

One of the key elements making up the JFK assassination mystery is Oswald's role in his Fair Play for Cuba charade.

The founders of the FPCC were Richard Gibson and Robert Taber, as mentioned in a previous chapter. Gibson was a writer for CBS News who eventually became a spy for the CIA. Gibson was also playing both ends against the middle by selling information to the KGB. Anthony Summers was one of the first to stumble onto Gibson's story nearly a quarter of a century ago. Summers interviewed Gibson who denied everything. Jefferson Morley has exposed new details of it in his latest research. He wonders why the CIA would dump a living source like Gibson. Was he giving bad intelligence? Was it because of his KGB treachery?

Originally, the FPCC was formed by a group of intellectuals who signed an ad in the *New York Times* designed to persuade news organizations and their audiences to perceive the good side of the Cuban revolution. This was in April 1960. The signers of this ad, a group of racially diversified high brows, were a threat because up until that time, black intellectuals had restricted their political endeavors to the racial question. Now they were protesting foreign policy. This was a no-no as was made clear years later with war protesters during the Vietnam War.

Morley points out that the CIA, FBI and Senate Internal Security Committee were immediately hostile to these developments. College students and professors began to form chapters and the FPCC was suddenly expanding into an organization they perceived to be a growing threat in the US.

The three forementioned agencies were the spearhead of efforts to suppress threatening groups like FPCC. Later, the hippy anti-war movement, Black Panthers, MLK, Malcom X, Weathermen, etc. became targets.

Oswald had connections to the FPCC, CPA and SWP. All three were targets of the Senate Internal Security Subcommittee (SISS), FBI and CIA.

COMMITTEE GOVERNMENT

As J.W. Lateer points out in his book The Three Barons, the Legislative Reorganization Act of 1946 enabled the employment of UN-elected professional staff by Congressional Committees. This is the catalyst that enabled witch hunting committees like HUAC and Joe McCarthy's Permanent Subcommittee on Investigations (PSI). This applied to commissions as well, and explains the motivation of the Warren Commission. This legislation also greatly enhanced the power of Southern congressmen like Richard Russell and James O. Eastland. The twin boogeymen, integration and Communism, were about to be hunted down by a mob of vigilantes carrying torches and destroying everything in their path. The result was a wasteland of ruined lives of innocent bystanders accused by neighbors and enemies with motivations of jealousy and hatred. With the creation of the CIA in 1947 in league with Hoover's omnipresent FBI, already on a crusade against Communism, the tools of the committees were in place. The cult of anti-Communist paranoia was on the rampage, fueled by the cold war.

> Abuse of power of the invisible power wielders is a natural hazard of the staff system.[145]

HUAC

The House UN-American Activities Committee, (HUAC), was established by the US House of Representatives in 1938. It investigated allegations of communist activity in the US during the early years of the Cold War. The committee wielded its subpoena power as a weapon and called citizens to testify in high-profile hearings before Congress. The use of intimidation produced questionable revelations about Communists infiltrating American institutions and subversive actions by well-known citizens. HUAC's tactics were controversial and contributed to the fear, distrust and repression producing the anti-communist hysteria of the

---

145   *Cases and Materials on Legislation, 4th Edition 1969, Nutting, Elliot and Dickerson.*

1950s. By the early 1960s, HUAC's influence was in decline, and in 1969 it was renamed the Committee on Internal Security.

Richard Nixon used HUAC in his rise to power by going after Commies in the State Department, the most famous of which was Alger Hiss. This Quaker on a white horse gained the publicity and notoriety necessary to propel him into the White House as a running mate for Ike in 1952.

S.I.S.S.

*T*he United States Senate's Special Subcommittee to Investigate the Administration of the Internal Security Act and Other Internal Security Laws, known more commonly as the Senate Internal Security Subcommittee (SISS) and sometimes the McCarran Committee, was authorized by S. 366, approved December 21, 1950, to study and investigate espionage, sabotage and protect the internal security of the United States.

A main concern was "infiltration of persons who are or may be under the domination of the foreign government or organization controlling the world Communist movement or any movement seeking to overthrow the Government of the United States by force and violence."

The chairman of the subcommittee was Patrick McCarran of Nevada. William Jenner of Indiana took over later after Republicans gained control of the Senate in 1952. In 1955 the Democrats returned to power and James O. Eastland of Mississippi became chairman. Eastman, known as the "Voice of the White South" and the "Godfather of Mississippi Politics," was a leader of Southern resistance against racial integration during the civil rights movement. Jay Sourwine, acted as legal counsel for SISS. He was very close to McCarren and served as his right-hand man.

SISS had the power to operate in secret and had no investigative limitations. The committee, sometimes made up of only "one" man (usually that man was McCarren), could call any witness it liked and swear them in without any records of the interviews being kept.

The witch hunting investigations of the 1950s included forming US foreign policy in Asia, the scope of Soviet activity in the US, subversion of the Federal Government, particularly the Department of State and Defense, immigration, the United Nations, youth organizations, TV, radio, and the entertainment industry, labor unions, educational organizations and sundry other segments of American life. Later it expanded into civil rights and racial issues, college campus disorders and drug trafficking. The subcommittee published over 400 volumes of hearings and numerous reports, documents, and committee prints.

We can now see that somehow Lee Harvey Oswald was being used as a tool in these witch hunts. In both New Orleans and Dallas he was acting as a provocateur for the Federal Government.

The investigations carried out by these witch hunting committees were focused mainly on Communist infiltration of US institutions. These included government agencies, colleges and universities, the entertainment industry, youth organizations, immigration, the defense industry, labor unions and others including FPCC. The State Department seemed to be a major target of the witch hunt. By the '60s the targets shifted to Civil rights, racial issues, campus unrest, and trafficking of drugs.

Although these crusaders of morality professed to be investigating fascist as well as Communist threats, little or no effort was made to explore the former's realm of influence.

The PSI,[146] McCarthy and RFK

The PSI or McCarthy Committee turned out to be the most visible of all the witch hunts. Robert Kennedy was assigned to the committee mostly because of the relationship McCarthy had with the Kennedy family, especially his father Joseph P., the patriarch. The fact that both were Irish Catholic added to the bond. Once the committee merged with the Labor Committee of John McClellan, it was at that point that RFK side tracked the Committee's investigation of Communism in the labor movement to a crusade against organized crime in that arena. It later was narrowed even further into an all-out effort to get Hoffa.

Thomas Dodd

After graduating from Yale Law School, Dodd was hired as an FBI special agent by J. Edgar Hoover. He, like Guy Banister, was involved in operations to bring down public enemy #1, John Dillinger. According to Drew Pearson, Dodd was actually physically involved in the famous raid of Dillinger's Little Bohemia roadhouse in Wisconsin.[147]

During WWII, Dodd worked for US intelligence. Later he played a role in the Nuremberg trials as the tribunal's executive trial counsel. Because of his leading role in this group, he was considered an international hero.

Dodd developed a reputation as a strong anti-communist and law enforcer, particularly against labor racketeers. As a result he was elected US

---

146 Permanent Subcommittee on Investigations
147 Banister was part of the team that actually killed Dillinger on a Chicago street after he left a theater. It's a strange coincidence that the demise of Dillinger, Lincoln and Oswald were all related to theaters.

Senator in January 1959. In September 1960, Eastland and Dodd blamed officials in the State Department for clearing the way for the regime of Fidel Castro to rein in Cuba,and that lower-ranking officials had misinformed Americans about the political climate of Cuba with assistance from the media. Eventually Dodd became acting chair of the Senate Internal Security Subcommittee (SISS). In 1963 he presided over the committee's investigation of the FPCC.

Frank Sturgis and other soured Castro followers testified before Dodd's committee. Sturgis later claimed to have intelligence connections to that same organization. An FBI report claimed that the FPCC had been infiltrated by CPUSA and the SWP. HUAC came to the same conclusion. Is it just a coincidence that Oswald wrote to both of these entities? News reports of congressional investigations (Dodd) and Justice Department inquiries focusing on the FPCC were being announced the very weekend of the assassination.

If seen through the lens of these investigations, Oswald's activities in New Orleans and Dallas make perfect sense. He started a fake branch of the FPCC in the right-wing saturated Crescent City. This effort would later provide a link between that organization and the president's assassination. His contact with the Socialist Workers Party, who were anti-Communist, and the CPUSA which is anti-SWP, also provided links to the Marxist Oswald. The provocateur had done his job well. After November 22,1963, there would be no more FPCC and any other leftist groups would be discredited … guilt by association.

Need more proof that Oswald was working for Dodd and/or Hoover? It was none other than Senator Dodd, who was also at the helm of the Senate's Juvenile Delinquency Subcommittee. Its main efforts involved "gun control"; specifically that of mail-order weapons. Realizing there was almost no control of over the sale of weapons by mail and that these weapons could reach children, the mentally ill, maladjusted individuals, hate groups, criminals, communists and assassins, Dodd decided to address the problem. The committee's efforts to control interstate mail-order weapons resulted in the creation of a list of notorious retailers of these arms. On the list was Klein's Sporting Goods of Chicago, as well as Seaport Traders of California. Could it be a coincidence that Oswald ordered his rifle from Klein's and his revolver from Seaport Traders? Why order these weapons separately? Why order them at all when they could be easily acquired on the streets of Dallas with no paperwork that could be traced? And why these two particular sources? Was it a coincidence that both just happened to be on the Dodd Committee's list? If these entities were taken to court it could be proven, through Oswald's testimony and the paperwork that linked his alias to them, that they sold weapons to a marxist ex-Marine with an undesirable discharge who had defected to the Soviet Union and belonged to the FPCC and was using a phony name.

In 1963, not only did Oswald's Fair Play for Cuba activity coincide with active programs by the FBI and CIA directed against that organization, but he also (allegedly) ordered interstate mail-order firearms from Klein's and Seaport Traders when both of these firms were also targeted by federal investigations. Peter Dale Scott notes: "in 1963 Seaport Traders and Klein's Sporting Goods were being investigated, by the ATF unit of the US Treasury's Internal Revenue Service, as well as by Senator Dodd's Juvenile Delinquency Subcommittee. Treasury and the Committee sought to demonstrate the need for more restrictive federal legislation to control the burgeoning mail-order traffic in firearms."[148]

Further, if Dodd had foreknowledge that Oswald would be blamed for shooting the President, the work of his committee could connect the unrestricted mail-order weapons sales to the death of a president. Certainly, that would be beneficial to the reputation of the committee and the last nail in the coffin of the FPCC.

Again, a lot of mystery surrounding LHO could now be explained if he were being manipulated by Dodd and this group. It would explain why he was reading rifle magazines at Alba's Garage in New Orleans and why he was collecting coupons for mail-order weapons.

But Oswald wasn't the only one working for Dodd in his efforts to incriminate the FPCC. One of Dodd's staff investigators created a disturbance while investigating juvenile delinquency on the Mexican border. He was found by Mexican police in the bathroom of a stripper, armed with a revolver. The same individual had earlier been arrested for wearing a weapon and impersonating a police officer. Worse than that, at the very moment Dodd was writing his mail-order weapons legislation, this very same investigator was apprehended transporting two Thompson sub-machine guns, a pistol and 5000 rounds of ammunition to Hyannisport, Massachusetts on a weekend that JFK was at home there for the weekend.

One must remember that Oswald, as a teenager in New York City, was put in a juvenile facility[149] briefly and considered a delinquent for his truancy. He was analyzed by a psychologist and found to be bright but suffer-

---

148   *Deep Politics, Chapter 15*
149   As an adolescent in NY City, Lee was sent to Borderntown Reformatory, a CIA funded institution in New Jersey.

ing from neglect and social disorders. It was recommended he be further tested and institutionalized. Instead his mother rescued him from getting the help he needed and aided him in an escape to Texas. Was this New York episode, when he was identified as a delinquent, later brought to the attention of Dodd's Committee? Did this make him an attractive subject for their future agenda?

Dodd was allied in his efforts to enforce gun control, stop juvenile delinquency, and defame the FPCC by the State Department (maybe Otepka?), the Justice Department (Hoover), the Treasury Department (Alcohol, Tobacco, Firearms) and the Bureau of Narcotics. The FBI was out to destroy the FPCC domestically. The CIA had a vendetta against it internationally. There is evidence that these were team efforts. COINTELPRO was a creature of Hoover as well as Angleton. It was used against FPCC and other groups as well, one of which was CORE. Oswald stood in line with blacks at a CORE voting drive in Clinton, LA in the summer of 1963. COINTELPRO actually stands for Counterintelligence Program, which was Angleton's lifelong obsession. To Angleton, the FPCC amounted to the presence of Cuban agents loose in America. Was one of these partners in crime responsible for directing Oswald, who had a record of delinquency, to contact groups under attack by these agencies in order to discredit them? Was he a provocateur whose mission was to link them to the Communist Party? Was Oswald piggy-backing his efforts to not only infiltrate and embarrass subversive groups but to discredit mail-order weapons dealers in Dodd's fight against juvenile delinquency. Two birds with one stone?

Dodd and Hoover were in bed together.[150] They shared their anti-Communist passions like brothers. The Justice Department, SISS and HUAC worked[151] together closely and had each other's backs.

Did someone close to Dodd and his committee order weapons in the name of "Hidell" for LHO? Researcher Charles Drago has found evidence that Dodd, or one of the allies above, did order a Manlicher Carcano rifle in the name of Oswald or Hidell in 1963. However, it is possible that this was done after the assassination. In which case Dodd and his committee were taking advantage of Oswald and the assassination to benefit their mail-order gun-control crusade.

---

150   Don't tell Clyde Tolson.
151   Much of the Dodd revelation is the work of researchers Fred Newcomb and the late George Michael Evica.

WHAT A DIFFERENCE A DAY MAKES[152]

Lieutenant J. C. Day, the man who claimed he discovered and lifted Oswald's palm print off the barrel of the Mannlicher-Carcano rifle, was not properly questioned by the Warren Commission (WC). Years after the WC disbanded, it came to light through an internal WC memo that the Commission was suspicious of the manner in which the palm print was obtained. When Day appeared before the Commission, the questioning to which he was subjected was non-probing and came close to friendly conversation. Later, when the Commission's doubts about the palm print began to surface, chief counsel J. Lee Rankin asked the FBI to secure more information from Lt. Day about the palm print. Day refused to make a sworn statement regarding his handling of the print, and that ended the matter. Lt. Day had the rifle from 1:25 till 11:45 P.M. on November 22 and did not find the palm print.[153] The question is why did the FBI, who had at that point, taken over the investigation, return the rifle to DPD at all??

It was Agent Vincent Drain of the FBI who received the rifle from Day and took it to Washington. Day later claimed that he told Drain of the print and told him not to disturb it. Drain denied Day ever said that. The FBI agent later said; "I don't believe there ever was a print." He postulated; "…there was increasing pressure on the Dallas police to build evidence in the case." Asked to explain what happened, Drain said; "All I can figure is that it (Oswald's print) was some sort of cushion, because they were getting a lot of heat by Sunday night. You could take the print off Oswald's card and put it on the rifle. Something like that happened."[154]

In actuality, the print was likely taken from Oswald's dead body at the funeral home. Mortician Paul Groody has revealed that agents, likely Dallas plain clothes detectives, asked to be alone with the body of LHO on the evening of his death. When they left he had to clean ink on Oswald's hands.[155]

Researcher Paul Hoch was one of the first to wonder if, when Oswald ordered his weapons, he believed he was doing so for the Dodd Committee.[156] As mentioned earlier, Oswald was collecting gun magazine cou-

---

152   Appologies to Dinah Washington
153   In an interview for Nigel Turner's *Men Who Killed Kennedy*, Funeral director, Paul Groody tells of a visit by "men in suits," who asked to be alone with Oswald's body at the funeral home. When they left, he said he found ink on Oswald's hands. Is this the origin of the palm print on the rifle?
154   *Reasonable Doubt*, Henry Hurt, p. 109
155   "Was Oswald's Palm print Planted on the Alleged Murder Weapon? Some Questions about the Latent Palm print," -Michael T. Griffiths
156   Paul Hoch, *Echoes of Conspiracy*, 11/30/77, page 3.

pons at Adrian Alba's garage. Why? He even asked Alba questions about ordering weapons through the mail after he had already done so. Was he doing his own research? Was it his belief he was working for Dodd?

In truth, Oswald may not have been really working for the Dodd Committee. However, it was his belief that he was. Someone was likely using this ploy to get him to order weapons by mail, not to incriminate Klein's and Seaport, but to incriminate himself in the upcoming assassination. A brilliant plan. But who? The FBI (Hoover)? CIA – Angleton or Phillips? Who are the patsies left with their pants down in this scenario? Oswald, FPCC, Dodd, Klein's, Seaport Traders? All of them will be damaged and embarrassed. A brilliant plan. Oswald may even have been told to take the gun to the TSBD when JFK was motorcading past it as part of a Dodd Committee strategy. If it were found in the building after the President passed by, it would be strong evidence supporting mail-order weapon control.

Another of Dodd's targets was narcotic trafficking. As an anti-narcotic crusader, Dodd was also deeply involved with the Federal Bureau of Narcotics. He was one of the few congressmen involved in JFK's national anti-narcotic conference. Was Oswald involved somehow in this endeavor? Was he infiltrating this arena as well? Contemplating the Dallas narcotics problem, the obvious names that come to mind are Marcello, Trafficante and Jack Ruby. Is this the connection between Oswald, Ruby and Tippit? Remember that an informant, believed by many to have been Lee Oswald, was reported to have notified the FBI that weapons stolen from a National Guard Armory were being transported, likely to Orcarberro's Alpha 66 group in Oak Cliff (Harlandale Ave). As a result, two men, Donnell Whitter and Lawrence Miller, were arrested on November 18 for possession of these weapons. One of the men arrested, Donnell Whitter, was known to have a gun-running relationship with Jack Ruby. Two days prior to the Whitter-Miller arrests, Oswald had visited the Dallas FBI office.[157]

As for Tippit, during testimony of Police Chief Curry on April 22, 1964, WC member, Allen Dulles asked Chief Curry about a rumor he had heard that Officer Tippit was in some way involved in narcotic trouble. Curry said he knew nothing about it. Was this a connection between Tippit and Ruby? Peter Dale Scott, in his book *Deep Politics and the Death of JFK*, documents a lot of evidence that Ruby was involved in international drug trafficking and that he was a payoff connection between narcotics and the Dallas Police Department as well as a contact on liquor and gambling raids.

157   See Chapter 13

So what started out as an ad in the *New York Times* written by a group of diversified intellectuals defending Cuba turned into a national political movement. Gibson was unprepared for this challenge, it seems. Even before Gibson became a CIA operative, the Agency was targeting FPCC. They sought to penetrate, manipulate, control and disrupt it as well as any Americans that sympathized with Castro's revolution. But the CIA was not alone in this endeavor. Since the CIA and FBI had been working together in COINTELPRO, a creation of Hoover and Angleton for counterintelligence ops against subversive groups, they cooperated to bring down the FPCC. The FBI domestically and the CIA internationally. Joining in on this endeavor was SISS (Dodd) and even the Department of State (possibly Otepka).

Gibson's conversations with June Cobb (CIA-LICOOKY-1) were wiretapped and he was subpoenaed twice by SISS. The FBI intercepted and opened FPCC mail. They turned the FPCC's accountant into an informant. Gibson decided that if you can't beat 'em, join 'em. He resigned from FPCC and joined the CIA in July 1962.

But spying on Cuban sympathizers wasn't enough. The Agency decided to act in the name of the FPCC to destroy it. To plant deceptive information that would embarrass the Committee, the CIA obtained the organization's mailing list and even it's stationery from the FBI. The agent behind this was John Tilton, who seemed to be working with George Joannides[158] of the psychological warfare branch of Miami CIA. Both reported to Jim Angleton. So, logistically, we can trace the efforts to destroy the FPCC back to James Jesus Angleton…. The Wizard of Oswald. As mentioned earlier, after the assassination Angleton used a mechanism called The Trust to flush out conspiracy theorists and Warren Commission critics. Similarly he was also using it before the assassination to flush out Castro sympathizers, using Oswald as bait in his creation of his own fake FPCC branch in New Orleans. The FPCC was an organization the Agency was out to destroy.[159] Linking it to the assassination was a false flag strategy. The question is, was it done with foreknowledge of the event?

In conclusion, it seems clear that the FBI and CIA were working together against the FPCC. There is evidence that a small group of CIA officers was keenly interested in Oswald in the fall of 1963. They were

158   Joannides files are among the most safeguarded yet unreleased files in the CIA's vault. He used the DRE and AMSPELL programs to set up Oswald and the FPCC. Later he was brought out of retirement as a liaison to the HSCA and worked to protect the agencies shenanigans from being exposed.
159   This was accomplished when Oswald was identified as both the assassin of JFK and a member of the FPCC.

running a psychological warfare operation, authorized in June 1963, that followed Oswald from New Orleans to Mexico City later that year. One of the officers supporting this operation was George Joannides. It looks like this COINTELPRO project began when Oswald moved to New Orleans in the summer of 1963. Jefferson Morley uncovered documents through the FOIA supporting this. Joannides was cleared for Special Intelligence in June 1963. The timing was perfect. This clearance designates access to wiretap information. Oswald was being used by the CIA and FBI in New Orleans to set up a fake FPCC organization, pass out leaflets, and stage a street fight with Cubans of the DRE, who were incidentally funded by Joannides. This lone member of the New Orleans FPCC branch went through the motions of having handbills, membership applications and cards printed at his own expense. He then sent honorary FPCC membership cards to CPA leaders Benjamin Davis and Gus Hall. What an ingenious way to link the Communist Party of America to the FPCC. This is exactly what the FBI, CIA, HUAC and SISS were trying to do to discredit it. Once his sheep dipping gave him the necessary bona fides, he was then sent to Mexico City to carry on the necessary charade to link him to Castro and Kostikov. This operation may have been piggy-backed on another super-secret project involving an Oswald impostor or involving the Mexican Federales. *A wilderness of mirrors.*

Oswald's street scuffle in New Orleans in August 1963, led to a brief court appearance where he and his anti-Castro antagonists were dealt with. These were not just hot-headed Cuban members of the DRE, they were CIA operatives as well in a program called AMSPELL. AMSPELL was overseen by George Joannides, chief of psychological warfare operations in Miami. According to a CIA memo, the group was funded for the purposes of "intelligence collection, propaganda, and political action." The DRE itself was funded by the CIA.

Joannides was chief of the psychological warfare branch of the CIA's Miami station in which the likes of David Morales, John Roselli and his buddy Bill Harvey were ensconced. Joannides worked for David Phillips who also just happened to be a psychological warfare specialist. As JFK would say; *in the final analysis,* all of these individuals and the whole creature, COINTELPRO, can be traced to Jim Angleton. He is at the top of the food chain!

Morley wonders if Joannides, with his Special Intelligence clearance, was privy to the LIENVY wiretaps of the Mexico City station coinciding with Oswald's adventures at the embassies. Is this why, in 1978, Joannides came out of retirement as liaison to the House Select Committee on Assassination for the purpose of misleading it and protecting the Agency's secrets?[160]

In 1966, investigative reporters, Drew Pearson and Jack Anderson, published a series of news columns condemning Dodd for unethical behavior including verbal abuse of staffers, financial misconduct and alcoholism. Dodd was finally censured for double-billing taxpayers for travel expenses and pocketing campaign funds. After a year-long investigation, the Senate Committee issued its report in April 1967. The committee concluded that Dodd had indeed double-billed taxpayers for travel expenses, and had pocketed over 25 percent of the money collected at political fundraisers he hosted during his re-election campaign. Those funds, the report found, were used for "personal purposes such as income taxes, home improvements, and payments to family members."

The committee also noted *indiscreet* behavior in Dodd's dealing with Julius Klein, a public relations consultant for several West German clients. Noting that he had received *favors* from Klein, the committee discovered that after receiving negative criticism from Senate Foreign Relations Committee hearings for his activities, he had lost some of his West German clients. Klein then coerced Dodd to travel to West Germany and meet with officials there on his behalf. Dodd did indeed go to West Germany, supposedly on Senate Judiciary Committee business, but it appeared that his purpose was influenced by Klein's requests.

SUMMARY

Thomas Dodd was a freshman Democratic senator from Connecticut. Former FBI agent and a star prosecutor of Nazi's at Nuremburgh. He was the "hammer" of the FPCC. Also actively against narcotic traffickers and juvenile crime. Chaired the Senate Subcommittee to Investigate Juvenile Delinquency. One of the concerns of the subcommittee was availability of firearms via mail order and the likelihood that guns were getting into the wrong hands. In January 63, Dodd held hearings into unrestricted delivery of weapons via the U.S. mails. He named two companies involved in these illegal practices; Klein's Sporting Goods of Chicago, and Seaport Traders, of LA. Both were under investigation by the ATF's predecessor agency, the ATTI who probably tipped off Dodd. That very month, on the 27th, Lee ordered a .38-caliber Smith & Wes-

---

160   He was, in fact, given a medal by the Agency for what amounted to intent to deceive a government committee.

son revolver by mail, from Seaport Traders of LA, using alias A.J. Hidell. $29.95. Using a false name to order a firearm interstate was a crime. Was the FBI informant also working for Dodd's Senate Subcommittee, or the ATTD, ordering guns from suspect stores under a false name as part of their investigation? Or is that what he thought?

In 1963, not only did Oswald's Fair Play For Cuba activity coincide with active programs by the FBI and CIA directed against the organization, he also (allegedly) ordered interstate mail-order firearms from Klein's and Seaport Traders when both of these firms were also targeted by federal investigations. Peter Dale Scott notes: "in 1963 Seaport Traders and Klein's Sporting Goods were being investigated, by the ATF unit of the US Treasury's Internal Revenue Service, as well as by Senator Dodd's Juvenile Delinquency Subcommittee. Treasury and the Committee sought to demonstrate the need for more restrictive federal legislation to control the burgeoning mail-order traffic in firearms."[161]

---

161   Peter Dale Scott, *Deep Politics*, Chapter 15

CHAPTER 10

OSWALD'S OTHER ROLE MODEL

"Patriotism is your conviction that this country is superior to all others because you were born in it."

– George Bernard Shaw

Lee Oswald's father died before he was born. Other than his older brothers, the only father figure in his early life was his step father Edwin Ekdahl. That connection however, was short lived. Oswald's shrewish mother soon destroyed her relationship with Ekdahl as she had many others.

It is well known that Lee's favorite TV show as a child was "*I Led Three Lives.*" It was the semi-true story of Herbert Philbrick, who as a member of a local Communist cell, spied on CPUSA for the FBI while pretending to be an innocent business and family man. His modus operandi was similar to that of Clark Kent. That Oswald was a Herb Philbrick wannabe, is a theme I explored in depth in my book, *The Other Oswald a Wilderness of Mirrors.*[162] But there is another role model that influenced Oswald's actions somewhat later. He identified with this man in his aspiration to become a soldier of fortune and a revolutionary figure. There is little doubt that William Morgan was a hero to Lee Harvey Oswald.

William Alexander Morgan was born in Cleveland, Ohio, on April 19, 1928, to affluent parents. Morgan was a *bad boy* in high school and was expelled four times from four different schools. He was also an habitual runaway. In 1943, at age 14, he joined a circus. His father succeeded in tracking him down in Chicago and bringing him home. By the time he was 16, he was arrested on grand larceny charges. He then dropped out of high school and joined the Merchant Marines. While working on the Toledo docks, he became involved with gangsters affiliated with mafioso.

Morgan joined the Army when he turned 18 years old. After basic training he undertook advanced infantry training stateside. He was then sent to occupied Japan. Like Oswald, Morgan spent time at the Atsugi Army-Air Force base. Like Oswald, he became involved with an attractive

Japanese woman who worked in a nightclub.[163] After going AWOL several times, he was court-martialed in 1947. He escaped from the Kyoto stockade by overpowering a guard and stealing his uniform and weapon. He was recaptured, court-martialed again, found guilty on charges of escape, assault and armed robbery. He was sentenced to five years' hard labor. He ended up serving three years in a federal prison.

As an ex-con with a dishonorable discharge, Morgan had few career opportunities when he returned to Toledo. As a result, he re-established himself as a street soldier with the Toledo mob, serving as a driver, runner and lookout for gambling houses. At this point, he once again fell back on his childhood fantasies and joined the Ringling Brothers Circus, re-inventing himself as a fire-eater or sword swallower, depending on who tells the story. He married a woman snake charmer named *Terese Bethel* and had two children. In 1954 the family moved to Miami.[164] Morgan was 26. Again the mob became his source of income. He became a clown and bouncer at a famous Miami nightclub. It was from the Miami Cuban exile community that he learned of the revolution taking place in Cuba. The mob was smuggling army surplus weapons into Cuba and Morgan accepted an offer to be part of this operation.

In 1956, Morgan was seen in Tampa, Fla., as well as further south in the Florida Keys. A former numbers runner for the Trafficante crime family, Michael Falcone, said that Morgan "was a familiar face around here in the mid-'50s." Falcone remembered, "He was with the outfit that was running guns to Cuba, a pretty lucrative undertaking back then." Falcone was not alone in his witnessing Morgan's gunrunning. Others have come forward to confirm that for about 16 months, Morgan traveled between Tampa and Miami, and occasionally to Houston, Texas, and Hope, Ark., arranging large shipments of Cuba-bound weapons.[165] One can connect the dots. Gunrunning-Tampa-Santo Traficante and possibly Tom E. Davis and Jack Ruby too.

Transcripts (1978) from the US House of Representatives Select Committee on Assassinations reveal that Morgan had dealings with Robert Ray McKeown, a Texas-based businessman and convicted gunrunner who was once approached by Jack Ruby for a letter of introduction to Fidel Castro. Ruby was also running guns to Cuba at the time. McKeown, had been deported in 1957 from Cuba by Batista. A close friend of former

---

163   I have not been able to determine if the nightclub was the Queen Bee.
164   He was a self promoter and often boasted of being a descendant of the murdered anti-Freemason activist with the same name.
165   "THE AMERICAN Comandante in the Cuban Revolutionary Forces: William Morgan," The Cuban History.com

Cuban President Carlos Prio Socarras, it was McKeown that allegedly helped spirit $300 million into the US when Prio moved to Miami. McKeown was also quite close with Fidel Castro.

Morgan vaguely alluded to contacts he had in Florida with the militant CIA-supported group Directoro Revolucinario. When Morgan was in Florida, he had contacts with CIA operatives that included future-Watergate burglars E. Howard Hunt and Frank Sturgis, and Mafia go-between Johnny Rosselli, according to former Intelligence officials.

In February 1958, using a made-up story of wanting to exact revenge for a close friend who had been murdered by Batista, Morgan convinced a group of exiles to allow him to accompany them to Cuba. Unable to join Castro in the distant Sierra Maestra mountains, he turned up in the highlands in the Escambray Mountains looking to join the anti-Batista rebels of the Second Front of the Escambray, headed by Eloy Menoyo. A *Time* magazine interview with former rebel Roger Redondo said he suspected Morgan worked "for the CIA or FBI" but that the American was allowed to stay and assist with training anyway.

Morgan helped train the rebels and within a few weeks was leading rebel bands in vicious attacks against Batista's troops. He was quickly promoted to the rank of major in the National Second Front of the Escambray, and by 1957 the coveted rank of Comandante.[166] *"He is the kind of American that Cuba needs,"* extolled Fidel Castro.

Morgan's exploits were sensationalized in the *New York Times* who dubbed him *"the Yanqui Comandante."* Portrayed as a national celebrity, there was no mention of his dishonorable discharge or prison record. In fact, embellishments were added to his legend, including his Korean War exploits as a master paratrooper. All this was total hogwash of course.

In September 1959 the US State Department revoked Morgan's US citizenship based on a section of the Immigration and Nationality Act that forbids US citizens to serve in foreign armies. Said to be devastated by the action, he argued that he had never done anything against American interests.

Known as "El Americano" and "the Yankee Commando," he painted himself as a freedom fighter to the American press and insisted that Castro was not a Communist.

Batista took exile in the Dominican Republic and together with his protector, dictator Rafael Trujillo, plotted the demise of Castro. Likely

---

166   He was one of only two foreign nationals (the other was Ché Guevara) to hold the rank of Comandante in the revolutionary forces.

the CIA was involved in this scheming as well. Morgan was approached and supposedly offered a million dollars to help them pull off a coup that included killing Castro. Morgan immediately warned Castro of the upcoming coup and Castro decided to use Morgan as bait to set a trap. The trap worked perfectly and Castro's forces crushed the opposition. William Morgan was once again a hero of the revolution.

After the revolution he settled down, and as weird as it sounds, Morgan started a frog farm, shipping frozen frog legs to the US. But when Castro changed direction and began nationalizing industries, seizing private property, curbing human rights, and aligning with the Soviet Union, Morgan was vocally critical of him. Approached by anti-Castro exiles in conjunction with CIA, Morgan agreed to lead a group of rebels in the mountains once again as part of the upcoming Bay of Pigs operation. He was, however, betrayed by Castro infiltrators of his own ranks and ordered to return to Havana by Fidel. In 1961, Castro put him against a wall and he was shot. It was one month prior to the Bay of Pigs debacle, in which he could well have been useful on the counter-revolutionary side.

In an article entitled "The American Comandante in the Cuban Revolutionary Forces: William Morgan," posted on May 16, 2012, the Comandante's ordeal before Castro's firing squad is portrayed in vivid detail as follows;

> According to eyewitnesses, Morgan was led out into an open field to face a firing squad of seven men. Standing with his hands tied behind his back, several floodlights were focused on him. A voice, out of the darkness, ordered him to kneel down. Morgan refused by shaking his head.
>
> "Kneel and beg for your life," the voice again commanded.
>
> "I kneel for no man," Morgan shouted back.
>
> Then an order was given, some say by Castro himself, and a member of the firing squad stepped forward and shot Morgan in his right knee. Morgan still did not go down, and another round was fired into his left knee. Morgan fell to the ground withering in pain. Forcing one of his wrists into his mouth, he bit down hard so as not to cry out in pain. Six years later in Bolivia, Guevara would do the same thing after he was shot as a CIA agent looked on.
>
> With Morgan on the ground, the voice shouted, "There! You see, we made you kneel."
>
> Morgan spat blood in response, and another marksman fired a round into his right shoulder. When Morgan still made no sound, his left shoulder was shattered by another bullet.

Then the captain of the firing squad approached and fired a full clip from his machine gun into Morgan's chest. Needlessly, another soldier fired five revolver rounds into Morgan's head.

A local priest, Rev. Dario Casado, who helped bury Morgan's body in nearby Colon Cemetery, said that there was nothing left of Morgan's face.

SUMMARY

William Morgan, like Lee Oswald, was one of those elusive soldiers of fortune who are difficult if not impossible to categorize. Sometimes in league with gangsters, sometimes with leftists or rightists and at the same time loosely integrated within the intelligence community. Oswald cited Morgan as a personal hero. Like Oswald, some speculate that Morgan was CIA the whole time, since there are periods of his life, dating back to his days in the military, that can't be accounted for. Both men were stationed at Atsugi, a CIA base. Both had affairs with Japanese nightclub women. At least in Oswald's case it seemed related to an intelligence assignment. Both were enamored with Cuba and wanted to go there. Oswald didn't make it, Morgan did. Both seemed to be failures with no direction or future in their youth. Both were involved with Cuban exiles and possibly with organized crime figures. Marcello in Oswald's case and Trafficante in Morgan's. One may even wonder if they were both on the CIA's radar in connection with its interest in juvenile delinquents.

William Morgan

June Cobb, Castro intimate, CIA operative and femme fatale, was friends with William Morgan in Cuba. Like Morgan, she believed it unthinkable that Communism would be embraced by Castro or the people of Cuba. When Castro had Morgan shot, Cobb, fearing for her own life, escaped Cuba. Her next assignment was Mexico City where she monitored Cuban agents, as well as Mexicans who were sympathetic to Castro. One of these was Oswald and her time there coincided with Oswald's visit.

A year after the assassination of JFK, Cobb reported to her CIA boss, David Atlee Phillips, that she had identified a trio of witnesses who could tie Lee Harvey Oswald to Cuban diplomats and spies in Mexico City. FOIA documents show that three sources, including a well-known Mexican writer, stated that they had seen Oswald at a "twist party" at the home of Ruben and Sylvia Duran, the woman whom Oswald had supposedly spoken to at the Cuban Embassy. Cuban diplomats and others who displayed anti-Kennedy sentiments were also present. The sources indicated that Oswald was not alone. He had two American compatriots with him, apparently traveling companions, who looked like *beatniks*.[167] If true, this could be evidence of Cuban influence in the assassination or perhaps an attempt to incriminate them.

The CIA's Mexico City station, its files reveal, downplayed Cobb's report. Her report contradicted the official story that Oswald was a lone nut, and that the Agency was powerless to have done anything to stop him. The CIA, therefore, withheld this information from the Warren Commission. A 2013 report by the CIA's in-house historian confirms that the agency had conducted a *"benign cover-up"* in the years immediately after Kennedy's assassination.

Cobb's main source was a Mexican novelist and playwright named Elena Garro de Paz. De Paz was also a cousin of Sylvia Duran.[168] The FBI interviewed her and rejected her account, even though other witnesses supported her. They did not pursue other leads Cobb provided either. Even if they had wanted to, it was too late by that time since the Commission issued its final report two weeks before Cobb's allegations were revealed. The investigation was rushed through so as not to have an effect on the upcoming 1964 election.

An interesting side note is Cobb's involvement as a translator for a book entitled *The Shark and the Sardines*, by Juan José Arévalo. The book was an allegory about US domination of Latin America. It was published in Spanish in 1956. An English version appeared in 1961 (translated by Cobb). By a strange coincidence, Lee Harvey Oswald borrowed this book from the Dallas Public Library on November 6, 1963. It was never returned.

In April 2007, the US State Department, acting at the behest of Morgan's Cuban widow, Olga, declared that Morgan's US citizenship was effectively restored, nearly 50 years after the government stripped him of his rights in 1959 for serving in a foreign country's military.

---

167   As we will see later, one of these may have been Thomas Eli Davis.
168   There is evidence that Duran herself may have been targeted for CIA recruitment.

CHAPTER 11

ALIBI FOR ABILENE

Abilene, Abilene
Prettiest town I ever seen.
Folks down there don't treat you mean
In Abilene, my Abilene.[169]

So where was Oswald on the weekend of the 17th of November? The WC couldn't account for his whereabouts. Was he in Tampa, Florida attending an FPCC meeting with Gilberto Lopez as attested to by FBI asset, Joe Burton and CIA asset, Frank Sturgis? Another possibility is that he was in Abilene, Texas.

A June 6, 1979, article in the *Dallas Morning News* revealed the story of a photographer named Harold Reynolds. In the early '60s, Reynolds had been friends with a Cuban exile leader named Pedro Valeriano Gonzalez (or Gonzales). The two men were neighbors and residents of Abilene, Texas. Gonzalez was president of the local anti-Castro group called The Cuban Liberation Committee. In addition, Gonzalez was friends with Manuel De (Tony) Varona . Varona, former Cuban prime minister under Carlos Prio Socarras was involved in the CIA-Mafia plots to kill Castro. Varona also was coordinator of the Cuban Revolutionary Council (CRC).

Reynolds story is that five days before Kennedy's assassination, on Sunday, November 17, 1963, he visited Gonzalez to show him some baby pictures. During the visit, Gonzalez's landlady knocked at the door of his apartment. Reynolds answered the door and the woman handed him a note she said she had noticed under the door of Gonzalez's apartment. She believed it had been there for two or three days. Reynolds read the note before giving it to Gonzalez.

---

169   "Abilene" is a song written by Bob Gibson, Albert Stanton, Lester Brown and John D. Loudermilk, and recorded by American country music artist George Hamilton IV. The song reached number one on the US country music chart for four weeks, and peaked at number 15 on the pop music charts.

Reynolds said that the handwritten message read; *"Call me immediately. Urgent."* On the note were two phone numbers and the name Lee Oswald.

When asked who Oswald was, Gonzalez said something like, *"Some attorney in Dallas."*

Reynolds thought that Gonzalez looked nervous and appeared to be sweating. Soon, Reynolds left to go up the street to deliver some photos. When he returned, he noticed Gonzalez's car parked a few blocks from his house and saw him standing in a pay phone booth. Reynolds said that it was unusual for Gonzalez to be using a pay phone at the time since he had a phone in his apartment. Reynolds wondered; *"Who was this Lee Oswald"* anyway? Whether this was the real LHO or an impersonator is not clear. After the assassination, Reynolds contacted the FBI. They seemed to have no interest in what he had to say.

But there is more to the story. After the assassination, Reynolds' wife said Gonzalez came to her home and demanded all photos and negatives that Reynolds may have taken of him and his friends. Reynolds said that when he saw Oswald's photo in the media after the assassination, he recognized him as resembling a man he had previously seen attending a meeting at Gonzalez's apartment along with a second and older American from New Orleans. His recollection was that Gonzalez was known for extreme anti-Kennedy sentiments as well as his friendship with Antonio de Varona, leader of the CIA-backed Cuban Revolutionary Council. Gonzalez had once said of JFK; *"Somebody is going to kill him."* Leaving Abilene soon after the assassination, Gonzalez was last heard of in Venezuela.[170]

Who was the older American from New Orleans seen by Reynolds entering Gonzalez apartment? Could it have been Clay Shaw or possibly Guy Banister? If so, this explains why Gonzalez was desperate to get the photographs and negatives back after the assassination.

Is it possible for Oswald to have been in Abilene at this time? His whereabouts the weekend before the assassination are still a mystery. Ruth Paine told the Warren Commission that Marina had told him not to come to Ruth's house that weekend. The Warren Commission was unable to determine his whereabouts on the 15th, 16th or 17th of November 1963. Why Marina did not want Lee to visit that weekend is unknown. The WC never bothered to ask her. As for the dates when Oswald visited Gonzalez with an older American from New Orleans, they are a mystery. That makes tracing Oswald's whereabouts at those times impossible.

---

170   Anthony Summers, *Conspiracy*, New York: McGraw-Hill, 1980, pp. 406-07, 588.

If this was, in fact, Oswald, it links him to a Cuban group with ties to the CIA/Mafia plots to kill Castro. Gonzalez's very powerful friend was Manuel de Varona and he had been Cuba's Prime Minister under former President Carlos Prio Socarras. Socarras, a violent anti-Castro millionaire, worked with the CIA in its Cuban invasion plans. He died of a gunshot wound in 1977 within weeks of the same fate befalling George de Mohrenschildt. Both were sought by the HSCA for questioning. Both were ruled suicide. It is known from research done over the years that Prio had been involved in the CIA-Mafia plots to kill Castro. Was he involved in the murder of JFK?

John Martino, an anti-Castro leader, told Texas businessman, Fred Claasen, that he had been a CIA contract agent. According to Martino, *"The anti-Castro people put Oswald together. Oswald didn't know who he was working for – he was just ignorant of who was really putting him together. Oswald was to meet his contact at the Texas Theater. They were to meet Oswald in the theater, and get him out of the country, then eliminate him. Oswald made a mistake.... There was no way we could get to him. They had Ruby kill him."*

As for Varona, on the same weekend of the Abilene encounter, and one week before the assassination, he attended a Cuban Revolutionary Council meeting in New Orleans. During this time he stayed at the home of Agustin Guitart, the uncle of Silvia Odio. It was Odio who was visited in September 1963 by men claiming to be anti-Castro freedom fighters. One of them looked exactly like LHO and was introduced as "Leon Oswald." One of the party later called Odio and made comments apparently designed to ensure that she remembered "Oswald." The caller said that Oswald thought the President should have been shot. All this links Lee Oswald, and/or Leon Oswald to Gonzalez, Varona, Prio and Odio and her uncle. Either LHO was involved in the conspiracy or was set up to look like he was before the assassination occurred.

WHAT WAS OSWALD'S ROLE?

When asked if Cuba had played a role in the assassination Oswald said; *"Will Cuba be better off with the President dead? Someone will take his place, Lyndon Johnson, no doubt, and he will probably follow the same policy."*

In the summer of 1963, Oswald was either working for Guy Banister's organization in New Orleans, or infiltrating it. Banister's projects included training anti-Castro Cubans for raids and possible invasion of Cuba as well as surveillance of pro-integration groups like CORE and the ACLU.

In addition Banister was involved in the CIA's efforts to discredit the Fair Play for Cuba Committee. Oswald's role seems to have been to set up a phony branch of this organization and flush out pro-Castro sympathizers who tried to join his group. As an Agent Provocateur, he also attempted to expose left-wing students and possibly even instructors at Tulane University for Banister. It is possible that Oswald attended some of the meetings where JFK's assassination was discussed. At that point, Oswald may have contacted the FBI or possibly they contacted him. Likely, he had already been an informant since 1962.

It is conceivable that his instructions were to infiltrate Banister's group of anti-Castro exiles. It was possibly his exposing of the camps that led to the July 31st, 1963 Pontchartrain raid.

At some point during that summer and fall, the exiles caught on to Oswald and decided to set him up as the patsy in the murder. Oswald was then impersonated and sheep-dipped to look like a pro-Castro Communist radical.

A link to Castro was manifested by his Mexico City charade. Oswald was manipulated into incriminating himself. Evidence was being planted to be used against him later.

Evidence that Oswald was an informant can be seen in his request to see an FBI agent when he was arrested in a New Orleans street fight over his handing out pro-Castro leaflets. On August 10, 1963, while passing out pamphlets[171] on Canal Street in New Orleans for the Fair play for Cuba Committee, he was arrested for *"disturbing the peace by creating a scene."* Oswald was questioned by Lieutenant Francis Martello, formerly of New Orleans police *intelligence.*[172] Oswald handed Martello a note on a piece of paper torn from his notebook. He pointed to a number at the top of the note and told Martello *"just call the FBI. Tell them you have Lee Oswald in custody." When they arrive, hand them this note."* Oswald asked to be visited by Warren de Brueys. Instead, Agent John Quigley showed up. The specific reason for Oswald requesting to speak with an FBI agent is something we can only speculate about now. Was it an opportunity to report as an informant? What we know is that from his jail cell, Oswald told a New Orleans police *intelligence* officer that he *"was desirous of seeing an agent [of the FBI] and supplying to him information with regard to*

---

171   *The Crime Against Cuba by Corliss Lamont. Lamont was an American socialist philosopher and advocate of left-wing causes.*

172   Martello was Guy Banister's police department contact and was among those who used the "Harvey Lee Oswald" transposition. Others who did so were the U.S. Army Intelligence, the 112th Intelligence Group, Office of Naval Intelligence (in teletypes sent on November 27th, 1963, Clay Shaw and a CIA courier named Donald P. Norton.)

his activities with the FPCC in New Orleans," according to an FBI report suppressed from the public until 1977. Agent John Quigley talked to Oswald in his cell for about 90 minutes, then left with some of his FPCC literature. The address, "FPCC, 544 Camp Street, New Orleans, LA," was stamped on the last page of one of the pamphlets that Quigley was given. A few days later, an FBI informant sent him a second copy with the same rubber-stamped address. Is it possible that the 544 Camp Street stamp was a message to the FBI that Banister's group, with CIA approval, was behind the Pontchartrain camps and raids being planned on Cuba? Moreover, in connection with this incident, a New Orleans FBI security clerk, William S. Walter, told the HSCA that he had been on duty the day of the interview. When Quigley requested a file check on Oswald, Walters turned up a security file as well as an informant file on him.

Another possible event hinting Oswald was an informant for the Bureau was the note Oswald wrote and personally delivered to the FBI in Dallas a week or so before the assassination. Was he attempting to warn the local FBI office of the impending assassination? Since Hosty was ordered to flush the note down the toilet, we will never know for sure what it really said.

Whether LHO was an informer or not, Reynolds's story relating to Gonzalez and his involvement with a "Lee Oswald," is evidence of a conspiracy. Can it be just a coincidence that Gonzalez left Abilene and was not seen again shortly after the JFK murder?

PROOFS OF CONSPIRACY

We may never know what role Oswald truly played in the assassination, but we can show that there *was* a conspiracy and that he definitely was not a lone nut.

The first proof is that Oswald was impersonated in Mexico City in late September 1963. Whether LHO was there or not doesn't matter. Whether he was *in* on the conspiracy or not, those behind his duplication knew ahead of time that he would be blamed on November 22nd, 1963. He, Castro and the Soviets were all being framed. *Foreknowledge.*

The second proof is the Odio incident. Once again, whether the *"Leon Oswald"* that visited Sylvia Odio was the real Oswald or an impostor, the incident proves foreknowledge of the events to come. If Leon was the real Lee then he was part of a conspiracy with these Cubans. If he was an Oswald impersonator, the real Oswald was being framed to take the blame.

Finally, the Abilene incident is yet another argument indicative of foreknowledge. Whether the individual in contact with Gonzalez was really Oswald or not, this Cuban exile group knew he would be the killer or patsy ahead of time.

In honorable mention we can add Rose Cheramie's foreknowledge to this list as well.

> In retrospect, so much had been held back it was surprising that the commission was still able to find Oswald guilty, or Kennedy dead ... evasions proved ill-advised, the cover-up causing more damage than the truth. The Warren Commission would be scorned and dismissed. The intelligence services disgraced. Secrets, when they came to be exposed, would serve only to confuse and complicate. The more people knew, the less they believed. History had been thrown to the wolves.
>
> – Lee Server, *Handsome Johnny*

CHAPTER 12

JUST HOP ON THE BUS, GUS[173]

"They muddy the water, to make it seem deep."
— Friedrich Nietzsche

I've always been amazed that Oswald is probably the only assassin in history whose main mode of transportation was the bus and sometimes a cab. He not only took buses to and from work and on trips to other cities, he even took them to attempt assassinations and make his escapes as well.

Although it's doubtful that it was Oswald, the Warren Commission pointed the finger at him as the perpetrator of an attempt on the life of right-wing extremist General Edwin Walker.[174] Walker was the target of an assassination attempt in his home on April 10, 1963, but escaped serious injury in the attack when a bullet fired from outside hit a window frame and fragmented. Although the bullet was identified as a 30.06,[175] the Warren Commission concluded, based on the testimony of Marina Oswald, that it was Lee who tried to kill Walker.[176] The whole incident is suspicious and seemed to be a publicity stunt to get Walker sympathy and boost his image as a hero on a white horse waging war against the Godless Communist menace. A witness saw two men leave in cars. Oswald supposedly took a bus.

Walker himself didn't believe it was Oswald who tried to shoot him. He wrote a letter to Senator Frank Church in 1975 telling him so. What is odd about the letter is the reference to Oswald being arrested as a suspect on the day of the shooting and subsequently released. That incident seems to be erased from the official record.

---

173   *Apologies to Paul Simon*
174   *Thanks to a tattle-tale named Marina Oswald.*
175   Oswald's rifle was a 6.5 Manlicher Carcano.
176   The first reports that it was Oswald that shot at Walker actually came from a neo-Nazi newspaper in Germany and their source was likely Walker himself.

Oswald is probably the only assassin who would take a bus to an assassination attempt while carrying a rifle. But then he supposedly tried to use a bus for a getaway after the JFK shooting as well. Since that bus was stalled in traffic, he was forced to switch to his second favorite mode of transportation, a taxi cab. Perhaps Tippit knew Oswald's routine and was anticipating his arrival via the Marsalis Street bus as it passed the GLO-CO gas station on Zang Boulevard on November 22, 1963.

So why did Oswald take the Marsalis Street bus and not the Beckley Street version? Where did the Marsalis bus go? The possibilities are interesting. One is Red Bird Airport. Another is the house on Harlandale Avenue rented by Alpha 66 Cubans. Although he left the bus, he still had a transfer on him when arrested. Was he on his way to catch the bus again when he left his rooming house?

Then, of course, there was the Mexico City bus trip in the fall of 1963. This adventure is one of the most mysterious episodes of Oswald's brief life. Did he even go to Mexico? Did he go alone? Did he travel by bus or car?

DID OSWALD GO TO MEXICO?

The Warren Commission tried to reconstruct Oswald's trip. They conveniently chose the only possible scenario that would exclude evidence of conspiracy. Oswald had to have gone alone and by bus since he was a lone nut and didn't drive. Case closed.[177] But they had a major problem in the testimony of Sylvia Odio. Odio, the daughter of a Cuban refugee who was jailed for his attempt to assassinate Fidel Castro, gave testimony that contradicted the bus trip scenario. She claimed that she was visited at her Dallas apartment in late September 1963, by three men who claimed to be anti-Castro and looking for her help regarding a letter soliciting funds for a Cuban exile organization called JURE.[178] Since her father was a political prisoner in Cuba, her name carried some weight. The visitors gave their "war" names as "Leopoldo" and "Angel" and the third man was an American. She remembered that one of them, looked more "Mexican" than Cuban and the American, named Leon, was Lee Harvey Oswald. Leopoldo called the next day and discussed Oswald, who he said was an excellent shot and had said that Cubans had no guts and should have killed JFK after the Bay of Pigs.

The Warren Commission dismissed the incident since it had already decided that Oswald had been in route by bus to Mexico City and couldn't

---

177   Shades of Gerald Posner.
178   Junta Revolucionaria Cubana

have been in Dallas. In an effort to rescue the Commission from its dilemma, G-man, J. Edgar Hoover produced three of the *usual suspects* who he claimed were Odio's visitors. All three men later denied it was them.

Was this really Oswald or another of his many doubles? Was it an impostor being used to set up Oswald? Was it Oswald associating with anti-Castro Cubans who wanted to kill Kennedy? Was it Oswald being manipulated by Cuban double agents pretending to be anti-Castro Cubans? A wilderness of mirrors.

Odio said the meeting took place on Wednesday, September 25. But it more likely occurred on September 26. On these dates, the Warren Commission timeline had Oswald on his way to Mexico City. Since he cashed an unemployment check at the Winn-Dixie Supermarket in New Orleans on the morning of the 25th and mailed a change of address form closing out his Dallas post office box no later than 11 A.M. on the 25th, the commissioners determined he boarded a bus in the afternoon. Therefore he couldn't have been in Dallas on the 25th. They concluded that he arrived in Mexico City early on the 27th since he registered at a hotel and made his first visits to the Cuban and Soviet Embassies. That is, if it was in fact really Oswald and not an impersonator.

Since Oswald didn't drive and was presumed to be traveling alone, the bus was a logical choice for a man of little means. Oswald, it seems, never had much money, but that didn't impede his globetrotting adventures. The only scenario that fit the WC lone nut itinerary was that Lee left New Orleans around noon or so on the 25th and arrived in Houston, 350 miles away, late in the day. He left Houston on the morning of the 26th and arrived in Nuevo Laredo in the afternoon.[179] After an hour or so stopover in Monterrey, he traveled to Mexico City and arrived there before 10 A.M. on the 27th. If Oswald visited Odio in Dallas, he had to be traveling by car or perhaps a private plane. New Orleans is 500+ miles from Dallas and Dallas 240 miles from Houston.

Either Oswald was on a bus heading to Mexico City and was being impersonated in Dallas, or he was in Dallas and being impersonated on a bus traveling to Mexico City. Another possibility was that he was in Dallas with traveling companions who had a car. But it's also possible he didn't go to Mexico City at all and was being impersonated in both Dallas and

---

179   Oswald, or someone impersonating him, made a point of being remembered by others riding on the bus. He discussed his FPCC work with a doctor and his wife and his Marine Corps adventures with a couple of girls from Australia. He told the girls he had been to Mexico City earlier in the summer and recommended they stay at the Hotel Cuba. He didn't follow his own advice and stayed at the Hotel Comercio instead. The Comercio was a safe house for anti-Castro Cubans and intelligence men.

Mexico City. Further evidence of Oswald being set up was the telephone call Odio received the day after the incident incriminating him with specific information that would later link him to the assassination.

Odio's testimony wasn't the only report that contradicted the WC version of events. A Secret Service report dated 12/2-5/63[180] reveals that an eyewitness identified Oswald as an individual he encountered in front of the Willard Hotel[181] in Washington, D.C., near the White House in late September 1963. The witness, Bernard Thompson, was a chauffeur for the Secretary of Agriculture, Orville Freeman. Thompson had parked Freeman's car in front of the hotel when an individual approached him and asked, *"Who's car is this? This must be some big officials car. This is a no-parking zone. You have no right to park here."* The man's tone of voice was very antagonistic according to Thompson who described him as a "rabble-rouser type." Thompson moved the car around the corner to avoid further confrontation. The man followed him and continued to be a nuisance. It seems Mr. Thompson was a personal acquaintance of Secret Service Special Agent Floyd Boring[182] of the White House Detail who filed the report on December 2, 1963. Thompson identified photos of *"Harvey Lee"* Oswald[183] as the man he saw. The date of the incident was either September 25 or 27. If this was Oswald, he couldn't have been in Mexico City at the same time.

Other than a hand-full of people on a Flecha Rojas bus traveling to Mexico, there are no credible witnesses who actually saw Oswald in Mexico City. CIA surveillance photos of the embassies failed to capture him on film. There *are* photos of a man who was not Oswald but apparently using his identity. Embassy recordings of Oswald's phone conversations don't match his voice either. Sylvia Duran, who dealt with Oswald at the Cuban embassy, described him as 5'4" and blond. Russian diplomats identified him years later, but at least one was an undercover KGB agent who was an early suspect of involvement in the assassination himself.[184] In addition, legendary researcher Mark Lane, makes a convincing case that LHO nev-

---

180   Treasury report 00-2-601.0
181   Ironically Robert Oswald stayed at the Willard Hotel during his interviews with the Warren Commission in 1964, as did John Wilkes Booth in 1864.
182   Vince Palamara, a researcher whose expertise is the Secret Service detail surrounding JFK, believes that three agents may have played a role in JFK's demise. They were Emory Roberts, William Greer and Floyd Boring. In an interview with Greer's son, Palamara asked him if his father liked JFK. There was no response. Later in the interview Vince asked the same question again. The answer was...."Well.....the President was Catholic." Greer was Irish Protestant. Kennedy Irish Catholic.
183   Harvey Lee? The scrabble game continues
184   This was Nechiporenko's book, *Passport to Assassination*. It's purpose seems to have been to reinforce Nosenko's version that the Russians had nothing to do with Oswald and weren't interested in him.

er went to Mexico City. The best evidence that he *did* go is his signature on a registration book at the Hotel Comercio, his visa photo and a ticket stub produced by Oswald's finger pointing wife, Marina. All of the damaging evidence the WC had on him came from her and Ruth Paine. There is, of course, the possibility that the signature could have been forged. The Comercio was a notorious lodging for spies, anti-Castro Cubans and intelligence operatives. Oswald was also seen by June Cobb in the company of Thomas Eli Davis.[185] She said they, along with a third man, held a meeting at the Hotel Luma.

There is strong evidence that Oswald did, in fact, visit Mexico City. He provided a photo and signature for his Visa application, and he had in his possession a bus ticket as well as a stub of a ticket for a bull fight.

DID HE GO ALONE?

Those who saw Oswald on the Red Arrow bus said he was seated next to a Baptist minister and missionary later identified as Albert Osborne aka John Howard Bowen. As George Michael Evica has pointed out, Allen and John Foster Dulles made extensive use of missionaries and other religious organizations as cover for intelligence agents and operations. Was Osborne a control for Oswald or did he just happen to be occupying the adjacent seat? Osborne was identified by six witnesses as the man who was seen sitting next to Oswald on the Flecha Rojas bus to Mexico City on September 26, 1963.[186] Was he a "handler" of Oswald?

Who was Albert Osborne? Albert Alexander Osborne, a soldier turned Soviet spy, was also known as John Howard Bowen. Bowen claimed to be an itinerant preacher and missionary, raised in an orphanage in Pennsylvania. He made frequent trips to and from Mexico to Texas, Alabama and beyond.

Documents unearthed in the 1970s show the FBI had suspected Osborne as a major suspect in its massive JFK assassination investigation. Bob Gemberling, a leading FBI investigator, stated that Osborne[187] was one of the few men we had a separate file on.

Newly released US government documents show that the Cambridge News received a call shortly after 6 P.M. on November 22, 1963, warning,

---

185   Gun running associate of Jack Ruby.
186   Although Oswald was reported to have company on the Red Arrow bus from New Orleans to Nueva Laredo via Houston, fellow passengers on the Flecha Roja bus (number 516) carrying him from Nueva Laredo to Mexico City said he was alone.
187   Strange that Oswald ordered his Fair Play for Cuba pamphlets under the name "Osborne." In addition Fellow Marine, Mack Osborne, was in Lee's squadron and shared a room with him.

"Call the American Embassy in London for some big news." Six PM in Great Britain is noon in the United States. The call was made from Grimsby, England 25 minutes before JFK was shot. Grimsby was the birthplace of Albert Osborne and he was living there at the time with his sister.

It's interesting that LHO had connections to two people who used the name Bowen as an alias. The other was Jack Bowen who worked with Oswald at Jaggars-Chiles-Stovall. This Bowen's name was on Oswald's library card as a sponsor. Although Bowen's wife was employed at the Dallas Library, she claimed no acquaintance with or knowledge of Oswald. This may all be a coincidence, but digging a little further reveals that Jack Bowen's real name was Jack Grossi. Grossi had a long criminal record and had spent a good deal of time in prison. He reportedly had mob connections, and his FBI file indicates that he knew Joe Bonnano and Pete Licovalli, and lived for a while at Licovalli's Grace Ranch. Although he and John Howard Bowen can have no genetic relationship, since both sobriquets are aliases, they do share geographical itineraries involving both Canada and the US. Later we will take a deeper look at how name sharing is used in the world of intelligence to muddy waters, leave dead-end trails and create *a wilderness of mirrors.*[188] Or maybe it's just irony. For example, it is well known the actor Woody Harrelson's father was the assassin Charles Harrelson. But did you know that Woody's mother's maiden name was Diane Lou Oswald?

Other recently declassified documents illustrate how things may suddenly come together when puzzle pieces are found. They also imply that Oswald did not go to Mexico City alone. They tell of a communique from one Rene Carbello[189] to Carlos Bringuer identifying one "El Mexicano" as having accompanied Oswald to Mexico City.[190] El Mexicano was also identified as head of the exile training camps at Lake Pontchartrain that Oswald, Ferrie and Mertz have been linked to. Further documents reveal that El Mexicano was Francisco Rodriquez Tomayo.[191]

But there's more, and the plot thickens. El Mexicano was apparently a paid agent of Castro's government.[192]

So, was it Oswald that visited Sylvia Odio or was it a double trying to incriminate him? Who were the other two visitors? Was the one who looked "Mexican" to Sylvia Odio, in fact, Francisco Tomayo, "El Mexicano"?

---

188   Another interesting connection between Jack Bowen and John Howard Bowen as well as LHO, is their interest in some kind of involvement in an import-export business.
189   Possible disinformation to sabotage the Garrison investigation.
190   HSCA 180-10141-10191
191   FBI 124-90158-10027
192   CIA 104-10180-10247 (Deputy Director of CIA to FBI)

If, as at least one source indicates, Tomayo was head of the Lake Pontchartrain training camp, it would seem he was anti-Castro. But he was later determined to be an agent of Castro as well as a paid assassin. If he was a double agent, where he and Odio's third visitor the two exiles Richard Case Nagell[193] said were manipulating Oswald to kill JFK for Castro? Or were they anti-Castro Cubans who convinced Oswald they were pro-Castro to set him up?

If Tomayo was "Leopoldo," who looked Mexican, who was "Angel?" Joan Mellen suspects Emilio Santana, whom Richard Bissell called "Oswald's Latin Shepherd." Santana, a Cuban burglar connected to New Orleans (1964), was alleged to own a Manlicher Carcano and to have been in Dealey Plaza on Nov. 22, 1963.[194] Another possibility is *Miguel Casas Saez, AKA Angel Dominguez Hernandez. Both he and Tomayo were Castro agents. Were they the two who Nagell reported were manipulating Oswald? And who was Leon? Was he the real Oswald or an impostor? If the report that Tomayo accompanied Oswald to Mexico City is correct, then it could have been the real Oswald being manipulated. If he were driven to Mexico City by Tomayo, his visit to Odio would have been within a possible time frame. A true wilderness of mirrors.*

DID OSWALD TRAVEL BY BUS OR CAR?

Do newly released documents[195] shed light on or merely add confusion to the odyssey of the bus travels of Lee Oswald? We will take a look and see. Although it looks like Oswald or his double traveled to Mexico at least part way by bus,[196] his return trip is a lot less credible.

Oswald canceled his reservations at the hotel on October 1st and reserved a seat on *Tansportes Frontera* to return to Nueva Laredo for October 2nd.

However, he did not travel on this bus or on any other bus line which travels to Nueva Laredo.[197]

Francisco Alvarado, ticket salesman and dispatcher for Transportes Frontera, prepared most of the handwriting on the October 2 manifest which "Oswald," "Laredo" and "seat 4" appeared. He stated he did not write the Oswald registration information and thought it was made by the baggage handler, Lucio Lopez.[198] Alvarado is certain that the individual

193   See *The Man Who Knew Too Much*, by Dick Russell
194   CIA 104-10067-10071
195   Released December, 2020
196   Although CIA 104-10015-10359 says LHO entered Mexico (apparently by car) at Nueva Laredo on 26 Sept, 1963.
197   Doc 321108146, (page 77) HMMA 23443
198   Chauffeurs on that trip don't remember Oswald, nor does Lopez.

listed as Oswald did not purchase a ticket and did not travel on the trip relating to the manifest. No ticket number was recorded for that person and a search of the company's records in Monterrey failed to locate a ticket which was not otherwise accounted for in connection with that particular trip. Alvarado had no idea how Mexican authorities arrived at the conclusion that Oswald traveled on that bus (Transportes Frontera) on October 2, 1963. He did not believe Oswald traveled on that bus.

Even stranger is a newspaper article by Peter Kihss from December 3, 1963, that is actually printed in Vol. 24[199] of the supporting, or should it be non-supporting, Warren Report evidence. Kihss writes;

> It is believed Oswald left New Orleans on Sept 24 after having sent his wife to Dallas the previous day with a friend. He vanished from his cheap apartment there that day without having paid the rent.
>
> He is believed to have hitchhiked to Dallas where he arrived on the 23rd.[200] It was his custom to travel by hitchhiking whenever possible.
>
> It was presumed that he probably hitchhiked north to Dallas on his return from Mexico City. He arrived in Dallas on the evening of October 3 and checked into the YMCA. The distance from Laredo to Dallas is 475 miles.

SYNOPSIS

Instead of clearing things up, the release of the new documents adds confusion and muddies the waters even more. The WC concluded that Oswald boarded a Greyhound bus in the afternoon on September 25th, left New Orleans and arrived in Houston, 350 miles away, late in the day.

Oswald then traveled on Continental Trailways bus No. 5133 which left Houston at 2:35 AM for Laredo. The bus was scheduled to arrive in Laredo at 1:20 PM on September 26, and Mexican immigration records show that Oswald in fact crossed the border at Laredo to Nuevo Laredo, Mexico, between 6 A.M. and 2 P.M. on that day. Two English passengers, Dr. and Mrs. John B. McFarland, testified that they saw Oswald riding alone on this bus shortly after they awoke at 6 A.M. A man representing himself as Lee Oswald presumably purchased a Houston to Laredo ticket after midnight in Houston.

However, WC assistant counsel, J. Wesley Liebeler wrote in a memorandum; "There is no evidence at all that Oswald left Houston on that bus ... there are problems. Odio may well be right. The Commission will look bad if it turns out that she is."

199   Page 585
200   How can you leave someplace on the 24th and arrive someplace else on the 23rd?

After an hour or so stopover, LHO traveled to Mexico City via Monterrey on Flecha Rojas (Red Arrow) bus number 516 and arrived there before 10 A.M. on the 27th. If Oswald visited Odio in Dallas, he had to be traveling by car or perhaps a private plane. New Orleans is 500+ miles from Dallas and Dallas 240 miles from Houston.

Two Australian women reported seeing Oswald on the bus in-route to Mexico City. Six people saw Osborne sitting next to him. But was this the real Oswald? Unlike the quiet and secretive LHO that we have come to know and love, this guy went out of his way to tell these strangers on the bus all about his personal life. He told them of his work for the FPCC, that he had been to Mexico City before[201] and even recommended a hotel they should stay at etc.[202]

His presence on this bus, however, is contradicted by CIA document ;104-10015-10359 that says LHO entered Mexico (apparently by car) at Nueva Laredo on 26 Sept 1963.

The Australian women who spoke with Oswald on the Monterrey to Mexico City leg of the trip claimed to have purchased *Transporte del Norte* bus tickets, yet describe a journey that has been documented to have occurred on a Flecha Rojas bus. The WCR simply states they were wrong about the bus line. There is *no record of a bus ticket* being purchased which would carry Oswald *from Nuevo Laredo to Mexico City*.[203]

A newly released CIA document reveals that the CIA suspected a man named William R. Dobkins, who was in contact with the Cuban Embassy in Mexico City, may have been the "twin" in the double Oswald theory. Their report on him states that he was of doubtful mental stability. That he claimed he served with Oswald in the USMC and told Oswald that his ranch was stolen by politicians. He said they talked of killing Johnson, Connally and Texas Railroad Commissioner James Langdon. Dobkins also threatened these people in a letter (1964) to Chairman of Texans for Goldwater. He claims he traveled to Mexico to arrange defection to Russia. Marguerite Oswald knew Dobkins and says he is similar to Oswald and that some of the travel activity attributed to Oswald may have been Dobkins.[204]

---

201   Newly released documents reveal that there was a rumor going around that Oswald had been there before (Mexico) to obtain a divorce.
202   He didn't follow his own advice and stayed at a different one, *The Comercio*.
203   Their is evidence that the Australian women who speak with Lee Oswald could not have been on the same bus which left Monterrey at 3:30pm and arrives in Mexico City at 10am. It is highly likely her and other first-hand witness testimony about these bus rides and the stay in Mexico is fabricated.
204   321108146 (page 100) June 18, 1967

HOW DID OSWALD RETURN TO DALLAS?

Rehashing the evidence once more, we know that Oswald canceled his reservations at the hotel October 1 and according to Mexican authorities, reserved a seat on *Tansportes Frontera* to return to Nueva Laredo on October 2. But there is no evidence he traveled on this bus or on any other bus line which travels to Nueva Laredo.[205]

As stated earlier, Francisco Alvarado, ticket salesman and dispatcher for *Transportes Frontera,* is certain that the individual listed as Oswald did not purchase a ticket and did not travel on the trip relating to the manifest. He testified that no ticket number was recorded for that person and a search of the company's records in Monterrey failed to locate a ticket which was not otherwise accounted for in connection with that particular trip. It was his belief that Oswald did not travel on that bus.

Gilberto Lozano, manager of the Mexi Terminal of the bus company, said *Transportes Frontera* had made a complete study of its records and procedures and arrived at the conclusion that the person designated as Oswald on the Oct 2, 1963, manifest did not purchase a ticket and could not have traveled on that trip.[206]

According to one CIA document,[207] Oswald drove back to the US via Nueva Laredo on October 3,1963. In another document,[208] the agency attempts to explain this as an error, stating, "Because of an error in one of the Stenographer's forms at the Immigration Office in Nueva Laredo, it is stated Oswald had traveled by car to US. However, no proof was found in search of papers that Oswald left by car." This document[209] mentions copies of a Greyhound International exchange ticket purchase order for one seat issued October 1, 1963, by Transportes Chihuahuenses Travel Agency. The ticket is for a trip from Laredo to Dallas in the name of H.O. Lee.

Still another CIA missive[210] states; "That day, October 3, Oswald drove back to US at the Nueva Laredo, Texas crossing point."

The new documents contradict themselves. Oswald traveled by bus... No, he traveled by car. He traveled alone.... No, he had company.... No, he wasn't there at all. You can find documents to support any of those arguments.

---

205   Doc 321108146, (page 77) HMMA 23443
206   321108146
207   104-10015-10359
208   321108146
209   Ibid, Page 71 (HMMA 2329)
210   104-10004-10256 (item 8) (page 97) Aug 8, 1966

CONCLUSIONS

The blame for the confusion surrounding the Mexico City travels of Oswald can be placed squarely on the Warren Commission. Instead of investigating and learning the truth, they started out with a conclusion based on the lone nut scenario and tried to make the evidence fit that conclusion without even considering that Oswald may have had help or that he was being framed.

The CIA came to the same conclusion about their methods and deduced:

> "The Warren Commission did not do an adequate investigation job. ... it's hard to believe the commission served the public well. Instead of ending all the rumors, they set the stage for a new, and more serious era of speculation."[211]

But the Commission's source for the Mexico City charade was, of course, the CIA. The CIA lied about the tapes being erased (cover up #1) and then played innocent to Oswald's activities by saying they had not realized that Oswald visited the Cuban consulate (cover up #2). To make cover up #1 work, the CIA needed the FBI to cooperate. When Hoover learned of this manipulation, he was livid. He was still mad about it in January 1964 when his subordinates sent him a memo on illegal CIA operations in the US which the Agency promised to keep the Bureau informed of. He responded to the memo with; *"OK. But I hope you're not taken in. I can't forget the CIA withholding the French espionage activities in the USA nor the false story re Oswald's trip in Mexico City only to mention two of their instances of double-dealing."*[212]

Oswald's whereabouts the night of September 24th is still one of the intriguing mysteries of his life. There is testimony that some time between 7 and 10 P.M., he made a call to a leader of the Socialist Labor Party in Houston. The Warren Commission believed Oswald took a Greyhound bus from New Orleans to Houston, but there are no records to confirm that conclusion. The FBI could not locate Oswald for the evening of Sept 24th, nor could they find any record of Oswald leaving New Orleans on ANY bus which could get him to Houston in time to perform activities, the evidence shows he did. But Oswald may have first traveled to Dallas before arriving in Houston, more than 200 miles away, to visit Sylvia Odio.

Two English passengers, Dr. and Mrs. John B. McFarland, testified that they saw Oswald on the second leg, riding alone on the bus from

211   321108146 ,page 92, Dec 25
212   John Newman, *Oswald, the CIA and Mexico City*

Houston to Nueva Laredo shortly after they awoke at 6 A.M. However, as mentioned earlier, WC assistant counsel, J. Wesley Liebeler wrote in a memorandum; *"There is no evidence at all that Oswald left Houston on that bus...there are problems. Odio may well be right. The Commission will look bad if it turns out that she is."*

Six passengers observed Oswald in the company of Osborne on the third leg, Flecha Roja (Red Arrow) bus (number 516) from Nueva Laredo to Mexico City. This Oswald may have been an impostor due to his out-of-character efforts to draw attention to himself.

Once in Mexico City, Sylvia Duran dealt with him and described him as 5'4" and blond. Writer, Elana Garro de Paz claimed that she saw Oswald at a "twist party" that took place on Sept 2 or 3, 1963. She also claimed that he was invited to the party by Sylvia Duran, with whom he had had sexual relations and that he arrived at the party with two American hippie types. If this is so, it wasn't Oswald. He wasn't in Mexico City till the 26th or 27th.[213]

Further contradiction comes from another memo noting that an investigation established that Mrs. Paz stated that the twist party took place not on September 1 or 2 but on the evening of October 1 or 2, 1963. Since Lee Harvey Oswald departed Mexico City, supposedly by bus at 8:30 A.M. on Oct 2, he could not have been identical with the American allegedly observed by Mrs. Paz at the party on that date either. The dates she suggested for the party occurred either before he arrived in Mexico City or after he left.

De Paz comes across as a vindictive paranoid gossip. The wife of Octavio Paz, she rented a room to June Cobb.[214] Paz claimed Cobb was a Communist and that she feared her. She related that Cobb had broken the legs and ribs of a pet cat and described her as promiscuous since she sleeps with men. She believed Cobb had been planted on her by the communists.[215]

While in Mexico City, Oswald reportedly made contacts with Quakers studying at the Autonomous University. One Quaker student at the University was an active agent of the CIA at the time. There is no way to know if this was the real Oswald.

Officers at the Soviet Embassy, mainly Nechiporenko and Kostikov claimed to have talked to Oswald when he visited there. None of the surveillance of the CIA, KGB, Mexican Police, or any one else has been able

---

213   Ibid, page 80, Nov. 25, 1963
214   Cobb was no communist. She was a CIA agent working at the Mexico City station under David Atlee Phillips.
215   Ibid, page 88, Nov 25, 1964

to produce a photo of him in one of the most heavily watched cities in the world at the time. Nor can any recordings of the embassies identify his voice.

It seems likely that Odio was right and as Liebeler predicted the Warren Commission looks bad.

DID OSWALD REALLY GO TO MEXICO CITY?

It's my belief that Oswald did go to Mexico City.[216] He went there as part of an AMSPELL Counterintelligence mission designed to discredit the Fair Play for Cuba Committee. This program was being run by George Joannides for David Phillips. Joannides and Phillips were layered cutouts for James Angleton and CI/SIG. That, at least, was Oswald's belief. However, another super-secret operation was underway that was piggybacked with AMSPELL.

This clandestine enterprise involved Oswald being impersonated and incriminated at the Cuban embassy. Voice recordings of a man calling the Russian Embassy are not Oswald's voice. Since the impostor clearly identifies himself as Lee Oswald, this is evidence of a frame-up. In addition, the photo of a man leaving the Soviet Embassy that the Agency claimed was Oswald was obviously not the real Oswald. This *"Mystery Man"* is proof of a cover-up. The Agency claimed to have no photos of Oswald at all. This seems ridiculous since there were multiple cameras staking out both the Soviet and Cuban Embassies 24-7. So was this photographic conundrum an honest mistake or a deliberate diversion?

JAR

Counterintelligence operative, Jane Atherton Roman, revealed in an interview that it was Mexico City Station Chief Win Scott, who deliberately substituted the *Mystery Man* photo. But why? If the CIA had photos of Oswald at the embassies, why not reveal them? One possibility is that they were protecting a *LIENVY* surveillance program. Thanks to the research of Jefferson Morley we now know that a CIA operative code-named *LIEMPTY-14*, who was actually a Mexican woman named Greta Goyenchea, took photos of the Soviet Embassy daily from her safe house, a building known as *LYRIC*. Her son, also a surveillance operative, stated that she *did* take photos of Oswald, that he was very important, and that had she not taken them she would have been fired. It now seems clear that Scott actually did have

---

216   He signed a visa application and provided a photo. He had a bus ticket stub among his effects after his death. He brought Marina a souvenir. He was seen on a bus.

photos of Oswald visiting the Soviet Embassy. Angleton cleaned out Scott's safe after his death and many of his files were destroyed. Were the photos destroyed as well?

Since 60 years have past and most everyone involved is dead, why not release the photos if they still exist? It seems the CIA is still covering up something it deems very dangerous to the Agency.

GREEN RAMBLERS AND RED BIRDS[217]

On November 22nd, 1963, at approximately 12:35-12:40, Oswald left the Schoolbook Depository. That much we know. How he did it is debatable. The WC says he walked east on Elm Street and caught the Marsalis Street bus heading back toward the TSBD. Since a bus transfer was found on him, this seems to be what happened. He then exited the bus and caught a cab to Oak Cliff.

However, Sheriff Deputy Roger Craig saw Oswald or a look-alike enter a green or gray Rambler in front of the building. Craig was supported by one or two others and photos taken at that time show a vehicle of that description at that location. The Rambler was being driven by a dark-complected Hispanic looking man. Craig told Captain Fritz about it and Fritz confronted Oswald during his interrogation. Oswald said it belonged to Ruth Paine and *"not to drag her into this."*

The problem here is one of contradiction. Philosophically, *a thing can not both be and not be under the same aspect.* Evidence of the historic scenario is the bus transfer, the cab driver's testimony and Mary Bledsoe's dramatic encounter with LHO on the bus, which I don't believe ever happened. Evidence for the second version of events is equally convincing. Two or more eyewitnesses, a photo of the car, and Oswald's statement that it existed. The only solution is that there were two Oswalds leaving the building at the same time. Since he was being seen in several places at one time frequently during that period, this is not so unlikely. But Oswald's comments on the Rambler indicate that he at least knew of it and possibly knew of the existence of the double.

If there were two Oswalds involved, one obviously escaped. I got to thinking about Air Force Sgt. Robert Vinson's account of his encounter with an Oswald double on the day of the assassination.

Vinson was posted at ENT Air Force Base as an administrative advisor for NORAD and had crypto-clearance. On the day of the assassination, he was hitching a ride on a military plane from Andrews AFB to Colorado

---

217   Not Falcons (Ford's version)

Springs. The flight he was taking was canceled and he had to scramble to get another to make it home. He found a C54 headed to Lowrey AFB in Denver. During the flight it was announced that JFK had been shot. At that point the plane made a 90-degree turn and headed south. Around 3 or 4 P.M. they were flying over a city that Vinson recognized from his window seat. It was Dallas. The plane then landed on a sandbar near the Trinity River and within city limits. The landing site was not a runway and was barren, but when they landed a jeep approached them and two men boarded the aircraft. One man was Hispanic, 6' or so 180-190 lbs. and the other Caucasian, 5'-9" and 140 or so. The men were dressed in off-white or beige coveralls similar to those worn by repairmen.

The plane took off and headed northwest. Their destination was Roswell Air Force Base where they arrived at dusk. Vinson was held at the base until about 9 P.M. and then caught a Greyhound bus to Colorado Springs.

Later that night, on TV, he saw Lee Harvey Oswald in custody of the Dallas police. To his shock Oswald appeared identical to the Caucasian who boarded the C54 in Dallas.

Bob Vinson kept this information to himself. In 1964 two men visited him and tried to recruit him into the CIA. Vinson turned them down. Then in February 1965 he was given a new assignment. He was now Administrative Supervisor for Base Supply at Nellis Air Force Base ... Area 51 in Nevada. His employer was the CIA.

Drop off the Key, "Lee," and get yourself free.

. . . .

PART IV

GUNS, DRUGS & ROCK N' ROLL

Introduction to Part IV
Birds of a Feather

Hate groups are a cancer on our free society. So many of our great people have been hurt by them.

–Jack Ruby

The chemistry of the JFK conspiracy soup was composed of a toxic mixture of drugs, guns and selected corrupt police, blended in a secret recipe of rogue intelligence operations, topped with a mafioso sauce and heated to a boil by hotheaded Cubans.

Part IV will show how diverse groups of like-minded fanatics with the same goals worked in tandem to change the world. A cabal within a cabal, they used their individual talents and know-how for the good of the cause. Believing themselves patriots, in denial of the actual horror of their mission, they succumbed to the hatred that filled their being. It was OK! After all, they were part of a great fraternity. They were *good old boys*.

Daniel Ellsberg, in his book *Doomsday Machine*, stated that when the missile crisis was over there was a "fury" within the Air Force. *"There was virtually a coup atmosphere in Pentagon circles. Not that I had the fear there was about to be a coup – I just thought it was a mood of hatred and rage. The atmosphere was poisonous, poisonous."*

Ellsberg added that distrust of civilian leadership became more intense under JFK. *"JFK believed that his generals, especially LeMay, were 'essentially insane, mad, reckless, or out of touch with reality.'"*

CHAPTER 13

A PLOT BY ANY OTHER NAME

Go down, Miss Moses, there's nothin' you can say
it's just old Luke and Luke's waitin' on the Judgment Day
"Well, Luke, my friend, what about young Anna Lee?"
He said, "Do me a favor, son, won't you stay
and keep Anna Lee company?"[218]

–The Weight

Т he plot to kill JFK has been given different names by different researchers. These code names supposedly derive from the conspiratorial groups themselves, whether they be CIA, mafia, military or Cuban exile groups. According to CIA operative, E. Howard Hunt, the plan was called *"The Big Event."* Author H.P. Albarelli's source, Pierre Lafitte, referred to it as *"Lancelot."* To researcher Gil Jesus, it is the *"Second Invasion of Cuba* or *Second Bay of Pigs."* Lamar Waldron and even Richard Nixon espoused similar references in their *"AMWORLD"* and *"The Bay of Pigs Thing"* rhetoric. Whatever moniker you choose, there are common deep political threads that they share.

THE WHOLE BAY OF PIGS THING

Т ime and again the release of JFK documents have been delayed. Although it is accepted that government moves slowly, sixty years would embarrass a sloth. But the procrastination in itself might be a revelation. It's not surprising that the focus of the withheld documents corresponds to the issues that researchers have also come to suspect were indicative of the conspiracy that led to the crime. The areas that the CIA deems the most sensitive and which they are protecting fiercely are: The CIA/Mafia plots to kill Castro, Oswald's Mexico City visit, a 1963 Pentagon plan for an "engineered provocation" that could be blamed on Castro as a pretext for toppling him (NORTHWOODS), the history of the CIA's Miami office (which organized a propaganda campaign against Castro's

---

218   Lyrics from "The Weight." The title is a homophone for the Wait. It's been a long wait indeed for the classified documents. Apologies to The Band.

Cuba) and the personnel file of the late George Joannides, a career CIA intelligence operative, whom staffers on the House investigation in the late 1970s believe lied to Congress about what he knew about a CIA-backed exile group that had ties to Oswald.

But what I find really interesting is their hesitation to release redacted files believed to contain new CIA information about the 1972 break-in at the Democratic National Committee in Washington's Watergate Hotel by former CIA operatives that led to the resignation of President Richard Nixon.

It seems clear that all of the above areas of intense secrecy revolve around Cuba and the efforts to eliminate Fidel Castro. But what about the Watergate break in? The White House tapes reveal that Nixon was obsessed that the *"whole Bay of Pigs thing"* might be revealed. Was it that he was somehow responsible for the CIA/Mafia plots to kill Castro? Did he know that this program was turned against JFK? Researchers have always been intrigued by the connection of many of the Watergate burglars with the assassination of President Kennedy.

WHAT GOES AROUND, COMES AROUND

Daniel Sheehan,[219] a constitutional and public interest lawyer, public speaker, political activist and educator, was part of a legal team led by F. Lee Bailey representing Watergate burglar James McCord. McCord and Gordon Liddy were the only two burglars to plead not guilty to the crime.[220] Sheehan's evaluation of the events leading to the Watergate break-in are enlightening. They take on the essence of a prelude to disaster and may be a clue to the reason related documentation is being withheld.

SHEEHAN'S ACCOUNT

According to Sheehan, President Nixon instructed Jeb Stuart Maguder to order the break-in of the office of Larry O'Brien to plant bugs. O'Brien was Head of the Democratic Committee. However, previously he had been a lobbyist for Howard Hughes. In the late 1950s when Nixon was vice-president and a member of the 5412 Committee, Hughes was

---

219   Over his career, Daniel Sheehan has participated in numerous legal cases of public interest, including the Pentagon Papers case, the Watergate Break-In case, the Karen Silkwood case, the Greensboro massacre case, the La Penca bombing case and others. He established the Christic Institute and the Romero Institute, two non-profit public policy centers. Sheehan has lectured on American history, politics and the JFK assassination at the University of California, Santa Cruz. Sheehan is currently Chief Counsel of the Romero Institute, where his focus is the Lakota People's Law Project. At one time, Sheehan was legal counsel to the Jesuit US national headquarters in Washington, DC.
220   Liddy wanted to kill Hunt for talking. Hunt's wife *was* killed. The same Liddy that wanted to kill columnist Jack Anderson.

a covert asset for the NSA as part of a creature known as Summa Corporation. Nixon and Hughes came to know each other quite well. [221] As Vice-President and member of the 5412 Committee, Nixon was a driving force in the upcoming invasion of Cuba at the time.

Although the historic version of events is that Robert Maheu was approached by the CIA (JC King or Sheffield Edwards) to get the mafia to kill Castro to coincide with or precede the invasion,[222] Sheehan reveals that it was actually *Nixon* who approached *Hughes* on the subject. Hughes, at first reluctant, then turned over the project to Bob Maheu. Maheu approached Las Vegas mob representative, John Roselli. Roselli then traveled to Chicago to report the proposition to his boss, Sam Giancana. Giancana astutely perceived that Havana was the territory of Santo Trafficante and this led to a series of meetings with the latter at the Fountainebleau Hotel in Miami, Florida. Trafficante wanted assurance that the proposition came from Nixon. So, the third meeting was attended by Sheffield Edwards.[223] Edwards, a former Army Colonel, was head of the CIA's Office of Security. His main task was to protect Agency personnel and facilities from enemy penetration.[224]

At the time of the meetings, Trafficante was deeply involved with the CIA's Operation 40 to sabotage Castro's regime. So he put together 15 assassins, some of which were CIA affiliated.[225] This group was called *S-Force*. These mercenaries were trained with Cuban exiles in five paramilitary bases in Florida and Louisiana. The hit team was then sent to Fort Huachuca, Arizona where they seemingly disappeared. However they

---

221   In the spring of 1961, the Kennedy Administration studied and *discarded the possibility* of prosecuting members of the Nixon family or Howard R. Hughes for criminal law violations that might have occurred in the loan of $205,000 from the industrialist to the Vice-president's brother in late 1956.

222   Sheehan also set the book straight on the revelation that JFK didn't cut off air support at the Bay of Pigs. He only forbade the involvement of US Marines. It is an irony that air support was based in Nicaragua (Somosa) and was on a different time zone. They arrived at the invasion site one hour too late. Brilliant planning for sure.

223   In 1960 Richard Bissell and Allen W. Dulles decided to work with the Mafia in a plot to assassinate Fidel Castro. According to Bissell, it was Edwards who first suggested the idea. Edwards argued that the advantage of employing the Mafia for this work is that it provided CIA with a credible cover story. The Mafia were known to be angry with Castro for closing down their profitable brothels and casinos in Cuba. If the assassins were killed or captured the media would accept that the mafioso were working on their own. Sheehan relates a slightly different scenario.

224   In April, 1950 Edwards set up Project Bluebird. This was the creation of teams to check out agents and defectors for the whole CIA. Each team consisted of a psychiatrist, a polygraph (lie detector), an expert trained in hypnosis, and a technician. This was the forerunner of MKULTRA. Some sources have William Harvey attending these meetings as well.

225   Mirroring Sheffield's plan of using the Mafia as a cutout to take the blame if things went wrong, Trafficante utilized some CIA affiliated assassins in his S-Force group for the same purpose; to shift the blame to the Company.

soon clandestinely reappeared in Oaxaca,[226] Mexico on a Ranch owned by Clint Murchison Jr., where they were trained by Carl Jenkins, a former member of Marine Corps and Special Forces, training specializing in utilization of triangular fire.

Fast forward to 1972. The order to bug O'Brien's office resulted from Nixon's fear that O'Brien knew about Nixon being behind the Castro assassination plots. Since the plot had been turned on JFK and S-Force did the deed, Nixon had blood on his hands.

One of the Watergate burglars, Bernard Barker, had on his person at the time of his arrest, a check that was cleared through the Banco International (Mexico City Bank) and specifically through the account of a lawyer named Manuel Ogarrio .

Financing of the Oaxaca base was handled by the skimming of casino money in Las Vegas. The money was placed in suitcases and driven in Cadillacs through Texas and New Orleans to the Miami National Bank owned by Meyer Lansky. Next it was wired from there to International Credit Bank in Geneva, Switzerland and subsequently to Banco International in Mexico into the account of attorney Manuel Ogarrio Daguerre .

Pat Gray (acting head of FBI after Hoover's death) warned Nixon through John Dean, that he, Gray, couldn't control the FBI investigation into the break-in. Actually, it was Mark Felt that he couldn't control. Felt was passed over when Hoover died and Gray, an outsider, was given the job. Felt, later identified as the *Washington Post* source, "Deep Throat," was in the process of traveling to Mexico to interview Ogarrio. This caused Nixon to send Erlichman and Halderman to the CIA to tell Helms to get the FBI to stop the investigation. They were instructed to threaten Helms by telling him; "*The whole Bay of Pigs thing will all come out if you don't.*"

SILENT COUP

Nixon, like JFK, MLK, and RFK, was a threat to the Federal Bureaucracy and National Security State. He had to go. Yet another lone nut assassination would result in even the most naive of Americans to become suspicious. It would just be too obvious what was going on. On June 23, 1972, a taped White House meeting between Richard Helms and President Nixon revealed that Nixon asserted that he knew who killed JFK. He even intimated that the CIA was involved. Soon after that, the Watergate affair resulted in Nixon's demise. A bloodless coup that ousted

---

226   Is it a coincidence that John Howard Bowen aka Albert Osborn is reported to have operated a school to train assassins in the very same location?

Nixon and instated Gerald Ford in the seat of power.[227] Ford, of course, was instrumental in absolving the CIA of JFK's murder during his tenure on the Warren Commission. Ford is the only president never elected to Executive office. According to Speaker of the House, Carl Albert; "We gave Nixon no choice but Ford." As for the Watergate fiasco, four of the five burglars were ex-CIA operatives.[228] These are the same guys who's resumé included the Bay of Pigs, the CIA/Mafia plots to kill Castro and the JFK assassination itself. As for the whistle-blowers that exposed the corruption of the Nixon White House, they turned out to be the usual suspects, what J. Edgar Hoover called "Wisner's Weirdos."

Frank Wisner was responsible for the CIA's Operation MOCKING-BIRD. It was later taken over by Cord Myer. The first media mogul to be brought into the fold was Phillip Graham and the *Washington Post*. The Post was an extremely conservative newspaper and a friend of the CIA. Doesn't it seem suspicious that they would go out on a limb and risk ruin by insinuating a conservative president would be a crook and that there was a White House conspiracy to destroy the Democratic Party's chances in the next election? It always did to me.

As we discovered in chapter four, Ben Bradlee was an insider and personal friends with Angleton, Helms and Wisner.[229] He had been in ONI during WWII and worked on covert projects for Wisner and Cord Meyer as a journalist. He was an asset for OSS Chief Wild Bill Donovan's Secret Paramilitary Group. It was Bradlee who helped his Georgetown neighbor, Angleton, acquire the diary of his sister-in-law, Mary Meyer.

The next player in this charade is Bob Woodward. Woodward had no journalistic background credentials at all when hired by the *Washington Post*. He had been a Naval Officer at the Pentagon. His duties included working with *intelligence agencies*. He had been detailed to the White House and interacted with Nixon aides. His source for information on the break-in came from FBI agent Mark Felt. In the FBI, Felt ran COINTELPRO, whose designed objective was to discredit politicians the FBI wanted to destroy. Politicians like Richard Nixon. COINTELPRO was a bastard child of Edgar Hoover and James Angleton. As for Felt, he was motivated by being passed over for Director when Hoover died. As revealed above, Patrick Gray, loyal to Nixon, was brought in from outside the agency for the job.

227 Vice-president Spiro Agnew was taken down also via tax evasion charges and forced to resign.
228 McCord, Barker, Hunt and Martinez.
229 He and his wife Toni Pinchot Bradlee (Mary Pinchot Meyer's sister) were close friends with James and Cicely Angleton. In addition, Richard Helms was a childhood friend.

THE USUAL SUSPECTS

"....Dallas County deputy constable Seymour Weitzman also ran toward the top of the grassy knoll – where he found a man carrying Secret Service identification. Weitzman later identified this man as Bernard Barker, a CIA asset and the future Watergate burglar who would lead the four-man contingent of Cuban–born Watergate burglars from the Miami area. Barker was an expert at surreptitious entries, planting bugs and photographing documents. He was a close associate of Florida Mafia godfather Santos Trafficante, and of Mob-connected Key Biscayne banker Bebe Rebozo – Richard Nixon's bosom buddy.

Barker was a veteran CIA asset. Along with JFK assassination suspects Howard Hunt, Frank Sturgis and David Ferrie, he had helped plan the unsuccessful 1961 CIA-sponsored invasion of Cuba, a mission fathered by Vice President Richard Nixon. The actual invasion was finally carried out at the Bay of Pigs under President Kennedy. The CIA recruited the Mafia to kill Cuban President Fidel Castro at about the same time the exile invaders waded ashore.

Barker's day job was a real estate agent on Key Biscayne. And he was a close friend and neighbor of fellow CIA asset Eugenio Martinez – the Watergate lock-picker. Martinez's real estate firm had extensive dealings with Bebe Rebozo, and had brokered Nixon's purchase of a house on Biscayne Bay.

In the immediate aftermath of the Watergate arrests, President Nixon was anxious about his pal Rebozo's vulnerabilities. On White House tapes released many years later, after hearing that Howard Hunt's name turned up in two of the burglars' address books, Nixon had a question for his chief of staff, Bob Haldeman: "Is Rebozo's name in anyone's address book?" Haldeman answers, "No ... he (Rebozo) told me he doesn't know any of these guys." Sounding rather dumbfounded, the president responds: "He doesn't know them?"

If Weitzman was correct in fingering Barker, the CIA man would have had no trouble obtaining Secret Service credentials. CIA operatives have a way of coming up with badges and other items to suit their various goals (As a Nixon White House spy, Howard Hunt once wore a speech alteration device and a red wig to a secret encounter.)

Barker wasn't the only future Watergate conspirator to reportedly show up in Dallas on Nov. 22, 1963. Under oath, CIA operative Morita Lorenz placed CIA agents Hunt and Sturgis at the assassination scene.

This claim was bolstered by two other local law enforcement officers who reported encountering men on the grassy knoll who identified themselves as Secret Service agents – yet the Secret Service maintained that none of its agents were in Dealey Plaza right after the shooting.

For the record:

Deputy Constable Weitzman told the Warren Commission he encountered "other officers, Secret Service as well" on the grassy knoll. In 1975, he told reporter Michael Canfield the man he saw produced credentials and told him everything was under control. He said the man had dark hair, was of medium height, and was wearing a light windbreaker. When shown photos of Frank Sturgis and Bernard Barker, Weitzman immediately pointed at Barker, saying, "Yes that's him." Just to make sure, Canfield asked, "Was this the man who produced the Secret Service credentials?" Weitzman responded, "Yes, that's the same man."

Dallas patrolman J. M. Smith also ran up the grassy knoll. At the top, he smelled gunpowder. Encountering a man, he pulled his pistol from his holster. "Just as I did, he showed me he was a Secret Service agent … he saw me coming with my pistol and right away he showed me who he was."

In the mid-70s, Dallas police sergeant David Harkness told a House committee, "There were some Secret Service agents there – on the grassy knoll – but I did not get them identified. They told me they were Secret Service."

According to a Secret Service report in the National Archives, "All the Secret Service agents assigned to the motorcade stayed with the motorcade all the way to the hospital, none remained at the scene of the shooting."

In the years following the Warren Commission Report, its findings have been repeatedly questioned. In 1979, the House Select Committee on Assassinations suggested that at least two gunmen were involved, and that the probable assassination conspirators were Mafia-connected...."

All of the Secret Service agents in the motorcade went to Parkland Hospital. Yet individuals with Secret Service *credentials* seemed to be in place in key locations at the time of the assassination.

Immediately after Tippit's shooting, police were called to two other sites in Oak Cliff where the dead officer's assassin was seen fleeing. One was the Abundant Life Temple which was discussed in chapter one. When they arrived there, they were called away to the Branch Library on Jefferson before they could search the temple. Once at the library they found Secret Service agents *protecting* it. Next they were called to the Texas Theater and the rest is history.

> More fake Secret Service agents protecting the Branch Library, where the Tippit shooter was seen to run into. The DPD aiding as well, note that they don't disclose the identity of said suspect.

> regarding the suspect being in the Branch Library on Jefferson. We con-
> verged on that location and there were Secret Service men and other patrol
> and CID officers present when all the people were ordered out of the
> building. One of the Secret Service men stated the person who came out
> of the basement with the others was not the suspect and that he had
> already talked to him a few minutes previously. We then went back to
> the car and a call saying the suspect was going down an alley reloading

THE CROOKED MAN[230]

"There are more things in Heaven and Earth, Horatio, than are dreamt of in your philosophy."

–William Shakespeare, *Hamlet* (1.5.167-8)

One of the strangest episodes of the Oswald impostor charades took place at the Ross Avenue Employment Office in Dallas in October 1963. Employment Counselor Laura Kittrell conducted an interview with a well-dressed black woman who was looking to become a trainee in an electronics factory. She had recently moved to Dallas from Encino California where she had been a domestic employee, working as a maid for Murray Chotiner. The date was October 7th.

During the interview Kittrell noticed a man in a black leather motorcycle jacket sitting at the desk of Don Brooks, another counselor. Later, when the interview was over and the black woman had left, the man in the leather jacket approached Kittrell and said, *"Excuse me, I don't mean to*

---

230   Apologies to Sir Arthur Conan Doyle

be butting in, or anything like that, but didn't I hear that colored woman tell you that she had worked for Murray Chotiner in California? He's a big gangster." Surprised, Laura explained that this was a government office and interviews are confidential. The man became angry and said, *"Well I'll be damned."* Then he slammed his fist down on her desk and loudly repeated, *"I'll just be damned."* He then got up and left the office. When Kittrell asked her co-worker Brooks who the man was, he told her his name was Lee Oswald. Littrell found it interesting that both the black woman and Oswald pronounced Chotiner's name as *"Shotner."* Littrell had pronounced it as it was spelled, "Chotiner."[231] She later learned that *Shotner* was indeed the correct pronunciation.

A few days later Laura was contacted by the claims investigator at the Main Street unemployment compensation office, Paul Elrod. He told her that Oswald would be sent to her to be re-interviewed. He informed her that the applicant had made a mistake on his claim. Elrod added, *"He's worried half to death. His wife is pregnant."*

When "Oswald" showed up for the second interview, she didn't recognize him as the man she had seen on October 7th. He seemed to be a different person with a different demeanor and attitude as well. She had to ask him his name to verify his appointment. He said he was Lee Oswald.

When asked about Chotiner during his second interview he reiterated, *"He's a crook."*

"Oh, now, I wouldn't say that," Kittrell replied.

"Well, he is, He's a crook, he is," Oswald repeated.

After a brief interruption during which she attempted to give directions in broken Spanish to a Cuban refugee, Oswald said, *"You know, your Spanish isn't half bad."*

Surprised, Kittrell replied, *"Oh, you speak Spanish?"*

"I speak three languages," Oswald proclaimed.

Intrigued, Kittrell answered, *"Indeed, and what is the other, German?"*

"Russian," he replied. *"Oh, I've been to Russia. Matter of fact, I married a Russian girl."*

"Oh really? Now how on earth did you happen to learn Russian?" Kittrell replied.

Oswald changed the subject.

"What do you think of the Cubans?" He asked.

"Oh, I think they're awfully nice."

231   For more detail on this incident see Kittrel's typewritten manuscript to HSCA describing Oswald interviews and William Weston's articles in the 4th Decade Nov. 2000/Jan. 2001 issues.

"No! No! I mean, what do you think of Batista?"

Laura explained that at first she had been pleased when Batista was overthrown, but after Castro started the mass trials, she lost all sympathy for the revolution. She stated she felt sorry for the Cubans.

"Even those who were for Batista?"

"Yes, all of them." Then she said, *"Tell me, what did you like best about Russia?"*

"The opera!" he answered.

During the conversation Oswald mentioned a job he had when he was sixteen years old in Encino, CA as a messenger boy on a motor scooter as well as some office filing and mailing at the E.T.I. Realty Company.

Four days after this interview the man returned and took an aptitude test. On October 21st the impostor Oswald told Kittrell that his "codes" needed changing. He had joined the Teamsters Union. Laura was confused by the inconsistencies between the interviews. In particular that in the first interview, he revealed he didn't have a driver's license. Joining the Teamsters, she believed, required one. Also he had said that his wife had had their second child. Later that she was still expecting.

After the assassination, Kittrell wrote to RFK and received a note of receipt from J. Edgar Hoover. However, she was never contacted and there was nothing in the WC report about her letter or the incident. During the Garrison investigation in 1967, she was interviewed by Bill Boxley. Eventually she gave her typewritten manuscript to the HSCA.

When Oswald appeared in photographs and newsreels after the assassination, she identified him as the Oswald in the motorcycle jacket she had talked to. It was not until years later, while leafing through the Warren Commission volumes that she identified the impostor or *"Teamster Oswald"* of the later interviews. The photo she identified was that of Larry Crafard.

HE'S A CROOK!

Murray Chotiner was born in Pittsburgh in 1909. In spite of dropping out of high school, he earned a law degree from Southwestern Law College. He worked for Herbert Hoover in 1932 and aided Earl Warren in his campaign for governor of California. He also managed Richard Nixon's 1950 campaign against Helen Douglas. Chotiner, notorious for his dirty campaign tricks, arguably contributed to Nixon's reputation along those lines. Nixon campaign advisor, Leonard Garment, depicted Chotiner as a *"hardheaded exponent of the campaign philosophy that politics is war"* and that *"politics is shabby most of the time, filled with lies and deceptions."*[232]

In 1956, RFK grilled Chotiner in a hearing of the McClellan Committee investigating the infiltration of organized crime into the textile industry. RFK and Carmine Bellino had dug into the lawyer's activities and discovered evidence that a New Jersey uniform company that had been convicted of stealing from the federal government had paid out $5,000 to Chotiner. An informant told Bellino that the money was meant for Richard Nixon to help prevent a possible prosecution by the Department of Justice. The investigation was eventually dropped thanks to Chotiner receiving support from Joe McCarthy. As a result of the damage done to his reputation by the hearings, Chotiner laid low in his association with Nixon until the 1968 election when he aided "Tricky Dick" in his defeat of Hubert Humphrey. Nixon rewarded him by appointing him general counsel to the Office of the Special Representative for Trade Negotiations. A year later he became special counsel to the president.

But before the 1968 election, the former Beverly Hills lawyer, who had close ties to organized crime figures including gambler Mickey Cohen, was working for Hubert Humphrey. This was less than a year before his appointment as special counsel to President Nixon. Soon after entering office, Nixon established *Operation Sandwedge*, a secret investigation of Edward Kennedy. Organized by H.R. Halderman and John Erlichman, the project had two main field officers, Jack Caulfield and Anthony Ulasewicz. Ulasewicz, then a member of Nixon's White House/Special Operations Group, was quoted as saying: *"When I first met Chotiner, the first thing he did was hand me a file on Rand Development Corporation and Its officers.."* "...Chotiner's file on the Rand Development Corporation disclosed that during the 1968 presidential campaign Rand was named as a defendant in a lawsuit started by some angry Minnesota businessmen. The charge was that the Small Business Administration and the Government Services Administration were guilty of fraud and conspiracy in the way of a government contract for some postal vehicles was awarded to a wholly owned Rand Corporation subsidiary, the Universal Fiberglass Corporation. The Universal Fiberglass Corporation, the lawsuit charged, was born for the sole purpose [of obtaining this contract]. *"Despite the apparent lack of qualifications, a crony of Senator Hubert Humphrey awarded the contact to the Universal Fiberglass Corporation. The Universal Fiberglass Corporation defaulted and disappeared under Rand Development's umbrella."* Murray Chotiner was trying to bring this situation to the attention of the media.[233] Caulfield later admitted that Ulasewicz's reports on Ted Kennedy went to three people: Nixon, Chotiner and Bebe Rebozo.

---

233   Ulasewicz, *Pres. Priv. Eye*, 1990

Chotiner's other alleged activities include an attempt to blackmail George Wallace about corruption in Alabama. In addition, Dwight Lee Chapin[234] was convinced that Chotiner was secretly involved in Watergate. Chapin said, *"There is a person who goes all the way back through this thing, and that is Murray Chotiner. He was in the White House ... he leaves; the break-in happens. Murray was the operator for Nixon on God only knows what."* Chotiner's law offices were one floor above those of CREEP.

John Simpkin posted an article that was published in the *Los Angeles Times* (31 March 1973) that claimed Chotiner had received copies of the tape recordings that had been made by Alfred Baldwin as a result of the bugging of Democratic campaign headquarters in the Watergate building.

It was Chotiner who told columnist Jack Anderson of a "gay sex ring" among White House Staffers. Anderson informed J. Edgar Hoover who warned Nixon of reports of homosexuality among his staffers. Nixon's paranoia wreaked havoc on his administration until he finally came to the conclusion that Anderson had been pulling his chain.[235]

Nixon hated Anderson to the extent that in 1972, his henchmen – the "plumbers" – conspired to have Anderson killed. Whether Chotiner played a role in this Machiavellian enterprise is unknown. On January 23rd, 1974, Murray Chotiner was involved in a car accident outside the Washington home of Edward Kennedy. Although he only suffered a broken leg, he died a week later.

CARNIVAL CHARACTERS

Curtis LeVerne (Larry) Crafard (Craford on his military documents) was only 22 years old in 1963. Prior to meeting Jack Ruby he worked odd jobs, mostly in carnivals. His marriage in 1962 resulted in a separation, a reuniting and a final breakup in August 1963. While working as a night watchman at the State Fair in Dallas, he met Jack Ruby who just happened to have had an investment in a show playing at the Fair. When the Fair closed, Ruby hired Crafard to build a cloakroom at the Carousel Club. Crafard hung on afterward doing odd jobs. He ran stage lights, cleaned up, answered the telephone and fed Ruby's dogs. William Weston believes Ruby hired Crafard because he resembled Oswald. It seems more than a coincidence that his impersonation of LHO at Kittrell's office occurred only one day after Ruby hired him, on October 21st. Several wit-

---

234   American political organizer, businessman, and Deputy Assistant to President Nixon during the Watergate scandal. Chapin was convicted of lying to a grand jury during the scandal and served nine months at the Federal Correctional Institution, Lompoc.

235   Meagan Day-Timeline Nov. 23, 2016

nesses said they saw Oswald at the Carousel at the time of Crafard's employment there. Hypnotist Bill De Mar told the FBI that Oswald was one of a group brought on stage for a memory expert routine. DeMar knew Crafard, so he couldn't be mistaken about who came on stage.[236]

One oddity involving witnesses of the Tippit shooting is that Ruby had a link to Virginia and Barbara Davis. It seems the telephone number (WH3-8120) that the Davises gave to police also showed up on a memo pad kept by Ruby employee, Larry Crafard.[237] Crafard used the pad to keep track of calls made to Ruby while he was out of the club. Why would the Davises be calling Ruby? Dallas Police Officer and personal friend of Jack Ruby, Harry Olson was working in the vicinity of the Tippit shooting and spent more than an hour talking with Ruby late on the night of the assassination. Olson was dating a Ruby stripper named Karen Carlin (stage name Kathy Kay). Olson left town a month after the assassination and moved to California. It is also strange that Crafard left Dallas for Michigan the day after the assassination and the Davises made a similar exodus within two weeks.

Another coincidence involves two suspects in the JFK assassination. The first, Turk Vaganov, worked at Texas Consumer Finance Corporation on 1310 Commerce Street. The address of the Carousel was 1310 ½ Commerce on the second floor of the same building. Jack Ruby apparently hung out in the office of the Texas Consumer Finance Co. and even took their male employees upstairs for coffee. An unidentified source told legendary researcher, Penn Jones that Oswald had worked at the Texs Consumer Finance Corpooration for briefly (for two 2 weeks). To me, this is very doubtful. (continued on next page).

Another suspect, Jack Lawrence, who worked at the same Lincoln-Mercury dealership where Guy Bogard was employed was known to have ties to Jack Ruby. Lawrence checked into the Dallas YMCA on October 5th, 1963 just three days before a Lee Oswald checked into the same establishment.

---

236   *William Weston, The Fourth Decade, January 2001*
237   *Crafard was supposedly asleep in the backroom of the Carousel when the assassination took place. Yet the Warren Commission called him to testify in a rambling 3900 question interview that took two days and covered all aspects of his personal life but almost nothing about the assassination. In their defense, they had to be aware that he didn't know anything about it unless he dreamed it while asleep at the Carousel. Of course it is important to know the details of the personal life of this accomplished(?) individual. It's almost as important as Ruby's mother's dental records (certainly of consequence if Ruby had bitten Oswald to death, but unfortunately he did not) and Oswald's pubic hair. These kinds of worthless reports alone could fill a volume of the report. In contrast, witnesses close to the events weren't very important and weren't even called unless they said Oswald did it.*

SUMMARY

So how can we make sense of the Kittrell saga? A million questions come to mind. One might ask why Crafard was pretending to be Oswald? How did Oswald know about Murray Chotiner, or even how to pronounce his name properly? He was supposed to be dyslexic. How was Ruby involved? It seems he had to be.

Chotiner was connected to both gangsters like Mickey Cohen as well as politicians like Humphrey and particularly Nixon. Ruby had underworld connections and once worked for Nixon as well as Johnson. Ruby was defended by flamboyant attorney Melvin Belli whose client, mobster Mickey Cohen, was also his close friend. Belli confided to his chauffeur that *"the fix was in"* in the Ruby trial. Belli was hired to make sure Ruby got the death penalty.[238]

The evidence indicates that Ruby stalked Oswald the entire weekend looking for an opportunity to eliminate him. He hung around the police station bringing sandwiches and coffee to his police friends. He tried to get into the room where Oswald was interrogated but was kept out.

When Ruby died of cancer in 1966, Belli told several people, including his law partner, Seymour Ellison that he believed *they* injected Ruby with cancer. He said, *"they* got Dorothy (Kilgallen) and *they* injected Ruby.[239]

The Warren Commission, amazingly, found no connection between Ruby and the mob. When they examined Jack Ruby's phone records, ... they saw what was essentially an inventory of the Mafia leaders that they had been investigating for the past two years at the Justice Department. RFK remarked that it looked like a list of the individuals that he had investigated in racketeer hearings. In addition, Ruby's clubs were owned by the Marcello organization. Ruby's ties to the mob went back to his childhood days in Chicago when he was a runner for Al Capone.

And what of Crafard? Whatever Crafard was doing it had to be at Ruby's behest. When impersonating Oswald, he told Kittrell of a job he had when he was sixteen years old in Encino, California as a messenger-boy on a motor scooter as well as some office filing and mailing at the E.T.I. Realty Company. Was this an effort to connect Oswald with Chotiner? But if so, why? If Crafard was being used as a pawn in a game to incriminate Oswald, why would he do so at an unemployment office of all places? Perhaps he and Ruby were trying to get Oswald's unemployment compensation extended even though he had found employ-

---

238   *Denial of Justice*, Mark Shaw
239   Ibid, p286. They being the CIA (specifically Dr. Jolly West)

ment at the School Book Depository. But again … if so why? And what was the obviously fictitious Teamster's Union story about? Finally, what was the innuendo of the reference to Cuba and Batista? It is well known that Ruby was involved in gun-running to anti-Castro Cuban's. Was all this part of the setup of Oswald's identity as a sheep dipped pro-Castro sympathizer? Ruby's partner in this gun running endeavor was Tom E. Davis. Davis, like Ruby's other crony Crafard, was known to use Oswald's name. That's two of Ruby's associates who were known to use Oswald's name. In essence impersonating him. There is no doubt that Ruby is the link in this game of deception.

It is apparent that we may never have all the answers to these questions and countless more. We can thank Jack Ruby for that. When he killed Oswald the door to the truth of who he was was lost forever.

> *Too often we enjoy the comfort of opinion without the discomfort of thought.*
>
> – John F. Kennedy

WHERE THERE'S SMOKE, THERE'S FIRE

What can be deduced by the fierce protection of the unreleased documents is that they all revolve around the CIA/Mafia plots to assassinate Castro. If that's all there is to it why not release them. The plot has been exposed by the HSCA and researchers have filled in many of the details. They are withheld because they tie together the CIA/Mafia plots, Operation NORTHWOODS, Oswald's trip to Mexico City, the JMWAVE base in Miami which ran the exiles, and the ZRRIFLE group. Throw in Joannides' cover-up of Oswald's interaction with Cuban exile groups and all the elements of a conspiracy to kill JFK come into focus. The involvement of rogue CIA agents, their counterparts in the mafia and Cuban exile community, military and right-wing fanatics are apparent. Was Richard Nixon the catalyst who started the whole ball rolling? Did guilt and fear of exposure lead to the paranoia that ultimately destroyed the 37th president?

NORTHWOODS

FALSE FLAGS AND A STRATEGY OF TENSION

I have to believe that the plot to kill JFK was an offshoot of Operation NORTHWOODS, a plan by the Joint Chiefs to commit acts of terrorism against American targets and to kill American citizens in order to place the blame on Castro. A plan designed to result in the American public's support an invasion of Cuba. NORTHWOODS was rejected by JFK's administration but was likely merely put on the back burner. False flag operations like NORTHWOODS are prevalent throughout history. Hitler's Reichstag fire is a prime example. Commit an act of terrorism and blame it on a Jew or a Communist or whoever your enemies are. In the NORTHWOODS scenario, it was Castro. The purpose being to enrage your constituents into giving you a free hand to commit atrocities they normally would find repulsive. Slogans are a great source of this venue of propaganda... *"Remember the Maine ... or Pearl Harbor"* are examples. A *strategy of tension* was the technical term adopted by the anti-communist movement beginning with *Gladio*. Use fear to gain absolute power. Get the masses to give up their rights willingly, *for the good of the Country*.

JFK's assassination is a perfect fit for NORTHWOODS. Kill a popular president, blame it on your enemy (Castro and or the Russians) and the result will be public support for an invasion of Cuba. Things didn't work out that way but that was the *phase one* plan.

In *Oswald Talked,* Ray and Mary La Fontaine brought to light an incident that links Jack Ruby's gun running to Cuban exile activities in Dallas. It began with an ATF investigation by Agent Frank Ellsworth of a Dallas gun shop owner named John Thomas Masen. Masen, an Oswald doppelganger, was a member of the Minutemen and an associate of H.L. Hunt. Ellsworth's interest in Masen had to do with violations of the National Firearms Act. It also appears that Masen's store was to be the only source of 6.5 mm ammunition, used by Oswald's rifle, anywhere in the Dallas area.

What peaked Ellsworth's interest in Masen was his association with Cuban exile Manuel Orcarberro, who had recently established a Dallas chapter of a violent anti-Castro group known as Alpha 66. The group's activities centered around meetings at a house located in Oak Cliff, not far from Oswald's rooming house. The house, at 3126 Harlandale Avenue, was rented by fellow Alpha 66 member Jorge Salazar. Orcarberro, Ellsworth learned, had been attempting to purchase arms for Alpha 66. An informant of Dallas Deputy Sheriff Buddy Walthers told him that Oswald had been to this house.

It is interesting that Orcarberro was also a member of the DRE, an anti-Castro group with whom Oswald had been involved in a scuffle on Canal Street in New Orleans the previous summer. Masen admitted to Ellsworth that Orcarberro was attempting to buy other weapons including machine guns, bazookas, and heavy equipment. Ellsworth thought the Minutemen were the right-wing group in Dallas most likely to have been associated with efforts to assassinate the President.

Jack Ruby approached gun-runner, Robert McKeown, for an introduction to Castro. One version of the story is that he wanted to sell Castro a large number of jeeps. Another is that he was haggling for a pardon of three prisoners held in one of Castro's prisons. In all likelihood he was offering the jeeps and maybe guns to Castro for their release. One of the prisoners was Santo Trafficante another may have been John Martino. Ruby told McKeown he represented *Las Vegas* interests. Where would Ruby get a large number of jeeps? Could it be from Fort Hood?

In the summer of '63 Masen had made a trip to Mexico *visiting friends.* He was fluent in Spanish and was affiliated with, and could well have been used by the anti-Castro Cubans or the Minutemen to incriminate his lookalike, Oswald.

In an interview with Dick Russell for an article for the *Village Voice,* Ellsworth said that *a man he had been investigating in the fall of 1963 for firearms violations,* was *"an absolute dead ringer for Oswald—identical build, weight, coloring, facial features, hair. They were like identical twins; they could've passed for each other."*

This man who was a ringer for Oswald, could drive a car, was skilled with a rifle and could well have been mistaken for LHO at rifle ranges, gun stores, cashing checks, visiting the safe house on Harlandale, or leaving the TSBD via a Rambler immediately after the assassination. Since he was known to have traveled to Mexico in the summer of 1963, it may have even been he who visited the Cuban Embassy and spoke Spanish in phone conversations with the Russian Embassy. Although Ellsworth would not reveal the name of this individual, it seems a certainty that it was John Thomas Masen.[240] Russell points out that although Masen was Oswald's twin in appearance, he was his opposite politically. Oswald was a virulent leftist and member of the FPCC. Masen a virulent rightist and member of the Minutemen.

Two of Masen's accomplices, Donnell Whitter and Lawrence Miller, were arrested on November 18 for possession of weapons stolen from a National Guard Armory. These weapons were likely headed for Orcar-

---

240   In a later interview with Ellsworth, Russell said that Ellsworth at first denied Masen was the twin. But at the end of the interview he said, "Look, you've got me boxed in. You're trying to get me to tell you something I'm not at liberty to tell without grossly jeopardizing myself and my agency. But if you can find Masen, the answer to what you've been trying to worm out of me will become immediately apparent."--*The Man Who Knew Too Much*, Dick Russell, p. 359

berro's Alpha 66 group. One of the men arrested, Donnell Whitter, had a gun-running relationship with Jack Ruby as well. The informant's identity has never been revealed, but it is logical that it was likely an FBI informant named Lee Oswald. Two days prior to the Whitter-Miller arrests, Oswald had visited the Dallas FBI office.

As the La Fontaine exposé reveals, one of the locations from which the arming of the Cuban exiles was coming, was Fort Hood in Killeen, Texas. Another was Red River Arsenal in Texarkana, Texas. Weapons and explosives were being pilfered by the truckload. Suspected of selling the surplus Army munitions at Fort Hood was Captain George Nonte. The source at Red River was thought to be a Property Disposal Officer named Ray McKnight.[241]

As researcher Gil Jesus points out, the FBI insisted that the ammunition that was used to kill the President was Western Cartridge Company ammunition for the Mannlicher-Carcano rifle. Western Cartridge only made copper-jacketed bullets for that rifle. But the bullet removed from the President's body was not copper-jacketed but an un-jacketed, fragmenting bullet, definitely not made by Western and apparently a reload. The only source of this type of ammunition was John Thomas Masen.

It is Gil Jesus' interpretation that once Masen denied selling the ammunition to Oswald the FBI dropped the investigation into him and his links to Alpha 66. Hoover feared that an investigation might lead to the revelation of the Bureau's foreknowledge of millions of dollars worth of stolen weapons leaving the bases and passing through Masen en route to groups like the Dallas Chapter of Alpha 66. The FBI had been allowing these endeavors to go on because Hoover approved of them. Hoover's FBI and the 112th Military Intelligence Group stationed at Fort Sam Houston in San Antonio, Texas, did absolutely nothing about these thefts. In fact, they intentionally blew the cover of Frank Ellsworth's investigation to protect themselves from discovery. Ellsworth was about to arrest Nonte and Masen when the DPD in cooperation with the FBI, arrested Ruby associates Donnell Whittier and Lawrence Miller with stolen weapons after a high-speed chase. In all probability on information provided by Oswald, an FBI informant. It is very likely that it was Lee who blew the whistle on Jack Ruby's operation.[242]

According to Gil Jesus, Ellsworth's Fort Hood inquiry into the thefts resulted in FBI men advising Nonte to warn Masen. This was needed to

---

241   FBI document dated 11/26/63-NARA 180 100 781 0055
242   If I were Ruby I'd shoot him for that.

assure weapons would be in the hands of the exiles for a second invasion of Cuba and or the *"2nd invasion of Cuba, 2nd Bay of Pigs, Big Event, or Lancelot operation."* An FBI teletype dated October 25, 1963, indicates that the FBI *"interviewed Nonte and briefed him on the scope of discreet inquiry to be made of Masen on contact."*[243]

Being tipped off by the Feds, Masen double-crossed Ellsworth by giving him a phony location for a weapons deal which would have entrapped him. The actual transfer of weapons was going on at another location, this one, involving Ruby's associates, was also a setup, but this time by DPD and the FBI. By beating the ATF to the arrest of Whitter and Miller, the FBI had scuttled the ATF investigation, preventing them from putting an end to the theft of weapons from Fort Hood, thus allowing it to continue. Ellsworth, upset that his operation had been blown, called a meeting on the morning of November 22 for a discussion on the weapons theft at Fort Hood. He was sure the Minutemen (Walker's supporters) were part of the operation due to Masen's involvement. The meeting included Ellsworth, James P. Hosty and an Army Intelligence agent named Ed Coyle of the 112th Military Intelligence Group from Fort Sam Houston. The 112th was supposed to help protect the president that day in Dallas, but was told to stand down, according to Col. Fletcher Prouty. The 112th is also the first source of the Oswald/Hidell alias information, Oswald's Russian defection legend and his street scuffle that summer in New Orleans.[244]

Lamarr Waldron's book makes a strong case that Robert Kennedy was planning a *second invasion* of Cuba around December 1st. However, in truth the term *2nd invasion* was actually a code name for his brother's assassination. Proof that Hoover knew about the plot was an air-tel dated November 1st, 1963.[245] The source of this air tel was likely a warning letter sent to Attorney General Robert F. Kennedy on October 22, 1963. An Army code breaker named Pfc. Eugene Dinkin in Metz, France, had overheard a plan involving *"an attempt to assassinate President Kennedy would occur on November 28th and that if it were to succeed, blame would be placed upon a Communist or a Negro."*[246] Dinkin wrote that the plan involved elements of the military and that a military coup might ensue. The date was

---

243   4 H 313

244   On the morning of Nov. 22, 1963, while the rest of the city buzzed in anticipation of President Kennedy's visit, the three agents discussed the Fort Hood case. In a 1993 interview, Hosty explained that Ellsworth was particularly interested in the possible involvement of the Dallas Minutemen in the thefts.

245   FBI File No. 105-125147-7 pg 3-4, dated 11/1/63

246   The exact language used by the Miami prophet, Joseph Milteer. A Milteer connection to Banister's New Orleans apparatis was discovered by the HSCA in the form of a business card in his posession belonging to G.Wray Gil Jr., son of Banister and Ferrie's lawyer.

off by a week but Dinkin told a Secret Service agent that, *"I knew of no exact date and gave November 28th as an approximate date."*

The FBI was aware that the weapons were coming from Fort Hood and that Nonte was involved, but had no idea where they were being sent.

Gil Jesus revealed that a weapons buyer from the CIA's JMWAVE station named Martinez was a source for Masen and that Masen and Nonte discussed how a killing in the stock market could be made with the fore-knowledge of the *Big Event*.

SA James P. Hosty's assignments were mainly right-wing subversive groups in Dallas. That being said, it raises questions about why left-wingers like Oswald and Lowery's Dallas Communist cell were part of his agenda. In the fall of 1963, Hosty was ordered to locate a man named George Perrel. It seems Perrel was involved in the procurement of weapons from Fort Hood. Perrel was an alias. His real name was Fermin de Goicochea, DRE secretary for military affairs in Dallas. Perrel, a student at the University of Dallas, would have likely had ties with high echelon Bircher and General Edwin Walker associate, Robert Morris. Morris had been president of that University in 1962. Now we can follow the guns from Fort Hood (Nonte) to Masen, then to Perrel, and finally on to the likes of Orcarberra and Alpha 66. Robert Morris had been a counsel to the Senate Internal Security Subcommittee under Senator Eastland. It was Morris that helped Air-Force officer Earl Lively in writing an anti-communist book stressing the Fair Play for Cuba Committee connections of Lee Harvey Oswald. He was being helped in this project by Lt. George Butler of DPD. It was also Robert Morris, acting as General Walker's attorney, that convinced a Mississippi grand jury not to indict the latter after Robert Kennedy had him arrested for his involvement in the *"Old Miss"* riots.

CONCLUSION

The accused presidential assassin knew about the inner working of a gunrunning network that was under investigation by federal agents in Dallas in the fall of 1963. These gunrunners trafficked in weapons stolen from US government arsenals. According to recently released FBI documents, two of them were suspected of supplying guns to anti-Castro groups that were planning to mount an invasion of Cuba in the last week of November 1963 and likely assassinate JFK as a prelude. If true, this could be conclusive proof that Oswald knew Jack Ruby and that he informed on his gun running activities to the FBI.

According to Col. Robert Jones (who testified to the HSCA in executive session) one of those agents assigned to Presidential protection in Dallas on November 22nd, 1963 was Ed J. Coyle.

The Military-Secret Service link could have gone through the Washington Secret Service agent who moved the motorcycles back and reduced their number, and also removed the agents from the President's limo. That agent, Winston Lawson, was a former Military Intelligence agent like Coyle and James Powell.[247]

If Lawson had a co-conspirator in the Military-Intelligence field in Dallas, it may have been the Commander of the local Military Intelligence Unit, Lt. Col. George Whitmayer, who for some reason was in the motorcade, but safely away from the shooting. He rode in the motorcade "Pilot Car" about 1/4 mile in front of the President's limousine.[248]

Coyle was the Military Intelligence agent in charge of investigating the thefts from Fort Hood and at the same time he was assigned to Presidential Protection in Dallas.

According to James Hosty, Coyle was transferred to Korea "so reporters couldn't get at him—since Korea is a combat zone." Hosty contends this was so because Coyle allegedly heard Dallas Police Lt. Jack Revill say on November 21st that he didn't want to guard that "son of a bitch Kennedy tomorrow." That the Army would transfer one of its agents halfway across the world to keep a lid on an indiscreet remark by a Dallas cop seems absurd. I am more inclined to believe that Hosty is telling another of his *"half-truths"* here and that it was Coyle who made the remark, revealing the Army's sentiment toward the President and making them a prime suspect in his murder, especially in front of a Dallas cop. Coyle's activities may shed some light on the weapons theft and its role in the assassination. Perhaps he was transferred to Korea to prevent anyone from questioning him at a later date.

---

247   4 H 313
248   *High Treason*, Groden and Livingstone, p.185; *Crossfire*, Jim Marrs, pg. 9

CHAPTER 14

ARRIVEDERCI ROMA, THE RED SCARE

*A large amount of false and exaggerated information has been fed to
the average citizen promoting the threat of Communist aggression. And
it has gone on for so long that the people now believe that lie. Communism is not the enemy. Johnson, Humphrey, and Nixon are the real
enemies. The American establishment is the enemy. I absolutely have no
hope for America. I could care less if this country were blown up by a
hydrogen bomb.*

– George de Mohrenschildt

I n order to understand a major historic incident like the assassination
of JFK, one must be cognizant of historic events that set the stage for
this radical event. It is a law of philosophy that every effect must have a
cause. The evidence strongly suggests the *cause* was the right-wing fear of
and obsession with the impending spread of Communism. This obsession
was fanatical to the point of paranoid schizophrenia. Hence, looking back
to the origins of this powerful ideology, it is necessary to re-examine its
conception. Its birth coincided with that of the Cold War, a time when anti-communism became a religion. A religion that would evolve into a jihad,
or holy war. A religion that spawned McCarthyism, the House UN-American Activities Committee (HUAC), the Hollywood Blacklist, the Rosen-
berg trial, loyalty oaths, hate, suspicion, prejudice and paranoia on a scale
comparable to the 17th century witch trials. In the process those responsible yielded abusive power to excessive levels. These power brokers included J. Edgar Hoover, Joe McCarthy, Richard Nixon, Martin Dies, James
O. Eastland and Thomas Dodd. The Red Scare was just that. In essence,
extreme anti-Communist paranoia resulted in the birth of a powerful cult
that would stop at nothing to eradicate the world of the red menace.

In late 1944 and early 1945 when WWII was in its final days, Allied
Intelligence, specifically the OSS and British G2, were making prepara-
tions for the next conflict. The new enemy was to be Soviet Communism.
Churchill's specter of an Iron Curtain in Europe sent chills up the spine of

the military industrial power elite. The personification of this group was Allen Dulles.

The wheels were turning long before the Third Reich succumbed to its death throes. Setting up a world anti-Communist organization became foremost in importance. To accomplish this task, Allen Dulles made a pact with the Devil. The demon's personification, General Rhinehart Gehlen,[249] was head of Nazi military intelligence. His spy network in the Soviet Union was already well established. This collaboration produced a two-pronged strategy utilizing Operation Paper Clip and a project called Operation Gladio.

CIA spymaster Frank Wisner was tasked to create the stay-behind networks of foreign agents in the Eastern Bloc countries to be used in the event of nuclear war. Wisners OPC was the most secret thing in the US Government after nuclear weapons, and was actually part of the nuclear war planning.

Frank Lindsay, Wisner's deputy, headed operational branches of the OPC which directed foreign agents like Otto Skorzeny in Wild Bill Donovan's Secret Paramilitary groups. Lindsay was assigned abduction and *assassination* missions. Angleton's deputy chief of CI SIG, Newton "Scotty" Miler's name is on the distribution list of several declassified CIA documents pertaining to Otto Skorzeny. Was Skorzeny a member of Angleton's personal assassination squad commanded by Boris Pash? This possibility would fit the Ralph Ganis (*The Skorzeny Papers*) interpretation of the three dimensional organizational apparatus of the assassination cabal: *Action Arm* – Souetre (Skorzeny); *Deception Group* – Oswald manipulation-Dallas Russian emigre community, de Mohrenschildt, Raigordsky, Bouhe-Tolstoy Foundation (secret arm of Skorzeny network)-Walker and the Birchers; *Support Elements* – Earle Cabell, Tolstoy group.

Judge Jesse C. Duvall of Fort Worth was presiding judge during Skorzeny trial in 1947. De Mohrenschildt met with Duvall about Oswald in 1961 to discuss Oswald's discharge. Roy Pike, friend and former trial case of Judge Duvall, came to Duvall's house 2-3 hours after Oswald had been shot and told him that Oswald had been seen at Ruby's club recently. Pike had worked at the Carousel under the name Tommy Ryan and had at one time been Ruby's book-keeper.

ALPHABET SOUP

Wild Bill Donovan's OSS and their British counterpart, William Stephenson's SOE, were both on the verge of extinction as the war

---

249   The Gehlen Org was eventually transformed into the BND under Chancellor Konrad Adenauer in 1956.

ended.[250] With the end at hand, the like-minded spy masters cunningly regrouped and organized cover corporate organizations to be manned by corporate officers who were actually their loyal ex-intelligence officers. Stephenson formed the British American Canadian Corporation (BAAC) and Donovan the World Commerce Corporation (WCC). The WCC functioned as an *import-export* company.[251] One former employee, Betty Lussier, who stated that an OSS official from Washington visited and informed me that I was the only one of our SI group to be kept on for work in a super-secret organization inside Spain. It was so secret that acting Ambassador Walter Butterworth made Lussier swear on a Bible not to reveal the organization's formation.[252] The company was a conduit for private companies to be used to support pro-US groups in a foreign country, similar to PERMINDEX and what later became Iran-Contra. What was being exported? Guns and money? What was being imported? Drugs? Laundered Nazi gold paid for the drugs and the drugs paid for the weapons.

Both BACC and WCC were born of a highly classified project called SAFEHAVEN. The Allies were concerned that the Nazis would use hidden assets they had acquired to build a Fourth Reich. The OSS and SOE carried out SAFEHAVEN objectives and tracked down and impeded German assets in neutral countries throughout Europe and the Americas. German corporations were targeted. One in particular was *Sociedad Financiera Industrial,* which served as a cover for a Nazi intelligence network extending into South America. It was controlled in Berlin by Otto Skorzeny and his commandos.[253] It seems suspicious that Bill Donovan would be the interrogator of Hitler's chief of commandos, SS Lt. Col. Otto Skorzeny.

Skorzeny surrendered to the Allies after the war and was held for two years as a POW and charged with violations of the *Laws of War.* His trial was attended by high-ranking members of the SOE and OSS who surprisingly came to his defense. He was found not guilty. After his acquittal he

250   Who needed spies in peace time? In addition, Truman disliked Donovan and thought the purpose of the OSS was to provide the President with important information and not be involved in covert action. This is the same purpose he proposed when he created the CIA. Talk about going from the frying pan into the fire! Add this to J. Edgar Hoover publicly labeling the OSS the American Gestapo, had the desired effect on Donovan supporter, FDR, supporting dissolution of the organization.

251   Didn't Oswald say he was going into the import-export business when he left the Marines? Wasn't Grossi/Bowen spouting similar sentiments? How about Osboune/Bowen? Clay Shaw?

252   *The Secrets War: The Office of the Strategic Services of World War II,* edited by George C. Chalou

253   *The Skorzeny Papers,* Major Ralph P. Ganis, Hot Books, 2018

was sent to a VIP POW camp for several months and then transported to a facility to await release. But he escaped in July 1948. Why bother? There, of course, was no manhunt and Skorzeny simply went underground. He was now free to conduct covert warfare against Communist expansion. He, like other *paper clippers,* was now part of Gladio and served as an exporter of weapons, operations consultant and assassination expert.

President Truman terminated the OSS on September 20, 1945.[254] OSS officers from the Special Operations Branch and Special Intelligence Branch were transferred to a new organization, the Strategic Services Unit (SSU).

By 1947, the OSS had evolved into the CIA. The fear of a possible Communist invasion of Western Europe resulted in a secret alliance, forged at the close of World War II by the CIA, the Sicilian and US mafias, and the Vatican. Known as Dulles' *"stay-behind"* army, these Guerrilla army units consisted of five thousand to fifteen thousand operatives. These *"stay-behind"* units were initially used to deal with possible invaders from the East. But as the Cold War intensified their mission evolved into thwarting the rise of left-wing movements in South America and NATO-based countries. At the same time, their tactics evolved from defense and sabotage, to rigging elections, outright terrorism and even assassination.

According to author and researcher Paul Williams, Operation Gladio soon gave rise to the toppling of governments, wholesale genocide, the formation of death squads, financial scandals on a grand scale, the creation of the mujahideen, an international narcotics network, and eventually, the ascendancy of Jorge Mario Bergoglio, a Jesuit cleric with strong ties to Operation Condor (an outgrowth of Gladio in Argentina) who became Pope Francis I.[255]

An initial problem arose as how to finance the Gladio armies and other CIA covert operations against Communist expansion. The Truman Administration had provided no funds for covert post war operations. The solution came from Col. Paul E. Helliwell, Chief of Special Intelligence for the OSS serving in China.[256] Helliwell had observed that General Chiang Kai-shek sold opium to Chinese addicts to raise money for his war against Mao Zedong. Why not sell drugs to addicts in America, specifically Harlem, to finance the stay-behind army and global anti-Communist covert operations? Helliwell approached his boss, General "Wild-Bill" Donovan.

---

254   Executive Order 9621
255   *Operation Gladio*, Paul Williams, Prometheus Books, 2015
256   Helliwell ran a small OSS detachment in Kunming, China. Included HL Hunt, Lucien Conein, Mitch Werbell and Ray Cline.

Donovan shared the idea with James Angleton, Allen Dulles and British Security Coordination (BSC) William Stephenson. They loved it! Donovan saw Helliwell's scheme as an opportunity to make good use of Lucky Luciano and the Sicilian Mafia.[257] The money for the opiates would eventually come from Nazi gold laundered by Dulles and Stephenson through the World Commerce Corporation.[258] Gladio funding incorporated the Vatican bank as a conduit.

The CIA/Mafia relationship was handled by *James Angleton* and Frank Wisner. The financial details were manipulated by Helliwell and Lansky through a Miami shell company called General Development Corporation. Angleton dealt with disputes between the CIA and the mob through New York lawyer and close associate, Mario Brod. In addition, Helliwell created the Castle Bank in the Bahamas. At this point Santo Traficante entered the picture, providing Cuban drug labs to cut the heroin. It was from Cuba that the drugs were shipped to Harlem.[259] Operation X was underway.

As the demand for heroin escalated with black jazz musicians[260] in Harlem, Helliwell's scheme was proving a huge success. Through his drug lords in Burma he was able to provide all that was needed. Cheaper "bars" of opium were soon provided to inner-city drug lords at rock-bottom prices to increase the number of dependent clients. Soon concern arose that the exponential demand would cause an epidemic. However, Helliwell, in denial, refused to accept that possibility and reasoned that the problem would be confined to poor blacks and would have little effect on white middle-class Americans.

At the end of WWII, Helliwell, E. Howard Hunt, Lucein Conein, Tommy Corcoran and Claire Chennault, of "Flying Tiger" fame, created the Civil Air Transport. This motley air-force transported weapons to the KMT in Burma and then loaded with drugs for their return flight to China. This proved to be the prototype for the CIA's Air America[261] that transported opium and cocaine during and after the Vietnam War.

---

257   Luciano used this to his own advantage. Establishing trade with Turkish and Chinese drug lords, he saved surplus merchandise for the women who worked in his brothels.

258   The initial funding for these guerrilla armies came from the sale of large stocks of SS morphine that had been smuggled out of Germany and Italy and of bogus British bank notes that had been produced in concentration camps by skilled counterfeiters.

259   Via ports of New Orleans, Miami and New York. The CIA protected these ports through agreements with International Longshoremen Association. Movement of the merchandise was facilitated by Jimmy Hoffa and the International Brotherhood of Teamsters.

260   Included were the likes of Billie Holiday and Charlie Parker. Many of these "junkies" died of overdoses.

261   Created by William Pawley

MEANWHILE BACK AT THE RANCH

During WWII the FBI built a special intelligence spy network in Latin America to compete with the OSS. This was especially true in Mexico. In 1947, Hoover was ordered, against his wishes, to merge this organization with the newly created CIA. Thus, a number of G-Men, including Raymond Leddy, Win Scott, and William Harvey, moved over to the CIA. Their true allegiance, however, was likely still with Hoover. The Old-Boy Network was born.

A split in American policy developed immediately. The old-money bankers of the New York Corporate Financial Network, epitomized by Chase Manhattan, pursued a global strategy moving toward understanding with the Soviets and a division of the Eastern and Western European markets. Their collaboration with the liberal wing of the CIA and Corporations such as Lockheed, Motorola and General Dynamics, as well as ITT formed the *Yankee* power elite into which the Kennedys were born.

The other side of the coin was the Western expansionist *Cowboys*, made up of the Fruit Companies, Texas investors, right wing oil millionaires like H.L. Hunt and Clint Murchison, Howard Hughes, and the Somoza brothers. The philosophy here was regional, exploitative, expansionist; happy to rule by military coup. These were fanatically anti-Communist patriots whose political embodiment were the likes of Richard Nixon, Lyndon Johnson, Edwin Walker, J. Edgar Hoover, Douglas MacArthur and Charles Willoughby.[262]

Thus, the US Government, on advice from Psy-War advisor C.D. Jackson of *Time/Life*, collaborated with Somoza and United Fruit (a CIA front on whose board of directors Allen Dulles sat) to overthrow the government of Guatemala. CIA renegade Rip Robertson went to work for Somoza. Also gaining a foothold in the region at this time was the ubiquitous Carlos Marcello. Gambling interests were looked over by Meyer Lansky, while the interests of United Fruit as well as Standard Fruit and Steamship were protected by John Roselli with help from his constant companion, John Martino, who in turn operated out of the Mexico City CIA station. Thus another Banana Republic was born; the illegitimate child of the CIA Fruit Companies and New Orleans organized crime interests. The system was tried and proven. It had worked before. It would work again under the direction of the Fruit

---

262   Jack Cannon, who served under Willoughby Ran Z Unit, a Gestapo type Zed group. According to a Garrison investigator Cannon was a rub out man for CIA. Soviet journalist, Michael Lebedev, claimed that it was an agent of Zed fired fatal head shot in Dealey Plaza. Cannon had been stationed at Fort Hood in the 1950's. It was Fort Hood that was a source of a stolen weapons operation that Jack Ruby was involved in late 1963.

companies, local client rulers, the likes of Somoza and Duvalier, the US Military and Organized crime. It had worked in Honduras since 1911 when both the government and the opposition financed themselves by narcotic trafficking to New Orleans ... a banana economy supplemented by narcotics.

In 1958, the World Anti-Communist Congress was formed in Mexico City. This new Anti-Komintern included representatives of the Asian People Anti-Communist League (APACL) and the Anti-Bolshevik Bloc of Nations (ABN) and was known to be linked to the international Anti-komintern of the 1930s under Hitler and Goebbels. America's representatives were Charles Edison of the John Birch Society and American Security Council and Lev Dobriansky, a professor at Georgetown University with close links to intelligence.

DID THE END JUSTIFY THE MEANS?

With the success of this drug based economic fluidity, the CIA became concerned that it's dealings with the Mafia might be exposed. With the aid of Rear Admiral Hillenkoetter and the ONI, all records relating to Luciano were collected and destroyed. As for the crusade against Communism, the biggest concern of the agency manifested itself with the rise of the PCI (Partito Comunista Italiano) in Italy. The Italian Communist Party was becoming the most powerful in that country. According to Victor Marchetti, it was at this point that the CIA became tight with the drug dealing Coriscan brotherhood as well. To deal with the Communist takeover of Italy, Angleton, Wisner, Dulles and Donovan needed mafia muscle provided by Luciano and company. Paying them was no problem with the influx of large amounts of drug money. However, they could not be compensated directly. Enter the Vatican bank, the only institution with immunity from US Treasury agents, Italian bank examiners, or international fiscal monitors. Through Luciano's syndicate, the CIA deposited $65 million of its drug money, sometimes delivered via large suitcases, just prior to the 1948 election. The money was then paid out by the Vatican bank to the mob through ecclesiastical organizations including Catholic Action.[263] Additionally, the Vatican played an essential role in Operation Paperclip providing a Nazi ratline to South America. Dulles' war on the Italian left was christened "Operation Demagnetize,[264]" its purpose was to do just that, demagnetize the Italian Communist Party (PCI), or break its magnetism. As head of the Italian Section of the OSS, it was Dulles that spearheaded this effort.

---

263   *Operation Gladio*, Paul Williams, Promethius Books, 2015
264   Secret Stay-Behind deal between CIA and SIFAR (Italian CIA equivalent)

MORE FORCES JOIN THE CRUSADE

The meetings of the Catholic Gladio stay-behind forces were held in Masonic lodges. These soon evolved into covert Masonic organizations. The most notorious was known as Propaganda Due or simply P2. Thus Italian Freemasonry, previously outlawed by Mussolini, enjoyed a rebirth with the wholehearted approval of a 33rd degree Mason named Allen Dulles. This created a split in the Italian Socialist Party that resulted in the birth of the Italian Social *Democratic* Party. Further, this was made possible via infiltration of American Freemasons. The mafia and P2 were natural allies, being secret organizations that had been previously banned by the fascists.

Founded in 1877, P2 had few members until Licio Gelli came to power and drastically expanded its membership within one year to over a thousand.

Gelli was a former fascist, having been a "black shirt" in Mussolini's army, having served as a liaison between Mussolini's government and the Third Reich. Gelli developed high-level contacts outside of Italy as well, most notably meeting with Alexander Haig, and contacts with Henry Kissinger and the CIA. It was Gelli who managed the ratline to Argentina. He became close to Juan Peron, who was amiable to protecting Nazi fugitives. Gelli enabled over sixteen hundred Nazi scientists and their families to immigrate to US to work in the space program. In addition to rat-lining Nazi's out of Europe after the war, Gelli smuggled $80 million in gold to the Vatican bank. In 1956 Gelli became a director of PERMINDEX. PERMINDEX was a branch of Gladio managed by Frank Wisner that provided weapons to anti-Communist forces in Hungary. Clay Shaw was on its American board of directors. It was Angleton, Wisner and Dulles that had recruited Gelli.

PROPHYLACTIC PROPAGANDA

Of the many outrageous ploys contemplated by the CIA for use against its communist adversaries, this one takes the cake. It is not clear if it was dreamed up by Frank Wisner or Carmel Offie.

Exploding cigars and sea shells, LSD and poison pills, staged second comings of Christ, contaminated diving suits, and other outlandish operations, most of which were brain childs of Edward Lansdale, were catastrophic failures in the war against Castro. These ideas seemed like outtakes from a bad James Bond movie. However, they were nothing compared to a plan dreamed up for Operation "Roll Back," in the 1950s.

This delusional CIA psychological propaganda ploy involved labeling extra-large condoms as "medium," and dropping them behind the iron curtain to demoralize the Soviets and their Eastern Bloc counterparts.

Although this project was never brought to fruition, and may possibly be an internet hoax, as some believe, there is some evidence of its existence in reality.

During the Cold War struggle between the US and the Soviet Union, the two countries competed for dominance in all possible areas, including military, science, sports, etc.

Apparently, planners within the CIA decided that masculinity be added to the script. The purpose was to undermine the morale of the people living behind the iron curtain, by implying that the males of the Western Bloc were anatomically superior to their communist foes and, in general, extremely well endowed. The CIA believed that this act of psychological warfare would make communist males doubt their masculinity and females of the regime would want to leave life in the "evil empire" for freedom and sexual bliss in the West.

It is known that Wisner's Office of Policy Coordination was responsible for executing similar covert operations at that time. Another of these bizarre tactics, including parachuting American toiletries behind the Iron Curtain to demonstrate their availability in the West.

PERMINDEX

PERMINDEX, an acronym for Permanent Industrial Exposition, was a trade organization headquartered in Basel, Switzerland, said to be a CIA-front company. On November 7, 1958, a State Department memo said that PERMINDEX had formed an alliance with the Rome World Trade Center or Central Mondaile Commercial (CMC). In 1959, Ferenc Nagy, who for a short time in 1945 was Prime Minister of Hungary, became president of PERMINDEX. It was Nagy's CIA history that catapulted him to the leadership of this organization. A long time asset of CIA Deputy Director for Plans, Frank Wisner, Nagy outlined the group's plans to build "Europe's first international shopping center for businessmen." The project was modeled after the International Trade Mart in New Orleans. Clay Shaw was head of the New Orleans Trade Mart and represented the United States on the board of directors for PERMINDEX, which was expelled from Italy for funneling money to political parties opposing Communists. Soon after Shaw was charged in the JFK case by Jim Garrison, Italian Newspapers, such as *Pease Sera* and *de la Sera* alleged that

Shaw was linked to the CIA. The link being his involvement in the CMC, the PERMINDEX subsidiary of which he was a board member.

The actual purpose of CMC was to fund and direct *assassinations* of leaders considered threats to the western world and petroleum interests. Their agenda was to furnish couriers and agents for re-channeling funds through Swiss banks for Las Vegas, Miami, and Havana gambling syndicates, to coordinate espionage activities of Solidarists and Division V of the FBI with groups in sympathy with their objectives and channel funds to these groups, one of which was the OAS. According to *Pease Sera,* the CMC had been a front organization developed by the CIA for transferring funds to Italy for "illegal political-espionage activities," and had attempted to overthrow French President de Gaulle. A later article named other individuals including Canadian businessman, Louis Bloomfield, as American agents and who established secret ties in Rome with Neo-fascist parties.

A link between Ferenc Nagy, PERMINDEX and the OAS is a man named Jacques Soustelle, one-time propaganda chief under de Gaulle. He had served as Governor General of Algeria in the 1950s. At odds with de Gaulle over Algerian independence, he soon became an active member of the OAS. He traveled to Washington, DC to meet with members of the CIA, notably the head of clandestine services, Richard Bissell,[265] to try and gain support for OAS rebellion by intimating that under de Gaulle's reign, Algeria would become a Soviet base. A year later, Soustelle went into exile and two years after that he would be accused of collaborating with the OAS to assassinate de Gaulle. It was de Gaulle's belief that the OAS was funded by PERMINDEX. Nagy was a contributor to Jacques Soustelle.

In 1962 the French Newspaper, *Les Echos,* wrote an editorial that linked PERMINDEX to the attempts on de Gaulle's life. Was it a coincidence that Guy Banister dispatched legal counsel Maurice Gatlin to Paris with $200,000 at a time when French intelligence discovered an identical amount in secret funds channeled to PERMINDEX accounts? Neither can it be discounted that some of the banking connections of the secret empire reached to Mafia leader Meyer Lansky and his Bahamas gambling operation – PERMINDEX was the basis for the movie "*The Parallax View.*"

Starting in late 1950s CMC-PERMINDEX acted as the covert funding and planning source for right-wing political terror in both Europe and the US, possibly including the assassination of JFK. Its board of directors includ-

---

265   Soustelle's arrival in US and meeting with the CIA was reported in the *New York Times.* Bissell was involved in the plots to kill Castro.

ed CIA, American and Italian Freemasons as well as Italian organized crime figures, Italian and German neo-fascists and neo-Nazis, Israeli Mossad, and French OAS paramilitary operatives. These were rabid anti-Communist and anti-Soviet terrorists willing to do whatever it took to stop the spread of Communism.

De Gaulle's opposition was the French Secret Army Organization (OAS), a right-wing terrorist group made up, in large measure, of French military deserters who were violently opposed to de Gaulle's giving Algeria it's freedom. They were financially supported by the CIA through front companies such as PERMINDEX[266] and Schlumberger Corporation, a large French-owned enterprise which serviced oil producers worldwide by using explosives to predict the potential of geological sites. By supporting the OAS against de Gaulle, Schlumberger found itself in an alliance with the CIA, who supplied the corporation with anti-personnel ammunition. Jean de Menil, a president of Schlumberger and member of the Dallas Petroleum Club, was a close friend of Oswald's Dallas mentor George de Mohrenschildt. After the demise of the OAS, the CIA got its munitions back when David Ferrie, and others[267] from Guy Banister's office in New Orleans raided a Schlumberger bunker at Houma, Louisiana and removed them. They were then stored at the Newman building at 544 Camp Street, New Orleans. The Banister operation acted as a supply line between Dallas, New Orleans and Miami, dispersing arms and explosives to Cuban exiles.

The OAS was nurtured by Allen Dulles out of fear that Algeria would go Communist, which would mean loss of rich economic resources. He also had no love lost for the French president.[268] JFK's Algerian Speech not only advocated Algerian independence but also independence for a Muslim country. It certainly did not endear him with the OAS or Dulles.

William Harvey of Staff D and head of ZRRIFLE, intimate of Johnny Roselli and a key operative in the CIA/Mafia plots to kill Castro, was exiled to Rome by RFK after he ordered unauthorized raids on Cuba during the Soviet missile crisis in 1962. In Rome, Harvey schemed and formed strong alliances with three men, Giovanni de Lorenzo, Renzo Rocca and Michele Sindona, all

266   Permanent Industrial Exposition

267   Sergio Arcacha Smith and Gordon Novel.

268   According to Larry Hancock, "documents showing that OAS terrorist and assassin, Jean Souetre had been allowed into the US in 1963, ostensibly as a diplomatic representative from the OAS but of course a representative without official French government credentials. That appears to have been at the initiative of the CIA and he was pitching various offices about the threat of Communist agents within the de Gaulle administration. It's pretty clear that his visit hadn't been approved but it's also clear the French would have officially protested if they had known, or if they found out."

linked to CMC. The HSCA considered David Atlee Phillips and William Harvey as central suspects in the JFK killing.

ALL IS FAIR IN LOVE AND WAR

The crusade to stop Communism escalated into an orgy of ruthless terrorism, assassination, corruption and insurrection. It created an epidemic of drug addiction on a previously unparalleled scale. The consequences of this endeavor resulted in a worldwide crime epidemic leading to millions of violent deaths and enormous allotments of resources for drug enforcement. A crusade that protected war criminals from prosecution and corrupted the Vatican into collaborating with the mafia. That the church profited enormously by laundering the dirty money of illegal drug trafficking seemed to be no sin in the eyes of the Holy See. Democratically elected governments were overthrown and brutal dictators friendly to the US were installed. Leaders who opposed these policies were simply eliminated. Where is that Communist threat now? What happened to the "domino effect," a concept that I am convinced even JFK believed a real threat, a concept that fifty-six thousand Americans were sacrificed to prevent. Even with their sacrifice the Vietnam war was lost. Why then was there was no expansion of Communism? What stopped the dominoes? Were they just a false flag to justify an unjust war? A war that produced enormous profits and provided still more drugs to feed the coffers for future covert enterprises. Was the end result of this 20-year Cold War struggle worth it? Was the threat real or just a paranoid illusion? Was the baby thrown out with the bath water? Philosophically, the effect does not seem worthy of the cause. We have to ask ourselves, did the end justify the means?

In the final analysis, which was more evil and to be feared more, Communism or Anti-Communism?

> *Oswald leads us everywhere and nowhere*
> —Jerry Koth, *Conspiracy in Camelot*

LICENSE TO KILL

World War II did not end in 1945. The Allies merely changed adversaries. Germany and Japan were replaced by the Soviet Union and Red China. A Gladio army was left behind in Europe, financed by narcotic trafficking revenue provided by the mafia and laundered by the Vatican bank. The CIA ran the show with the blessing of the Pope and the mob prospered. An anti-communist pogrom of terror was used against communist party efforts to win free elections in Italy and France. Beating up candidates, stuffing ballot boxes, bombing and burning meeting halls, bribery, buying votes, and assassination were considered justifiable in this "holy" war. A triple alliance of Intelligence agencies, mafioso and religious institutions united in a cold war of good against evil as they saw it.

We have seen how Unitarians, Quakers, Old Church Organizations and other religious groups were used as a clandestine apparatus by US Intelligence. The Catholic Church was no different. As far back as the crusades, the Church used military religious orders like the Knights Templar to rain terror on those they perceived to be a threat.

In *Church of Spies*, Mark Riebling identifies the conditions that must be observed to make murder an acceptable option to the church. He writes, *"Church teachings stated the conditions under which citizens could kill tyrants. Catholic doctrine permitted capital punishment, and though a priest himself could not shed blood, a* Christian Knight *could wield the sword of justice at the bidding of a priest."*

The assassin of a head of state had to be a Christian Knight. This would be acceptable to the Vatican. It just so happens that the church did have a legendary military society that dated back to the Crusades. This was *The Sovereign Military Order of Malta*. To become a member of this secret society, one had to be knighted by the Pope. Are there any such knighted personages who might be willing to kill a *tyrant* like JFK? As it turns out there are quite a few. Those knighted by the church in the Order of Malta include James Jesus Angleton, William Donovan, William Colby, William Casey, John McCone and General Rhinehard Gehlen. Gehlen was a Nazi Intelligence czar and organizer of Gladio in Europe. Those not named Gehlen were all OSS/CIA power brokers.

Another violent military religious order is *The Shickshinny Knights of the Order of St. John of Jerusalem*. This radical right-wing Catholic organization was founded in 1956. They considered themselves to be the *Real Knights of Malta,* and many members of the armed services belonged to this group. Author James Day lists the most notorious as General Charles Willoughby, General Pedro Del Valle, General Lemuel Shepherd, General Bonner Fellers, Col. William Potter Gale (founder of a paramilitary unit called the Rangers, who were affiliated with the John Birch Society), and Col. Phillip Corso (started the rumor that Oswald was an FBI informant). General Edwin Walker was made a member of the Order's Military Affairs Committee in 1965. His ties to Willoughby and H.L. Hunt are well known as is his partnership with Billy James Hargis in JBS fundraisers and the famous Freedom Ride of 1963. But the most interesting member of this august society was David Ferrie. Religious militarism was his obsession.

As mentioned before the Knights Templar were disbanded by the pope on November 22nd, a date that will live in infamy.

It is interesting that when the OSS evolved into the CIA there were temporary intelligence units that existed in the interim. Strange creatures like the OPC and WCC that were akin to private intelligence agencies. They were made up of the stalwarts of the old OSS and Wild Bill Donovan was their mentor. These became the nucleus of a private intelligence group that would later act independently inside the CIA, working secretly and accounting to no one. This list includes Allen Dulles, James Angleton, Bill Donovan, Frank Wisner and Bill Harvey. This private intelligence agency was the force manipulating the war against communism in Italy and France. Working with them were the mafia and the Vatican. This led to the inclusion of the Corsican mafia and later the Cuban exiles joined their arsenal of anti-communist fanatics. This was a secret team that acted on its own and without legal authority. The rogue unit that was likely behind the assassination of JFK.

Gladio was financed by importing opium, financed with laundered Nazi gold money, and turned into heroin in Corsican labs. It was then marketed to inner-city blacks in Harlem. The WCC and OPC, off-springs of the OSS and precursors of the CIA, maintained assassination squads behind the iron curtain. They created assassination training camps and used mafia killers, ex-Nazi murderers and Corsican assassins. One of the key players was George Hunter White. His employers over the years included the FBN, US Immigration, the OSS and CIA. He was part of Operation Underworld and worked with the Trafficante drug network. His list of credits also included the MKULTRA project.

CHAPTER 15

SPARKY, THE MOB AND THE DPD

The Dallas police department was rotten from top to bottom.
—Seth Kantor

I t was a matter of common knowledge in 1963 Dallas that Jack Ruby knew most of the Dallas police on a first name basis. They frequented his clubs and were given free drinks and some reports say access to his strippers. Dallas County Sheriff Steve Guthrie told the FBI that Ruby was a front man in Dallas for the Chicago syndicate. He testified that he believed that Ruby *"operated some prostitution activities and other vices in his club"* in Dallas. With these observations in mind, it becomes obvious that the Warren Commissions version of Ruby's connections between the Dallas Police and organized crime were fiction to cover-up his true role.

That is not to say that the Commission attorneys assigned to investigate Ruby weren't suspicious of his connections. That area of the report was allocated to WC Attorney's Leon Hubert and Burt Griffin. They did a commendable job and were developing leads that if pursued, would likely have uncovered conspiracy. However, Earl Warren proved himself disinterested in their revelations. In the end Hubert resigned because Warren was ignoring their findings and suggestions.

His colleague, Burt Griffin, accused Dallas Police Sgt. Patrick Dean of lying in his commission testimony. Dean reported this to Henry Wade. Wade called LBJ and LBJ confronted Earl Warren. This resulted in Warren shipping Griffin back to Washington and forbidding him to question any more Dallas police officers. When Dean went to Washington to testify, Warren actually apologized to him! More on Dean later.

Robert Kennedy had investigated organized crime and their connection to labor unions in his work for the McClelland Committee in 1957. After his brother's assassination, RFK had investigators do private research and found that phone records of Oswald and nightclub owner Jack Ruby, who killed Oswald two days after the president's assassination, *"were like an inventory"* of mafia leaders that the and the government had been investigating.

ROOM 317

Warren took Ruby's word over the testimony of more than a half-dozen witnesses who said they saw him at various times over the weekend of the assassination stalking Oswald. On Friday, November 22nd, Ruby was seen trying to enter the office of Capt. Will Fritz on the third floor of the police department. This was the room that was being used for Oswald's interrogation. The time was around 3 P.M. Dallas reporter, Victor Robinson saw Ruby try to enter Fritz' office. He heard an officer stationed at the door say, *"You can't go in there Jack."* Although Robinson is the only witness to hear this brief conversation, four other witnesses saw Ruby in that same hallway at approximately the same time. These were vice squad detective, A.M. Eberhart, DPD Detective Roy Standifer, KBOX news editor Ronald Lee Jenkins, and *Dallas Morning News* reporter, John Rutledge. All four personally knew Oswald's killer. Ruby denied being on third floor of DPD on Friday afternoon. Warren believed him and declared that the witnesses were all mistaken.

Also on Friday, prior to the incident on the third floor, reporter Seth Kantor not only saw but spoke to Ruby at Parkland Hospital at about 1:30 P.M. Kantor was a respected newsman who was trained to be observant. His testimony was corroborated by another witness, Wilma Tice. She provided the FBI with a description that matched Ruby. Wilma and her husband, James Tice, soon begin receiving threatening phone calls and Mrs. Tice reported incidents of prowlers at night while Mr. Tice was working at Love Field. A third witness was a former radio newsman named Roy Stamps. Stamps was an acquaintance of Ruby and said he had met him on about 45 different occasions prior to November 22nd, 1963. Stamps told Texas researchers that he was in the hall at Parkland Hospital holding open a telephone line to his radio station when he saw Ruby enter the building. He said Ruby was carrying some television equipment and trailing behind a TV crew he was apparently helping. Ruby used this same technique to enter the midnight press conference later that evening. Pretending to be a reporter, he tagged along with two real ones and acted like he was writing notes on a pad. He was using the real reporters who were walking on either side of him wearing press badges, as cover. Warren decided Kantor was mistaken since Ruby denied being at Parkland. In 1979, The HSCA reversed Warren's interpretation that Kantor was mistaken about his Parkland meeting with *Ruby*. The HSCA Stated that *"While the Warren Commission concluded that Kantor was mistaken, the Committee determined he probably was not."*

Since Ruby was filmed impersonating a newsman at the midnight press conference, he had to admit he was there. He couldn't deny it with the existence of photographic proof. Ruby stayed in the basement for two hours and was the last to leave. He then showed up in the KLIF newsroom at 2 A.M. and then the *Times Herald* news office until 4:30 A.M. No doubt with the help of amphetamines, he hung out in newsrooms to find out if Oswald had confessed or incriminated the conspirators.

Protocol required that Oswald be transferred from the city to the county jail.[269] On Saturday, Chief Curry announced that the transfer would occur around 4 P.M. that day. At the designated time, Ruby was seen by Sgt. D.V. Harkness at the vehicular entrance to the Sheriff's jail (about 4 P.M.). Five reporters observed Ruby hanging out both inside and outside the Dallas Police Station on Saturday afternoon. He was seen outside the building by an NBC producer watching a TV monitor and the same producer later saw Ruby on that very monitor later patrolling the third floor. Four other newsmen also saw him on the third floor as well. One of them, Thayer Waldo, took a business card from Ruby.

At 6 P.M. it was announced Oswald would be transferred on Sunday morning. After the announcement Ruby was not seen in the area the rest of the evening.

That weekend Oswald was paraded through the hallways of the Dallas Police Department incessantly for no less than 12 interrogation sessions in room 317 of the Homicide Department, plus interviews with the press. To many it appeared that they were purposely setting the prisoner up for elimination by would be vigilantes time and time again.

About 2:30 on Sunday morning, the Sheriff's office and the FBI office in Dallas (not DPD) each received an anonymous call warning that a committee of 100 citizens had voted to kill Oswald within 24 hours. *"We will be there and we will kill him."* Dallas Secret Service and FBI recommended transferring him secretly during the night. Gordon Shanklin called Chief Curry and told him he needed to cancel the morning transfer. Curry refused and that sealed Oswald's fate. Even a few of the police officers thought this suspicious. If the suspect had been moved secretly during the night, Ruby would have been off the hook with his mob overseers; Campisi,[270] Civelo and their boss

---

269   When Ruby was arrested he also was transferred to Sheriff's jail. When the moment came, he broke away from his police escorts and ran to transfer car, diving into back seat and laying on the floor the entire trip. His handlers revealed that he was shaking afterward. Was Ruby expecting the same fate as Oswald? Perhaps he knew of the ties between Sheriff Decker and Joe Civello.
270   The first visitor to see Jack Ruby in jail was Joe Campisi who owned the Egyptian Lounge. Campisi's excuse was that Sheriff Decker (Civello's friend) had asked him to visit. Jack Ruby had dinner there the night before the assassination.

Carlos Marcello. He couldn't be held responsible for an unforeseen clandestine maneuver that he had no control over. Was that the purpose of the call? At least one of the recipients of the anonymous call thought the voice sounded like Jack Ruby's. It seems probable that he didn't call DPD because most of the officers knew him well and his voice was likely to be recognized.

On Sunday morning, the transfer was delayed from 10 A.M. until after 11 under suspicious circumstances. The basement transfer was to be restricted to the press only. Dan Rather described the gathering to *"a tsunami of reporters."* So how did Ruby get in? According to one of the crew working for KLIF radio, Ruby offered to cover the transfer for KLIF. He said he was a friend of Henry Wade and could get pretty good news stories. Had this proposal been accepted, it would have enabled Ruby to enter the basement legitimately as a credentialed reporter. No one would have said; *"You can't go in there Jack."*

Ruby staged a visit to the Western Union office near the Dallas jail in order to make his shooting of Oswald look like a spur of the moment act, rather than premeditated. However, he may have given away his true intentions when he placed his billfold in his car trunk and put the key in the glove compartment before going into the Western Union office. It is a usual practice for criminals to protect their wallets from falling out during the commission of a crime.

I'LL GET BY WITH A LITTLE HELP FROM MY FRIENDS

Earl Warren asked DPD if any of their men aided Ruby in his mission. They replied with a straight face that none of their force would be guilty of such a thing. Warren believed them and that was the end of the matter. Chief Curry said that only a handful of the officers on the force knew Ruby. This was a gross understatement and amounted to an outright lie. Warren willingly accepted Curry's opinion as fact.

So who are the prime suspects in conspiring with Ruby to kill Oswald? The most likely officers to be involved were Patrick Dean, Blackie Harrison, Lt. George Butler and Harry Olsen. JD Tippit was already dead by Sunday morning and could not have assisted Ruby in getting access to the basement. However, that doesn't mean that he wasn't a possible conspirator to kill Oswald on Friday.

According to a witness at Ruby's trial; "Mr. Ruby replied that somebody had to do it, somebody had to take care of him, we couldn't do it." By we, he meant the Dallas Police Department. It's my take that the purpose of the Tippit shooting was to incite the Dallas Police to kill the cop killer, Oswald. When they failed and had him in custody, they couldn't get away with it without a little help from their "friend," Jack Ruby.

PATRICK DEAN AND BLACKIE HARRISON

It was Patrick Dean who was in charge of the basement transfer. It was he that prematurely signaled that the car to be used to transfer Oswald to the County jail was ready before it actually was. Blackie Harrison, a very large man, provided cover for Ruby among the crowd of reporters. He is seen in news footage standing next to Ruby as Oswald entered the garage. It was Dean who assigned Harrison to the basement.

Two lines of police were supposed to protect Oswald in the basement. But not only was the car not ready, but the police line hadn't yet been formed. Sgt. Lavelle said the newsmen weren't kept back where they were supposed to be. Police were backed up along the walls instead of shielding Oswald. Twice on media news film, Harrison is seen looking over his shoulder at the entrance ramp to the basement instead of watching for the prisoner he was to protect. Was he watching for Ruby? Timing was critical. If Ruby got there too early, he might be spotted and thrown out. Dean was part way up the exit ramp. Together they coordinated the incident that was about to occur. Once Ruby was in place, Dean gave the all-clear signal and Oswald walked into a trap with no protection. A sitting duck among an army of Dallas' finest. Jack Reville suspected Blackie Harrison of conspiring with Ruby to get him down the ramp. When Harrison testified before the Warren Commission, he did so accompanied by a lawyer. Why would a policeman need a lawyer when he wasn't on trial for anything?

J. Edgar Hoover's position on organized crime was that it didn't exist. That position proved an embarrassment when a conclave of major Mafioso were discovered by police meeting at the home of mobster *"Joe the Barber"* Barbara in Apalachin, New York, on November 14, 1957. This event and the testimony of Joe Valachi in 1963 were to prove fatal to the American crime syndicate. Although Marcello did not attend the Apalachin affair, he was represented by Dallas boss Joe Civello. When Civello returned from the meeting, one of his first undertakings was having dinner with Dallas Police Sgt. Patrick Dean. Dean was a close friend of Civello as well as Ruby.

HARRY OLSEN

Another suspicious Dallas police officer is Ruby's close friend, Harry Olson. The day of the assassination, Olson was working a side job guarding an *estate*[271] on Eighth Street in Oak Cliff near the Tippit shoot-

---

271   Actually a run down house. The house in Oak Cliff that Harry Olson was guarding that day was located at a spot in Oak Cliff which gave him visual observation of any of five streets which Oswald might have used in moving to his destination at the Texas Theater.

ing. His story was that he had broken his knee cap and was inactive from the force. His girlfriend Kay Coleman was a stripper at *Ruby's* club, The Carousel. She had an apartment four blocks away at 325 N. Ewing. Jack Ruby lived at 223 S. Ewing Avenue. Olson told the Warren Commission that Coleman visited him that day at the Eighth Street residence. Late that night, Ruby, Olsen, and Coleman spent two or three hours' conversing about the assassination at a downtown parking garage. Ruby later said that Olson suggested, *"they should cut the guy up in little pieces."* Olson Left town a month after the assassination and moved to California.

LT. GEORGE BUTLER

In 1948 George Butler was assigned to Chief Carl Hansson's office working narcotics for DPD and following mobsters. He and his partner Pat Gannaway[272] arrested Paul Rowland Jones as part of a bribery attempt. Jack Ruby was linked to Jones and was interrogated behind closed doors at a Kefauver Committee hearing by Butler in 1950. Ruby became of interest when Jones and his associates began hanging around Ruby's club after the trial.

According to ex-FBI agent William Turner, Jones told the FBI that Butler wanted a payoff from the mob until he heard the Texas Rangers were wise to his negotiations. Mobster Pat Manning promised Butler that gambling was all the mob wanted, and he would prevent other stuff from happening. In 1958 Butler testified at the *Investigation of Improper Activities in the Labor or Management Field*. RFK was asking the questions. Butler testified for the most part about how the mob moved in the late '40s with their coin-operated machines into Dallas and had an 18 million dollar enterprise. What he didn't reveal, however, was that in addition to gambling, the mob was also involved in illegal narcotics and prostitution in Dallas during this period. So Butler was lying to RFK. And perhaps RFK was letting it happen for political reasons.

Butler also provided information to researcher Penn Jones Jr. in 1961. Jones said that Butler told him 50% of the Dallas Police Department were also members of the Ku Klux Klan. He even wanted Jones to start a statewide Klan newspaper with him![273]

---

272   Special Service Division Chief Gannaway, who Bill Simpich calls the master of the Dallas spooks, like Butler, is everywhere in this case. He worked Narcotics, Vice and Criminal Intelligence for DPD. There are innuendos he had CIA ties as well. Another Gannaway link to Ruby is Commission Document 86. It reports that FBI SA Frank M. Ivey was advised by a Texas police officer named Robert L. Forche that the, Forche, was introduced to Jack Ruby by Mary Hartford. He believed Hartford to be Ruby's mistress. Hartford was formerly a secretary to Captain Pat Gannaway.

273   William Turner, *Ramparts Magazine*, June 1967

Butler was also involved with the Dallas Cuban Exile community and the Sylvia Odio incident. A Cuban exile named Colonel Castorr was a friend of General Edwin Walker and the H.L. Hunts, as well as Gerry Hemming and Joe Grinnan. Castorr's wife, Trudi, was an energetic worker for the Dallas Cuban Catholic Relief Fund and their activities. The Castorrs were considered in many circles one degree of separation from the JFK Assassination. Harold Weisberg interviewed Colonel and Trudi Castorr in 1967 in regard to John Birch Society Meetings. Trudi revealed that she made phone calls to Lt. George Butler of the DPD. She discussed at length how Butler was friends with Sylvia Odio and got inside information from the whole Dallas Cuban crowd.

Odio's friend, Lucille Connell sent many letters to Silvia while she (Silvia) was staying with another Dallas society matron, Mrs. John B. Rogers. When Silvia moved out, Mrs. Joanna Rogers found these letters from Connell and was concerned about their contents. She discussed this with Colonel Castorr and Trudi who suggested these letters be given to Lieutenant Butler. These letters have never surfaced nor was Butler asked to testify before the Warren Commission.

Like DPD, the Dallas Sheriff's Office was also involved with criminal elements. Sheriff Decker had once acted as a character reference for Dallas mob boss Joe Civello in a pardon application. It was Decker who had his men *stand down* and not participate in protecting the President during his Dallas motorcade.

George Butler joined the Dallas Police Force in October 1946. Paul Rowland Jones, an underworld crime boss, contacted Butler and offered him money to help him establish his gambling operation in Dallas. Butler arranged a meeting between Jones and Sheriff Steve Guthrie. Jones offered Guthrie an annual sum of $150,000. This conversation was recorded and Jones was eventually convicted of attempted bribery. Jones appealed his three-year sentence on grounds that he had been entrapped by a well-established corrupt law-enforcement system in Dallas.

Seth Kantor said that ; *"Butler's … knowledge of organized crime was so intimate that he had been the key man in the department contacted by the Chicago mob when they chose to move into Dallas in 1946 and make police payoffs"* and later he was *"loaned by the Dallas police department to aid three different US Senate investigatory groups as an expert on gangster operations."*

Did Butler play a role in helping Ruby kill Oswald? In his testimony to the commission, Thayer Waldo of the *Fort Worth Star Telegram* said that during the basement transfer of Oswald, Butler *"was an extremely nervous man, so nervous that when I was standing asking him a question after I had entered the ramp and gotten down to the basement area, just moments before Oswald was brought down, he was standing profile to me and I noticed his lips trembling as he listened and waited for my answer. It was simply a physical characteristic. I had by then spent enough time talking to this man so that it struck me as something totally out of character."*

DID RUBY KNOW OSWALD?

John Armstrong's research has revealed that a Dallas radio personality named Chuck Boyles ran a late night talk show on KLIF radio in Dallas and frequently discussed the assassination with callers. One evening an unidentified woman called and told Boyles, and his listening audience, that there were telephone calls between Ruby and Oswald. The woman explained that she worked as a telephone operator in the Whitehall exchange and not only remembered the calls, but said the telephone company had records of the calls. The woman explained that when Ruby tried to call Oswald, and was unable to get through because the pay phone Oswald was using was busy, he would call the operator and tell her that his call was an emergency. The operator would then interrupt the call, ask the callers to get off the line, and make a record of the call as required by the phone company. The woman said that Ruby used this trick so frequently that she remembered his name and numerous calls.

These "emergency call records," mentioned by the unidentified telephone operator, may have been given to the Dallas Police by the Area Commercial Manager of Southwestern Bell, Raymond A. Acker. Acker took the phone company records to the Dallas Police Department after the assassination and told the police they were proof of calls between Ruby and Oswald. Acker said that after he gave the records to the Dallas Police, he was told to go home and keep his mouth shut. Phone calls within the Dallas area, which included Irving and Oak Cliff, were not toll calls and were not recorded by the phone company. The only local calls that were recorded by the phone company were "emergency" calls (which the operator said Ruby placed to Oswald). Some of Jack Ruby's emergency phone calls may have caused Oswald to return calls to the Carousel Club. In the days leading up to the assassination Ruby's handyman, Larry Crafard, received many calls from an unknown male who never identified himself or left a message. Crafard told the Warren Commission, *"This gentleman would call maybe two or three times a day asking for Jack. He would ask where he could reach Jack. It sounded like it was pretty important that he reach Jack, and that he would never leave a number where Jack could call him back at."* When Crafard asked Ruby about these strange telephone calls he was told to mind his own business.

On November 26, 1963, Larry Crafard told SA John Flanagan that Jack Ruby's home phone number was WHitehall 1-5601. On November 29, 1963, Crafard told SA Theodore Cramer that Ruby's unlisted home telephone number was WHitehall 1-1050. Oswald's rooming house was WH 3-8993. There is no indication the FBI checked telephone company records for emergency calls placed to or from these numbers.[274] It is strange that Larry Crafard left Dallas for Michigan the day after the assassination. The Davis sisters made a similar exodus within two weeks and Harry Olson left town a month after the assassination and moved to California. Coincidences?

Larry Crafard admitted to investigator Peter Whitmey that he was a hit man in the early 60s. Crafard's brother supported this claim a few years later and added that his brother was heavily involved in the events of that weekend in November 1963. it's worth noting that Crafard, while in the army, was a crack shot. Crafard had been working with carnivals for years … where he'd learned to be a crack shot and a quick draw artist. J. D. Tippit's killer definitely was very fast on the draw (he fired four shots into the kill zone before Tippit could draw his weapon). This action suggests Oswald was not the killer. It's possible that Larry Crafard could have been at the corner of 10th & Patton at 1:09 P.M. that day. He soon escaped Dallas alive. The fact that he hastily grabbed a hand full of change from Jack Ruby's desk and went to the highway and started hitch-hiking north to the sparsely settled woods of Michigan simply screams of his guilt in the events of 11/22/63.

Another possible link between Oswald and Ruby is George Bouhe. Bouhe was a White Russian exile leader and benefactor of the Oswalds. He tutored Marina in English and paid for her dental work. He also lived next door to Jack Ruby.

On 1 November, Lee opened a post office box in the Dallas post office Terminal Annex. He would list the FPCC and the ACLU as being eligible to receive mail at this box. Coincidentally somebody else opened a post office box in that same office. On November 7, 1963, Jack Ruby rented post office box No. 5475 because he hoped to receive mail responses to advertisements for the twist-board exercise device, which he was then promoting. Although it is conceivable that Oswald and Ruby coincidentally

---

encountered one another while checking their boxes, the different daily schedules of the two men render even this possibility unlikely. Moreover, Oswald's withdrawn personality makes it improbable that the two would have spoken if their paths had crossed.

What did Ruby and Oswald have in common? Both came from dysfunctional families. Both spent time in Youth Houses for truancy. Both were analyzed by Dr. Renatus Hartogs. Both may have been bisexual, although Oswald's preferences are not clear.[275] Both were involved in some way with the Cuban revolution. Both served in the military. Both had ties to Carlos Marcello and organized crime. Both hated Walker and fascism.

An anonymous letter appearing in *Playboy* that was sent to the editor after Jim Garrison's October 1967 *Playboy* magazine interview:

"I read Playboy's Garrison interview with perhaps more interest than most readers. I was an eyewitness to the shooting of policeman Tippit in Dallas on the afternoon President Kennedy was murdered. I saw two men, neither of them resembling the pictures I later saw of Lee Harvey Oswald, shoot Tippit and run off in opposite directions. There were at least half a dozen other people who witnessed this. My wife convinced me that I should say nothing, since there were other eyewitnesses. Her advice and my cowardice undoubtedly have prolonged my life—or at least allowed me now to tell the true story ..."

This tipster's story matches that of Aquilla Clemons perfectly.

Another example of "witness neglect" was reported by 10th Street neighbor Frank Wright. Wright later told Tippit researchers that "I was the first person out. I saw a man standing in front of the car. He was looking toward the man on the ground (Tippit). The man who was standing in front of him was about medium height. He had on a long coat, it ended just above his hands. I didn't see any gun. He ran around on the passenger side of the police car. He ran as fast as he could go, and he got into his car. … He got into that car and he drove away as fast as he could see.… After that a whole lot of police came up. I tried to tell two or three people (officers) what I saw. They didn't pay any attention. I've seen what came out on television and in the newspaper but I know that's not what happened. I know a man drove off in a gray car. Nothing in the world's going to change my opinion." (Hurt, pp. 148-49)

There is evidence that the Dallas Police intimidated witnesses. Acquilla Clemens was threatened. When Vincent Salandria, Harold Feldman and Marguerite Oswald visited Helen Markham's home for an interview, her son Bill told them his mother was threatened that "there would be

---

275   Rose Cheramie portrayed them as lovers.

trouble" if she talked. They also saw DPD cars leaving her house when they showed up for a second visit. Salandria said of the Markhams; *"I have never seen that kind of terror, their teeth were chattering."*[276]

WC attorney William Ball couldn't even get Markham to admit she recognized anyone in the line-up she saw. He finally had to blurt out; *"Was there a number two man in there?"* That worked. Similarly, when Howard Brennan did not positively identify Oswald in a line-up, even after seeing him on TV, a Dallas police officer asked him, *"Does the second man from the left look most like the man you saw?*

Of course, the line-ups were totally unfair. Oswald stood out like a sore thumb. He also had to give his name and place of employment (the TSBD). Everyone knew by then that shots had come from that building. Witnesses viewed the line-ups in pairs, which is a no-no in procedure.

Buell Frazier was slapped around, questioned military style for hours and coerced unsuccessfully to sign a confession of involvement in the assassination. Billy Lovelady and Jose Molina received similar treatment.

DID RUBY KNOW TIPPIT?

Tippit used to live near a nightclub owned by Jack Ruby's sister. Ruby later took over that club. Ruby's sister, Eva Grant, was quoted as saying, *"Jack called him buddy ... Jack knew him, and I knew him. He used to come into the Vegas Club (run by Grant for Ruby) and the Carousel Club.... He was in and out of our place many times."*

In an interview with a JFK researcher, Jack Tatum, a witness to the Tippit shooting, told him that he saw Tippit at Ruby's club.[277]

Thayer Waldo, a Fort Worth newspaperman, told Mark Lane that Ruby met for two hours with Tippit and Bernard Weissman at the Carousel Club on November 14, 1963. Weissman was responsible for the full-page ad in the *Dallas Morning News* on November 22 attacking Kennedy. He was a protege of General Edwin Walker, and linked to the Minutemen. Tippit's long history of "part-time" jobs included many establishments owned by criminal elements connected to Ruby, Cuban exiles and narcotics dealers.

During testimony of Police Chief Curry on April 22, 1964, WC member, Allen Dulles asked Curry about a rumor he had heard that Officer Tippit was in some way involved in narcotic trouble. Curry said he knew nothing about it. Was this a connection between Tippit and Ruby? Peter Dale Scott, in his book *"Deep Politics and the Death of JFK,"* documents a

276   *The Realist*, September 1964
277   John Simkin, Spartacus-educational website, September 1997, (updated August 2014).

lot of evidence that Ruby was involved in international drug trafficking and that he was a payoff connection between narcotics and the Dallas Police Department as well as a contact on liquor and gambling raids.

THE MANY FEDORAS OF JACK RUBY

Jack Ruby's trademark fedora wasn't the only hat he wore. The others, however, were metaphorical. His roles included; businessman, mob courier, FBI stoolie, gun runner, drug runner, pimp, and DPD payoff bag man. He was in cahoots with cops on the take, Cuban exiles, Carlos Marcello's underlings, Santo Trafficante and Jimmy Hoffa and the Teamsters. He was in debt and susceptible to servitude and even blackmail.

On November 22, 1963, a man was arrested and taken in for interrogation because he had been "acting suspiciously" in the Dal-Tex Building that overlooked Dealey Plaza at the time JFK's assassination was taking place. The man told the police his name was Jim Braden, he was in Dallas on oil business and had gone into the building to make a phone call. Braden was released without charge. What Braden didn't tell police is that he had recently changed his name. His real name was Eugene Hale Brading, a name that boasted a long criminal record obtained while living in California. Arrested 35 times he had convictions for burglary, illegal bookmaking and embezzlement. He was notorious as a bag man for organized crime. On 21st November 1963, Brading arrived in Dallas with a man named Morgan Brown. They stayed in Suite 301 of the Cabana Motel. It was later established that Jack Ruby visited that motel around midnight on the 21st. Earlier that day, as stated above, Brading visited the offices of the son of Texas oil billionaire H.L. Hunt. It is believed that Jack Ruby was in the offices at the same time as Brading.

Braden/Brading was coincidentally near the Ambassador Hotel on June 5, 1968, at the time of the Robert Kennedy assassination.

The Cabana Motel was built with Teamster funds. Mob lawyer, Melvin Belli, stayed there when he represented Ruby in his trial. Jean Aase[278] & Lawrence Meyers stayed there and dined with Ruby at Campisi's Egyptian Lounge the night before the assassination.

Morgan H. Brown

Photo source; S.r. Dusty Rhode @ JFK's COUP

---

278   Aase's phone records include several calls from David Ferrie.

Morgan Holton Brown was one of the few people to flee Dallas immediately after the assassination. Brown and his wife were arrested in August 1964 in Brentwood Heights, CA. The *Los Angeles Times* reported that Brown, described as a "wealthy oilman," and his wife were accused of holding a policeman captive and threatening him with death. The patrolman, John Ensign, said he was on patrol and spotted Brown, who he knew was wanted on a Santa Barbara County complaint. The officer was forced to disrobe, held captive, and threatened with death. According to a witness, Brown closely resembled a fake Secret Service Agent seen on the grassy knoll immediately after the shooting in Dallas.

THE MR. HUNT LETTER REVISITED

Sometimes history can be so difficult to believe that we require fiction to make it seem plausible.

– Old Sicilian saying

In 1977, a copy of a letter was published by Penn Jones, the retired owner of a small Texas newspaper and self-published author of four books about the assassination. The *New York Times* reported that three handwriting experts had authenticated the letter. Oswald's widow also identified her husband's handwriting." Experts summoned by the House Select Committee on Assassinations in 1978 concluded more prudently that they were unable to reach a "firm conclusion" because of the absence of the original document.

Although the HSCA concluded an evaluation couldn't be made from a Xerox copy, One of the experts said it's done all the time and she would go to court and testify it was Oswald's handwriting under oath.

THE LETTER

Nov. 8, 1963

Dear Mr. Hunt,
I would like information concerning my position. I am only asking for information. I am suggesting that we discuss the matter fully before any steps are taken by me or anyone else.
Thank You,
Lee Harvey Oswald

Nov. 8, 1963

Dear Mr. Hunt,
I would like information
concerning my position.
I am asking only for information
I am suggesting that we discuss the
matter fully before any steps are
taken by me or anyone else

Thank You,
Lee Harvey Oswald

The Mr. Hunt in the letter was assumed to be CIA operative E. Howard Hunt,[279] although many concluded it might just as well be Oil billionaire, H.L. Hunt. Since the timing of the letter being made public coincided with the Watergate scandal, Howard Hunt seemed the more logical choice.

Most researchers assumed the letter to be a hoax. In the 1990s this assessment was apparently proven. In their book, *The Sword and the Shield; The Mitrokhin Archive and Secret History of the KGB*, Christopher Andrew and Vasili Mitrokhin, revealed that the letter was forged by the KGB who predictably, were anxious to lose no opportunity to promote active measures which supported the increasingly popular theory that the CIA was behind Kennedy's assassination. Its chief target was the former CIA officer turned Watergate conspirator E. Howard Hunt, who had been accused by Mark Lane of being in Dallas on the day of the assassination. According to Mitrokhin, the letter, using phrases and expressions taken from actual letters written by Oswald during his two years in the Soviet Union, was fabricated in a clever imitation of his handwriting. The implication, clearly, was that Oswald wanted to meet Hunt before going ahead with the assassination. After being "checked for authenticity" by the Third Department of the KGB's Operational Technical Direcorate, photocopies of it were sent to three of the most active conspiracy authors with a cover letter from an anonymous source who claimed to have given the original to FBI director Clarence Kelly, insinuating FBI suppression.

---

279   Since one of the copies came from Mexico City, some researchers believed that incriminated E. Howard Hunt since he was known to be in Mexico City around that time.

Mitrokhin said that the KGB was frustrated when after the note was made public, an American press campaign made an effort to divert public attention from Oswald's connections with the American intelligence community by focusing on H. L. Hunt as the recipient of the note instead. They took this as a CIA counterplot to deflect suspicion from the KGB's intended target. The targeting of a Watergate conspirator, E. Howard Hunt, was seen by them as an effort to disrupt the KGB plan.

The KGB's efforts contributed little to the growing belief in a conspiracy. If the Watergate scandal wasn't enough of a breeding ground for proof of corrupt conniving by government agencies, the obvious cover-ups of Hoover's FBI and Allen Dulles in their dealings with the Warren Commission sealed the public's lack of faith in the Warren Report. And that seemed to be the end of speculation on the Hunt Letter.

But fast forward to 2018 and like everything else in the JFK case another version of events reared its head. A lawyer and close associate of Harold Lafayette Hunt decided to share his intimate relationship with 1963's version of the richest man in the world. The informant's name was John Currington and he didn't have an agenda. He was not a conspiracy theorist or someone trying to make a buck. He was an old man who decided to share what he knew with the world before it was too late. He chose writer Mitchell Whitington to co-author the book, *H.L. Hunt, Motive & Opportunity*. One of the incidents Currington shared dealt with the infamous Hunt letter. According to Currington, the letter actually showed up in Hunt's interoffice mail system shortly after the assassination. Currington was instructed by Hunt to turn it over to the FBI. Currington's view is that Hunt feared that Oswald was possibly a listener to his *Life Line* radio program or was a reader of *Facts Forum*, his right wing newsletter. Both of these vehicles spread his pro-fascist and racist views as well as his hatred of Kennedy. There is evidence that Currington had previously produced a copy of the Hunt letter, published in the *National Enquirer*, in the 1970s soon after Hunt's death.

If this is true, and there is no reason for Currington to make it up, this means that the note was certainly written to H.L. Hunt and not E. Howard Hunt. It also means that the KGB couldn't have forged it to embarrass the CIA during the Watergate fiasco since the letter had already been in existence since 1963. Thus it was written before the assassination and not forged later. Further, it confirms that the FBI kept it secret for fourteen years! One wonders if the CIA leaked it to the press at a time when they were under fire for Watergate and accusations were surfacing that they were involved in the assassination. Possibly to take the heat off themselves and shift it to the Texas oil men. Or maybe it was really written by Oswald and that's why it was kept secret to begin with. If Oswald was acting on behalf of Hunt, there is little doubt that he would not be allowed to testify and incriminate the most powerful man in Texas.

At 5:30 P.M. on Nov. 23rd, 1963, Hunt called John Currington and asked him to check on the security at the police station where Oswald is held. Currington did so under the guise of legal work he was doing at the time. He had no problem entering and leaving the premises on three separate occasions. On one of the forays, he actually encountered Oswald in an elevator handcuffed to Captain Fritz![280] If Currington wanted to, he could have shot Oswald right there. About midnight Hunt's trusted assistant reported back to his boss about the lack of security he had encountered. Hunt instructed him to contact Joe Civello and ask him to visit Hunt's estate, Mount Vernon, for a private meeting. Currington complied. At 6 A.M. on Sunday the 24th, Civello met with Hunt at his home. A little over five hours later Jack Ruby killed Lee Harvey Oswald.

Joe Civello was not only a close friend of Ruby but was the mob boss of Dallas. He answered only to Carlos Marcello, who was the Don of Louisiana and Texas. By coincidence, Ruby just happened to have two transcripts of Hunt's "Life Line" radio program in his pocket when arrested.

A short time after the assassination and Oswald's elimination, on a Saturday morning at approximately 6:30 A.M., Hunt again called Currington and asked him to go to Hunt's offices in the Mercantile building and tell any employees there to take the day off. He also told him to lock a door connecting the two buildings that on any other day was left open. The Mercantile National Bank and Mercantile Securities Building were next to each other and took up the whole block. Hunt arrived at 8:30 A.M. A short time later a woman, whom Currington recognized as Marina Oswald, came into the lobby and took an elevator to Hunt's office. Twenty minutes later she left the building and got into a car with government plates.

Of course Marina has denied meeting Hunt at any time. Currington, however, is positive it was her. Why would the right-wing oil man be meeting the wife of JFK's assassin? Did he want to know what Oswald had told her? Did he want to pay her off? Only Marina knows the truth and she is an octogenarian and won't be around for long.

There is no doubt that Hunt was an extremely wealthy and powerful man. There is no doubt Hunt hated JFK, RFK and MLK. All you need

---

280   Fritz greeted Currington with "Meet the son of a bitch that shot the president."

for proof is to read *Facts Forum* or listen to *Life Line* broadcasts from the '60s. Hunt sank a very large amount of money into these propaganda outlets. He told Currington that the Kennedys *"had to go."* Currington related that in 1962 Hunt asked him to contact Civello, as he would do the night prior to Oswald's murder, and ask him if he would recommend a bank in Chicago. Hunt then opened a $250,000[281] checking account in the bank Civello had recommended. Was this a slush fund to be used in JFK's assassination? Chicago is the territory of Sam Giancana, a member of the CIA/Mafia plots to kill Castro.

MORE DISCLOSURES BY CURRINGTON

Currington, a first-hand witness to Hunt's activities, provides details of many other suspicious activities undertaken by Mr. Hunt.

1) Currington revealed that it was on Hunt's advice that his close friend Lyndon Johnson decided not to run in 1968.

2) In Spring of 1968 Hunt traveled to Los Angeles and stayed at the Ambassador Hotel where he had never stayed. His usual residence was the Beverly Hills Hotel on his many trips to that city. He asked Currington to contact a man named Wendell Niles. The oil man met privately with Niles, who gave him info on Bobby's itinerary in Los Angeles. After RFK was shot, it was Niles that contacted Hunt to inform him of the assassination. Hunt then had $40,000 delivered to a contact at the Ambassador Hotel. This was 4 to 6 weeks after the assassination of RFK.

3) After the killing of Martin Luther King, Hunt called attorney, Percy Foreman, and told him he was sending Currington to see him. Currington laid a briefcase with $125,000 on Foreman's desk. Foreman was James Earl Ray's attorney at this time. Foreman soon talked Ray into pleading guilty. Hunt hated MLK as much as the Kennedys.

4) It was also Percy Foreman who got Joe Civello's five-year sentence, a result of his arrest at the famous mob conference in New York state (Appalachia) in the 1950s, reversed.

5) The Teamsters and Jimmy Hoffa tried to unionize Hunt's food enterprises. This was a real cause of concern for Hunt. Currington alleged that Hunt eventually made a deal with Hoffa to keep union recruiters away from his business. Hunt's end of the bargain with Hoffa involved sending $125,000 to the union leader. In addition Hunt promised him a parole and a pardon (arranged through

---

281    $2,000,000 in today's money

Richard Nixon). Hoffa's attorney Sidney Zachary handled the transaction. The money changed hands at the Cabana Motor Hotel in Dallas.[282] After receiving a briefcase from Currington containing $125,000, Zachery left Dallas, flew to Atlanta and had dinner at a restaurant. Strangely, the restaurant caught fire while he was there. Unbelievably, only one death resulted from the fire. That was Sidney Zachary. Currington had no idea what happened to the briefcase. Later, additional payments were made to Hoffa and the Teamsters via a Louisiana Government Official.

ON THE LAMB?

As a response to both the JFK and MLK killings, H.L. Hunt left Dallas for brief periods until things cooled off. The hate messages spewed by his media outlets had focused heavily on these two individuals and death threats resulted from some of the loyalists of the two victims. After the MLK killing, J. Edgar Hoover conveniently called Hunt to ask for a personal meeting. Hunt immediately flew to Washington to meet him.

BIRDS OF A FEATHER

Very convincing books have been written and strong cases made that the assassination was carried out by the Mafia, the CIA, the Cuban Exiles, Texas Oil men, LBJ, the KGB, Fidel Castro, the Mossad, Hoover's FBI, the Military Industrial Complex and others. These suspects all had motive and opportunity. If all of them were represented by independent concentric circles on a single page, there would be a small area where they all overlapped. For example, the CIA, Mafia and Cuban exiles are simply different sides of a three-headed coin as demonstrated by the Watergate participants, those of Operation 40, the conspirators in plots to kill Castro etc. To be successful in politics you have to scratch the backs of competitive entities. Favors and protection, financing and blackmail are standard procedure for success. When the similar motivating factors such

---

282   It's a strange coincidence that Jack Ruby was seen visiting the Bon Vivant Room of the Cabana Motel about midnight on Nov. 21, 1963. Mob courier, James Braden (aka Eugene Hale Brading) was staying there at the time with his friend ex-convict, Morgan Brown. Braden had been arrested in the Dal-Tex building shortly after the assassination. In addition, Ruby's friend Lawrence Meyers and his mistress, Jean Aase (West) were also guests at the Cabana at the time. Another Cabana guest was Meyers brother Edward. Braden and Ruby had both visited the office of H.L. Hunt's son, Lamarr earlier that day as confirmed in both an FBI report and a witness, Hunt Security Chief, Paul Rothermal. Edward was in Dallas to visit the same Pepsi bottlers convention as Richard Nixon. David Ferrie, as it turns out, had connections to these suspicious characters. In the weeks preceding the assassination, Braden had visited Room 1701 at the Pere Marquette Building in New Orleans. At the time, Ferrie was working down the hall as an investigator for Carlos Marcello. At the time Oswald left New Orleans, Ferrie made a long distance phone call to a number belonging to Jean Aase (West) in Chicago.

as patriotism, acquisition of power, profits, racism, religion and hate come into play, rival and sometimes opposing groups will work together for a common cause.

H.L. Hunt was one of the most powerful men in the world in 1963. He was close to politicians and mafia figures as well. He counted J. Edgar Hoover and LBJ as intimates. If his anti-Communist obsessions were shared by others, he would have no problem financing illegal ventures behind the scenes. The important thing was that nothing could ever be traced back to him. Cutouts were essential.

A reliable source for Polish intelligence, and an American entrepreneur and owner of a number of firms closely connected to the petroleum circles of the South, reported in late November that the real instigators of this criminal deed (JFK's assassination) were three leading oil magnates from the south of the USA -- Richardson, Murchison and Hunt, all owners of major petroleum reserves in the southern states who have long been connected to pro-fascist and racist organizations in the South. While I don't believe they were solely responsible, I have no doubt that they had motive and opportunity to help finance such a venture.

In the clandestine world of intelligence, misinformation is the weapon of choice. We live in a fog of plausible deniability and countermoves designed to confuse and distort information. Counterintelligence analyst, Ann Egerter, referred to CI/SIG as the spy agency that spied on spies. Her boss, Jams Angleton, defined Counterintelligence as "… *the activity of gathering intelligence so as to confront, penetrate, and frustrate the other intelligence agencies."- "It is a Wilderness of Mirrors,"* he said, quoting T.S. Eliott. If it is designed to confuse the enemy, it is certain to confuse researchers.

SUMMARY

Always go too far, because that's where you'll find the truth.
                                                    –Albert Camus

There is ample evidence that Jack Ruby stalked Lee Oswald the entire weekend of the assassination looking for an opportunity to eliminate him. He hung around the police station bringing sandwiches and coffee to his police friends. He tried to get into the room where Oswald was interrogated but was kept out. He attended a midnight press conference in the basement of the jail disguised as a reporter. When Henry Wade explained to reporters that Oswald was a member of the *"Free Cuba Committee"* (an anti-Castro group), Ruby corrected Wade and said, *"That's Fair Play for Cuba Committee, Henry."* How did Ruby know that?

Jack Ruby told an FBI informant to "watch the fireworks" in Dealey Plaza on the day President John F. Kennedy was assassinated, the latest release of JFK files reveals. Although the President was assassinated on 22 November 1963, the interaction between Ruby and the FBI informant, identified as Bob Vanderslice, was not officially relayed to the FBI until March 1977.

My research has uncovered so much irony in the JFK case that it amazes me. The bizarre links between those involved are astronomical. Jack Ruby's "motive" for killing Oswald was that he didn't want Jackie to have to suffer through Oswald's trial, that he loved JFK, that he wanted to show that Jews had guts, and that he was infuriated by the fact that it was a Jew, Bernard Wiseman, that he believed was responsible for the Wanted for Treason full-page ad in the *Dallas Morning News* on November 22, 1963. Ironically, Wiseman later moved to Detroit where his dry cleaner was Earl Ruby.

FOLLOW THE MONEY

There is no doubt that Lee Oswald was impoverished. He moved from place to place taking low-paying temporary jobs and barely survived on unemployment compensation during the intervals in between. Yet he was able to pay off large loans in short periods, travel the world, order handbills and membership cards for an enterprise of which he was the only member. During his excursion to the Soviet Union, he stayed in the most expensive hotels, one in Helsinki and another in Moscow.

There are, of course, rumors that he was being paid as an FBI informant. This was of serious concern to the Warren Commission and became the subject of an off the record emergency meeting. Many researchers believe the CIA was providing him funds covertly. The mob is a suspect as well.

Currington's allegations insinuate H.L. Hunt as another potential financial backer.

I ran across a news clipping published during the period immediately after the assassination and even before the Warren Commission began its inquiries. The ar-

FUNDS WIRED TO OSWALD

Western Union Recalls Sending Message Prior to Assassination

Lee Harvey Oswald received small amounts of money via Western Union for several months prior to the assassination of President Kennedy, The Times Herald learned Saturday.

He sent a telegram himself—printed in a curious, crowded script—only a few days before the tragic afternoon.

Oswald was remembered at Western Union because he invariably argued with those persons who assisted him.

The sender of the sums of money—ranging up to $10 or possibly $20 at a time—was not known. Neither was the recipient of Oswald's message. Presumably, the FBI is investigating all messages involving both Oswald and his slayer, Jack Ruby, prior to the tragic weekend.

MESSAGES RECALLED

Oswald's messages at Western Union were recalled after he was shown on television.

This latest aspect of the case was revealed to The Times Herald at a time when hordes of federal agents were searching out all available clues and President Lyndon B. Johnson was appointing a potent presidential commission to investigate both the assassination and the slaying of the assassin.

The FBI already had been instructed to collect all available evidence and report it. In Washington, the Justice Department said Saturday it could not say anything at this time.

PROBE CONTINUING

"The investigation is continuing and all questions will be answered in the final report, but they will not be answered piecemeal.

"The report specifically will say what the FBI knew about Oswald,

See PROBE on Page 6

ticle, identified as being from the Wilcox Exhibit (no. 3002), reported that Oswald received small amounts of money via Western Union in the weeks leading up to the assassination. In addition it maintained that Oswald himself sent a telegram written in a *"curious crowded script"* (code?) only a few days before November 22, 1963. Strangely, neither the sender of the small $10 and $20 donations nor the recipient of Oswald's coded message, are known. It seems that employees of the Western Union office remembered Oswald when they saw him under arrest on television. He was hard to forget since he apparently gave them a hard time while doing business with them.

DOROTHY

> I *don't own a gun, I didn't have that gun. They planted that on me when they arrested me.*
>
> –Lee Oswald to Gus Rose

The real-life Dorothy who was caught up in *this tornado* of conspiracy, unlike the fictional Dorothy Gale, did not survive. Her name was Kilgallen and if anyone could have solved the JFK assassination mystery it would have been her. She slyly convinced Judge Joe B. Brown to allow her access to Jack Ruby for an interview. Brown liked the spotlight and to him Kilgallen was a movie star. One critic described him as a high school dropout who acquired a law degree by correspondence course. A third of his trials were overturned on appeals. Ruby's would be as well. Brown was writing a book about the case even as the trial was taking place. He would not allow a change of venue fearing he would not be the presiding judge if that happened.

What Dorothy learned from Ruby is not known for sure, but she told intimates that she would blow the case wide open in a new book she was writing. She was soon found dead supposedly of overdoses of drugs and alcohol. The extenuating circumstances of her demise exude suspicion. After her death all her notes for the book disappeared. She wisely had given a copy to a close friend. The close friend soon died a suspicious death and her copy disappeared as well.

Jack Ruby had been a Chicago syndicate Lieutenant who was essentially thrown out of town by the mob. He relocated to Dallas to become a payoff man with DPD. His involvement with Paul Roland Jones in an attempt to bribe Sheriff Steve Guthrie used mob-connected Dallas police Lieutenant George Butler as a go-between. The deal fell through when the Texas Rangers got wind of it. Jones was later arrested by Federal Narcotics Agents for smuggling opium into Texas from Mexico, The FBI was tipped off by an informant named Hyman Rubenstein. Hyman was the brother of another FBI informant named Jack Ruby.

Guthrie was corrupt as was his successor, ex-bootlegger, Bill Decker. A mob payoff man with mobster Benny Binion. Decker was also very close to Dallas syndicate head, Joe Civello, a lieutenant of Carlos Marcello. Sgt. Patrick Dean was also very close to Civello. Marcello controlled the Carousel Club managed by Ruby. Marcello was also the source of loans made by Ralph Paul to Jack Ruby in 1963. Ruby is also linked to Jimmy Hoffa and the Teamsters. Most of his sundry phone calls in October and November of 1963 were to Hoffa's minions. Hoffa became involved with Santo Trafficante, Carlos Marcello, Costello and Meyer Lansky in the French Corsican aided drug smuggling in the 1940s.

There is no way all these connections can be written off as coincidence. Dallas was the center where all of JFK's enemies linked up. In the middle of it all was the Dallas Police Department. DPD embodied mob influence, racist segregationists (KKK and Birchers), military intelligence (488th Intelligence Detachment) and CIA connections as well.

OSWALD VS WADE[283]

Dallas District Attorney Henry, "conviction at all cost," Wade, ended his first year as DA with 1002 convictions and only seven acquittals in 132 trials. Homicide Captain Will Fritz's clearance rate was 98% compared to a nationwide average of about 50% in other big cities. This dynamic duo seemed unbeatable in the South in 1963. Oswald would have stood no chance of a fair trial in Dallas. Even Jack Ruby, who was caught red-handed on TV murdering Oswald, had his trial verdict overturned

283   An "aborted" version or Roe vs Wade. Oswald's abortion was post-birth +24 years.

due to unfair venue. A treatise of *"Do not take Jews, Negroes, Dagos, Mexicans or a member of a minority race on a jury."* One of Wades' assistants wrote a training manual cautioning the choosing of *"free-thinkers,"* and *"extremely overweight people,"* adding, *"You are not looking for a fair juror but rather a strong, biased and sometimes hypocritical individual who believes defendants are different from them."*[284]

The Center for Public Integrity exposed 215 cases that appellate courts found prosecutorial for misconduct at trial in Texas and more than a third were in Dallas County.[285]

Today, Oswald would not have been convicted. His rights had been totally ignored by DPD. Numerous times he was paraded through the municipal building that weekend. Each time he loudly pleaded that *"someone come forward"* and give him legal representation. Yet the Dallas police claimed he didn't ask them for any. There version was that he wanted NY attorney John Abt (who represented communists) and wouldn't settle for anyone else. When asked if Oswald requested a lawyer, Captain Fritz replied;*"Oswald had not asked for counsel to that time."*

Mark Lane's Defense Brief for Oswald was printed in the December 19, 1963, issue of the National Guardian. The article included the take of the ACLU on the trial that never was;

"It is our opinion that Lee Harvey Oswald, had he lived, would have been deprived of all opportunity to receive a fair trial by the conduct of the police and prosecuting officials in Dallas under pressure from the public and News Media."[286]

They felt that *"Oswald's trial would have been nothing more than a formality."* The American Bar Association agreed.

---

284   *Prayer Man*, Bart Kamp, p. 173
285   Ibid
286   NARA 124-10371-10166

CHAPTER 16

THE GUNS OF NOVEMBER

The victim of mind-manipulation does not know that he is a victim. To him, the walls of his prison are invisible, and he believes himself to be free.
— Aldous Huxley

There is a strange background noise that permeates the environment of the events preceding the assassination of JFK. It is the residue of covert gun and drug running activities. This may reveal clues to who the real participants in the plot might be. Supplying armaments is a common denominator used by US Intelligence, Organized Crime and the Military to achieve their goals. For a second invasion of Cuba, whether sanctioned or not, weapons would be needed. These weapons, in turn, had to be paid for. Funding was accomplished through drug smuggling. It seems clear that a significant aspect of the second invasion planning manifested itself in the plots to kill Castro. At some point, the *target* of these plots flipped from Castro to JFK. If we are to know what groups and individuals were a part of the conspiracy, we need a better understanding of who was involved in these activities.

As revealed in chapter 11, it all began at the end of WWII, even before the collapse of the Axis powers. The West anticipated the next conflict would be with the Soviet Union. Anti-Communist paranoia led to Project Gladio. The goal of Gladio was establishing a stay-behind army in Europe to engage in partisan activities should Soviet aggression push westward. It later evolved into clandestine suppression of Communist political movements, particularly in Italy. The methods used were propaganda, infiltration, sabotage, terrorism and assassination. It was a *strategy of tension*. The anti-Communist army needed weapons. An international weapons cartel was developed. These weapons had to be paid for and an international drug cartel was established to provide the slush funds. Gladio terrorists were financed through front companies like PERMINDEX. Mercenaries trained anti-Communist brigades made up of Hungarians, anti-Castro Cubans, and other revolutionary forces around the world, whether real or contrived. Training camps in Florida, Texas, Louisiana and Mexico were established and soldiers of fortune hired to lead and arm the rebels. Private armies serving US Intelligence overseers.

The running of guns to arm Cuban exiles for an invasion of their homeland provides us with links to the main characters of the JFK conspiracy. The exile boot camps in Louisiana and Miami, where CIA instructors trained a private army of mercenaries for use against Castro, was a meeting place for soldiers of fortune, French-Corsican terrorists, mafioso soldiers and neo-Nazi radicals.

Former Deputy Chief Counsel of the House Select Committee on Assassinations, Robert Tanenbaum, has revealed that his committee viewed a CIA training film that he considered a "shock to the system." *"The movie was shocking to me because it demonstrated the notion that the CIA was training, in America, a separate army,' he said. 'It was shocking to me because I'm a true believer in the system and yet there are notorious characters in the system, who are funded by the system, who are absolutely UN-American! And who knows what they would do, eventually. What if we send people to Washington whom they can't deal with? Out comes their secret army? So, I find that to be as contrary to the Constitution as you can get."* What is even more shocking is what the film reveals. According to Tanenbaum, depicted in the film among the Cuban exiles were Guy Banister, David Atlee Philips, [287] Alpha 66 operative Antonio Veciana[288] and Lee Harvey Oswald. Inexplicably, the film would later disappear from the Committee's files. The Banister detective agency was also involved with collecting intelligence on the American civil rights movement, and was deeply involved with white supremacist organizations.[289]

Wendall Roache, a senior patrol inspector for the Immigration Service, testified under oath that David Ferrie took these movies at a Cuban exile training camp north of Lake Pontchartrain.[290]

After the Cuban Missile Crisis, RFK used the FBI to clamp down on these camps. JFK had promised to stop the raids and not invade Cuba as part of his agreement with Khruschev to extricate the Soviet missiles from Castro's island. There are strong indications that Oswald was working undercover for the FBI by spying on these camps. It was likely he that helped set up the Pontchartrain raid. RFK may have recognized him as one of his

---

287   CIA Western Hemisphere chief and propaganda/psy-war specialist.
288   Cryptonym-AMSHALE
289   *Let Justice Be Done,* Bill Davy
290   *A Farewell to Justice,* Joan Mellen, p48

own after the assassination and deduced that the assassination was payback for what the anti-Castro Cubans felt was yet another betrayal.[291]

The Ponchartrain Camp trainers included David Ferrie, Jean Souetre and/or Micheal Mertz, Soldiers of fortune like Jerry Patrick Hemming, Loren Hall, Lawrence Howard, William Seymour and Thomas Eli Davis. Davis was a gun runner with ties to Jack Ruby, Otto Skorzeny and international weapons dealer, Victor Oswald.[292]

These arms were smuggled via a supply route from Miami to New Orleans, and were stored at Guy Banister's Camp Street address, and then to Texas. Weapons were being stolen from Fort Hood as well as Red River arsenal in Texarkana.

Another operator in the trafficking of arms was Jack Ruby, who had his hands in both tills, being involved in dealing drugs as well as guns.

Jack Ruby can be linked to CIA terrorist, QJWIN, via Tom E. Davis, a soldier of fortune involved with Cuban exiles in Miami and New Orleans and, not surprisingly, the French OAS. On March 15, 1959, Ruby phoned and met with Davis, a CIA-connected gunrunner in Beaumont, Texas. At the time, Davis was serving a five-year sentence of probation for a 1958 bank robbery and was working for the CIA. He helped train anti-Castro units in Florida and South America. Soon, Ruby and Davis were supplying arms and munitions to anti-Castro Cubans. Ruby had been involved in Cuban gunrunning operations with the likes of Robert McKeown as well as Davis.[293] Ruby's best friend, Lewis McWillie, was a gun runner as well, working for Santo Trafficante. In addition, McWillie ran Trafficante's casinos in Cuba and later in Las Vegas.

I found an amusing news clipping dated January 4, 1961, involving McWillie. The incident occurred during the Eisenhower administration. A high school teacher named Laverne E. Kautt, age 54, was punched in the face by McWillie at Miami International Airport following the arrival of their flight from Havana. Kuatt had been in Cuba with members of the Fair Play for Cuba Committee and made a speech praising Castro and labeling

291   When did RFK know about Oswald? Was it in 1960 when he sabotaged Otto Otepka's investigation of the defector? Was Oswald part of the FBI crackdown on the CIA's exile training bases in Louisiana and Florida? Was Oswald infiltrating them and reporting back to RFK as an FBI informant? Did the Cubans, Ferrie and Banister find out and set him up as a patsy?
292   No relation to LHO.
293   After Castro overthrew Batista in January 1959, Ruby began to provide weapons, now with CIA support, to anti-Castro Cubans. When JFK was assassinated, Davis was in jail in Algiers, charged with running guns to the secret army terrorist movement (OAS), who were then attempting to assassinate French Premier Charles de Gaulle. Ruby also had another close friend and owner of Dallas radio station KLIF, Gordon McLendon. In 1978, the House Select Committee on Assassinations discovered that McLendon was then working closely with JFK assassination suspect David Atlee Phillips.

Eisenhower and other American leaders as "a bunch of imperialists." McWillie asked him to repeat what he said, tore off his glasses and "let him have it." Instead of McWillie being charged with assault, the teacher was disciplined by his school board. His superintendent said he would be fired if he was found to be a communist. It was the McCarthy Era!

When asked by his lawyer, Tom Howard, if he knew of anything that would be damaging to his defense, Ruby said, "*Thomas Eli Davis.*"[294] Davis was also an informer for FBN and met with French drug traffickers including Souetre and likely Mertz and Trafficante. The drug running network was run out of Marseilles by Santo Trafficante and Carlos Marcello using the French Coriscan cartel. Michael Mertz was their supplier in these activities.

Reporter George Carter's version of the acquaintanceship of Davis and Ruby is that Davis met Ruby at a party in 1958. Seth Kantor's version is that Davis walked into Ruby's club with a plan to use strippers in a stag movie. Kantor claimed Ruby and Davis shipped arms to Cuba and the WC knew all about it.

Davis's wife, Carolyn Hawley Davis[295] confirmed that Tom Davis knew international drug dealer, Victor Oswald[296] and met with him and Otto Skorzeny in Madrid. She also confirmed that Davis and Lee Oswald knew each other and had been together for a few days in Mexico City at a hotel. June Cobb

---

The Miami News
Wed, January 4, 1961

Boot For Socked Teacher?

A Chicago school teacher, punched in the nose by a Miamian for his alleged praise of Fidel Castro, faced disciplinary action today by his school board.

Lewis McWillie, 50, of 3631 SW 18th Ter., former manager of Havana's Tropicana night club, belted Laverne E. Kautt, 54, at Miami International Airport after they landed from Havana last Monday.

Kautt, a teacher of typing, bookkeeping and transcription at a Chicago high school, had been in Cuba with members of the Fair Play for Cuba Comittee.

DEFENDED

McWillie said that at the Havana airport, Kautt made a speech defending Castro and calling President Eisenhower and other American leaders "a bunch of imperialists."

At Miami, McWillie invited Kautt to repeat his remarks. He said Kautt made a move as if to hit him and that he then yanked off the teacher's glasses and "let him have it."

VIOLATION

Chicago Assistant School Superintendent Richard C. McVey said Kautt would be fired if he is a member of the Communist Party.

McVey added that such membership is a violation of the non-Communist oath all Illinois teachers must take.

Kautt denied the comments attributed to him and called the fracas a "misunderstanding."

---

294   Ruby told Howard that "he had been involved with Davis, who was.. entangled in anti-Castro efforts and that he (Ruby) had intended to begin a regular gunrunning business with Davis. Ruby warned Howard about this connection, and feared that if it were to be revealed by either an investigative reporter or a witness it would blow open the CIA's role in JFK's assassination. .nance). Being connected to Schlumbergers meant connected to PERMINDEX as well.

296   Victor Oswald, like everybody else in our investigation, was a former OSS officer,

also saw Davis and Oswald together at Hotel Luma in Mexico City[297] and her friend, Elena de Paz identified Davis as being one of the "hippie types"[298] accompanying Oswald at the Duran twist Party. Cobb described Davis as tall, lanky, blond hair, with a lethargic, drawling manner and cow-boy-like.[299] Win Scott told Cobb not to discuss Davis anywhere, or "*commit it to any sort of writing, official or unofficial.*"

One source says Davis was arrested Dec. 8, 1963, in Tangiers, Morocco for gun dealing with anti-Algerian terrorists (OAS). Another source says he was *released* from jail in Algiers on November 22, 1963.[300] It is likely he was arrested twice and both are right. Either way, at the time of his arrest, Davis was carrying a letter in his own hand-writing referring to Oswald and the JFK assassination. If the second source is correct then the letter was evidence of advance knowledge of the assassination. He was released almost immediately through the efforts of QJWIN, a principal asset in the Agency's ZRRIFLE assassination program.[301] Davis was not only in New Orleans in the summer of 1963, but told newsman George Carter that he used the name "*Oswald*" while in North Africa.[302] Ruby's relationship with Davis allegedly began prior to a 1959 deal on which they collaborated to buy and ship jeeps to aid Castro in Cuba.

When arrested in Tangiers, Davis was charged with trying to sell two Walther pistols. Although the sale ... of pistols was a minor offense, Moroccan officials decided to detain Davis because of an unsigned letter in Davis's handwriting referring in passing to "*Oswald and the Kennedy assassination.*" The letter was addressed to Attorney Thomas G. Proctor,[303] a political contributor to Lyndon Johnson. The letter closed by advising Proctor to contribute to LBJ's campaign. Odd??

---

297   *In 2015 June Cobb told H.P. Albarelli that in Sept '63 she was aware of Davis's presence in Mexico City with LHO but not aware of his identity. (p 178 Coup in Dallas)*

298   *Davis wore a goatee and looked more beatnick than hippie. But to a foreigner the designations were indistinguishable.*

299   *H.P. Albarelli Jr., Coup in Dallas*

300   *Army cryptologist Eugene Dinkin reportedly intercepted the Kennedy plot among the coded message traffic tied to the CIA-OAS group Davis was involved with. Dinkin began a campaign of trying to warn authorities and even RFK on October 25th in Luxembourg. Both Albert Osborne-a.k.a. Bowen and the unfortunate Dinkin were flown out of Luxembourg on December 5, 1963, three days before the alleged arrest of Davis.*

301   *CIA Inspector General's report*

302   *Crossfire, Jim Marrs, p207.*

303   *Proctor had dealings with Victor Oswald in Spain and was, in fact, his legal counsel. Proctor was also an associate of June Cobb. It is interesting that he and George de Mohrenschildt had lived at the same address in NY at different times. Being an official representative for Chase Manhattan Bank in Spain also provides a link to Warren Commissioner John J. McCloy.*

Researcher H.P. Albarelli, discovered that Moroccan authorities had questioned Davis about an American named Howard Loeb Schulman who was allegedly in Tangier peddling pro-communist propaganda. Reports that Oswald and Schulman were in Tangier at the same time were determined to be erroneous by the FBI. On December 20th, Hoover sent a memorandum by courier, the subject of which was *"Lee Harvey Oswald, Internal Security."* The memorandum scarcely mentioned Oswald but focused on Davis and Schulman. Another memorandum revealed that Schulman was arrested by Moroccan police after having reportedly stated that he was wanted by US authorities in connection with the assassination of JFK. I have been unable to obtain any information on the elusive Schulman and he remains a mystery. The only source on him seems to be Hoover's reports. They portray Schulman as professing pro-Castro sympathies and making an unauthorized trip to Cuba. They also give indications that he had suicidal tendencies.

THOMAS ELI DAVIS III
GUN RUNNER AND SOLDIER OF FORTUNE

Davis enlisted in the Army after high school. Reports of him being involved in Army intelligence are unconfirmed. There is also confusion over FBI reports stating he was stationed in Korea during that war and was even a POW. Since his military records were destroyed, there is not much really known about his military history. He was honorably discharged in Feb of 1957. However, since his service was from 55-57, it seems impossible that he could have served in the Korean conflict or that he was a POW. Was this a cover story? Dick Russell's take is that Davis served a five-year stint and was discharged in 1958 and that Davis told the FBI he was part of a Ranger battalion in Korea.  Davis told a nephew that he had been personally involved in the Bay of Pigs invasion. Was this guy a disinformation agent or what?

In addition to using Oswald's name, he mimicked LHO in his ability to receive passports on a moment's notice. Journalist, Seth Kantor wondered how Davis received his New Orleans passport so quickly in spite of the fact that he was a convicted felon. Shades of Oswald.

Davis also attempted recruiting men for an invasion of Haiti. Oddly, Hoover claimed this effort involved an innocent attempt to acquire background information for an article he was planning to write. What Hoover failed to mention was that Davis had never written any articles and never acted as a journalist at any time. Davis died from accidental electrocution in Jacksboro in 1973, supposedly in the act of stealing copper wire.

Like Richard Case Nagell, Davis feigned robbing a bank. This was in Detroit in 1958.[304] He handed a teller a note but changed his mind. He was arrested and pleaded guilty. He got a suspended sentence with 5 years probation dependent on getting *psychiatric* treatment at a Michigan facility. Like Nagell, he did actually spend time in such a facility. His stay was at the Lafayette Clinic.[305] Lafeyette Clinic was funded by CIA as part of *MKULTRA*. Nagell's Lafayette files, like the military files of Tom Davis, were destroyed. Jolyon West was one of the contractors that visited Lafeyette. Lashbrook[306] and Gittinger were there also. Davis's doctor, Ernst Rodin had been a member of the Hitler Youth movement and briefly served as a Nazi soldier before leaving Europe. His protege was Jolly West.[307] West, of course, treated Ruby shortly before his death. West was an MKULTRA doctor and administered LSD liberally. He was involved in the Patty Hearst trial and was part of Angleton's CHAOS program that involved Charles Manson. Davis and Nagell weren't the only individuals with information regarding the assassination to be institutionalized for "psychiatric" treatment. Others include Ralph Leon Gates[308] and Abraham Bolden. The patients were drugged and suffered sleep deprivation and psychic driving, techniques associated with the MKULTRA program.

Jack Ruby may have been an MKULTRA subject as well. He reported to psychiatrist Dr. Walter Bromberg, that he remembers going down the ramp and seeing Oswald, but doesn't remember anything else until he found himself struggling with officers." Sounds exactly like Sirhan Sirhan's version of the RFK assassination. Post-hypnotic suggestion to erase memory of the crime is an essential part of the MKULTRA process.

Oswald has been suspected of being an MKULTRA subject in light of his stationing at Atsugi and his earlier proximity to CIA-funded Bordentown Reformatory in New Jersey as an adolescent in NY City. His in-

---

304   Nagell was a United States Army veteran and former CIA double agent. He was arrested on September 20, 1963, after he entered the State National Bank in El Paso, Texas and fired two shots into the ceiling of the bank.

305   Nagel received psychiatric treatment at Walter Reed Hospital.

306   It was Lashbrook who was present when Frank Olson plunged to his death from a NY City hotel in 1953.

307   For more on West, Lashbrook and Gittinger see *The Other Oswald, A Wilderness of Mirrors*.

308   Gates picked up a hitchhiker in Oak Cliff with a package of "curtain rods," who discussed how the president could be shot from a window. He dropped him off near the TSBD two days before the assassination.

terview by Dr. Renatus Hartogs[309] was used by the Warren Commission as evidence of Oswald's psychological abnormality. Author, Dick Russell, has uncovered that Hartogs played a role as a doctor in the CIA's MKULTRA program. Hartogs had been involved in mind altering drug experimentation at the New York Psychiatric Institute (NYPSI). During WWII the OSS and from 1951-54 the CIA and Army Intelligence conducted behavior modification and mind control experiments at Bordentown. Is it a coincidence that George Hunter White used the Bronx zoo, Brooklyn Park and the Museum of Natural History as rendezvous to meet clients? When Oswald was a kid in New York he hung out at the zoo regularly when playing hooky from school. His half-brother, John Pic took Lee to the Museum as well. Dr. Carl Pfeiffer was involved in mind-control projects for the CIA and gave LSD and amphetamines to boys at Bordentown in efforts to induce psychosis. Another psychiatrist at NYPSI was Dr. Sydney Malitz. Malitz was involved with his boss Dr. Paul Hoch in the death of a professional tennis player named Harold Blauer who died after being injected with a mescaline derivative at the New York institute in a project funded by the Defense Department. Hoch, like Hartogs was a German born doctor who came to the US with the help of Allen Dulles. Hoch also worked at Bordentown and was involved in contracts with the CIA and US Army involving psychosurgery, convulsive therapy, LSD, mescaline and other drugs. As for Malitz, he was involved at Camp Dietrich (along with Frank Olson) experimenting on children and teenagers without their consent.

Robert Webster's employment at RAND Corporation and Christopher Bird, as well as H.J. Rand's link to MKULTRA Sub-Project No. 79, is evidence of his involvement in mind control projects. Also, his link as *Guide* 223 to Air-Force Intelligence[310] and Project LONGSTRIDE while in the Soviet Union are suggestive as well.

Make note of the name Dr. Willis Gibbons on the above document. Gibbons was chief of the CIA's Technical Services Section and Sydney

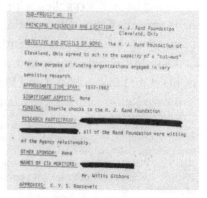

---

309   A 1996 article in the New York Times revealed that Hartogs was accused by a woman whom he had treated of inducing her to enter a sexual relationship with him during the course of her therapy. Hartogs had to pay a compensation of $350,000.
310   The CIA often used Air Force cover for projects.

Gottlieb's boss! After the death of Frank Olson, Sheffield Edwards summoned Gottlieb and Gibbons to meet him as soon as possible in Gottlieb's Quarters Eye office. Could this have been to coordinate a cover-up in Olson's death?

THE MOST DANGEROUS MAN IN EUROPE[311]

Otto Skorzeny was Hitler's go-to guy for impossible missions. It was he that in 1943, rescued Mussolini from confinement in the Abruzzi mountains. The Nazi SS officer made this daring raid using gliders and a handful of commandos.

After the Valkarie assassination attempt on the Fuhrer, it was Skorzeny who carried out the torture for the would-be assassins. In 1944, he led an SS unit to the Budapest royal palace and arrested the Hungarian leader Admiral Miklos Horthy. In the course of the Germans' Ardennes offensive during Christmas week 1944, Skorzeny directed the infiltration of hundreds of English-speaking Germans clad in US uniforms behind the Allied lines. This was a war crime in itself.

Skorzeny surrendered to the allies after WWII. At his trial, high-ranking members of SOE and OSS came to his defense. Allen Dulles and the OSS were champing at the bit to get Skorzeny into their fold as Operation Paper Clip began to unfold. Not surprisingly, the Waffen SS Colonel was found not guilty. Strangely, he then *escaped* and went underground. It seems this scenario was orchestrated by SOE and OSS officers. He then became part of a secret paramilitary group formed to conduct covert warfare against Communist expansion in Europe and prepare for war against the Soviet Union. He was also used to liquidate double agents and others who were threats to the west. The group worked in concert with CIA and MI6. This is obviously part of Operation Gladio. The German government admitted in 2014 that a *"shadow army"* to defend Germany against Soviet invasion had been in existence in the years following WWII. Skorzeny was part of this contingency or stay-behind army. He, like General Reinhard Gehlen, had extensive knowledge and contacts with former German intelligence networks that were absorbed and utilized by US intelligence in the immediate post war period.

Skorzeny located in Spain and started an import-export business that in actuality was a cover for black-market connections and underworld networks. One of these was the ODESSA network that helped smuggle Nazi war criminals out of Allied Europe to Spain, South America and other

311   What the Allies called Skorzeny during WWII.

friendly destinations so they could avoid prosecution for war crimes and perhaps form a nucleus for a Fourth Reich. His agents provided information crucial to US Intelligence. He also became an arms dealer, front man, and advisor. He established an *industrial complex* in Madrid that became a cover for his private intelligence network. His role was supplying clandestine intelligence and support to the CIA and US military. Ironically, it was two members of the Warren Commission who were instrumental in the establishment of Skorzeny as a covert asset and were aware of his secret network. They were Allen Dulles and John J. McCloy. *Skorzeny's commando organization for hire was named International Fascista.*[312] *McCloy had been High Commissioner of Germany after WWII and was instrumental in pardoning Nazi war criminals, including many convicted in the Nuremberg trials. During his reign a third of the Nazi prisoners at Lansburg Prison were set free. He was a known admirer of Adolf Hitler, played a role in Japanese American interment in the US, and later was appointed alongside his good friend Allen Dulles on the Warren Commission.*

Mae Brussell's research concluded that "SS Colonel Skorzeny's CIA agents participated in terror campaigns waged by Operation 40 in Guatemala, Brazil, and Argentina. Skorzeny was also in charge of the Paladin mercenaries, whose cover, MC Inc., was a Madrid import-export firm."

According to the author, Ralph Ganis, who obtained Skorzeny's personal papers, *"Skorzeny became an independent paramilitary adviser to US and French Intelligence*[313] *in the early 1950s … the presence of these men in the Skorzeny papers indicates the experience level and lethality of Skorzeny's paramilitary network"*[314]

Ganis also provides convincing circumstantial evidence indicating that Skorzeny's profile regarding his travels and operations with the CIA indicate that he was involved in the elusive QJWIN program.[315]

In 1947, the CIA purchased Southern Air Transport (SAT). Based in Miami, Florida, this cargo airline then became a front company for the Agency. It was immediately put at the disposal of Otto Skorzeny. In the 1980's this fleet played a role in the Iran-Contra affair, carrying weapons bound for Iran from the US to Israel, and carrying weapons destined for

---

312   Mae Brussell article "The Nazi Connection to the JFK assassination," *The Rebel* January 1984.
313   Reading between the lines suggests that French Intelligence asset, Micheal Mertz was an operative under Skorzeny in the QJWIN project used in Bill Harvey's ZRRIFLE program. French-Corsican terrorists like Mertz and Souetre were mercenaries and international assassins for hire.
314   *The Skorzeny Papers*, Ralph Ganis, p242
315   Ibid, p328

the Nicaraguan Contras from Portugal. It was the shooting down of an SAT flight in Nicaragua in October 1986 that helped expose Iran-Contra.

This CIA document refers to an article published in Peru in 1966 that exposes a plan to kidnap Castro called "Project Tropical," was approved by Allen Dulles but vetoed by JFK. The kidnapper was to be Otto Skorzeny.

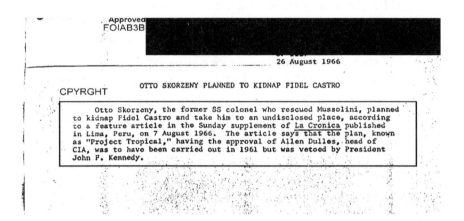

Approved
FOIAB3B

26 August 1966

CPYRGHT
OTTO SKORZENY PLANNED TO KIDNAP FIDEL CASTRO

Otto Skorzeny, the former SS colonel who rescued Mussolini, planned to kidnap Fidel Castro and take him to an undisclosed place, according to a feature article in the Sunday supplement of La Cronica published in Lima, Peru, on 7 August 1966. The article says that the plan, known as "Project Tropical," having the approval of Allen Dulles, head of CIA, was to have been carried out in 1961 but was vetoed by President John F. Kennedy.

JEAN RENE SOUETRE

Souetre was a decorated military hero and winner of five military citations, including two combat medals. A paratrooper in the French air commandos, he deserted in 1961 and joined the OAS (French Secret Army Organization). This group rebelled against de Gaulle over his giving independence to Algeria, a decision influenced by President Kennedy. This organization was essentially a right-wing terrorist group made up, in large measure, of French military deserters. Souetre was at one time one of the two most wanted men in France. Suspect in not just one, but at least two assassination plots against National Heads of State including Charles de Gaulle, his reputation as a terrorist and assassin was not unfounded.

According to a CIA document on Souetre released in 1992; *"On 5 March 1964, Mr. Papich[316] (FBI) advised that the French Legal Attache in Paris and also the SDECE (French Intelligence) had queried the Bureau in New York City concerning the subject (Souetre) stating that he was expelled from the US at Fort Worth or Dallas 48 hours after the assassination (of JFK). He was in Fort Worth in the morning and Dallas in the afternoon. The French believe that he was expelled to either Mexico or Canada."*

---

316   Sam Papich was an FBI agent and in 1961 was investigating Sam Giancana. He informed Hoover of the CIA/Mafia assassination plots against Castro. Later he became the FBI's liaison officer with the CIA.

Apparently, he wasn't alone. He was accompanied by Jean Paul Filiol, a fellow French terrorist. Strange, what would terrorist/assassins be doing in Dallas on Nov. 22? I wonder? Probably just a coincidence (hardly likely).

Souetre's version of these events is that it was Micheal Mertz, who often used his (Souetre's) name, who was in Dallas in November, '63. Mertz was known to have been in New Orleans in the early '60s. He had infiltrated the OAS as a double agent, also working for French Intelligence (SDEC). Mertz was a legendary figure during WWII. A marksman and leader, he was decorated by de Gaulle himself for capturing 400 enemy prisoners and killing 20 Gestapo agents. He was captured and escaped four times.

JFK Records Act documents (1992) tell of Souetre being seen at Cuban exile training camps at Lake Pontchartrain. Was this Souetre or Mertz? Others frequenting the camps included Frank Sturgis, Gerry Patrick Hemming, David Ferrie, who was an instructor there, and Lee Harvey Oswald. Souetre also supposedly met with William Harvey at Plantation Key, with E. Howard Hunt (of Watergate and Bay of Pigs infamy) in Madrid in March-April 1963, and with General Edwin Walker in April-May 63 in Dallas.[317]

The OAS is known to have had contact in New Orleans with anti-Castro groups. It was at the Pontchartrain camps, as an operative in the OAS Mandeville cell, that Souetre worked closely with elements of the CIA helping to train Alpha 66 and 30th November anti-Castro groups. Their headquarters was 544 Camp Street in New Orleans.[318] Both Frank Sturgis and Gerry Patrick Hemming worked with the New Orleans branch of the Cuban Revolutionary Council (CRC) which was headed by Sergio Arcacha Smith. At one time E. Howard Hunt ran operations out of the CRC Camp Street address.

In the document below, the *Madrid clandestine interrogation center* appears to refer to the role of William Harvey in getting *mechanics* in place on 22 November 1963. These European untraceable assets were to be provided by Skorzeny. The connection between the QJWIN for ZR/RIFLE programs link Harvey, Skorzeny and Souetre in clandestine operations. Jean René Souetre and Jean-Paul Filloil, both were in Dallas and deported within hours of the assassination. Were they members of sniper teams run by Harvey?

317   *The Man Who Knew Too Much*, Dick Russell interview with Gilbert Le Cavelier
318   *JFK: The French Connection*, Peter Kross, p.264

HARVEY #3

Exh. #13

3 May 1962

MEMORANDUM FOR RECORD

SUBJECT: Minutes of Meeting of Special Group (Augmented) on
Project Mongoose, 3 May 1962

PRESENT: General Taylor; Mr. Kennedy; Mr. Johnson; Mr. Gilpatric,
General Decker, General Lansdale and General Craig;
Mr. McCone, and Mr. Harvey

1. General Lansdale gave an interim report on the progress
of stepping up recruitment of Cubans into the U. S. Army. He said
the consensus is that there are not more than a thousand suitable
individuals from whom additional recruits could be selected. The
Attorney General commented that the President wishes to have a large
number. General Lansdale said that various alternatives for training
of such Cubans are being looked into.

It was agreed that such a cadre of Cubans would be an asset
to the U.S., which might be used in a number of ways. General
Lansdale, supported by General Taylor, pointed out that in this
connection the matter of holding the individuals and giving them
useful employment after they are trained is an important and a
difficult one.

2. Mr. Harvey gave a rundown on progress to date with agent
teams and in the general field of intelligence, including the
Opa-locka interrogation center and the Madrid clandestine interrogation center. He outlined various difficulties encountered, and said
that three agent teams have been infiltrated and that five W/T sets
are in place. Approximately 72 actual or potential reporting sources
are also in place. A significant development is that Major Duque has
refused to allow agents responsive to him to be dispatched on purely
intelligence-gathering missions. (This sort of attitude had been
forecast earlier as a possibility, but it now assumes particular importance in view of Duque's stature.)

3. Mr. Harvey also commented on the two attempts made to intrude
into Havana TV programs. The Group asked that a check be made, as
soon as possible, on how effective these operations were. They also
asked that a copy of the scripts used be made available. The Group
felt that it is worthwhile to check this capability out, as is now
being done, but questioned whether once proved effective it should not
perhaps be kept in reserve for a more meaningful time.

Thomas A. Parrott

cc: General Lansdale

CIA HAS NO OBJECTION TO
DECLASSIFICATION AND/OR
RELEASE OF THIS DOCUMENT
12 Jan 94

PROPERTY OF
THE WHITE HOUSE OFFICE

How can Souetre or Mertz be tied to the conspiracy to kill JFK? Both
were terrorists and assassins. Both had been used by Bill Harvey in his
ZRRIFLE assassination program as well as by the mafia for the same
purpose. Mertz, at least, was part of an international drug cartel affiliated
with the likes of Santo Trafficante and Carlos Marcello. Both were expert
marksmen and trained assassins. Both harbored hatred for JFK over the
Algerian affair. I believe both were part of the QJWIN program. Soue-

221

tre was the chief trainer for Otto Skorzeny in his Madrid camp. He was also tied to General Walker and running guns through Banister's New Orleans network. He met Bill Harvey at Plantation Key, FL, as well as Lake Ponchartrain. He met LHO at the CIA training camp in Florida, as well as Ponchartrain. He met with E.H. Hunt in Madrid in April or May 1963. He met with Bringuier in New Orleans and then went to Dallas to meet with Walker on April 30th. From there he went to Ponchartrain with Thomas E. Davis to help train exiles.

SUMMARY

Thomas E. Davis said he was arrested in Algiers on the day of the assassination and was using the name Oswald at the time. It actually appears that he was arrested twice in Tangier. The first time being Nov. 22 and the second, Dec. 8th. He frequently used Oswald's name as an alias in his travels. However, it's not clear if it was Lee or Victor Oswald he was pretending to be. Davis was released in Tangier through the efforts of QJWIN. The QJWIN operation was an assassin recruiting project run by the CIA. QJWIN is now known to have been Jose Marie Andre Mankel, however, it seems that there were others. These were QJWIN2, QJWIN3 etc… It is known that Otto Skorzeny was a leading figure in the QJWIN program. Since the program recruited Corsicans, Jean Souetre and Michael Mertz are likely participants. All of these men were involved in gun and drug running. Journalist Seth Kantor wrote that Davis settled in Beaumont, TX and began to run guns to CIA units training in Florida and South America. His trip to Morocco was done to run guns to "secret army terrorists" (OAS) attempting to kill de Gaulle. These attempts were financed by PERMINDEX, a CIA front of which Clay Shaw was a board member.

Lee Oswald was seen in Mexico City in the company of Tom E. Davis by CIA operative June Cobb[319] as well as Carolyn Hawley Davis. Oswald, or a look-alike, was also seen in Tangier in 1962 and 63 at a beatnik hangout with Davis and a man named Marc David Shleifer. Schleifer was an American Marxist and journalist deeply involved with the FPCC. it's very doubtful this was really Oswald but someone using his name is a possibility. Oswald was supposedly seen with Howard Schulman in Tangier. But the FBI determined this to be a false flag.

---

319   For more on June Cobb see *The Other Oswald, A Wilderness of Mirrors.*

It seems that efforts to tie Oswald with conspirators was an international modus operandi. The Odio incident in Dallas, Davis and others in Tangiers and the FPCC meeting in Miami with Policarpo Lopez.

The gun running phase of operations reveals connections between Tom Eli Davis, Jack Ruby, Lewis McWillie, Victor Oswald[320] and Otto Skorzeny,[321] Mitch Werbell,[322] Guy Banister and David Ferrie, French terrorists Souetre and Mertz, military dealers, Nonte and McKnight (Fort Hood and Red River), John Thomas Masen and Manuel Orcarbrerra.

Shadows of MKULTRA's influence permeate episodes of *"psychiatric"* treatment of individuals who *knew too much* and were threatening to reveal the truth. These included Thomas Eli Davis, Eugene Dinkin, Richard Case Nagell, Robert Webster, Ralph Leon Gates and Abraham Bolden and Lee Harvey Oswald. All were institutionalized in facilities funded by the CIA for psychiatric treatment involving sleep deprivation, psychic driving and drugs. The name Jolly West rears its familiar head in many of these incarcerations.

Harvey was banned to Rome after his efforts to sneak militants into Cuba for unauthorized raids during the Missile Crisis of 1962. I found a strange document emanating from Harvey in Rome immediately after JFK was shot. It involved an investigation done by the Italian government. The report was requested by Italian Defense Minister Andreotti and pertained to the weapon found in the TSBD. The report, printed in the Italian and foreign press, stated that the weapon used by Oswald was identified as a Model 91, 7.35-caliber, 1936 modification of Austrian origin derived from the Steyer. The report goes on to say the statement in the press that the rifle was a Manlicher Carcano of Italian origin is in *error*. Further, it identified the Mauser as a Hungarian rifle whose clip loader was adopted for the Italian "model 91."

---

320   Victor Oswald was a Swiss National, member of OSS, in business with Skorzeny in Madrid (international arms trafficking) and had a hand in training camps outside New Orleans (Banister-Camp Street-weapons-Cubans-Ponchartrain). *The Skorzeny Papers* by Major Ralph Ganis makes it clear that Victor Oswald was a major partner of Skorzeny. Ventures included arms sales, aircraft and aircraft parts, machine parts and industrial equipment. Shipped to Middle East and Latin America and Africa.

321   A 1958 CIA memorandum describes Skorzeny as; "Grand master of arms traffic for Algeria is former Nazi officer of the SS, Subject, who is installed in Madrid is a principal military advisor to Nasser in Egypt."

322   Soldier of fortune and arms merchant who developed small arms for intelligence services including Mexican DFS. He was a developer of silencers for assassins. His expertise in silencers no doubt played a role in Dealey Plaza.

CHAPTER 17

CANADIAN CAPERS

We seek a free flow of information.... We are not afraid to entrust the American people with unpleasant facts.... For a nation that is afraid to let its people judge the truth and falsehood in an open market is a nation that is afraid of its people.

— JFK (February 26, 1962)

In his book, *De Dallas à Montréal,* Screenwriter and video director, Maurice Phillipps explored the phenomena of coincidence in many pieces of information concerning the assassination of John F. Kennedy leading to Montreal and to Canadian characters. He deduced that his conclusions reveal the ignorance of Americans to the importance of the Montreal Mafia and it's connections to the American Cosa Nostra. Let's examine Phillipp's list of trails leading from Dallas to Montreal:

A 1964 FBI document (CE 2195) revealed that on a bus trip to Mexico City in September 1963, Lee Harvey Oswald was accompanied by an ex-chaplain in the Canadian Army using the alias Jack Bowen.[323] Once back in the United States, this Montreal resident was issued a passport at the Canadian Consulate in New Orleans. The name on the passport was that of Albert Alexander Osborne. Canadian officers granted him this passport even though no one could testify to his true identity. Even stranger, the address he gave the authorities was in reality that of the Montreal YMCA. Another interesting coincidence is that the Canadian Consulate in New Orleans was conveniently located in Clay Shaw's International Trade Mart.

WHO WAS ALBERT OSBORNE?

Documents unearthed in the 1970s show the FBI had regarded Osborne as a major suspect in its massive JFK assassination investiga-

---

323   Osborne was identified by six witnesses as the man who was seen sitting next to Oswald on a Red Arrow bus to Mexico City on September 26, 1963. Strangley, the name Jack Bowen was on Oswald's library card as a sponsor. As revealed earlier, that Jack Bowen was a co-employee of Oswald's at Jaggars-Chiles-Stovall. Like Oswald's travel companion on the Mexico City bus trip, the Dallas Jack Bowen was an alias. His real name was Jack Grossi. Two Jack Bowens? Pairs of everything permeate the assassination.

tion. Bob Gemberling, a leading FBI investigator, stated that Osborne was one of the few men "we had a separate file on." Albert Alexander Osborne, a soldier turned Soviet spy, was also known as John Howard Bowen. Bowen claimed to be an itinerant preacher and missionary, raised in an orphanage in Pennsylvania. He made frequent trips to and from Mexico to Texas, Alabama and beyond. Osborne was described elsewhere as the head of an assassination squad based in Mexico.

As mentioned earlier, Osborne was likely the source of the phone call to the *Cambridge News* warning of big news less than one half hour before JFK's assassination was announced.

The Garrison investigation revealed that, as an agent of the CIA, Clay Shaw associated with Mortimer Bloomfield,[324] a Montreal lawyer and former Major in the OSS. Both were on the board of directors of CMC PERMINDEX. PERMINDEX at one time was based in Montreal. According to Garrison witness Jules Ricco Kimble, Ferrie invited Kimbell to accompany him on a flight to Montreal in the summer of 1963.[325] Clay Shaw was also a passenger on that flight. Kimble later admitted to have furnished, in 1968, a false identity to James Earl Ray, the patsy in Martin Luther King's assassination. The passport given to Ray had been forged in a Montreal office used as a front by the CIA.

Montreal businessman, Norman Le Blanc, was heard discussing the purchase of a cheap carbine sold in a magazine as one that would be "*good to kill Kennedy.*" This occurred in New Orleans months before the assassination. Le Blanc, later implicated in Watergate with his friend Robert Vesco, was close to Giuseppe Cotroni, a Montreal gangster and associate of Jack Ruby's close friend, Lewis McWillie, as well as Santo Trafficante, Meyer Lansky, and Norman Rothman.

Three months before the JFK assassination, the Canadian office of US Customs reported that Lee Harvey Oswald was seen in Montreal and positively identified distributing Fair Play for Cuba Committee pamphlets with a group of FPCC members.[326] The Royal Canadian Mounted Police perceived this report as serious enough to make further inquiries and attempted to identify Oswald's pro-Castro companions even though the FBI tried to dismiss the Customs report as hearsay. In his book, *JFK:*

---

324   Osborne also allegedly met with an agent of Canadian Louis Bloomfield (PERMINDEX) in Laredo in early November 1963. Could this have been to plan the movement of the hit men?
325   According to a document in files at the Assassination Archives and Research Center in Washington.
326   One of the witnesses, Customs Investigator Paul Tremblay, knew Oswald since he, Tremblay, had worked on a Cuba related case. At the time Mertz had a home in Montreal. Is there a pattern here? Was Oswald's being merged with Mertz?

The French Connection, Peter Kross wrote that Corsican drug kingpin and OAS assassin, Micheal Victor Mertz, was also arrested for passing out leaflets on a street in Paris, was involved in a brawl and arrested. This was three months before Oswald played out the same scenario in New Orleans ... trade craft. In Oswald's case, he actually described the incident in a letter to V.T. Lee, the National Chairman of the FPFC before the event took place.

The RCMP also conducted an investigation into Oswald's revolver. Although officially mail ordered in California, it really came from Montreal through a subsidiary of Century International Arms, which coincidentally was the same CIA Montreal company implicated in the Iran-Contra arms-for-drugs scandal.[327]

One of Castro's prisoners visited by Jack Ruby in 1959 was Lucien Rivard. A member of Montreal Cotroni family, a branch of Joe Bonanno's New York organization. Rivard was arrested in 1964 in a large heroin raid. Paul Mondolini, a Corsican trafficker and accomplice of Micheal Victor Mertz, furnished the drug via Mexico City to Rivard. According to a CIA document, Mertz, using the name of rival OAS terrorist Jean Souetre, was expelled from Dallas by the Immigration and Naturalization Service on November 23, 1963. While detained in Montreal's Bordeaux jail and awaiting extradition to the United States, both Rivard and his superior Joe Bonanno had important figures of the Canadian government intercede for their release. The result was the *Rivard Affair*, one of the biggest scandals in Canadian history. Rivard escaped Bordeaux and thus became a folklore hero. The Rivard Affair finally forced the Canadian Minister of Justice to resign.

The same Canadian government which helped Rivard also gave a new identity to Oswald's companion, Bowen/Osborne, on his trip to Mexico. Did the Montreal Mafia as well as Canadian intelligence operatives, who are also OSS veterans and accomplices of the CIA, play a role in the JFK assassination?

LOST HORIZON

A November 1967 article in *Winnipeg Free Press* reported that an FBI man named Merryl Nelson was told a story by a local businessman (name withheld for security reasons). A Canadian magazine, *Maclean's* also covered this event and identified the businessman informant as Rich-

---

327   A photograph in *Soldiers of Fortune Magazine* displays a weapons box with the name Century International Arms clearly visible.

ard Giesbrecht, father of four, and according to the article, a devout sincere and sensible Mennonite.[328] To summarize an article written by Paris Flamonde in 1969,[329] Giesbrecht's story follows:

Giesbrecht reported a conversation he overheard on February 13, 1964, in the Horizon Room, a cocktail lounge at the Winnipeg International Airport. Giesbrecht was seated near and overheard two men discussing the assassination of President Kennedy. He described one of the men as having *"...the oddest hair and eyebrows I'd ever seen. The eyebrows were wide and sort of streaky. The hair was very shiny and it started quite far back on his head."* The man also had heavy-rimmed glasses and reminded Giesbrecht of comedian Stan Laurel. Later he identified this man as David Ferrie. He described the man Ferrie was speaking to as middle to late forties, reddish-blond hair and a badly pockmarked neck and jaw. His accent sounded Latin and he wore a hearing aid. The men's clothing was casual. They wore light colored tweed suits and loafers. He perceived both as homosexuals. The thrust of the conversation revolved around how much Oswald had told his wife about the "plot" to kill JFK. The name Isaacs was mentioned and his relationship with Oswald discussed. The men wondered how a man like Isaacs could have gotten himself involved with a "psycho" like Lee Oswald. It seems that Isaacs was caught on television video near the President when he arrived in Dallas. Presumably, this was at Love Field. They further related that Isaacs was under surveillance by a man named Hoffman, or Hochman, who was to "relieve" him of and destroy a 1958 model automobile Isaacs possessed. Ferrie added that *"we have more money at our disposal now than at any other time."*

The conversation then turned to another topic and the two began speaking of a meeting to take place at the Townhouse Motor Hotel in Kansas City, Missouri, on March 18th. Giesbrecht overheard that they mentioned that a rendezvous in the banquet room that would be registered under the name of a textile firm. They added that there had been no meeting held since November 1963.

Ferrie mentioned that an "aunt" (or "auntie"? – gay patois for an older homosexual) named what sounded like *"Romeniuk"* would be flying

---

328   The lead was provided to SA Merle Nelson by Constable Wershler of RCMP in a letter on May 5, 1964. Wershler had also been contacted by an unidentified social worker, who had recalled an intriguing classified ad she had seen after reading about Giesbrecht's allegations on the front page of the *Winnipeg Free Press* (May 2). In the Personal section on April 7-8-9 read as follows. "Int. Airport Lounge, Feb 13, 1964. Gentlemen interested in textiles Kan. Cy. Apply to Box 400, Free Press."

329   "The Winnipeg Airport Incident," Paris Flammonde, *The Kennedy Conspiracy*, Meredith Press, New York, 1969, pages 29–32

in from California. The name was mentioned several times; Ferrie asked about some merchandise coming out of Nevada and the other man indicated that things had gotten too risky and that the house, or shop, at a place called Mercury had been closed down. He further explained that a "good shipment" had reached Caracas from Newport.

The Warren Commission was discussed and it was felt that its investigation would continue whether Oswald was found guilty or not.

As the conversation abated, Giesbrecht became a little "jittery or excited," and decided to leave and contact the police. The last thing he overheard was a remark by Ferrie that he had flown a plane like the one standing outside the window of the cocktail lounge.

As Giesbrecht departed he noticed another man had been watching him for some time from another table. The man was about thirty-five, with light hair, flushed-cheeked, six feet tall and two hundred pounds, with a slightly deformed nose. His left hand appeared to be tattooed or scarred.

When Giesbrecht left he was followed. When he attempted to visit the Royal Canadian Mounted Police office on the next floor of the airport, his path was blocked by a large man. Getting to a telephone, he began relating the situation to an RCMP corporal at the downtown headquarters. However, noticing that the man following him was rapidly approaching, he hung up and raced off. Finally, he successfully eluded the man, or was abandoned by him. He telephoned his lawyer who contacted the United States Consulate, which in turn notified the FBI.

The *Maclean's* article mentions Geisprecht's confusion at the Bureau's behavior. Initially FBI agent Merryl Nelson's reaction was *"This looks like the break we've been waiting for."* However, a few months later, he remembered being informed that he should forget about the entire episode as it was *"too big,"* and that *"we can't protect you in Canada."*[330] It was on February 23, 1967, that Giesbrecht saw a photograph of David Ferrie in a newspaper. He thought the picture looked familiar; then he realized it was one of the men he had overheard in the airport.[331]

Soon after the Winnipeg *Free Press* broke the story, one of Jim Garrison's aides got in touch with Geisbrecht. At last there was an official who actually wanted to pursue his evidence. Telephone calls were exchanged, including

---

330   Giesbrecht's lawyer, Harry Backlin told the FBI "I checked out the man (Geisbrecht) and I firmly believe that what he has divulged to me is fact." The FBI, however, concluded that Giesbrecht had a vivid imagination.

331   A corroborating witness turned up. A woman named "Lorraine," age 22. On Nov 18 or 19, 1963, while waiting for a flight to arrive at Winnipeg Airport, went to Horizon Room about 11AM. While sitting in a booth she overheard three well dressed men talking. They talked of someone that was going to be killed on Friday in Dallas.

conversations between Giesbrecht and Garrison.[332] In September, according to *Maclean's*, he tentatively agreed to testify at Clay Shaw's forthcoming trial.[333]

Garrison accepted that Ferrie, who was easily recognizable because of his red wig and false eyebrows, as one of the Winnipeg men. Some believe that the other man was Maj. L.M. Bloomfield, former OSS officer, living in Montreal. Like Clay Shaw, Bloomfield was a board member of the CIA-sponsored Centro Mondiale Commerciale in Rome.

Flamonde felt the incident was of sufficient importance to warrant a personal inquiry and he called Giesbrecht in Winnipeg from New York. Giesbrecht agreed to answer a few questions. That conversation, between the witness and the Flamonde, went as follows:

> Q. Is there any doubt in your mind that the conversation you overheard [at the Winnipeg Airport] referred to the conspiracy relating to the assassination of the President?
>
> A. Oh, yes. Most definitely [it was].
>
> Q. There is no doubt in your mind?
>
> A. No, none at all.
>
> Q. From the photographs you have seen of David Ferrie, how certain are you that he was one of the two men talking?
>
> A. Well, I'll put it this way. It was a photo three years after—that I'd seen this man—three years after—without even seeing a story on it, that immediately this stuck out. And I had identified this man three years previous, but not knowing it was a man by the name of Ferrie, you know.
>
> Q. When was the first time you ever saw a photograph of Ferrie?
>
> A. About five or six months ago.
>
> Q. Therefore there would have been a three-year lapse between seeing the man and the photograph?
>
> A. Right, right.
>
> Q. Yet, on the basis of that, what would you say your certainty that it was Ferrie was? Fifty percent? Eighty percent?
>
> A. I would say a hundred percent.

Flamonde thought that Giesbrecht's mention of the name sounding like "Romeniuk," might be Romanian or at least eastern European. He

332   Garrison investigation, the Boxley (Wood) files.
333   However, after receiving threats and listening to his wife's reservations, he decided not to do so.

230

asked Giesbrecht whether any mention had been made of the Old Catholic Church, or related religious bodies, to which the businessman replied, "No comment."[334]

Flamonde sought more information regarding the mysterious men at Winnipeg Airport. Giesbrecht continued:

> A. I don't know the size of them. I didn't see either one of the two standing up. The color of the hair? The one that I thought was Ruby [*sic*; Ferrie?] would have been a very light brown or red, and the other fellow, he would be blondish, grayish, you know, blond-gray, between red and blond, turning gray.
>
> Q. Right. Do you have any idea who the man was, other than Ferrie?
>
> A. At that time, or now?
>
> Q. Now.
>
> A. Well, I again would say "no comment" there.
>
> Q. Right. But you have no doubt about the one man being Ferrie?
>
> A. No, no doubt in my mind.
>
> Q. So, in summation, we may say that in your mind there is no question that it was Ferrie, you have no comment at this time on whom the second man might have been, you have no comment on whether you have been contacted by any intelligence agencies recently.
>
> A. Right.

What's Going on Here?

> *Some are born more equal than others.*
> –The Pig, *Animal Farm*, George Orwell

So what can be deduced from this incident? It doesn't seem Giesbrecht had any reason to make up a story like this. He seemed to be a respected businessman and family man as well. He reported it to authorities immediately. I believe him. The only individual in his story that can be identified with any assurance is David Ferrie. His unmistakable appearance makes him a poor choice for clandestine work. It has also been established that Ferrie made trips to Canada. Garrison witness Jules Ricco

---

334   Flamonde suspected the involvement of the shadowy clergy of some branches of the Old Catholic Church in this country had repeatedly appeared in the background in intelligence ops. (authors note: Ferrie belonged to the Old Catholic Church.)

Kimble accompanied him and Clay Shaw and picked up a Latin or Cuban on such a trip in the summer of 1963. In addition he was asked by Ferrie to accompany him again a month or so later. Kimbell turned him down on that occasion. Could the man conversing with Ferrie have been Shaw? It's not likely. The man had a Latin accent and wore a hearing aid. Louis Bloomfield[335] has been suggested, but again the Latin accent doesn't fit. Ferrie was known to be close friends with Eladio Del Valle. It could have been him. But that is speculation.

We do know the name of a person they were discussing, however. The man was named "Isaacs." Let's take a look at who this might be. There are several men with the name Isaacs that had associations with Oswald.

- When the Oswald's returned from the Soviet Union in June of 1962, they appeared at the Special Services Welfare Center in New York City. There they received help from a social worker named Martin Isaacs. Isaacs interviewed Oswald's family. He granted the Oswald's a loan, put them up overnight in a Times Square Hotel, and booked them on a commercial flight to Dallas, via Atlanta.[336] It seems quite unlikely that this is the Isaacs, Ferrie and his friend were speaking of.

- Charles Isaacs was a customer service manager for American Airlines. Interviewed January 6, 1964, due to the fact that his name, phone number and place of employment had been listed in Jack Ruby's notebook. It seems that Mrs. Isaacs had at one time worked for Ruby as a wardrobe designer and had confronted Ruby in regard to a "check that bounced." The Ruby connection is interesting.

THE ISAACS APPARATUS

A man who fits the bill best, however, is Professor Harold Isaacs, a former Communist spy, who later become a paid agent of the Japanese. If you remember, he was discussed in Chapter two. Originally a Trotskyite, he was a journalist in Shanghai in the 1930s and had a direct link to Charles Willoughby, the Intelligence chief under General Douglas MacArthur.[337] Effectively a triple agent, men like Isaacs were never what they appeared to be. It was never quite clear whom he might be working for.

---

335   Louis Mortimer Bloomfield died in 1984. A few years before his death he donated 31 boxes of documents to the Library and Archives Canada. This included correspondence with some well-known politicians such as George H. W. Bush. The one condition Bloomfield placed on the donation was that public access to the papers would be restricted for 20 years after his death. However, when researcher, Mauice Phillipps gained access to these materials in 2004 he found that Bloomfield's widow, Justine Stern Bloomfield Cartier, was still refusing permission for them to be released into the public domain.

336   WCH VIII, 324, Bishop 317

337   Willoughby was known as MacArthur's "little fascist."

The CIA funded a project out of MIT through the "Isaacs apparatus" to bring over a group from Japan to embark on a study of the Japanese "Science of Thought." More likely than not, it was a part of the MKUL-TRA Project. In Nippon, they were called "*Thought Police*." Were the Japanese able to take known communists and turn them into fascists? Sounds like something Willoughby would champion enthusiastically. Dr. Isaacs, it seems, had close ties with a linguistics-oriented group of Japanese in Tokyo led by Chikao Fujisawa. The goal of this CIA project was the same as that of Isaacs and Fujisawa; the indoctrination of student radicals around the world. An author and a linguist, Fujisawa was fluent in five languages including Russian. He authored "*A Prophecy of the Dawn of a New Age*," "*The Great Shinto Purification Ritual*" and "*On the Divine Mission of Nippon*." On the one hand, it was known that Fujisawa was a purged war criminal hired by the U.S. Army to indoctrinate Americans.[338] On the other hand, that the same man worked for Soviet intelligence. The contradiction was unsettling.

During Oswald's tour of Japan, it is known that he became involved with a group of Japanese Communists. Was this the Isaacs apparatus? Did his cousin Marilyn encourage this contact? Was she on a CIA mission to arrange contacts for possible defectors to the Soviet Union? Was she chosen because of her relationship with Oswald? Was she infiltrating the Isaacs apparatus or was she working for Isaacs? Was Oswald a "dangle"?

CD1080 tells of Isaacs' international travels and concentration on study in India. Strangely, although this WC document is entitled "Marilyn Dorthea Murret," it makes no mention of her. FBI document CD942 links Murret to Isaacs revealing that Murret traveled extensively in the Far East and spent long periods of time in India.[339]

Could Isaacs have been involved with Oswald? Could he have been in Dallas on November 22, 1963, as Ferrie's conversation indicated? An independent researcher at MIT discovered that Isaacs taught the course, "*Changing Outlook and Identities in the World*," every year throughout the 60s except for 1963-64. Thus he could have been in Dallas at the right time. In addition, Mary Ferrell found listings for Harold R. Isaacs as well as Charles R. Isaacs in Dallas directory for the years 1961-63. Being that Oswald was known to have been involved with Communists in Japan and that his cousin Marilyn Murret was linked by the FBI to Isaacs, the connection is possible. The links to Oswald, Murret, Isaacs, and the CIA are extensive.

---

338   Possibly part of Operation "Paper-Clip."
339   *Coup d'etat in America*, Alan J. Weberman and Michael Canfield

It was CIA funds that set up the MIT Center for International Studies. Like Langley, a guard watched the door and the participating academicians must show badges when entering or leaving. The center was founded by Walt Whitman Rostow, an economics professor who served in OSS in WWII and later was chief of the State Department's Policy Planning Staff in the Kennedy and Johnson Administrations. A book entitled *The Dynamics of Soviet Society* (1953) was produced by Rostow and colleagues and financed by the CIA. It was published in two versions. One classified for circulation within the intelligence agencies and a sanitized version for public consumption. The MIT Center for International Studies was a CIA think tank.[340]

Cord Meyer and Priscilla Johnson (McMillan) were once members of the World Federation which advocated One World Government. Later, these two, like Isaacs, became staunch anti-communists. Another World Federalist supporter was the eccentric heiress Ruth Forbes Paine, mother of Michael Paine.

One of Wisner's WCC Emigre Resistance Movement projects involved both the Harvard Russian Research Center and the MIT Center for International Studies. This may provide another possible link to the source of Oswald's defection to the Soviet Union. We know that Oswald's cousin Marilyn Murrett was believed to be involved with the Harold Isaacs Apparatus and that Isaacs worked at MIT. Oswald was stationed in Japan and possibly interacted with Isaacs when he became involved in a communist cell in Tokyo. Was Oswald's motivation to defect inspired by this group involving Wisner, Cord Meyer and Isaacs. Strange that Priscilla McMillan was one of only two news reporters able to get an interview with the turncoat while he was in Russia. Note that this does not replace the Sollie/Angleton origin of the false defector dangle, but merely adds their cohorts, Meyer and Issacs/Murrett to the mix. On returning to the US, Oswald is handed off to the Russian Emigre Community in Dallas where de Mohrenschildt and later the Paines become his overseers.

Getting back to the Giesbrecht allegation, the man said to be watching Isaacs was named Hoffman or Hochman. A possibility here is Troy Hauckman of the Minutemen. This man was to "relieve" Isaacs of and destroy a 1958 model automobile Isaacs possessed. A possible tie in here is the transfer of weapons from a Dodge to a Thunderbird involving Jack Ruby associates, Donnell Whittier and Lawrence Miller. They were arrested but the driver of the vehicle fled the scene. Was this Ruby associate Charles Isaacs?

---

340   *The Invisible Government,* David Wise and Thomas B. Ross

As for the reference to "sales meeting" at the Townhouse Motor Hotel in Kansas City, Missouri, on March 18th, is there any hint of what this might mean? The reservations made were in the name of a textile firm. It seems an odd coincidence that Watergate burglars were allegedly attending a sales meeting of a dummy corporation in a hotel banquet room the night they were caught breaking into the offices of the Democratic Party National Committee. The Town House Motor Hotel was located on the corner of Kellogg and Broadway, the main street of Witchita, KS, (FBI report). Or was it Town House Motor Inn, also located in K.C. This was the Inn where the Minutemen held their first national conference. It's known that David Ferrie made six phone calls to an oil producer living in Witchita, KS in the fall of 1962. Vice-versa, he also made several calls from Witchita to New Orleans in early '63. Of course another place of business with the name Town and Country is the one in New Orleans, operation center of Carlos Marcello.

Giebrecht also mentioned that Ferrie asked about some merchandise coming out of Nevada. The man he was conversing with indicated that things had gotten too risky and that the house, or shop, at a place called Mercury had been closed down. He further explained that a "good shipment" had reached Caracas from Newport.[341]

Was this a shipment of arms? What was Mercury? A possibility is that this referred to a right-wing periodical called the *American Mercury*. The military editor of this publication in 1963 was none other than Gen. Edwin Walker. He had replaced Gen. Charlies Willoughby.

In checking out this information, the FBI's LV office discovered there was a *shop* in *Mercury*, Nevada, (location of the Atomic Energy Commission's testing site).

CONCLUSIONS

The research of Flamonde, Weberman, and Whitney is intriguing. Is it a link to a conspiratorial cabal involving Ferrie, Shaw, Ruby's gun running associates, Isaacs and Oswald? Or is it possible the Winnipeg Airport escapade was merely CIA disinformation? The event conveniently occurred just as Garrison was getting his investigation under way.

As for the Phillipps' hypothesis that the murder of JFK was the result of a conspiracy uniting both mafia and intelligence people, it seems more convincing. Could Rivard and Bonanno be the missing link between the powerful Hoffa-Marcello-Trafficante-Giancana circle that ordered JFK's

---

341   The name "Caracas" was in Oswald's notebook.

execution? Were Corsican executioners rewarded with heroin? It appears that Lucien Rivard, and thus Joseph Bonanno and the New York Mafia, were solidly linked with Canadian political figures.[342] The usual suspects in assassination literature that have links to Montreal include Dave Ferrie, Clay Shaw, Micheal Victor Mertz, L.M. Bloomfield, Lee Oswald, James Earl Ray and Albert Osborne, alias Jack Bowen.

Truth crushed to earth, will rise again.
–MLK

---

342   *From Dallas to Montreal, The Montreal connection to the JFK assassination*, Maurice Phillipps

PART V

SEVEN DAYS IN MAY

INTRODUCTION TO PART V

BAD CHOICES

When JFK investigators asked John Whitten in 1978 why Bill Harvey
might have told his wife to destroy his papers, Whitten's reply was caustic.
"He was too young to have assassinated McKinley and Lincoln. It
could have been anything."

I n 1962 JFK read a book called *Seven Days in May*. The story told of a
US Military Coup d' etat led by a general of the Joint Chiefs of Staff
opaquely based on General Edwin Walker or maybe General Curtis
LeMay. Kennedy loved the book and perceived its relevance to his own
circumstances. Kennedy too had clashed with an Army general with extremist views early on in his administration. The President encouraged
Hollywood director John Frankenheimer,[343] to make a movie and even
allowed him use of the White House when JFK was out of town. Apparently, the President feared such a cabal really was possible. Discussing it
with Frankenheimer he said, "First of all it would have to be a young president, and he would have to have had a 'Bay of Pigs.'" He added, "Then, if
there was a second 'Bay of Pigs,' a second conflict with his military power and the national security state." Finally, he said, "If there were a third
'Bay of Pigs' ... yea it could certainly happen.... But it won't happen on
my watch." Sadly, JFK did not live to see the film he helped bring to the
screen. The movie starred Burt Lancaster, Fredrick March, Kirk Douglas
and Ava Gardner. It was arguably one of the best cold war films made. Its
theme proved a prophecy of John Kennedy's destiny.

In retrospect, we can see that JFK's first Bay of Pigs was just that. The
second was the Cuban Missile Crisis. The third could have been any of
sundry events he orchestrated; NSAM 263 to end involvement in Vietnam, opening back channel negotiations with Khruschev and Castro, the
nuclear test ban treaty, executive order #11110 issuing silver certificates

---

343   Robert F Kennedy spent the night of June 4th, his last night alive, sleeping over at the
Malibu home of film maker John Frankenheimer who directed and produced the 1962 film *The
Manchurian Candidate as well as Seven Days in May*. Frankenheimer was a media consultant to JFK
and, as is a confirmed fact on record, he personally drove Bobby Kennedy to the Ambassador Hotel
the next day.

(Kennedy greenbacks), threatening the oil depletion allowance, or the American University speech. All of these things combined sealed his fate and signed his death warrant. In the final analysis, *thirteen days in October* became the catalyst for JFK's *Seven Days in May*. The result was a reduced fraction equaling *four days in November*.

By 1963, JFK was isolated from his advisors in the Security State. They wanted war, especially in Cuba. He didn't. They saw him as a traitor, soft on Communism and afraid to stand up to Khrushchev. He let them down at the Bay of Pigs as well as the missile crisis and the Berlin standoff. He was backing down in Laos and Vietnam as well. Worse than that he was going over the heads of the Joint Chiefs, CIA and NSC and dealing directly with Kruschev and Castro. As they saw it, he would very likely be re-elected and that was just the beginning. They nurtured fears that a dynasty would evolve, and that after JFK's second term there would be eight years of Bobby followed by eight more of Teddy. This looked like a real possibility. JFK had to go.

In retrospect, it appears to me that JFK contributed to his own demise by consistently making poor choices in the appointments of his staff and advisors. Perhaps he thought appointing enemies would result in compromises. They didn't. Resentment and even hatred permeated this entourage. No doubt these choices played a role in his demise. These appointees may have taken advantage of their proximity to orchestrate a plot.

THE COWARDLY LION

Vice President *Lyndon Johnson* hated the Kennedys and felt humiliated by them. Many have long suspected his involvement in the assassination. It was he and Connally that persuaded Kennedy to travel to Dallas. The murder happened in *their* home state. It was LBJ who appointed the Warren Commission, the purpose of which was to produce a cover-up. It was he that had the most to gain by JFK's death. He benefited by becoming president, a position he coveted. In all likelihood he would have been dropped from JFK's ticket in 1964. He avoided a possible prison sentence resulting from ongoing investigations into the Billy Sol Estes and Bobby Baker scandals. These investigations were dropped once he inherited his powerful position in the government.

In a photo of the Vice-president's car in Dealey Plaza at the moment of the first shot, Johnson is nowhere to be seen. He seemed to be hunched over near the floor talking on a walkie-talkie device. Is it possible he knew the shots were coming ahead of time?

LBJ's allegiance with J. Edgar Hoover is conspiratorial in itself. He gave Hoover full reign of the investigation and made it the source for the Warren Commission's evidence. Although it was not yet a federal offense to kill a president, Johnson had the Dallas Police turn over all of the evidence they had to the FBI.

There was no love lost between the Kennedys and Hoover. The former were looking forward to the Director's upcoming mandatory retirement due in January 1964. Johnson issued Executive order 11154 exempting Hoover from compulsory retirement and appointed him for an *indefinite* period of time. Hoover certainly had foreknowledge of what was to happen in Dallas. In retrospect, Johnson was a terrible choice for JFK as a running mate. One has to ask would JFK have been assassinated if his vice-president was someone like Adlai Stevenson?

Secretary of State, *Dean Rusk* advocated military force as a deterrent to Communism. He proved himself a military hawk during the Vietnam War. He was connected to the Rockefellers and there were rumors of his imminent dismissal by JFK prior to the assassination.

Secretary of Treasury, *C. Douglas Dillon* had been chairman of the Rockefeller Foundation and counted *John D.* as a close friend. As Treasury Secretary, Dillon was head of both the ATF and the Secret Service. The stand down of the latter played an important role in the success of an ambush in Dealey Plaza. Dillon was close to the Dulles brothers. He had worked with John Foster in past Republican campaigning. Brother Allen called Dillon *"Doug"* during his Warren Commission testimony. Dillon had supported Richard Nixon and not JFK in the 1960 election.

Appointing *Henry Cabot Lodge* as Ambassador to Vietnam was a huge faux pas. Kennedy was trying to get the ambassador to work out a compromise with the Diem brothers. Instead Lodge was initiating a dialog with their enemies that led to a coup d'état and their liquidation. It was *Lodge* who ran the show in South East Asia and flagrantly ignored the directives of his Commander in Chief.

National Security Advisor, *McGeorge Bundy* played a crucial role in foreign policy as well as defense decisions in Kennedy's administration. A supporter of the domino theory, he was a strong proponent of the war in Vietnam. Following in the footsteps of McNamara, Bundy later became president of the Ford Foundation. Kennedy trusted Bundy and instructed him as well as Maxwell Taylor to come up with a strategy for troop withdrawal from Vietnam in late '63. JFK had signed NSAM 263 an October 11 of that year, and needed a blueprint to carry it out.

Instead, Bundy did the opposite. In a cover letter he attached to NSAM 263, he made no mention of troop withdrawal. At a cabinet meeting held in Hawaii on November 20, what was discussed was the war escalation plans that would be set forth in a future Lyndon Johnson directive, NSAM 273. Bundy's signature reads November 21, 1963. This indicates a foreknowledge of the assassination.[344]

Kennedy also believed in and trusted *Maxwell Taylor*. Like Bundy, Taylor was also ignoring his orders to plan a withdrawal from Vietnam and was actively involved in the escalation of that war. The betrayal of these two men whom he counted on as supporters is revealing.

Walt Rostow, Deputy National Security Advisor under McGeorge Bundy, was possibly JFK's most influential advisor on foreign policy. Rostow, born of *White Russian* Jewish immigrants, served in the OSS during WWII. It was Rostow who was to later counsel President Johnson that his own personal inspection of Israel's Dimona site found *no* evidence of nuclear weapon production. It was Rostow who wrote Johnson's first State of the Union speech. Convinced the Vietnam War could be won, he was LBJ's most vocal war hawk.

Robert McNamara was JFK's Secretary of Defense. His thinking at the time was closer to Kennedy's than the other cabinet members. He also socialized with Kennedy's family and was eventually a pall bearer for RFK. McNamara worked with JFK to morph US military strategy from the Eisenhower doctrine of "massive nuclear retaliation" to a "flexible response" relying on conventional weapons. However, when McNamara served under Johnson in the next administration, he seemed to transform from dove to hawk. Where he once backed Kennedy's vision of Vietnamizing the war, he later became an advocate of escalating the number of US troops and using bombing to expand the conflict. He was also a clear advocate of the generally accepted domino theory in the Asian conflict

General *Lyman Lemnitzer* was appointed Chairman of the Joint Chiefs of Staff in 1960 by President Eisenhower and not by JFK. His involvement in the Bay of Pigs disaster, Operation NORTHWOODS, and a plan to launch an all-out first strike against Russia and China by the fall of 1963, were all anathema to JFK. *Lem*, as he was called by his close associates, was replaced by General Maxwell Taylor in November 1962 and became Commander of NATO. Lemnitzer was a close associate of Allen Dulles.

---

344   This revelation comes from the Pentagon Papers and Fletcher Prouty's book; *JFK; The CIA, Vietnam and the Plot to Assassinate John F. Kennedy.*

General Curtis LeMay

The military advisor that hated JFK the most was General Curtis "bombs away" LeMay. An *extreme* hawk whose politics were miles to the right of Attila the Hun, LeMay was responsible for the firebombing of Tokyo in WWII. This would have been a war crime with dire consequences had the allies lost the war. LeMay was pushing JFK for an all-out first strike against not only the Russians, but the Chinese as well. Wiping out every commie on the globe was his life's ambition. During LeMay's arguments for the Pearl Harbor-like attack JFK walked out of the meeting. LeMay argued that we'd *only* lose 30 to 40,000 Americans and it would be well worth it. To LeMay if, after a nuclear war there was one of us left standing and none of them ... we win! LeMay was also reported to have tried to force the military to bomb the Soviet missile bases in Cuba against Kennedy's orders.

LeMay argued that in nuclear war, the president should not be part of the decision-making process at all. "After all, who is more qualified to make that decision ... to go nuclear ... some politician who may have been in office for only a couple of months or a man who has been preparing all his adult life to make it? Especially a politician who had held back air support from the invasion force at the Bay of Pigs, refrained from knocking down the New Berlin Wall, and who had refused to send combat troops to Vietnam, and earlier rejected sending forces to Laos as well.[345]

By weird coincidence, there seems to be a connection between LeMay and the Manson murders case. One of the victims in the Tate murders was Jay Sebring. Sebring was involved with mob affiliated characters from Chicago and Las Vegas.[346] They were customers of the hair stylist and he partied with them. One of these individuals was Charlie Baron.[347] Baron, a casino executive and mobster, was close to Sebring. He was said to have been capable of murder according to sources from the drug culture that the hairdresser was associated with. Baron had a strange associate in JFK's Air-Force Chief of Staff, *Curtis LeMay*. Can it be coincidence that behind the scenes in the Manson case are the specters of organized crime, Military Intelligence and MKULTRA's mind control involving LSD?

Tom O'Neill's research on this subject reveals a common denominator in this multidimensional conspiracy. This was a man named Reeve Whitson. O'Niell describes him as Mr. *Anonymous*, a "walk in."[348] Reportedly, a

345   Daniel Ellsbert, *Doomsday Machine*, p.113
346   Giancana and Rosselli?
347   See *CHAOS* by Tom O'Neill for details of this bizarre case.
348   The same type of mysterious anonymous "walk ins" played important roles in the JFK

CIA operative, Whitson was said to be a more or less invisible entity. His endless array of connections included Hollywood elites, Curtis LeMay, Nazi Otto Skorzeny, mobster Charlie Baron, Manson victim Jay Sebring and even Charles Manson himself. More significantly, he seemed to be working closely with Vincent Bugliosi.

The choices JFK made for his cabinet may have been patterned after those of the Lincoln administration. Lincoln chose a team of rivals rather than yes-men, with mixed results. It is likely that Kennedy's father, Joseph P. Kennedy, used his influence to affect his son's choices. The most disastrous of which was the appointment of brother Bobby to the post of Attorney General. This choice proved a catalyst for disaster. JFK himself was against it at first but later acquiesced. This idea of patriarchal influence was reinforced by Theodore Sorrenson, who believed that it was the elder Kennedy that was also responsible for the nominations of Rusk and McNamarra.

and Tippit murders.

CHAPTER 18

STRANGE BEDFELLOWS

Hatred in a dying man may be excusable. But among the living it can become an intolerable thing. It never gives its victim a moments peace.
— Paladin, *Have Gun Will Travel*, "The Lady," 1958

Sometimes it's hard to see the forest for the trees. You need to step back to observe the overall picture. For example, in the immediate aftermath of the assassination of the president, it was *not* known that the CIA and Mafia were working together for a common purpose (to kill Castro). Most of us had little knowledge of the even earlier allegiance between the two occurring during WWII. Later, anti-Castro Cubans appeared to be prime suspects. Relatively few were aware at the time that they were financed mercenaries of the CIA. As a result, when books blaming the Mafia or Cuban exiles for JFK's demise began to surface, confusion reigned and researchers were divided on whether the CIA, radical Cubans or the Mafia was responsible for the dastardly deed. More division was to come as suspicion was focused on other groups. Far-right extremists like the John Birch Society and the Minutemen were to blame. Religious zealots and racist segregationists such as the States Rights Party, motivated by racial hatred, were certainly not beyond suspicion. Military hardliners with no respect for the president and considered him a traitor soft on Communism were behind the murder. Was it a military coup? Right-wing oil tycoons had the motive and finances to see it through and paid the bill. It seemed everyone had a different theory as to where the guilt should be placed ... step back folks and look at the big picture.

There is a common denominator here that links all these groups regardless of their seeming divergence. Their common link is that they are all members of a cult of thought as strong as any religious passion and as all consuming as any patriotic or nationalistic belief can be. In an era when indoctrination and fear went hand in hand, they all were of one mind and passionately joined in their obsession with one common cause

... *anti-communism.* In their view this boogieman lurked under every bed, behind the smiles of your neighbors, in dark alleys and even behind the masks of constituents of our own government. Cult leaders like Joseph McCarthy and J. Edgar Hoover stirred the masses to a fever pitch with their anti-Communist fervor. Unlike the rabble-rousers of earlier times who preached from stumps and soap boxes to small crowds, these crusaders used the technological magic of radio and television to reach the masses. It worked! Fear and paranoia ruled the land. A *strategy of tension* was created.

The CIA was running amok and had octopus-like tentacles that reached into all areas of American and European politics. They infiltrated law enforcement in the US and abroad, political groups they considered subversive, they manipulated religious groups, the media and sundry other bastions of society. They used front companies as cutouts to provide plausible deniability. In Dallas, the White Russian emigres were entwined with Big Oil conglomerates. Both were fiercely anti-Communist. The CIA used this group to manipulate the patsy and separate him from his family, liberating him for clandestine assignments.

WHITE RUSSIAN KNIGHTS

The White Russian community in Dallas was a *munchkin land* of fiercely anti-communist aristocrats. Simultaneously, they were deeply seeded into the Big D Oil community. There is little doubt that the CIA used this wealthy right wing group as a source of information and as tools in clandestine activities. It seems the perfect environment to nurture the future patsy and his non-English-speaking wife. So who was responsible for connecting the young refugees with their babysitters? Oswald's benefactors, the White Russians in Dallas, had ties to the Tolstoy Foundation and the Russian Orthodox Church (both subsidized by the CIA). Michael Paine's brother and father-in-law both worked for AID,[349] as did George de Mohrenschildt.

The Tolstoy Foundation was part of Frank Wisner's Emigre Resistance Operation used in Operation Gladio. It is no accident that the Oswalds ended up in the care of these Russian Emigres. Ilia Mamantov worked for Sun Oil, owned by the Pugh family, who were Birchers. The OPC/WCC, run by Wisner, used the Emigre Resistance Movement as a first line of defense against the spread of communism in Europe. In the US, it used resources like George de Mohrenschildt, Ilia Mamantov, Don Isaac

---

349   AID was a CIA cover for clandestine activity abroad.

Levine, the Dallas White Russians and their Big D oil contacts and others like Spas T. Raikin to carry out their agendas.

ISSAC DON LEVINE

A newsman for the *Kansas City Star* and *NY Tribune* and later an editor of *Plain Talk* (an *anti-communist* monthly), Levine was a central figure in the Alger Hiss case.[350] Levine first brought Whittaker Chambers' accusations against Hiss to the attention of Secretary of State, Adolf Berle Jr.

Levine was hired by Frank Wisner in 1951 in a program to exploit Russian and Ukrainian emigre populations. Otto Skorzeny was part of this program. Levine set up an American Committee for the Liberation of the Peoples of Russia (funded by CIA). It was part of an OPC project called QKACTIVE.

Levine arrived in Dallas almost immediately after the assassination of JFK and met with Marina in an attempt to gain exclusive access to her story. In truth, his book was never published. The real purpose of his relationship with Marina was to "coach" her as a witness. He was aided in these efforts by Ilia Mamantov, and C.D. Jackson of *Life* magazine.

PAUL RAIGORODSKY

Raigorodsky was an expert on the Dallas Russian emigre' community, He stated that the centerpiece of that community was the Tolstoy Foundation. He was on its board of directors. Tolstoy Foundation had several former OSS and intelligence personnel on it's board. The Tolstoy Foundation acted as a major cover for US intelligence operations vetting Russian emigres for national security or for recruiting potential espionage agents. Translation; the Tolstoy Foundation was a CIA front used for recruiting covert operators. Sounds to me like George de Mohernschildt would be a perfect recruit.

GEORGE DE MOHRENSCHILDT

De Mohrenschildt was Oswald's mentor. It was he who manipulated the young ex-Marine to move to Dallas from Fort Worth. It was he who got Lee a job at a firm, *Jaggars-Chiles-Stoval*, a firm that did sensitive photographic work for the US Military. It was he that separated Lee from Marina under the guise of their abusive domestic quarrels, coercing others in the exile community to take her in. It was he that introduced the Oswalds to Ruth and Michael Paine and eventually handed them off to the same when he left for Haiti.

350   Which links him to Richard Nixon by association.

George said that it was a Dallas CIA officer, J. Walton Moore, that persuaded him to baby-sit Oswald. Apparently, a deal was struck to assist de Mohrenschildt in a Haitian oil deal of great interest to the Baron.

Although the testimony of both de Mohrenschildts to the Warren Commission was damning, George later recanted and became very remorseful concerning Oswald. He wrote a memoir that later became a book depicting his friend as a patsy. In essence, he became convinced that he, as well as Oswald, had been manipulated. By the time he was called before the House Assassinations Committee in the 1970s, he was a broken man and possibly a danger to the conspirators. His mysterious death on the eve of his scheduled testimony was ruled suicide. Few believe it was.

EVERETT GLOVER

A key event in the life of LHO was a party at the home of this Russian exile soil scientist working for Magnolia Oil. It was at this party that the Oswalds, the Paines and the de Mohrenschildts met.

Glover had met George and his wife Jean previously in the late 1950s at a skating rink. The friendship was renewed in 1962 at another party at the home of Lauiston Marshall. At that party, George introduced Glover to his close friend, Sam Ballen. Glover and Ballen hit it off and found they had a mutual interest in tennis. They agreed to play together the next day. Oddly, when they did, George showed up unannounced.

Glover had previously met Ruth and Michael Paine as fellow members of a madrigal[351] singing group at his Unitarian church.[352] So now we have a unification of Quakers and the Unitarians in the personification of the Paines. Ruth's excuse for being at the party and attaching herself to Marina was that she was looking for someone to teach her Russian. Since she already spoke it and even taught it, this is not a very convincing motivation.

At the party, Oswald made an impression on these anti-communist emigres that they could not forget. He espoused the virtues of Marxism and came across as a generally obnoxious and self-centered individual. It was probably his mission to do so. What it accomplished was getting the emigres to dislike him and also feel sorry for Marina. The end result being their willingness to take her in and separate the couple.

But there were others at this "party." Present that evening were the de Mohrenschildts, Lee and Marina Oswald, Ruth Paine, Volkmar Schmidt, Richard Pierce and Betty McDonald, and research employee Norman

---

351   Madrigal is an acapella vocal rendition of 16th century music, point-counterpoint.
352   See *The Other Oswald, A Wilderness of Mirrors,* for the connection between the CIA, Quakers and Unitarians.

Fredricksen and his wife Elke. Magnolia Oil chemist, Volkmar Schmidt shared Glover's home. It was Schmidt and Glover who planned the party. However, Schmidt was called away on business and did not attend. Schmidt had cornered Oswald at a party the previous week at the home of the de Mohrenschildts. The topic was General Edwin Walker. Schmidt later believed it was he who encouraged Oswald to attempt to kill Walker. These White Russians seemed to be party animals. In August 1962, there was another party at the house of Peter Gregory.

The party accomplished several things. It established Oswald publicly as a Marxist. It provided a convenient explanation of how Lee and Marina met Ruth Paine, putting it in an innocent light. And through Volkmar Schmidt, it provides a pathway leading Oswald to the Walker shooting.

In the early '60s, the CIA still had a good patriotic reputation. If asked, most citizens would willingly help them out and felt it their duty to do so. Demonizing Oswald in preparation for his role could be easily accomplished without suspicion.

PETER GREGORY

Like Glover, Gregory was a Russian emigre and oil geologist. Like Ruth Paine he wanted to use Marina Oswald as a Russian tutor, not for himself, but for his son. After moving to Dallas, Oswald had approached Gregory to ask for certification as a translator of Russian documents. Through Gregory, who was a translator of Russian, Oswald was introduced to the White Russian community. Gregory's son has recently published a book about he and his father's experiences with the Oswalds. In the book, Oswald is portrayed as a wife-beating oaf. Gregory's father, however, is portrayed as a saint who was benevolent to the Oswalds. It was he who got Lee the job at Jaggars, Chiles and Stoval (not... it was de Mohrenschildt who did that), he was the translator for Marina (not... it was Mammantov). Ruth Paine is mentioned once in his book as a "friend" of Marina. Nothing about Michael. Astounding as it may seem, George de Mohrenschildt is not even mentioned at all.

Coincidentally, Paul Gregory was a neighbor and close friend of Lloyd Adams. It was Adams that manufactured the famous twist board promoted by Jack Ruby. Ruby visited Fort Worth with Adams and subsequently left Adams home phone number with Larry Crafard. He instructed Crafard to "give this number to Mike Shore, only." Shore, of LA, California, is the man who helped aquire Melvin Belli as defender in the Ruby trial. Shore also assisted Lawrence Schiller in selling Jack Ruby story.

GEORGE BOUHE

He was a prominent member of the White Russian expatriate community. It was he who introduced the Oswalds to the de Mohrenschildts. Bouhe became Marina's English tutor and financed her dental work. When Jim Garrison informed Marina that Bouhe just happened to be a neighbor of Jack Ruby, the man who killed her husband, Marina admitted that she was aware of it. How did she know? Her source was Bouhe himself! He had visited her for the purpose of telling her about it. He said it was just a coincidence.... *So* many coincidences in this case. As researcher Steve Jones pointed out, *was this not a possible connection between Oswald and Ruby?* Apparently, the Warren Commission didn't think so. Bouhe lived in an apartment located at 4740 Homer. Jack Ruby had lived at 4749 Homer.

George Bouhe and Jack Ruby were seen together by neighbors using a swimming pool shared by their separate apartment buildings.

We are asked to believe that all the right wing forces in the cold-war universe flew through the cosmos and crashed simultaneously into the small world of Lee Harvey Oswald in Dallas in the Fall of 1963? It was just a coincidence that CIA agents, Cuban exiles, White Russians, HUAC, SISS, General Walker and the Minutemen, fascist oriented Dallas Oil tycoons, patriotic mafioso characters all dominate his small world. No liberals or Communists or Socialists seem to be represented among his acquaintances? Of course, the Warren Report assures us that this is all coincidental.

SPAAS T. RAIKIN

Raikin was not a part of the Dallas White Russian community. However, I am including him here because he was of the same ilk and played a role in Oswald's legacy. Although not Russian, he was of Eastern European roots and a rabid anti-Communist with ties to the Central Intelligence Agency.

Raikin was politically active during the Cold War era, protesting human rights abuses by communist regimes. He was secretary-general of the *American Friends of Anti-Bolshevik Bloc of Nations*, a right-wing group that staged a demonstration when Soviet Premier Nikita Khrushchev visited New York in 1959. He was also a member of its powerful lobbying faction. Researcher Peter Dale Scott also came across Raikin's name in a 1960 publication of the *Asian People's Anti-Communist League*, with which Raikin, the lobbyist, was in personal contact.[353] A CIA Office of Security file, released in 1993, noted:

---

353   *Time Magazine,* "The Truth About Hoover," December22, 1975, p.20.

250

"Spas T. Raikin was employed by the CIA in 1957 when he worked for its Joint Press Reading Service in New York City."[354]

The American Friends of the Anti-Bolshevik bloc of Nations (the ABN), of which Raikin was secretary general, was an extreme right-wing, anti-communist organization with Nazi and fascist roots in the Ukraine of the Soviet Union. The ABN was supported heavily by General Charles Willoughby.

It was Raikin who fulfilled the role of a one-man reception committee greeting Lee Harvey Oswald, his wife, Marina, and baby daughter, June, as they came down the ramp of a Dutch steam merchant on Fifth Street Pier, Hoboken, Jew Jersey. They arrived from Rotterdam, Holland on June 13, 1962. As the SS *Maasdam* approached the pier, Spas T. Raikin, a case worker with the Travelers Aid Society[355] of New York, expected to see newsmen and investigators waiting to question Oswald. He was surprised that there were none. The dock was quiet and practically empty. Raikin had never met Oswald. All he had was a sheet of paper with the name of the traveler he was supposed to meet: Lee Harvey Oswald. Raikin's job was to escort him off the boat and take him to the Travelers Aid office in New York.

The official story is that Oswald was of no interest to the State Department, FBI, US Intelligence or even the Media. No one was there to greet or arrest the ex-Marine who defected and claimed he would give secrets to Soviets. Raikin was just an agent of the Travelers Aid Society. Do you buy that? I don't. Raikin was a cutout for US Intelligence. Plausible Deniability is always the modus operandi.

But recent research by author James Day links Raikin to the clandestine world of the CIA's usurpation of religious groups as assets. Raikin's fight against communism began before before he came to the United States. As a Bulgarian, Spas T. Raikin did not just want to fight communism, he wanted to do so "*in the name of the Bulgarian Orthodox Church.*" Day sites a1956 FBI report stating that Raikin looked to escape to Greece to join such a church group there, that is if such a group existed. If there was none, he aspired to form such a *militant illegal* church group of his own to fight communism inside Bulgaria.

Raikin did have a religious background. He studied theology and taught it at Sofia Theological Seminary. He later wrote in his autobiography he was "*assigned to recruit Theology students to join with other students from other schools for a brigade.*" He doubled this assignment by "*carrying*

354   *The Man Who Knew Too Much*, Dick Russell, p. 156
355   A social welfare group that provided assistance to immigrants, stranded tourists and ex-pats

on surreptitious activities which were squarely anti-communist in conception and in execution."

Day wondered if Raikin ever did find that militant church. Did his work for Travelers Aid constitute an example of the existence of a militant and illegal church?

Day writes; *"In Greece, Raikin managed to land a scholarship from the World Council of Churches (WCC), according to the Hoover Institution's biographical sketch on Raikin. The FBI, however, noted Raikin was sent to Chicago by the WCC to "assist" a Bulgarian political exile. Either way, clearly Raikin undertook assignments for the WCC in some capacity; he was deeply tied to the Bulgarian Orthodox Church, a member of the WCC until 1988."*[356]

COL. LAWRENCE ORLOV

When George de Mohrenschildt first knocked on the Oswalds' door bearing gifts, he did so in the company of Orlov. Orlov then promptly melted into the background and disappeared. Why was he with de Mohrenschildt at this critical juncture? Like de Mohrenschildt, Orlov had Intelligence connections and was friends with Dallas CIA man, J. Walton Moore. Likely it was Orlov who linked Moore with de Mohrenschildt. Coincidentally, Orlov just happened to be a Unitarian involved with Big D oil and the White Russian Community in Dallas.

---

356   The JFK Assassination: Christian Identity Terrorists in Dealey Plaza?, James Day, *Medium*, 2024

CHAPTER 19

BIG OIL AND MILITARY INTELLIGENCE AND D.P.D. ... OH MY!

The Communists, since 1917, have sold communism to more people than have been told about Christ after 2,000 years."
–Conservative radio commentator Paul Harvey, September 1960:
He urged his readers to support the "counter-attack" ... mounted (of course[357]) in Dallas.

The head of the intelligence component of Dallas Civil Defense was Jack Crichton.[358]

THE MANY HATS OF JACK CRICHTON

On Jan 18, 1960, Tracy Barnes called a meeting. Those in attendance included E. Howard Hunt and the team responsible for the Guatemala Coup of 1954. The purpose of the meeting was to discuss executing a similar operation against Cuba.

Richard Nixon was the Cuban case officer and assembled a group of businessmen headed by George H.W. Bush and *Jack Crichton*, both Texas Oilmen, to gather funds for Operation 40.[359] The plan was put together by the 5412 Group, a subcommittee of the NSC (National Security Council). Lyndon Johnson later called Operation 40 *"Murder Inc. in the Caribbean."* In *Deadly Secrets*, Warren Hinckle and William Turner described Operation 40 as an "assassins-for-hire" organization. Involved in its operations were Sam Giancana and Santo Traficante. The Cuban plan called for Castro's assassination and included a false flag attack on Guantanamo naval base to coincide with an invasion by a Cuban exile brigade.[360]

357   Authors comment.
358   Pronounced "CRAYTON"
359   All three just happened to be in Dallas on the day of the assassination.
360   According to Fabian Escalante (*The Secret War: CIA Covert Operations Against Cuba*), in 1959, Crichton and Bush raised funds for the CIA's Operation 40. Originally it was set up to organize sabotage operations against Fidel Castro and his Cuban government. However, it evolved into a team of assassins. One member, Frank Sturgis, claimed: "this assassination group (Operation 40)

WHO WAS JACK CRICHTON?

According to Conservapedia, "*Jack Crichton (October 16, 1916 – December 10, 2007), was an oil and natural gas industrialist from Dallas Texas, who was among the first of his ranks to recognize the importance of petroleum reserves in the Middle East. In 1964, he carried the Republican banner in a fruitless campaign against the second-term re-election of Governor John Connally, then a Democrat, who switched parties nine years later.*"

When Crichton was enrolled at Texas A&M University, his classmates included future industrialist Harry Roberts, "Bum" Bright and Earle Cabell, later a mayor of Dallas, Crichton wrote an award-winning essay, "*The Political Career of Huey P. Long.*"

In 1990, Crichton wrote in *The Dallas Morning News* that he first realized the vastness of the Middle Eastern oil reserves prior to 1950. In 1951, he helped to establish the San Juan Oil Company in Dallas, where he became the vice-president of operations. He later became president of the Yemen Development Corporation and the Dorchester Gas Corporation and was involved in mining copper, zinc, gold, silver and nickel through his Arabian Shield Development Company.[361]

Crichton served in the U.S. Army in WW II as a field artillery officer and an OSS special agent. He won the Air Medal, five Battle Stars, and the Bronze Star. He retired as a colonel in the Army Reserve. Crichton's OSS service during WWII was just one facet of his persona. He wore another hat in November 1963. He was President of NAFCO Oil and Gas, Inc. and counted among his associates, Clint Murchison, H.L. Hunt, Earl Cabell, D.H. Byrd, Sid Richardson, George H.W. Bush and George de Mohrenschildt. In fact, he, de Mohrenschildt and several other oil men were involved in negotiations with Fulgencio Batista, the military dictator of Cuba. In August 1953 Crichton joined the Empire Trust Company. He eventually became a vice-president of the organization. According to Stephen Birmingham, the author of *Our Crowd: The Great Jewish Families of New York;* "...the company had a network of associates that amounted to '*something very like a private CIA.*'" The Empire Trust was also a major investor in the defense contractor General Dynamics.

In 1956 Crichton started up his own spy unit, the 488th Military Intelligence Detachment in Dallas. Crichton served as the unit's commander under Lieutenant Colonel George Whitmeyer, who was in overall com-

---

would upon orders, naturally, assassinate either members of the military or the political parties of the foreign country that you were going to infiltrate, and if necessary some of your own members who were suspected of being foreign agents...

361   Conservapedia

mand of all Army Reserve units in East Texas. In an interview, Crichton claimed that there were "about a hundred men in that unit and about forty or fifty of them were from the Dallas Police Department." Crichton served as the "intelligence unit's only commander ... until he retired from the 488th in 1967.[362]

In 1961, Crichton joined with fellow Dallas conservatives to establish the program *"Know Your Enemy,"* which aimed to combat communist influence that *"was undermining the American way of life."* In 1962, Crichton opened a command post underneath the patio of the Dallas Health and Science Museum with the goal of maintaining the continuity-of-government were the United States attacked.

KNOW YOUR ENEMY

In Dallas in 1963, *JFK* was *the enemy. Big D* was the Capital of ultra-conservatism. In their *slanted to the rig*ht eyes, he was undermining the *American way of life.*

Crichton's activities at the time of the assassination are suspicious, to say the least. In November 1963 he was involved in the arrangements of the visit that President John F. Kennedy made to Dallas. His close friend, Deputy Police Chief George L. Lumpkin, a fellow member of the 488th Military Intelligence Detachment, drove the pilot car of Kennedy's motorcade. Also in the car was Lieutenant Colonel George Whitmeyer, commander of all Army Reserve units in East Texas. If these units were standing down, why were their leaders not?

Crichton was the first person to interview Marina Oswald after the assassination. Why wasn't it the FBI or Dallas Police? In addition, within hours of the assassination, he contacted a White Russian immigrant named Ilya Mamantov who worked for Sun Oil Company as an oil geologist. Manantov was an ultra-right-wing professor at Southern Methodist University in Dallas, who taught petroleum law. He also *happened* to be an acquaintance of Ruth Paine.

Crichton asked Mamantov to act as a translator in his interview with Marina.[363] Crichton knew Mamantov personally as a fellow petroleum geologist. He also knew him because Mamantov was a precinct chairman of the Republican Party, for which Crichton became the 1964 candidate for governor of Texas. Since Mamantov and Marina were the only speakers of Russian, we must take it in faith that the answers given by Oswald's wife

---

362   *Family of Secrets* , Russ Baker, (2008)
363   *Bloody Treason*, Noel Twyman, p.521

were what Mamantov said they were. According to Russ Baker, the author of *Family of Secrets*, they *"were far from literal translations of her Russian words and had the effect of implicating her husband in Kennedy's death."*

Crichton met with H.L. Hunt shortly after the assassination. Why? As mentioned, Crichton was linked with *Big Oil* in Dallas. In his book *Blood, Money and Power*, Barr McClellan states, *"Big Oil in Dallas during the fifties and sixties was what the OPEC oil cartel was to the United States in the seventies and beyond. One of the main concerns of this group was the preservation of the oil depletion allowance."* If JFK were re-elected, that entity would likely have been eliminated.

Strangely, another Army Intelligence officer, James Powell, was seen on the sixth floor of the TSBD near where the Manlicher Carcano was found. He later found himself trapped in the building when it was sealed off after the assassination.

At the actual moment of the assassination of President Kennedy and the wounding of Governor Connally, Crichton was attending an annual luncheon held that year at the Adolphus Hotel on Commerce Street in Dallas. Held yearly on the same weekend, the luncheon's purpose was to honor the TAMU and University of Texas football teams, who traditionally met on the gridiron on the Friday after Thanksgiving.

Crichton recalls:

> I walked over to Elm Street to see the Kennedy delegation ... President Kennedy and Jackie made a handsome couple. She was resplendent in her pink dress and pink pillbox hat. The crowds on the sidewalks applauded, and waved as they drove by ... I entered the hotel.... The room was almost filled, and people were seated at the individual tables.... We had the invocation, and many guests began to eat their lunch. Suddenly we heard sirens screaming and someone from outside ran up to the head table and excitedly said, 'The President, Vice President, and Governor Connally have all been shot.' I stood and announced the news. There was stunned silence in the room. Someone then produced a radio, and the news confirmed that the President (and Connally) had been shot."

BRANDY BRANDSTETTER

Hotelier, corporate executive, and U. S. Army intelligence officer Frank M. Brandstetter was born in Transylvania in 1912. He came to the US at the age of sixteen and worked at immigrant factory jobs, finally ending up in the restaurant and hotel business. He enlisted in the army in 1940. His spectacular achievements were legendary; He uncovered and averted a plot by German POWs in England during the Second World War, led a small party on a dangerous mission behind German lines for General Matthew Ridgway to demand a surrender from Field Marshall Walther Model, parachuted into battle on D-Day, and was involved in a confrontation with an angry Cuban mob intent on destroying the Havana Hilton. As a result, Brandstetter received the highest commendations. Brandstetter's leadership qualities soon carried over to the business world. He skillfully turned a few undeveloped casitas in Acapulco into Las Brisas, the top resort in the world in 1972. Later in life he became general manager of Seagrams de Mexico (1976-1977) and director of the Diplomatic and International Account Sales with Seagrams Overseas Sales Company. Brandstetter's papers include references to Edgar Bronfman and Gordon McClendan.[364] Brandy became involved with Santo Trafficante when Conrad Hilton sent him to manage the godfather's Havana Hotel.[365] He became close friends with Jack Crichton and David Atlee Phillips and became a member of the 488th. Brandstetter's commanding officer during the war was fellow 488th member, George Lumpkin. It was Jack Crichton and the 488th that lured Brandstetter to be in Dallas on November 22, 1963.

JAMES POWELL & THE 112TH MILITARY INTELLIGENCE UNIT

Special agent James Wesley Powell was an investigative photographer for the 112th Intelligence Corps Group based in Dallas's Rio Grande Building about ½ mile east of Dealey Plaza. This was one of seven regional commands of the 112th, which was headquartered along with the Fourth Army down at Fort Sam Houston in San Antonio. It was from sources in the 112th that personal information about Oswald and his Russian sojourn was almost instantaneously made known to the authorities and the media. This smacks of setup and foreknowledge of the assassination.

Approximately 30 seconds after the last shot, Powell snapped a photo of the facade of the Texas School Book Depository that remained unknown until the HSCA investigation. Down at the Rio Grande, the 112th's security officer Edward Coyle had just returned from a meeting with Frank Ellsworth of the ATF and the FBI's James Hosty at the ATF offices at 912 Commerce Street. The AM radio in the office suddenly

---

364   McClendon was a Dallas radio broadcaster known as "the Maverick of Radio." He was commissioned in the Office of Naval Intelligence during WWII and was a close friend of Jack Ruby.
365   Hilton also employed Warren Broglie who ended up at Luma Hotel in MC. Oswald and T.Davis were seen meeting there in the fall of 63.

went blank. Soon the phone rang and it was Powell telling them that the President had been shot. When Coyle reached Elm Street, he recognized Powell standing inside the front lobby of the depository and pointed him out to DPD Lieutenant Jack Revill of Police Intelligence. Revill was the Police Intelligence liaison to the 112th. However, Coyle never mentioned Powell in his WC or HSCA testimonies. The 112th changed names several times, it was the 112th Counterintelligence Corps Group in 1957, the 112th Intelligence Corps Group in 1961, and the 112th Military Intelligence Group in 1966. On June 30, 1974, the unit encased its colors for the first time at Fort Sam Houston, Texas. As mentioned earlier, James Powell, was seen on the sixth floor of the TSBD near where the Manlicher Carcano was found. He later found himself trapped in the building when it was sealed off after the assassination.

Powell's photo of the TSBD facade was taken about 30 seconds after the last shot. Since the photo was not made known until the HSCA investigation in the late 70s, comparisons could not be made with the only other known photo that included the 6th floor sniper's nest immediately after the last shot. Newsman Tom Dillard took that photo only 5-7 seconds after that shot. As it turns out, there is a major discrepancy between the photos. In Powell's photograph, boxes are seen in the center of the window. These boxes are not present in the Dillard version. The HSCA was forced to conclude that *"the additional boxes visible in the Powell photograph were moved during the interval between" the two photos."* This box rearrangement would have delayed Oswald's legendary flight down the stairs to the second floor lunchroom. Not only did the FBI hide this evidence from the Warren Commission. Anyone with the 112th who knew about it; at the very least Powell himself, never came forward.

Edward Coyle's ARRB testimony indicates that Powell never intended to give up any of his photos in the first place. He was an investigative photographer for the 112th, half a mile from his office, with the President in town, yet he needed somebody to bring him a camera?! Had he not been trapped inside the TSBD when police sealed off the building, we would probably never have known about this important piece of evidence. Coyle was very close to Dallas FBI agent James Hosty. In fact, he called him "Jimmy." According to Edward Coyle's ARRB testimony in 1996, he was Head of Security Section of the Dallas 112th Army Intelligence Unit and Liaison to the Dallas Secret Service at the time of the JFK assassination. In testimony to ARRB staff member, Tim Wray, Coyle said; *"... my boss, the Colonel, had a comment, and I'm not sure whether he made this before the thing or after, but he was quite surprised that we were not asked to participate in the security of the president during the motorcade and while he was in Dallas." He added; "We weren't asked, ONI wasn't asked, OSI wasn't asked, the FBI wasn't asked. He says that the Dallas Police Department and the Secret Service said that they had everything taken care of."*

At 3:15 P.M. on November 22, 1963, Colonel Robert E. Jones, of the 112th Army Intelligence Corps. telephoned the Department of Justice/ FBI to notify them Oswald had been arrested for killing Tippit. According to him, his source was news broadcasts. Later he changed his story and said the source was a DPD officer sometime between one and two o'clock. Oswald was arrested at 1:50 P.M. At the time of Jones's call Oswald had just entered the interrogation room. Jones produced an extensive file on Oswald that included the Hidell alias, Russian defection, news clippings and the skinny on his New Orleans FPCC activities. How did he have all this stuff so soon? It is actually the first time the Hidell name is mentioned by authorities.

The Warren Commission called no members of the 112th to testify. The HSCA did call some of them, including Jones, in 1977. Jones testified that he suspected Oswald of being an intelligence agent. He also thought he did not act alone in the assassination.

IN SUMMARY; WHERE THERE'S SMOKE, THERE'S FIRE

In November 1963 Jack Alston Crichton was involved in the arrangements of the visit that President John F. Kennedy made to Dallas. His close friend, Deputy Police Chief George L. Lumpkin, a fellow member of the 488th Military Intelligence Detachment, who drove the pilot car of Kennedy's motorcade, would later tell the House Select Committee on Assassinations that he had been consulted by the Secret Service on motorcade security, and his input had eliminated an alternative route.[366] Also in the car was Lieutenant Colonel George Whitmeyer. The pilot car stopped briefly in front of the Texas School Book Depository, where Lumpkin spoke to a policeman controlling traffic at the corner of Houston and Elm. So, it appears that Crichton and Lumpkin played a role in the decision to change the motorcade route from continuing down Main Street to turning on Houston and then onto Elm.

As mentioned earlier, in 1956 Jack Alston Crichton started up his own spy unit, the 488th Military Intelligence Detachment in Dallas.[367] In an inter-

366   What did you say, George???
367   Russ Baker points out in *Family of Secrets* (2008) Crichton served as the "intelligence unit's only commander... until he retired from the 488th in 1967."

view Crichton claimed that there were "about a hundred men in that unit and about forty or fifty of them were from the Dallas Police Department." Crichton served as the unit's commander under Lieutenant Colonel George Whitmeyer, who was in overall command of all Army Reserve units in East Texas. Why were Whitmeyer and Lumpkin in the pilot car of Kennedy's motorcade?

Also, Crichton went up against John Connolly in the Governor race of 1964. He was very critical of both Connolly and LBJ, calling for them to make public the findings in the Billie Sol Estes investigation. George H.W. Bush backed up Crichton's calls and both men went on the political attack. So we have Bush and Crichton vs LBJ and Connally. Why?

Bush and Crichton were political allies as well as business associates. Both were involved in the financing of the Operation 40 assassination squads. Crichton was connected to army intelligence and had been an OSS Operative in WWII. Bush was CIA connected and eventually became its director. Both were deeply tied to Dallas Oil and were Kennedy haters like their oil business associates, H.L. Hunt and Clint Murchison. Crichton played a role in questioning Oswald's widow through fellow oil man, Illya Mamantov who was an acquaintance of Ruth Paine. The convenient tie-in of Dallas Police,[368] particularly Crichton's good friend, Lumpkin, adds fuel to the fire. The speculation that D.P.D. played a role in framing Oswald and aiding Ruby has long been haunting the events of November '63.

FOLLOW THE YELLOW BRICK ROAD
DID CRICHTON PLAY A ROLE IN THE EVENTS OF 11/22/63?

Jesus, let me tell you, let me ... in so many ways Jack Crichton is critical ... is the critical lynch pin to solving any mystery in the JFK assassination, but any real investigator must have all the pieces to the Crichton puzzle, I mean it.

–Col. Albert Haney, Florida,1990s

THE EVIDENCE:

Crichton was a very powerful and well connected right wing conservative.

- His Empire Trust[369] network acted as a private CIA.

- The Bronfman dynasty was a primary investor in Empire Trust as well as in PERMINDEX. Chairman of PERMINDEX, Louis

---

368   Forty or fifty of them were members of the 488th.
369   The Empire Trust, investment bank based on Bronfman fortune and PERMINDEX, hired Crichton in Aug '53 Crichton.

Bloomfield was a Bronfman attorney. The links to PERMINDEX are transparent.[370]

- He commanded an entire Intelligence detachment (488th).

- He was part of the influential right wing oil cartel of Dallas and had the ears of billionaires like H.L. Hunt. Crichton was, in fact, head of H.L. Hunt Foundation.

- He was well connected to the Dallas Police and many of them were part of his 488th command.[371]

- He used his influence to be the first to interview Marina Oswald and used his personally chosen translator to do so. The translator was a member of the same right wing Dallas oil cartel.

- He, as well as Oswald's widow made visits to H.L. Hunt shortly after the assassination.[372] Why?

- He and his crony, George Lumpkin, played a role in the choosing of the motorcade route. Where there is smoke, there is fire.

- It was Jack Crichton and the 488th that lured Brandy Brandstetter to be in Dallas on November 22, 1963. Brandstetter was associated with Gordon McClendon. McClendon was one of Jack Ruby's closest friends ... according to Jack Ruby anyway.

- Crichton had a relationship with Skorzeny in Spain after the war. In 1952 while working with Delta Drilling of Tyler, TX.

- De Mohrenschildt also a friend and involved in Meadows-Korzybski venture.

- Delta Drilling was an integral part of the 1952 Meadows-Skorzeney venture in Spain.

- Crichton's diary mentions: "his unit's participation" and "concealment involvement" with Dallas leg of President Kennedy's Texas trip.

- The head of the intelligence component of Dallas Civil Defense was Jack Crichton.

Members of the 488th'

Jack Crichton

George Lumpkin

---

370   PERMINDEX was a direct extension of Bill Donovan's World Commerce Corporation, and WCC worked closely with New Orleans Trade mart.

371   At least 50% of DPD were members of the 488th.

372   Crichton met with HL Hunt the day after the assassination.

Jack Revill

Pat Gannaway[373]

William Westbrook

Frank Brandstetter

Jack Earnest

LIKELY MEMBERS OF THE 488TH INCLUDE:

Boise B Smith

Gerald Hill

Don Stringfellow

LIKELY ASSETS OF THE 488TH INCLUDE:

George de Mohrenschildt

---

373   It was DPD Capt. Pat Ganaway that falsely claimed a roll call had taken place at the TSBD and Oswald only one missing. It was also he that revealed Oswald's Russian episode.

CHAPTER 20

THE PALACE GUARD

I told the FBI that I heard (two shots from behind the grassy knoll fence), but they said it couldn't have happened that way and that I must have been imagining things. So I testified the way they wanted me to. I just didn't want to stir up any more pain and trouble for the family.
– Kenny O'Donnel, White House Aid and Presidential Advisor

A president is an easy target if he isn't protected. JFK was a sitting duck. You can argue all you want about the integrity of that Secret Service, but in the end you will have to admit that they did nothing to protect their charge. The only agent that reacted at all was Clint Hill and he was assigned to *Lace* and not *Lancer*.[374]

How was the Dallas motorcade different from all the others of Kennedy's brief administration? Vince Palamara has covered this topic very well in his books on the subject. He looked at films of earlier motorcades and interviewed the agents themselves.

The motorcade route itself broke sundry Secret Service's rules. Hairpin turns, slowing to 5 miles an hour, leaving windows in tall buildings open and not having agents in positions to watch them for suspicious activity, were all violations. The SS also played a role in choosing the route. Changes were made to the motorcade route at the last minute. The positions of the vehicles were rearranged from their usual slots. The newsmen and their cameras were pushed toward the rear of the parade where they could not take photos of the tragic events that were about to happen. The president's physician, Dr. Burkley, was also moved toward the rear of the procession where he would not be able to react if needed. The motorcycle officers were kept back and did not ride in there normal locations on the sides of the president's limousine. There were no agents riding on the bumper or side handles of the car either. At least one agent Henry Rybka, was left behind at Love Field. When he tried to mount JFK's vehicle as he normally did, he and Agent Don Lawton were waved off the vehicle by

---

The Secret Service code names for Jackie and JFK were Lace and Lancer.

Agent in Charge, Emory Roberts. In addition, when the shooting started in Dealey Plaza, Agent John Ready tried to react but was called back by the same agent, Emory Roberts. Many of the men were out drinking into the early morning hours on the eve of the motorcade. They should have been punished or even fired for breaking the SS rule of no drinking on duty. They weren't. Why? The driver of the limo, William Greer, looked back and brought the car to nearly a complete stop, speeding up only when he was satisfied that the President was dead. He had been trained to floor the gas pedal and get the President out of harm's way as quickly as possible.

That is not to say that all the agents were responsible. The obviously suspicious individuals are Emory Roberts and William Greer for sure. Floyd Boring is suspect as well, although he wasn't in Dallas. Winston Lawson is a fringe suspect to me. The Secret Service is part of the Treasury Department, which points a finger at its head C. Douglas Dillon, since that is where the buck stops. Lawson told the WC that JFK did not want his protectors on the vehicle. Palamara interviewed the other agents and found that absolutely not the case.

Further suspicious acts incriminate the palace guard as well. Taking JFK's body illegally from Parkland Hospital at gunpoint was incriminating, although they may have been ordered to do so by LBJ. Washing out the vehicle at Parkland and thus destroying evidence is also an indication of a cover-up. Replacing that very evening, the windshield that reportedly had a bullet hole in it says volumes. Consigning Governor Connally's clothes to the cleaners amounts to undeniable contamination of evidence. Later sending SS100X[375] to Detroit to be rebuilt, essentially wipes out a crime scene and amounts to a criminal act. This does not even take into account the failure to provide a chain of custody for the trail of the "*magic*" bullet. Making matters worse, recently Agent Paul Landis has come forward and said he retrieved that bullet, which wasn't so magical at all. In his version of events, it never left the seat Kennedy was sitting in, let alone induce all of Connally's wounds. Not only did he keep this secret for 60 years, he recounted that he just laid it on a stretcher without telling anyone. Which stretcher? Why didn't he give it to a superior or an FBI agent or even a Dallas policeman? He just dropped it on a stretcher and walked away? The Parkland Hospital doctor's testimony indicates that some of the doctors, McClelland for instance, were told never to mention an entry wound again by a Secret Service or FBI agent. This is proof of a cover-up already under way on the very weekend of the assassination! They knew

---

375   Secret Service code name for the presidential car.

that early that Oswald was to be the patsy and was located in the rear of the Presidential vehicle. Therefore all the shots had to have come from the rear...whether they actually did *or not.*

Of course the Secret Service wasn't the only agency to act suspiciously. The Dallas Sheriff had his men "stand down," as revealed by deputy Roger Craig. The 112th Military Intelligence Unit, usually assigned as a support group, also was in "stand down" mode.

By observing the performance of the Secret Service at the times of threats to other presidents, one can see the profound difference in their response. In assassination attempts on FDR, Truman, Ford and Reagan, the agents acted quickly, professionally and bravely to save the lives of their charges. In Dealey Plaza they did nothing.

But the Secret Service wasn't the only agency involved in providing protection for the President, or perhaps in leaving the President unprotected. As discussed in Chapter 18, Military Intelligence played a role as well. In addition, it was they who were the source of the earliest reports on Oswald's background as a Russian defector, his description and history was immediately released to the media. As Peter Dale Scott has pointed out, it was the 488th that was also responsible for the false Marina story involving Oswald's rifle[376] and the Stringfellow report.[377] Scott calls these actions *phase one* efforts to tie Oswald to the Communists in Cuba and Russia to the assassination designed to encourage an invasion of Cuba.

Mamantov's creative interpretations of Marina's responses to questioning were particularly damning to her husband. Not surprisingly, he was selected for the task in a phone call between Deputy Police Chief George Lumpkin and Jack Crichton. Crichton commanded the 488th; and Deputy Police Chief, Lumpkin was deputy commander of the unit under Crichton. Lt. Col. George Whitmeyer, Crichton's superior in the Army Reserves, rode in the motorcade's pilot car along with Lumpkin. The car inexplicably stopped in front of the TSBD.[378] Lumpkin was not the only DPD member who belonged to the 488th. Crichton admitted that about half of the intelligence unit's 100 men were also members of the DPD. Did these members and assets of the unit play roles in the events of No-

---

376   Mamantov translated Marina Oswald response on the description of Oswald's rifle to say that it looked like the rifle he owned in Russia. (Marina's actual words, before mis-translation, were quite innocuous: "I cannot describe it [the gun] because a rifle to me like all rifles.")

377   Assistant Chief Don Stringfellow, Intelligence Section, Dallas Police Department, notified 112th INTC [Intelligence] Group, this Headquarters, that information obtained from Oswald revealed he had defected to Cuba in 1959 and is a card-carrying member of Communist Party."

378   Owned by D.H. Bird, who was also director of Dorchester Gas Producing. A company owned by Crichton.

vember 22nd? The list of members and resource assets included; Jack Revill, William Westbrook, Frank Brandstetter, Jack Earnest, Boise B. Smith, Gerald Hill, Don Stringfellow, asset named George de Mohrenschildt, and Pat Gannaway.[379]?

PAT GANNAWAY

Gannaway was one of the first to hint that LHO was a Communist on November 22nd and that he had lived in Russia and had a Russian wife. It was he and Chief of Intelligence Section of the DPD, Don Stringfellow, both members of 488th, that made the false claim that a roll call was taken at the TSBD and that Oswald was the only one missing. In 1948 he and his partner George Butler, Gannaway arrested Paul Rowland Jones as part of a bribery attempt. Jack Ruby was linked to Jones and was interrogated behind closed doors at a Kefauver Committee hearing by Butler in 1950. Ruby became of interest when Jones and his associates began hanging around Ruby's club after the trial. In spite of this Gannaway denied that there was any mob activity in Dallas. As for the roll call, Gannaway's source was supposedly Oswald's boss, Roy Truly. The article below quotes Truly as denying Oswald was the only one missing.

THE MAD HATTER

Crichton's haberdashery included another hat, that of *Chief of Intelligence for Dallas Civil Defense*. So, in addition to Commander of the 488th Military Intelligence Detachment, big D oil and natural gas industrialist, ex-OSS agent, and vice-president of Empire Trust (and it's private Intelligence network), he was involved in a civil defense unit. This unit worked out of an underground Emergency Operating Center. Russ Baker described this facility's purpose as "continuity of government operations."[380] It was part of the National Plan to link Federal, State and local government agencies in a communications network in case of a national emergency. This acted, more or less, as a doomsday machine designed to keep essential network communications going in a major emergency like a nuclear war. This, in essence, would create a shadow government to carry on in the event the actual government and/or the president were dead.

---

379   Special Service Division Chief Gannaway, who Bill Simpich calls the master of the Dallas spooks, like Butler, is everywhere in the JFK case. He worked Narcotics, Vice and Criminal Intelligence for DPD. There are innuendos he had CIA ties as well. Another Gannaway link to Ruby is Commission Document 86. It reports that FBI SA Frank M. Ivey was advised by a Texas police officer named Robert L. Forche that he, Forche, was introduced to Jack Ruby by Mary Hartford. He believed Harford to be Ruby's mistress. Hartford was formerly a secretary to Captain Pat Gannaway.
380   Known as COG.

Considering the outage of key communications immediately after the assassination,[381] one cannot help but wonder if Scott's *phase one* scenario, a version of Operation NORTHWOODS, was to be a nuclear strike against the Soviets as retaliation for the false-flag evidence of their alleged involvement in Kennedy's assassination.

Conclusion

What adds so much confusion to the *Crime of the Century* is the multitude of guilty looking adversaries who possessed motive and wanted JFK eliminated. The CIA, FBI, National Security State, SISS and HUAC, Anti-Castro Cubans, organized crime, Joint Chiefs, Military Intelligence, KGB, Castro, big D oil tycoons, right wing extremists; Minutemen, Birchers etc. JFK's enemies were sundry and powerful. But once again, we are not seeing the forest for the trees. Many of these entities were made up of the same people! People who wore more than one hat. The CIA, Mafia and Anti-Castro Cubans were all sides of the same coin and worked together as a team. The Birchers, Minutemen, white supremacists, oil tycoons, SISS and HUAC all held the same beliefs and worked together as the radical Right. Joint Chiefs, Military Intelligence, CIA, NSA were also like-minded and collaborated for the same goals. The KGB and Castro worked together but not well. Since the Coup required a coordinated effort inside our government, and because of the *phase one* efforts to frame them, the Communists are unlikely suspects.

If we take away the labels of all of JFK's antagonists what we have left are like-minded individuals with the same goals. Fueled by patriotism, anti-Communist fervor, racism, hatred of Kennedy and his policies, and radical Right wing ideology, the powerful group was indeed amiable to and capable of a coup d'état.

The most suspicious evidence of a team effort by intertwined adversaries presents itself in the odd relationship of the 488th Military Intelligence Unit and the Dallas Police. Half of the 488th's members were also members of DPD. In addition, a majority of the Dallas Police were Birchers and Klan members as well. DPD also had a working relationship with the Dallas organized crime syndicate. Crichton is a key to this whole charade. His being Chief of Intelligence for Dallas Civil Defense opens up another layer to the multitasking organization of the conspiracy. It was key Military Intelligence operatives, selected Secret Service agents, and *multi-affil-*

---

381   Phone communications were out as well as communications were disabled on the plane carrying the President's Cabinet members to Hawaii. Could Collins radio have been involved? It was they who installed the hardware on Air Force 1, Air force 2 and the Cabinet plane as well.

iated Dallas Police that made up the Palace Guard in Dallas in November 1963. All Right wing, like-minded, Southern *good old boys*.

Peter Dale Scott notes that SS agent Winston Lawson is the man who installed the radio frequency transmissions for the motorcade which was part of the 1950s doomsday COG scenario. [Collins Radio?] These tapes form a key document of the assassination, yet they were never reviewed by the Warren Commission. Lieutenant Colonel George Whitmeyer, commander of all Army Reserve units in East Texas, and a fellow member of the 488th MID, Dallas Deputy Police Chief George L. Lumpkin, drove the pilot car in the motorcade through Dealey Plaza. SS agent Lawson, formerly of Army Intelligence, was in the car behind them driven by Dallas police chief Jesse Curry. Lawson had to change his story and admit later that his testimony to the WC regarding the position of the motorcycle escort was "mistaken" that they were not flanking JFK's limo but actually rode just behind. DPD Captain Curry testified that this arrangement was designed by Lawson himself.

CHAPTER 21

A VORTEX OF DUPLICITY

Three things cannot be long hidden: the sun, the moon, and the truth.
– Buddha

As overseer of the *Wilderness of Mirrors*, James Angleton used contradiction and duplicity to sew confusion among his counterparts and foreign adversaries. In my book, *The Other Oswald, A Wilderness of Mirrors*, I alluded to the illusive technique of using doubles of everything to muddle the case against Oswald. Too much evidence in a case of this magnitude is strongly suggestive of a frame-up. To accept the official story, we are asked to believe that the Keystone Cops (Dallas police) solved the Crime of the Century within an hour. These caped crusaders quickly captured a lone nut Commie who killed the President as well as a heroic policeman. Strangely, he did so without motive. Adding to this scenario, another lone nut, with links to organized crime, murdered the first lone nut. This lone nut did have a motive. He, a Jew who loved a Catholic president. It didn't seem to matter that this love conflicted with the fervent hatred his fellow mobster friends nurtured for their commander-in-Chief. These same superbly efficient Keystone Crusaders then accidentally let down their guard long enough to allow Oswald's Semitic, but Christian loving, assassin to stroll into their headquarters, penetrate a large body of protectors without any problem, and slaughter a prisoner in their charge even though they had been warned in advance that it would happen.

Had Oswald gone to trial, and he likely would have needed a change of venue to get a fair one, a good lawyer would have had a lot to work with. Mark Lane's *Rush to Judgment* could have served as a defense brief. In fact, it likely would have been he who wound up defending the patsy. Oswald's mother asked that Lane be Lee's representative during the Warren Commission meetings.

Exposing the plethora of double evidence in this case would have placed the prosecutors on the hot seat. Oswald was denied legal representation, although he asked for it more than once. All the pairing of evidence smacked of a frame-up. Two rifles, two packages to wrap the rifle, two revolvers, two wallets, two sets of ID, two jackets, two shoe stores, two School Book Depositories, two Oswalds and two separate 201 CIA files (Lee Henry and Lee Harvey) on Oswald, two separate entrances with different street addresses for his FPCC operation in New Orleans, and several versions of the Neely Street photos. A surplus of planted evidence with no chain of custody and much of it coming from *anonymous* sources would be a valuable resource to a good defense lawyer. Then there is the identity sharing charade of covert operatives. There were at least two Oswalds running around Dallas in the weeks before the assassination. Other clandestine operatives shared identities as well. Souetre/Mertz and Bishop/Phillips for example, and as has come to light more recently, June/Jerrie Cobb. A CIA agent involved in Oswald's Mexico City adventure, Cobb, it appears, had a doppelganger named Jerrie. It still isn't clear if she was an alternate personality, a twin sister or just an alias. But somehow these two were used like Webster and Oswald to confuse and frustrate the enemy and cloud investigation.

The following excerpt is from my book, *The Other Oswald, A Wilderness of Mirrors*;:

MEET JUNE COBB—SHE'S A SOLDIER OF FORTUNE

"All that is needed to make this tale of espionage and intrigue a James Bond adventure is a beautiful *Mata Hari*. Enter Viola June Cobb,[382] an adventure-loving world traveler.[383] Cobb was a femme fatale, who courted dangerous missions and flirted with death. The *"official"* story is that while at University in Mexico she met Rafael Herran Olozaga, a student and a chemist, whose grandfather and great-grandfather had both been presidents of Colombia. Romance enticed her to travel with him and his brother, Thomas, who was a pilot, to the jungles of Ecuador. Together they lived among the Indians where he and his brother farmed opium. While there she took a position at Pan American Airways in public relations. The romance didn't last. Some said she left Olozaga when he became addicted to his own crop. Others that her lover left her for another woman.[384]

[382] AKA Joyce H. Pineinch, AKA Clarinda E. Sharp. Born Ponca, Oklahoma August 24, 1927.
[383] Career Travels: Mexico 1947-48 (educational study), Ecuador with fiance 1949, Columbia 1951-52 with fiance, Cuba 1959 working with Cuban Government, Mexico and Guatamala 1961 (expelled from Guatamala for political reasons), Mexico City 1981-65, New York City 1966- (resigned CIA).
[384] The "official" story of her life reads like a bad romance novel.

In 1951 Cobb contracted leishmaniasis, a rare tropical disease, which resulted in spending several months at Mount Sinai Hospital in NYC.[385] At some point after her return to the US, she turned Olozaga in to authorities. According to FBN Agent George Gaffney, "*A woman with CIA connections offered information to an agent.*" If she was *connected* to the CIA at this time, it was long before her *official* 1960 recruitment.

The likely "*truth*" is, as John Newman contends, that she met Olozaga in Mexico City and not at the University of Oklahoma. In addition, she was probably working for the FBN[386] undercover and the South American adventure was a mission to infiltrate drug traffickers. The Olozaga brothers were a source for Cuban cocaine.[387] Did she

Viola June Cobb

"squeal" on *Rafa*, as she called her lover, out of jealousy? Or did she blow the whistle as part of her duties as an undercover FBN agent?

The "*official*" story of her life continues by relating that in 1959 she was working as a journalist in New York when Castro visited the Big Apple after taking power. The Cuban leader, possibly taken with her beauty, invited her to come to Cuba and work as an English-language translator to the American media, a good choice since she spoke fluent Spanish. Becoming enamored with the revolution, Cobb moved to Cuba and accepted the position. Rumor has it that she was one of Castro's lovers. Her office on his senior staff was just down the hall from the Cuban dictator. She saw him, his brother Raul and Che Guevara daily. It was her belief that Castro was doing a "tremendous" job in reconstructing the economy of Cuba. She also believed it unthinkable that Communism would be embraced by Castro or the people of Cuba. In June 1960, she was *officially* recruited by the CIA[388] as a contract agent. While spying on Fidel she watched him as

---

385   She was treated by Dr. I. Snapper. By 1952 they had become lovers. He took a position at a Chicago hospital and she became his secretary .

386   Federal Bureau of Narcotics

387   By 1951 they had gone from producing opium to cocaine.

388   June 1960. Previously declassified CIA document show that Cobb's information was valuable in preparing the spy agency's detailed psychological profiles of Castro and his deputies and in monitoring their activities. Her cryptonym was AMUPAS-1. She was recruited by a Mr. Hermsdorf in Cuba. Her 201 file was 201-278841.

he metamorphosed into a Communist. Disillusioned with the revolution and fearful of her fate after her friend, another American, Captain William Morgan,[389] was tried and shot as a traitor, she fled Cuba and was assigned to the Mexico City CIA Station in June 1961. Her CIA cryptonym was LICooky-1.[390] The objective of the LICOOKY PROJECT was to identify and report on plans, activities and associates of Central American Communists, resident or visiting Mexico City. She monitored Cuban agents, as well as Mexicans who were sympathetic to Castro. Cobb's time in Mexico City coincided with the Oswald circus.

The *"truth"* is that she was probably working for the CIA all along to infiltrate Castro's regime. John Newman believes that she went to Cuba in April 1959 and not September of that year as she claimed. The spring-summer of 1960 recruitment by the CIA was also a cover story to make it look like she went to Cuba on her own out of admiration for Castro.[391] She actually went there as a CIA agent to spy on Castro.

A year after the assassination, she reported to her CIA boss, David Atlee Phillips, that she had identified a trio of witnesses who could tie Lee Harvey Oswald to Cuban diplomats and spies in Mexico City. FOIA documents show that three sources, including a well known Mexican writer, stated that they had seen Oswald at a "twist party" at the home of Ruben and Sylvia Duran,[392] the woman who Oswald had supposedly spoken to at the Cuban Embassy. Cuban diplomats and others who displayed anti-Kennedy sentiments were also present. The sources indicated that Oswald was not alone. He had two American compatriots with him, apparently traveling companions, who looked like *beatniks*. If true, this is evidence of Cuban influence in the assassination or an attempt to incriminate them.

The CIA's Mexico City station, its files reveal, downplayed Cobb's report. Her report contradicted the official story that Oswald was a lone nut, and that the Agency was powerless to have done anything to stop him. The CIA, therefore, withheld this information from the Warren Commission. A 2013 report by the CIA's in-house historian confirms that the agency had conducted a *"benign cover-up"* in the years immediately after Kennedy's assassination.

---

389   Cobb befriended Morgan and testified on his behalf before the Senate Internal Security Subcommittee in 1962.
390   Her crypt was AMUPAS-1 while in Cuba and US. It was changed to LICOOKY-1 in Mexico City.
391   *Countdown to Darkness, The Assassination of President Kennedy, Vol II,* John M. Newman
392   See these documents in appendix H

Cobb's main source for the *twisted* Oswald story was a Mexican novelist and playwright named Elena Garro de Paz. De Paz was also a cousin of Sylvia Duran.[393] The FBI interviewed her and rejected her account, even though other witnesses supported her. They did also not pursue other leads Cobb provided. Even if they had wanted to, it was too late by that time since the Commission issued its final report two weeks before Cobb's allegations were revealed. The investigation was rushed through so as not to have an effect on the upcoming 1964 election.

In a 1978 interview with Dan Hardway, David Atlee Phillips described Cobb as; "*Blond, flew an airplane; track record for hitting a lot of beds in Cuba; had a twin sister who was an aviator.*"[394] Cobb was an Adjutant of the Civil Air Patrol Squadron of Norman, Oklahoma. Her commission was Second Lieutenant. During wartime the CAP was an auxiliary of the Armed Air Forces. Oswald and David Ferrie were involved in the CAP in Louisiana. D.H. Byrd, owner of the Texas Schoolbook Depository in Dallas, was a founder of the CAP. She had no known twin sister, much less one that was an aviator. Could she have had a CIA double like Oswald and Webster? Or was she lying when she said she didn't fly? Perhaps she too had an MKULTRA background. One personality was a pilot and the other never left the ground.[395]

An interesting side note is Cobb's involvement as a translator for a book entitled *The Shark and the Sardines*, by Juan José Arévalo. The book was an allegory about US domination of Latin America. It was published in Spanish in 1956. An English version appeared in 1961 (translated by Cobb).

Arévalo had been elected president of Guatemala in 1944 in what was considered by many to be the first fair and democratic election in Guatemalan history. During his term in office (1945–1951), he initiated a moderate agrarian reform that continued under the administration of Jacobo Arbenz, who succeeded him as president in 1951.

Arévalo's book, *The Fable*, echoed the strong anti-imperialist sentiment prevalent throughout the continent against US government meddling in Latin America. In the introduction, Arévalo writes: "*The Eisenhower Administration and US foreign companies with investments in Guatemala, especially the United Fruit Company, became concerned about the course of the*

---

393   There is evidence that Duran herself may have been targeted for CIA recruitment.
394   (180-10142-10078)
395   New information regarding the alleged sister-pilot has now come forward and will be addressed later in this chapter.

agrarian reform. In 1954 the Central Intelligence Agency orchestrated a coup d'état that overthrew the Arbenz government."

By a strange coincidence, Lee Harvey Oswald borrowed this book from the Dallas Public Library on November 6, 1963. It was never returned.[396] Even stranger, the address the Dallas Library had for Oswald was 602 Elsbeth Street."

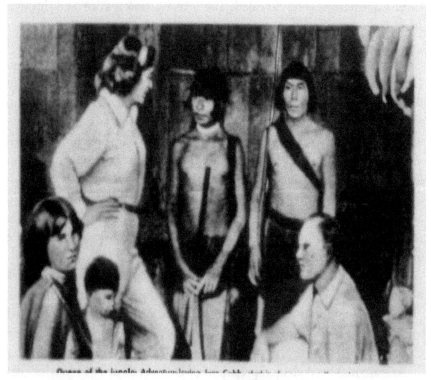

Cobb speaks with Amazonian natives in Ecuador. Picture from Parade Magazine article by Jack Anderson titled "Meet June Cobb—She's A Soldier of Fortune." August 1962

JERRIE COBB

Jerrie Cobb was an American pilot and aviator and part of the *Mercury 13 program*. This was a group of women who underwent the same physiological screening tests as the *Mercury Seven* astronauts. Cobb was the first of

---

396   "After the assassination of JFK, the FBI asked Lillian Bradshaw, library director for the city of Dallas, for records of Lee Harvey Oswald's transactions at the library. The search took months, according to a current display at the J. Erik Jonsson Central Library, because circulation records, stored on microfiche, weren't indexed. Eventually, library officials determined that Oswald had checked out a book that was overdue at the time of his death: *The Shark and the Sardines*, by Juan José Arévalo. The 1961 book, written by a former president of Guatemala, was a pointed denunciation of US foreign policy in Latin America. It's been reprinted but the original editions are now a rarity. The one checked out by Oswald was never returned." -Bruce Tomasco, Dallas Morning News, November 2013.

the group to complete the tests successfully. Jerrie set aviation records for non-stop long-distance flight, the world lightweight aircraft speed record and the world altitude record for lightweight aircraft, all while still in her 20s. She was named by *Life* magazine as one of nine women of the top 100 most important young people in the United States in 1960.[397]

Jerrie Cobb

The LICOOKY Project

A new book by Mary Haverstick, *"A Woman I Know,"* has unveiled a double-identity operation that links June and Jerrie Cobb as, at the very least, shapeshifting alter egos. Haverstick has documented that Jerrie used June's name in espionage activities, and that June had multiple social security numbers and paid taxes under pseudonyms. June even

---

397   Wikipedia

loaned her birth certificate to someone, possibly Jerrie, for travel to Cuba. It seems that the CIA was running a double identity project that involved these two women for clandestine operations in Mexico, Cuba and around the world.

Was David Atlee Phillips description of Cobb as; *"Blond, flew an airplane; track record for hitting a lot of beds in Cuba; had a twin sister who was an aviator."* Was this a tease to add confusion to the story of these two women? They were not sisters. Were they the same woman using two identities? Were they different women using the same identity?

Haverstick believes that they are two separate people but will not swear to it. If they are, their similarities are astounding.

They were both born in Oklahoma. June was born in Ponca City in 1927 to Jasper E. Cobb and Jesse Lois Sharp. Jerrie in the city of Norman in 1931. Her parents were Col. William Cobb and Helena Butler Stone Cobb. However, Jerrie spent the majority of her childhood in Ponca City!

June graduated from Ponca City High School, then attended the University of Oklahoma for one year. Jerrie attended Classen High School and Oklahoma College for Women also for one year.

Both women were in the Civil Air Patrol. June was an adjunct of the Norman squadron, attaining the rank of 2nd class Lieutenant. Jerrie earned her pilot's license in high school at age 17. In 1946, both were living in Oklahoma City. June helped organize the local Civil Air Patrol squadron and Jerrie was a junior member of the same unit.

Both girls soon left Oklahoma for international travels. Both ended up in South America. June traveled to Guayaquil, Ecuador and was hired as a PR in aviation. Jerrie also ventured to Guayaquil and was promptly arrested for spying. Each seemed to be infringing on the other's tradecraft.

Both were able to communicate in Spanish. They then shared itineraries, traveling to Colombia, Ecuador, Venezuela and the Amazon jungle. Their flying adventures included romantic involvement with men they would later call the loves of their lives.

Both then visited Cuba at the same time Castro was beginning his revolutionary operations.

Both were employed by Time-Life and were involved with movie projects.

Both worked for oil companies.

Both testified to Congress about their biographies.

Both were described as blond. Jerrie was, June wasn't. But then Oswald wasn't 5'10" and didn't weigh 165, but his clone, Robert Webster, was.

* * *

We have seen this version of trade craft before. Two or more individuals being merged to confuse and complicate covert activities. John Armstrong's Harvey & Lee[398], Souetre & Mertz, Osborne/Bowen, Oswald & Webster.... Names, activities, locations, physical characteristics, identities, all documented with fake birth certificates, social security numbers, passports, fake identification, employment and travel records, use of doubles; whatever is deemed necessary to wipe trails clean.

Haverstick's research is first-class. She has uncovered more skulduggery involving the Bobbsey ... er ... Cobb twins in a relatively short time than the entire research community has in decades. Unfortunately, her final conclusions are sure to elicit severe opposition from that same community. She believes, although she says she is not certain, that Jerrie Cobb was not only the Bubushka lady, but JFK's assassin. Even worse, she has concluded that the weapon was a camera gun. In her defense she has documentation showing that Bill Harvey's ZRRIFLE program was developing a secret weapon along those lines. In addition, she has evidence placing Jerrie and her plane at Red Bird Airport in Dallas on the day of the assassination.

In addition she convincingly links June Cobb to the QJWIN program and even suggests June was actually QJWIN him/herself, it would seem Jerrie was in essence working for June in this caper as part of ZRRIFLE. The author documents Cobbs links to Bill Harvey in Mexico City as a cutout in dealings with Juan Orta. Orta, a Cuban official close to Fidel, was to be his assassin via a poison pill delivered by American mobsters (Roselli-Giancana). The pill was to be slipped into a chocolate milkshake according to ex-Cuban Intelligence agent Fabian Escalante. Haverstick deduces that at the same time these machinations were taking place, documents show that June Cobb was also dealing with Orta in efforts to get him to defect. That, Haverstick believes, was just a cover and June Cobb was, in actuality, the go-between in the ZRRIFLE Castro assassination plot. In other words, the mob didn't give Orta the pills, Cobb did. It was Cobb, and not Jose Mankel, who was actually the *real* QJWIN.

As I see it, whether the camera-gun wielding Bubushka lady aspect of the story has any truth or not, it is inconsequential. It doesn't matter. The rest of the information in the book is of immense value. Through its revelations, we can see the inner workings of how CIA counterintelligence

398   Armstrong documents that two boys used the same identities and attended different schools, worked in different places, served in different military units and even seemed to share birth certificates.

functions in regard to duplicating individual's identities. Through this wilderness of mirrors, the web spinning of James Angleton becomes evident. Once again, back tracking from Cobb to Harvey or Cobb to Phillips or Cobb to Pearson, leads us to James Jesus Angleton.

One of the mysteries surrounding June Cobb involves the Elena Garro de Paz revelations. It was Cobb who first reported the *twist party* story to David Phillips as proof of a Communist conspiracy. For some reason her efforts were thwarted by Mexico City Station Chief Win Scott. Subsequently, the Warren Commission was never advised of these accusations. De Paz sought desperately to get her information to authorities, including Robert Kennedy. Surprisingly, Cobb then made an about-face and, according to de Paz, frightening her, injuring her pet cat and insinuating her life might be in danger. It was at this point Cobb admitted to de Paz that she was a CIA agent and that de Paz could report to her rather than the FBI, police or anyone else. When de Paz later moved to New York, the discovery of Cobb's presence in that city terrorized her once again.

But Cobb wasn't the only one to attempt to notify Win Scott of the de Paz story. Diplomat Charles Thomas, a Foreign Service officer, stationed in Mexico from 1964 to 1967, uncovered details of Oswald's alleged affair with Sylvia Duran, the woman who had interviewed him at the Cuban Embassy. Thomas assumed that the CIA and FBI would be interested in his new evidence. He assumed wrong.

Instead, Thomas was punished for making inquiries about JFK's assassination. Although he had excellent job recommendations, he was inexplicably dismissed from the Foreign Service in 1969. His daughter Cynthia Thomas told a reporter, "*It was nonsensical, Charles was the best sort of American diplomat.*"

Charles Thomas lost his position in the State Department and was unable to find employment anywhere. He made one last effort to bring the de Paz allegations to light by forwarding a letter to a government official. The official sent it to the CIA. A 46-word rejection letter came back saying they weren't interested. The letter was signed by an official neither Thomas or his wife had ever heard of. His name was James Angleton.

In 1971, Charles Thomas put a gun to his right temple in the second-floor bathroom of his home in Northwest Washington, and pulled the trigger. The family doesn't believe it was suicide.

The reports Thomas sent to Win Scott and Secretary of State, William P. Rogers were ignored. Why?

Another interesting aspect to the Charles Thomas incident is the fact that before venturing to Mexico to talk to Paz, he was sent to Haiti. While there he was approached by a business man named George de Mohren-schildt and his attorney, CIA affiliated Charles Norberg. They wanted him to invest in a Haitian business venture of some kind. It may have been at this time that Thomas became aware of CIA drug experiments going on with the blessing of the Haitian government. No doubt George Hunter White was involved in the project. Another player in the Haitian adventure was none other than Thomas Eli Davis, a mercenary attempting to put together a coup against Papa Doc. Davis of course, was a gun-running partner of Jack Ruby. They may have have been involved in running drugs as well.

Norberg, another Allen Dulles recruit, is interesting because of his involvment in bioweapon testing in the 1950s. In addition he was a legal advisor for MANKIND RESEARCH, a CIA front company experimenting in mind and behavior control. A key player in this facility was Christopher Bird of Rand Development Corporation. There is a definite link by association between all of these characters, drugs, mind-control, Oswald and Webster.

Warren Commissioners wanted to interview Sylvia Duran but Earl Warren would not allow it. When asked why not, Warren replied; *"she was a communist and we don't interview communists."*

Although the Agency photographed Oswald in Mexico City and taped his phone conversations, none of this evidence ever reached the Warren Commission. Scott's public attitude that *"we did not believe it was a conspiracy,"* was contradicted by his own memoirs which suggested the opposite.

Like Thomas, CIA official, John Whitten (aka John Scelso), was also punished for asking questions about Mexico City.

In 1963 Whitten was chief of the Mexico desk. Immediately after JFK's assassination Whitten was assigned by CIA director Richard Helms to gather all Agency reports on Oswald. Concerned with Oswald's Cuban contacts he launched a counterintelligence investigation of the accused assassin. The result was, as he put it himself, that he was "sandbagged" by CI Chief James Angelton.

On Christmas Eve 1963, Whitten was relieved of his duties. *"Helms wanted someone to conduct the investigation who was in bed with the FBI,"* Whitten said. *"I was not, and Angelton was."*[399]

399   "WHAT JANE ROMAN SAID," *A Retired CIA Officer Speaks Candidly About Lee Harvey Oswald*, Jefferson Morley, History Matters

Why would Helms and Angleton not share information with their colleague who was placed in charge of the agency's investigation of Oswald?

Angleton treated Scott in the same manner, suppressing the Mexico City station chief's dissent on the official story.[400] Angleton confiscated Scott's unpublished manuscript immediately after his death with the same haste that he used acquiring Mary Myer's diary. Scott was then demonized by the Agency as *"going to seed."* A sad legacy for an employee who had received the Distinguished Intelligence Medal in 1969.

So why did Cobb change sides and engage in a cover-up of the *Commies did it* scenario? Why did Win Scott file her original report as well as that of Charles Thomas away under lock and key? Why was the Warren Commission kept in the dark about these accusations? Was it because the CIA had abandoned the phase one, *Castro did it,* scenario and were now promoting phase two, the *Lone Nut version?*

Since I originally wrote about Cobb, some new revelations have led us down new roads of inquiry. There seem to be connections between June Cobb and Lee Oswald that must be more than coincidental. We know that June Cobb was working for David Phillips in Mexico City when Oswald strolled into town in late September 1963. We know that they were both involved in the CAP, she in Norman, Oklahoma, and he in New Orleans, Louisiana. D.H. Bird, owner of the Texas Schoolbook Depository, was one of the CAP's founders. New information revealed by author Walter Herbst reveals that in 1977 the University of Oklahoma admitted it was part of the CIA's MKULTRA program. It was designated Sub-project 43 and the ubiquitous Dr. Jolly West was part of it. Naturally, LSD experiments were conducted. The University resides in Norman, Oklahoma. Norman, Oklahoma just happens to be scribbled in Oswald's notebook. Others known to have spent time in Norman are Thomas Eli Davis and Loren Hall. Like Cobb, Davis was an FBN informant. In 1959, Davis was admitted to Lafayette Clinic in Detroit for treatment. Lafayette Clinic was also involved in the CIA's MKULTRA project and Jolly West just happened to be working there as well.

As stated earlier, June Cobb was being treated at Mt. Sinai Hospital in New York City for leishmaniasis, a rare tropical disease. Like all the institutions mentioned above, Mt. Sinai Hospital was a CIA-funded institution used in the MKULTRA program. Dr. Harold Abramson worked there in LSD experiments on adolescents. It was Abramson who became Frank Olson's psychiatrist after he was given LSD without his knowledge.

---

400   Scott rejected the lone assassin theory in his memoirs.

However, Abramson had no psychiatric credentials and was actually an allergist. Abramson was the first one called by Olson's roommate the night he died. Abramson also worked at Ft. Dietrich in LSD research. Olson was a threat to blow the whistle on the bioweapon research he had been a part of at Dietrich.[401]

Cobb was treated for several months at Mt. Sinai. Could she have been involved in the MKULTRA experiment? She then stayed on to work there as an administrative assistant. Was this because of her relationship with Dr. Snapper, her love interest? Or was it a CIA cover. She became Snapper's secretary when he moved to a Chicago hospital in 1952. In that same year she worked briefly for *Time* magazine (Henry Luce). By 1955 she had returned to Columbia to work for the Columbia American Culture Foundation and briefly taught at an American School there. This was probably an intelligence assignment similar to Marilyn Murrett. Teaching was a good over-seas cover.

In Cobb's undercover work for the FBN she dealt with drug-running mobsters like Santo Trafficante, Carlos Marcello, Sam Giancana and even Jack Ruby. Herbst wonders if her turning in the Olozaga brothers to the FBN had a sinister motive. That being to give the Trafficante-Marcello Corsican drug operation a monopoly.

In her CIA/FBN undercover covert role, June was also involved with mercenaries like Frank Sturgis while she was in Cuba. She was close to William Morgan but may have betrayed him in efforts to manipulate a coup against Castro. After Morgan was shot by the Cuban dictator, Cobb fled Cuba. She then became involved in infiltrating left-wing groups thought to be communist infiltrated. One of these was the FPCC. Once again LICooky and LHO cross paths. She managed to get an an interview with FPCC leader, Richard Gibson.

They met in her hotel room while the CIA listened in from the next room with hidden microphones. This seemed to be some kind of propaganda ploy. Gibson's revelations completely confirmed all of the world conquest rhetoric that instilled fear in the anti-communist right. According to Cobb and her accomplices, Gibson admitted that the FPCC wanted to destroy the world, that they were funded by Castro, that they were involved in the Algerian revolution, that they were stirring up Negroes in the South, that Gibson was in cahoots with Lumumba in the Congo and that Castro was financing their organization.[402]

---

401   1 Ironically, The Statler Hotel, where Olson met his demise was also the same place Cobb first met Castro.

402   It Did Not Start with JFK, Walter Herbst

This sounds too pat and phony to me and seems to be an "I told you so!" effort by the CIA to give credence to their war against the group. In support of this view, Gibson, at some point, defected to the CIA. Perhaps it was before the interview, which would make it a false-flag operation.

Was the mind control Project Out of Control?

It is becoming obvious that June Cobb was a chameleon like James Angleton. Seemingly, a small player in the clandestine charades, but far more important. Apparently at the center of the ZRRIFLE project and somehow up to her neck in MKULTRA as well, she maintained a low profile. She may even be a QJWIN candidate or at least a player in that operation.

Her involvement in the ZRRIFLE plots against Castro involved Juan Orta and the poison pill plan. She had links to Bill Harvey, John Roselli and Sam Giancana. She infiltrated Castro's inner circle. She was in the middle of the Mexico City intrigue with David Phillips and Jim Angleton. She was the first to report the Garro de Paz accusations and then later intimidated de Paz. She was close to William Morgan. She was involved in the Corisican drug network as an undercover FBN agent. She knew Thomas Eli Davis and possibly Jack Ruby as drug and gun runners. Like Oswald, she was infiltrating the FPCC and was part of his Mexico City game.

But new revelations insinuate that she had some kind of involvement with the MKULTRA mind control experimentation. She attended the University of Oklahoma in Norman. It was an MKULTRA facility. Doctors known to do LSD experiments there were Jolly West and Harold Abramson. For unknown reasons, Tom Eli Davis and Loren Hall had been there too. Lee Oswald had "Norman, Oklahoma" scribbled in his notebook.

She was incarcerated at Mt. Sinai Hospital for months. It was also a CIA funded MKULTRA facility. Dr. Abramson just happened to work there as well.

Oswald is linked to MKULTRA through his Bordentown incarceration as a teenager, Atsugi, as a Marine, Tulane University and Louisiana State Hospital.[403] All of these institutions were involved in the MKULTRA project. Doctors Malitz, and Hoch worked at both Bordentown and Louisiana State Hospital as well as the New York Psychiatric Institute. These were also CIA/MKULTRA funded. Hock had been a Hitler Youth and was likely Operation Paper Clip affiliated. Hartogs at Bordentown was German. Nazis are an important part of the CIA's anti-communist endeavors.

---

403   Where Dave Ferrie was known to take young CAP cadets.

Doctors Sydney Malitz and Harold Abramson are also linked to the Ft. Dietrich LSD and bioweapons facility involving Frank Olson. It is from this facility that the Anthrax attacks of 2001 originated. Dr. Bruce Irvin, a disgruntled mad scientist there, seemed to be trying to wake the world up to the danger of the government's bioweapons program. Sounds like what Frank Olson was trying to do fifty years earlier. Both died as a result of their efforts.

Tom Eli Davis was somehow involved very deeply in all this as well. He was hospitalized at Lafayette Clinic (MKULTRA facility) and the ubiquitous Jolly West just happened to work there with his always-present bag of LSD. Lafayette Clinic was the domain of Dr. Ernst Rodin, a Nazi doctor and another product of the Hitler Youth and a Paper Clip acquisition. In addition to Rodin, Lafayette employed Professor John Gittinger. As chief psychologist for the Central Intelligence Agency, Gittinger was responsible for locating, assessing and recruiting foreign nationals to be agents for the CIA. He also was responsible for compiling psychological profiles of foreign leaders, including Fidel Castro, the Shah of Iran, Nikita Khrushchev and Ferdinand Marcos. And he decided whether defectors were bona fide or plants. But Lafayette was just a sideshow. He worked for 28 years in Norman, Oklahoma at the University of Oklahoma. It is also revealing that he was called to testify at a congressional committee investigating the Watergate affair. Gittinger was a protege of Dr. Sydney Gottlieb and was accused of doing mind control experiments on children. As mentioned earlier these experiments were based on those conducted in the 1930's by Nazi doctors at concentration camps.

Frank Olson's roommate the night of his death, Robert Lashbrook was also a fixture at Lafayette Clinic.

CHAPTER 22

LANCELOT

What a miracle of momentous complexity is the poet!
– E.E. Cummings description of James Jesus Angleton

In his datebook, H.P. Alberalli's source, *Pierre Lafitte*, links James Angleton to an assassination plot against JFK known as *Lancelot*. Dick Russell's analysis of the Lafitte material is relevant to the roles of Dulles and Angleton in this project.

As Gladio evolved from a stay behind army in Germany into a terrorist organization in Italy, the next stage presented itself in Algeria and France. Anti-communist committees in the US began to concentrate on threats to French colonial dominance in Algeria. They advocated the *integration* of Algeria and France. However, JFK favored Algerian independence and de' Gaulle agreed.

Behind the scenes, motivation for *integration* was likely tied to the discovery of sizable oil reserves in North Africa. Alberalli cites a 1952 scheme launched in Spain by Dallas oil man Algur Meadows and ODESSA's Otto Skorzeny as a link to plans of Texas oilmen to stake claim to these large oil reserves. Propaganda for *integration* was published by Bircher and White Citizens Council member Kent Courtney. Courtney and Banister were closely linked in New Orleans in the summer of 1963 and were no strangers to a provocateur named Lee Harvey Oswald.

The John Birch Society spread its ideology via the American Opinion Speakers Bureau. The featured speakers included Billy James Hargis and his "Christian Crusade," and Skorzeny's business associate, Clifford Forster, who was the creator of *integration*.

In October 1963, even though Algeria had been granted her independence a year earlier, Allen Dulles was still advocating the *integration* chit in his speech before the Dallas Council on World Affairs. Lafitte's notes establishing Dulles' presence in the Emerald City ... er Big D, was also part of Lancelot planning. The Dallas Council on World Affairs was founded in 1951 by Bush family crony, Neil Mallon, at the behest of his good friend Allen Dulles. In 1951 Dulles was still Director of the CIA and the DCWA became an Agency asset.

Kent Biffle of the *Dallas Morning News* published a recapitulation of Dulles' speech the next day and cited Dulles's accusation the Soviets were arming Algerian troops in an attempt to get a foothold in North Africa. Biffle also announced that oil man, Jack Crichton would present a report to the Petroleum Engineers on his Romanian tour on November 1st. Crichton's speech detailed Romanian suffering under the Russian yoke, using propaganda and rhetoric to incite anti-Communist paranoia, fear and hatred in Dallas, inciting the locals to a fever pitch. Lafitte met with Crichton a few days later at the Tech building. Crichton was also involved with Meadows in the Meadows-Skorzeny oil scheme.

Biffle is an interesting guy. His name was found in Oswald's papers. This caused the State Department to take an interest in him. They discovered that he tried to contact Oswald by phone in 1959 at the Metropole Hotel in Moscow.

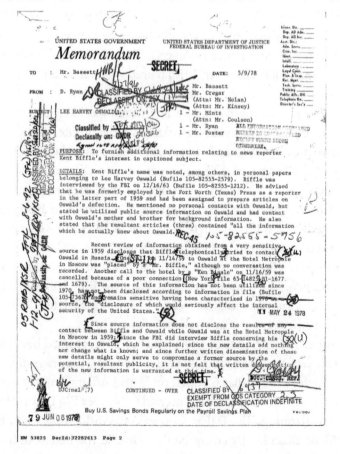

In late April of 1961, Dulles backed a coup plan to be led by a handful of retired French generals. De Gaulle's opposition was the French Secret Army Organization (OAS), a right-wing terrorist group made up, in large measure, of French military deserters who were violently opposed to giving Algeria it's freedom. They were financially supported by the CIA through front companies such as PERMINDEX,[404] whose Board of Directors included Clay Shaw; and Schlumberger Corporation, a large French-owned enterprise, which serviced oil producers worldwide by using explosives to predict the potential of geological sites. Jean de Menil, a president of Schlumberger and member of the Dallas Petroleum Club, was a close friend of Oswald's Dallas mentor George de Mohrenschildt.

The OAS was nurtured by Allen Dulles out of fear that Algeria would go Communist, which would mean loss of rich aforementioned oil resources. He also had no love lost for the French president.[405]

An assassination attempt on de Gaulle in 1962 is eerily reminiscent of Dallas. A motorcade with de Gaulle and his wife in the back seat of his limo is attacked. Without warning the air exploded in a hail of gunfire in three bursts from automatic weapons. In all, the vehicle was hit about ten times as a dozen OAS snipers riddled the car and its escorts. More than a hundred bullets poured in on the motorcade from multiple locations. The rear window of the presidential vehicle was shattered instantaneously. A missile struck the door frame only two inches from de Gaulle's head and another narrowly missed the French first lady. Two motorcycle escorts were killed, but unlike JFK, the President's loyal and well-trained security forces reacted quickly and he escaped unharmed.[406] One of the snipers was Jean Souetre.[407]

The OAS soon became a pool from which competent professional assassins could be hired and used for international contracts by organized crime or clandestine agencies. The CIA's Bill Harvey used them in the *Executive Action* program, ZRRIFLE. Soutre had connections to the Mafia and Jack Ruby. He also had contacts with the right-wing fanatics in Dallas and New Orleans, and was in touch with anti-Castro Cubans.

---

404   Permanent Industrial Exposition
405   According to Larry Hancock, "documents showing that Jean Souetre (more on him shortly) had been allowed into the US in 1963, ostensibly as a diplomatic representative from the OAS but of course a representative without official French government credentials. That appears to have been at the initiative of the CIA and he was pitching various offices about the threat of Communist agents within the de Gaulle administration. It's pretty clear that his visit hadn't been approved but it's also clear the French would have officially protested if they had known, or if they found out."
406   Kennedy's motorcycle escort melted away when he entered the kill zone. Only one secret service agent reacted at all and he was Clint Hill, who was assigned to Jackie.
407   The movie *Day of the Jackal*, based on John Forsythe's book was inspired by Souetre.

So what is seen in Lafitte's book, as described in the above diatribe, are connections between Dallas oil men, including Jack Crichton, Allen Dulles, James Angleton, Bill Harvey, Jack Ruby[408] and organized crime, American committees, Birchers, Otto Skorzeny, the OAS (Souetre/Mertz), PERMINDEX, Clay Shaw and anti-Castro Cubans in an assassination plan called *Lancelot*.

Jean Pierre Lafitte was the namesake and descendant of the famous pirate who aided Stonewall Jackson in the Battle of New Orleans in 1812. There is even a city named by and for him in Louisiana, called *Jean Lafitte*. The twentieth century version of Jean Lafitte was an assassin and CIA operative involved in Operation Gladio. Author Walter Herbst reveals that Lafitte used the Hidell alias as well as others such as Jack Martin and Mertz and that he once employed Jack Ruby. Lafitte also worked at Reily Coffee. Richard Case Nagell also used the alias Hidell and had a card near-identical to Oswald's ID among his possessions when arrested in El Paso in 1963.

THE PATSY

With Lancelot in place, all that was needed was a patsy to take the fall. But not just anyone would do. The structure of the plot necessitated that the blame be placed on Castro and Khruschev. To fill the bill, the fall guy had to embrace Communist ideology and have links to subversive organizations. Angleton's choice was someone he knew would fit the bill well. Someone whom he had controlled for at least four years. It may even have begun when Oswald was an adolescent, living in New York City. In 1953, thirteen-year-old Oswald was charged with truancy. Sent to a youth house, he was given a psychiatric examination by a resident psychologist, Dr. Renautus Hartogs. Hartogs, who later testified to the Warren Commission about Oswald's personality disorders and abnormal psyche, found the case fascinating and requested that a three-week study be done at Bordentown Reformatory. Bordentown was being used as part of the CIA's new MKULTRA program. The Bordentown facility was run by Dr. Carl C. Pfieffer and conducted experiments involving hypnosis, LSD, mescaline, truth serum and amphetamines.[409] One of their goals was to come up with an *anti-interrogation* drug for use in spy craft. The

---

408   And through Ruby as well as QJWIN, Thomas Eli Davis.
409   Pfeiffer was also head of another MKULTRA hospital in Atlanta, GA. This one used adults mostly "volunteers" from prisons who were rewarded with lighter sentences. These volunteers knew nothing of the purpose of the program and were, in essence, guinea pigs. One was convicted murderer, Whitey Bulger.

program was also a study of adolescents with certain psychological profiles. These *troubled* individuals were tracked over the years to determine if they were useful to the agency in the future. Hartogs had also worked with MKULTRA doctor Sydney Mallett of Columbia Presbyterian Hospital on the use of hypnosis.

In 1995, in an unpublicized session of the President's Committee on Radiation in Washington, D.C., a New Orleans therapist named Valerie Wolf used two of her patients to expose extensive CIA brainwashing programs. With her help and therapy, the patents managed to uncover memories of being subjected to CIA brainwashing programs as young children (in one case, starting at age seven).

Their brainwashing included torture, rape, electroshock, powerful drugs, hypnosis, and death threats. According to their testimony, the CIA then induced amnesia to prevent their recalling these terrifying sessions.

Both Wolf and her patients stated they recovered the memories of this CIA program without regression or hypnosis techniques. In other words, these patients spontaneously discovered this information about themselves and their pasts.

Even though the committee's main concerned was with radiation, Valerie and her patients were permitted to testify because, amazingly, several doctors who had administered the mind-control experiments have also been identified by other Americans secretly exposed to radiation.

Prominent names surfacing in the testimony: Richard Helms, former head of the CIA, Dr. Sidney Gottlieb, who ran MKULTRA and Dr. John Gittinger, Gottlieb's protege. These men and others were directly accused of participating in grisly mind-control efforts on children.

Predictably, this testimony received no media attention, in itself evidence that the CIA and the media cooperate.

This program, "Operation Mockingbird," has been going on since at least 1947. Many "journalists" actually worked for the CIA.

MKULTRA utilized many of the tactics that the Germans developed in the 1930s and during World War II in their concentration camps.

THE WIZ-KID OR IS IT WIZARD'S KID

Four years after his Bordentown experience, Oswald enlisted in the Marines and was sent to Atsugi, Japan, a CIA base, to work on the top secret U2 project. Atsugi was also an MKULTRA facility. What a coincidence! In Japan, Oswald became involved with a Japanese girl at the exclusive Queen Bee nightclub, essentially a *bees' nest* of international spies, and became entangled with a Communist cell in Tokyo. He was likely recruited by ONI or CIA at this point and told fellow Marine, David Bucknell, that he was being sent to Russia on an intelligence mission.

While in Japan, Oswald reportedly was involved with Richard Case Nagell of FOI, in an effort to recruit a Russian officer, Nikolai Eroshkin, at the Soviet Embassy in Tokyo. Later in Mexico City he would repeat this type of assignment and meet with a KGB officer, Kostikov, at the Soviet Embassy in that city.

Another phase of LHO's training took place at the base at Nags Head, North Carolina. Here he was schooled in illusionary warfare and *propaganda*. Let's see ... *anti-interrogation* training at Bordentown and *propaganda* at Nags Head. Hmm ... in what profession would he need these skills?

Nags Head was also the center for an ONI program to create a false defector program, designed to send disgruntled young Americans to the Soviet Union in hopes they would be accepted by the Commies as real.

A CIA accountant in Tokyo at the time, James Wilcott, testified under oath to the HSCA that he wrote government checks to pay for the *Oswald Project*. It was he who paid our spies and Oswald, under a code name, was one of these.

The CIA tried to discredit Wilcott. He was harassed, his tires were slashed and sugar poured in his gas tank. When he obtained employment elsewhere, his employer was harassed to the point of having to fire Wilcott.

Oswald was granted an early discharge from the Marines on a trumped-up excuse involving an injury to his mother. Instead of watching over her, he immediately disembarked on a trip to Russia. This excursion has the fingerprints of intelligence all over it. He only had a $200 bank account and the trip cost $1800. He entered the USSR via Finland, an end-run maneuver that he could not have been aware of on his own.

When he arrived in Moscow, he had to fake a suicide attempt to scare the KGB into accepting him. He then put on a show at the US Embassy in that city, loudly offering secrets to the Soviets and throwing his passport down and declaring that he wanted to give up US citizenship. The American Counsel, Richard Snyder's telegram reporting this incident was cc'd to James Angleton's CI/SIG.

When Oswald returned to the US he was not debriefed or arrested for treason. He was met by Spas Raikin of the Traveler's Aid Society. Raikin was also a member and lobbyist of the Anti-Bolshevik Nations. He also had close ties to the CIA. Raikin was likely a cutout for James Angleton to use in babysitting Oswald upon his return to America. Angleton also kept track of his vest-pocket operative by opening his mail both in the Soviet Union and in the States after his return. The cutout for this job was Reuben Efron. Efron also was Angleton's eyes and ears during the testimony of Marina Oswald to the Warren Commission.

Once in Texas, Oswald was monitored by George de Mohrenschildt at the behest of CIA agent J. Walton Moore. De Mohrenschildt's Warren Commission testimony condemned Oswald as guilty. However, later the Baron suffered great remorse and wrote a book called *Lee Harvey Oswald as I Knew Him*. In it he proclaimed his young friend as a patsy. He told journalist Dick Russell, that the assassination was a massive conspiracy and that the WC report "defiled Oswald's corpse." Rantings like this hastened his demise. He was found dead days before a scheduled interview with the HSCA.

Just prior to the assassination, de Mohrenschildt passed off his babysitting duties to Ruth and Michael Paine and accepted his reward for these duties, a big oil deal in Haiti.

The next project involving Oswald was a propaganda operation against the FPCC that began in New Orleans.

EPILOGUE

FOLLOW THE YELLOW BRICK ROAD

The Warren Commission is contradicted by its own evidence.
— Jefferson Morley

Recently much has been added to *what we know now*. Of these new revelations, the most important is the Paul Landis bomb shell. Landis was one of the Secret Service agents riding in the follow-up car on November 22nd, 1963. It is an amazing story for several reasons. First, it is astounding that he kept this information to himself for 60 years! It is also astonishing that, in spite of his close proximity to arguably the most important historical event of the century, he was unaware of the controversy involving the single-bullet theory. How could he have isolated himself for so long?

His version of events on that dark day are as follows; After arriving at Parkland Hospital, he witnessed the President's body being taken from the limousine by his partner, Clint Hill and another agent. He stepped into the back seat area of the car and picked up and examined two shell fragments that were lying on the seat the President had occupied. He replaced these and then noticed a complete and nearly pristine bullet lodged in the folds of the seat at the approximate location where the First Lady had been sitting. Here is where things get weird. Afraid that the bullet, which he realized was important crime scene evidence, would be taken as a gruesome souvenir, he picked it up. Makes sense so far. Then, instead of giving it to an SS superior, FBI agent, Dallas Policeman, or even informing *anyone* of its existence, he put it in his pocket. Being that he was under stress, this behavior can be understood. But what he finally did with the missile is absolutely baffling to me. He placed it on the table where JFK was being treated in the Emergency room. Then he didn't tell *anyone* about it for 60 years!

The logical assumption, at this point, is that this was the bullet that later fell off a gurney in an elevator and became Arlen Specter's magic bullet.

However, this assumption is muddied by his assertion that he placed the missile on a metal table and not a gurney.

Why this is so important is that it completely negates any possibility of the single-bullet theory's accuracy. If this missile was lodged in the back seat of the presidential vehicle, it could not have traveled through the President and caused all of Connally's wounds. Without the single-bullet theory, Oswald could not have acted alone. Case closed.

The autopsy established that JFK's back wound was a shallow one. A doctor at Bethesda probed it digitally and said it was only as deep as the first segment (from tip to knuckle) of his finger. The wound was never tracked due to instructions from military overseers who continually interfered with the autopsy. In addition, there were many witnesses who testified that the first shot sounded like a fire cracker. This sounds like a defective discharge. Even the FBI at first suspected that the bullet had fallen out during attempts at medical CPR. It is obvious via the Landis revelation, that when Kennedy fell into his wife's arms in the vehicle, the bullet exited his back and lodged in the seat.

The neck wound was not caused by this bullet as Specter would have us believe. But there is also a problem with the neck wound being an entrance wound as the Parkland doctors observed. The problem is that if it was an entrance wound, where did the bullet go? Once again there was no tracking done of this wound for the same reasons stated concerning the back wound. In addition, the autopsy doctors did not know it was a bullet wound since a tracheotomy had obliterated it. The only possibility is that the missile somehow went *downward* after entering the neck and is still in JFK's body. I don't think that is feasible. I think Josiah Thompson got it right way back in the 1960s. The throat wound was one of exit for a very small piece of skull or tiny bullet fragment resulting from the head shot. JFK's reaction of bringing his arms to a horizontal position was not to grab his throat, in fact, if you look closely, he doesn't. It is a reaction to getting punched in the back by a missile that barely penetrated and later fell out.

Still, this doesn't explain the two large fragments Landis found on the seat and left there. If one shot missed the limo, one hit JFK in the back, at least one and maybe even two hit Connally and one, or again possibly two, blew Kennedy's skull to pieces; that makes at the very least four shots. If we had the fragmented bullet on the seat that makes five. But where did that one come from? It may have been the same missile that made a hole in the windshield, although it seems unlikely that this could have missed all of the occupants. In addition, if FBI agents Sibert and O'Neill, are right, another missile was discovered during the autopsy. If you are a hard core lone nutter and still believe in the magic bullet, the one found by Landis still proves more than one shooter since Oswald could only have fired three times max.

There is little else in *The Final Witness* of much interest. It reads like an autobiography and it is a bit of a chore to wade through to get to the important part. But a couple of comments are intriguing. Landis mentions that for a brief period after the assassination, his fellow agents speculated, partly in jest, that LBJ was likely behind JFK's death. Interesting. I also liked the references to Onassis as being "sneaky" and trying to lose Jackie's bodyguards on several occasions.

Another devastating blow to the Warren Report is a new documentary that aired on *Paramount+* entitled: *JFK: What the Doctors Saw*. In it the surviving Parkland doctors who saw JFK's wounds in Trauma Room 1 on November 22, 1963, are finally brought together to tell their story. Sadly, not all of them are still with us. The most important of the deceased being Dr. Charles Crenshaw. He was the only emergency room witness who risked his reputation to reveal the truth in two books he wrote later in his life. The unanimous version of events presented by these doctors is that JFK was shot from the front as well as the back. This, of course, is irrefutable proof of conspiracy. But even more important is their revelation that these doctors were threatened and warned not to ever repeat what they saw. What that means is that the cover-up had already begun within hours or days of the event. It means that they knew *that early* that Oswald was to be the patsy and was not the lone assassin!

An agent that later admitted threatening one of the doctors said he regretted it but that the orders came from Washington, DC. Logically the source of the orders was LBJ, J. Edgar Hoover or possibly his Secret Service boss, Douglas C. Dillon.[410]

The third area of new revelations involves George Joannides. It has gradually come to light that Joannides was a propaganda specialist under David Atlee Phillips. In 1963 Joannides was running the Cuban exile group, DRE in New Orleans for the CIA. The Agency was pouring $51,000 a month into this anti-Castro organization. It is now apparent that Lee Harvey Oswald was involved in this propaganda operation to derail the FPCC. His street fight with DRE leader, Carlos Bringuier and his henchmen, the radio debates that followed, handing out pamphlets

---

410   Dillon was head of the Treasury Department that oversaw the Secret Service.

and starting a one-man branch of the committee in the *Emerald* … er … *Crescent* City all smacks of an operation in which Oswald participated as a provocateur. The radio debates were recorded and saved for later use against Oswald. This is indicative of the purpose of the exiles, or at least the constituents of the debate; Carlos Bringuier, Bill Stuckey and INCA[411] head Edward Scannel Butler. They knew in advance that this recording would be important evidence in the conviction of Oswald and a nail in the coffin of the FPCC. The question is, did they also know in advance that JFK would be assassinated? It seems odd that the first to be made aware of these recordings by Bringuier and Butler was the Senate Security Investigation Subcommittee. Was this all this being set up in advance to be used at the right moment to blame Castro and the FPCC for Kennedy's death? It's no coincidence that although the CIA funded INCA, it had other benefactors behind the scenes. Anti-Castro crusader, Dr. Alton Ochsner and William Reily, Oswald's employer at the Reily Coffee Co. Reily also backed Sergio Archacia Smith's Crusade to Free Cuba Committee.

Lee Oswald worked hard to establish his identity as a pro-Castro Marxist. He offered to join Carlos Bringuier's group, the DRE, to help them train exiles, and later double-crossed them by passing out pro-Castro leaflets on a nearby street corner. This led to a street scuffle that seemed staged to attract media attention and establish his credentials as a left-wing provocateur. Proof it was staged is contained in a letter Oswald wrote to V.T. Lee of the Fair Play for Cuba Committee, describing the confrontation five days before it even took place!

As for Joannides, it was he who was brought out of retirement to be the CIA's contact with the HSCA probe and worked to successfully sidetrack its New Orleans investigation to protect the Agency. The CIA's Joannides files are still secret and one of the most closely guarded by the *Company*.

Jefferson Morley has spent years undertaking legal action against the Agency to try to get these important documents released.

Joannides was chief of the psychological warfare branch of the CIA's Miami station. If the Agency was involved in a coup, it was run out of Miami's JMWAVE station. Its main front company was *Zenith Technological Enterprises, Inc.* and JMWAVE's staff included the likes of David Morales, Ted Shakley, John Roselli and his buddy Bill Harvey. They oversaw the Cuban exiles and trained them in commando tactics, espionage and seamanship. Their operations included exile raids on Cuba.

---

411   Information Counsel of the Americas, an anti-Communist propaganda organization.

Let's see where the yellow brick road (the path paved by *what we know now)* leads us. We may not have munchkins to guide us, but like Dorothy we are very determined to find the Wizard. That road is sprinkled with red-baiting and colored by yellow journalism. What we can deduce is that Oswald was a false flag patsy who worked as a provocateur for Joannides in a propaganda operation against the FPCC. Joannides used the DRE and Ed Butler's INCA in concert to embarrass FPCC and link them to Castro's Communist regime via the Marxist, Lee Harvey Oswald. Backtracking from Joannides leads us to his boss, David Atlee Phillips. Phillips was also a psychological warfare specialist. His credits included personally overthrowing the Arbenz democratically elected government in Guatemala armed only with propaganda and without firing a shot. David Phillips, in turn, is a cutout for James Jesus Angleton. The bottom line is that all of these individuals and the whole creature, COINTELPRO, the program to destroy the FPCC, can be traced to Jim Angleton. When you reach the end of the yellow brick road, you will find the Wizard.

ABBOTT AND COSTELLO MEET THE GHOST[412]

Lou Costello: I'm asking YOU who's on first.

Bud Abbott: That's the man's name.

Lou Costello: All I'm trying to find out is what's the guy's name on first base.

Bud Abbott: No. What is on second base.

Lou Costello: What's the guy's name on first base?

Bud Abbott: No. What is on second.

Lou Costello: I'm not asking you who's on second.

Bud Abbott: Who's on first.

Lou Costello: I don't know.

Bud Abbott: He's on third, we're not talking about him.

Lou Costello: Now how did I get on third base?

Bud Abbott: Why you mentioned his name.

This abbreviated version of the classic *reparte'* between the famous comedy duo goes round and round eventually resulting in Costello's repeating a response of..........THIRD BASE!

If we apply this same logic to what has been discussed in this book, it becomes clear that it is somehow illogically logical. For example, if Joannides is on first base and David Atlee Phillips is on second, logic leads us to..........THIRD BASE! And third base is James Angleton. This same

412   *The Ghost: James Jesus Angleton*

logistical reasoning pattern can be followed time and time again to lead us back to third base and the Wizard.

June Cobb leads us to David Phillips, Phillips to Angleton..........THIRD BASE!

Ruby to Marcello, Giancana, Roselli, Trafficante.....Mario Brod.....Angleton ....THIRD BASE!

CHAOS to Jolly West, Jack Ruby...........THIRD BASE!

COINTELPRO to J. Edgar Hoover, FPCC, Clinton, LA, Shaw, Ferrie, Angleton..........THIRD BASE!

Mary Meyer, Ben Bradley, Cord Meyer..........THIRD BASE!

Bill Harvey, ZRRIFLE, Angleton..........THIRD BASE!

French OAS terrorists, Clay Shaw and Guy Banister, PERMINDEX..........THIRD BASE!

Robert Webster, Lee Oswald, mole hunt, Angleton..........THIRD BASE!

If you were asked then who was on third (the puppet master) your answer was "I don't know." Now we do know. It was James Jesus Angleton.

All roads are Yellow Brick and all lead us to the Wizard.

THERE'S NO PLACE LIKE HOME

It has taken decades to get from third base to Home. During that time, the Wizard has been a Ghost, out of sight in the background wreaking his havoc in secrecy for 60 years or more. That is how it used to be. But no longer. The diligent research of people who cared has brought us to the enlightened gnostic home plate of truth. The Wizard has been exposed for what he is.

We now know what we didn't know then!

Bibliography

Accessories After The Fact,Sylvia Meagher, Vintage Books, 1967

A Certain Arrogance, George Michael Evica, TrineDay, 2011

A Farewell to Justice, Joan Mellen, Potomac Books Inc., 2005

A Reporter at Large, May 28, 2012, issue

A Woman I Know, Mary Haverstick, Crown Publishing, 2023

Assassination Chronicles, Spring 1996

Brush with History, Eric R. Tagg, Shot in the Light Publishing, 1998

Church of Spies, Mark Riebling, Random House Audio, 2015

Coup D'Etat in America, Alan J. Weberman and Michael Canfield, Quick American Archives1992.

Crossfire, Jim Mars, Caroll and Graf, NY, 1989

Coup in Dallas, H.P. Abarelli Jr., Skyhorse Publishing, 2021

De Dallas à Montréal (From Dallas to Montreal), The Montreal connection to the JFK assassination, Maurice Phillipps (no relation to David Phillips or his alias Maurice Bishop)

Deep Politics and the Death of JFK, Peter Dale Scott, University of California Press, 1993

Denial of Justice, Mark Shaw, Post Hill Press, 2018

Handsome Johnny, Lee Server, St Martin's Press, 2018

Harvey and Lee, John Armstrong, Quasar Ltd., 2003

H.L. Hunt Motive and Opportunity, John Currington as told to Mitchell Whitington

Interloper, Lee Harvey Oswald Inside the Soviet Union, Peter Savodnik

It Did Not Start With JFK, Walter Herbst, Sunbury Press, 2021

JFK Assassination Debate-John Simpkin,The Education Forum, August 9, 2005

JFK, Oswald and Ruby, Burt W. Griffin, McFarland & Co., 2023

JFK: The French Connection, Peter Kross, Adventures Unlimited Press, 2012

Laura Kittrel, typewritten manuscript to HSCA

"Last post for Oswald," Garrick Alder, *Lobster Magazine*

"Lee," A Portrait of Lee Harvey Oswald, Robert Oswald, Coward-McCann Inc.,NY 1967

Lee Harvey Oswald's Cold War, Greg Parker, New Disease Press, 2015

"LHO on Campus," Dennis Bartholomew, *Fourth Decade*, vol.4, nr. 3, 1997

Marina and Lee, Priscilla McMillan & Marina Oswald, Harper & Row, 1977

Meagan Day-Timeline Nov. 23, 2016

New Evidence Regarding Ruth and Michael Paine, Steve Jones

On The Trail of Clay Shaw, Michelle Matte, 2019

Operation Gladio, Paul Williams, Prometheus Books, 2015

Oswald and the CIA, John Newman, Carroll and Graf 1995

Oswald's Mother website, George Bailey

Oswald: Russian Episode, Ernst Titovets, Custodian Books, 2010

Oswald's Tale, Norman Mahler, Random House, 1995

Oswald Talked, Ray and Mary La Fontaine, Pelican Publishing Co., 1996

Suppressing the Truth in Dallas, Charles Brandt, Post Hill Press, 2022

Survivor's Guilt, Vince Palamara, TrineDay, 2013

"The American Comandante," *American Experience* documentary, PBS, Nov 17, 2015

"The American Comandante In The Cuban Revolutionary Forces: William Morgan," TheCubanHistory.com, May 16, 2012

The Final Witness, Paul Landis, Chicago Review Press, 2023

The Invisible Government, David Wise and Thomas B. Ross, Bantam Books, 1964

The Man Who Knew Too Much, Dick Russell, Carroll & Graff Publishers, 1992

The Other Oswald, Gary Hill, TrineDay Books, 2020

"The Ghosts of November," Anthony and Robbyn Summers, *Vanity Fair,* Dec. 1994

The Ruby Cover-Up, Seth Kantor, Zebra Books, 1978

The Skorzeny Papers, Major Ralph P. Ganis, Skyhorse Publishing, 2018

The Sword and the Shield; The Mitrokhin Archive and the Secret History of the KGB, Christopher Andrew and Vasili Mitrokhin

The Three Barons, J.W. Lateer, TrineDay 2017

The Winnipeg Airport Incident, Paris Flammonde,

The Kennedy Conspiracy, Meredith Press, New York, 1969.

"The Yankee Comandante, " The New Yorker, David Grann, May 21, 2012

Travalanche, April 19, 2021, "William Morgan: Comandante of the Carnival."

William Weston, *The Fourth Decade* Nov. 2000/Jan. 2001

"The Winnipeg Airport Incidents," Peter Whitmey, The Fourth Decade, November 1995.

"The Winnipeg Airport Incident Revisited," Peter Whitmey, The Fourth Decade, March 1999.

"The Second Invasion of Cuba," Gil Jesus,*JFK Conspiracy forum,* 2019

Uncovering Popov's Mole, John Newman, 2022

We Are All Mortal, George Michael Evica

"What the Curious Case of Richard Gibson tells us about Lee Harvey Oswald," Jefferson Morley, *JFK FACTS,* 2023

Who's Who in the JFK Assassination, Michael Benson, Citadel Press, 1993.

Index